# Keynesian, Sraffian, Computable and Dynamic Economics

"I had the chance to meet Stefano as a student in the Faculty of Economics of the University of Modena. I think my role in applying Mathematics in modelling economic situations may have stimulated Stefano (and his friends) to do the same. We came from the same region Romagna and this made our relationship easy, and at the same time it was deep and enduring. This *Festschrift* is a testimony to the personal and intellectual esteem with which many scholars hold Stefano."

—Gianni Ricci, Emeritus Professor, *University of Modena, Modena, Italy*

"It is fitting that a volume in celebration of Stefano Zambelli should incorporate so many features of his own work: theoretical rigour and creativity, profound and insightful analysis spanning across different disciplines with ease. It is even more exciting that it includes fresh new contributions from outstanding thinkers. Truly a volume to value."

—Jayati Ghosh, *Centre for Economic Studies and Planning, Jawaharlal Nehru University, India*

Kumaraswamy Velupillai
Editor

# Keynesian, Sraffian, Computable and Dynamic Economics

## Theoretical and Simulational (Numerical) Approaches

palgrave
macmillan

*Editor*
Kumaraswamy Velupillai
Solna, Stockholms Län, Sweden

ISBN 978-3-030-58130-5 ISBN 978-3-030-58131-2 (eBook)
https://doi.org/10.1007/978-3-030-58131-2



This Palgrave Macmillan imprint is published by the registered company Springer Nature Switzerland AG.
The registered company address is: Gewerbestrasse 11, 6330 Cham, Switzerland

# Contents

# Notes on Contributors

**Charlotte Bruun** is an associate professor at University College of Northern Denmark, previously Aalborg University. She was an early adapter of agent-based economics, combining it with Keynesian macroeconomics in her 1995 dissertation, partly supervised by Stefano Zambelli. She is working on possible theoretical underpinnings for the idea of doing sustainable business.

**Edgardo Bucciarelli,** PhD, is an Italian economist. He is Associate Professor of Economics at the University of Chieti-Pescara (Italy). His main research interests lie in the area of complexity and market dynamics, decision theory, experimental microeconomics, classical behavioural economics, economic methodology, and foundations of mathematics. He cooperates with several international academic institutions.

**Sara Casagrande** is a post-doc research fellow in comparative European Studies. She holds a PhD in Economics and Management at the University of Trento, Italy. Her research fields include cyclical development, economic simulation, and macroeconomic theoretical and applied issues. Her present research activity relates to European integration process and institutional variety.

**Shu-Heng Chen** is a distinguished professor in the Department of Economics, National Chengchi University (NCCU), Taipei, Taiwan. He is the director of the AI-ECON Research Center. He serves as the editor-in-chief of *the Journal of New Mathematics and Natural Computation* (World Scientific) and *Journal of Economic Interaction and Coordination* (Springer). He holds a PhD in Economics from University of California, Los Angeles.

**Guglielmo Chiodi,** Former Professor of Economics at the University of Rome "La Sapienza", Italy, he is president of the interdisciplinary association 'Nuova Accademia'. His articles on monetary theory, the theory of value and distribution, with special regard to Classical, Sraffian and Marxian economic theory have appeared in many journals and books.

**John B. Davis,** Professor Emeritus of Economics, Marquette University and University of Amsterdam, is author of *Keynes's Philosophical Development*, *The Theory of the Individual in Economics*, *Individuals and Identity in Economics*, co-author with Marcel Boumans of *Economic Methodology: Understanding Economics as a Science*, and Robert McMaster of *Health Care Economics*.

**Donald A. R. George** is Honorary Fellow in Economics at the University of Edinburgh. He advocates a pluralist approach to economics. Donald has published extensively on a wide range of topics, including economic dynamics and workers' co-operatives. He is a founding editor of the *Journal of Economic Surveys.*

**Geoffrey Colin Harcourt** is Emeritus Reader in the History of Economic Theory, Cambridge, 1998; Emeritus Fellow, Jesus College, Cambridge, 1998; Professor Emeritus, Adelaide, 1988; and Honorary Professor, School of Economics, UNSW Sydney, 2010–2019. He has published 33 books and over 400 articles, chapters in books, and reviews. His research interests include post-Keynesian theory, applications and policy, intellectual biography and history of economic theory.

**Brian Hayes** is an essayist who writes on topics in mathematics, computation, and the sciences. He began his career as an editor at *Scientific American* and later edited another magazine, *American Scientist*. His most recent collection of essays is *Foolproof, and Other Mathematical Meditations*.

**Selda Kao (Ying-Fang Kao)** is a data scientist at the Experimentation, Artificial Intelligence and Machine Learning Team, Just Eat, London, UK. Selda (Ying-Fang) obtained her PhD in Economics from the University of Trento, Italy. Her research includes classical behavioural Economics, computable economics, causal inference and machine learning.

**Cassey Lee** is a Senior Fellow at the ISEAS—Yusof Ishak Institute, Singapore. Prior to joining ISEAS, Dr Lee held academic appointments at the University of Wollongong, Nottingham University Business School (Malaysia) and University of Malaya.

**Francesco Luna** has spent the last 20 years at the International Monetary Fund, working as desk economist in transition economies and more recently training country officials from Eastern Europe, Central Asia, and the Middle East. His research interests include Computable Economics and Computable Agent Based modeling. Luna has taught at the University of Venice "Ca' Foscari" and Oberlin College.

**Nicola Mattoscio** is an Italian economist. He is Distinguished Professor of Economics at the University of Chieti-Pescara (Italy) where he heads the PPEQ Sciences Department. He is the editor-in-chief of *Global & Local Economic Review* and *Il Risparmio Review*, as well as the Maestro of two generations of economists. He is the founder and director of the Federico Caffè & Corradino D'Ascanio Research Center. He has authored over 100 publications.

**Dharmaraj Navaneethakrishnan** holds a PhD in Economics and Management from the University of Trento, Italy, a master's degree in Engineering Management from MAHE, India, and a bachelor's degree in Mechanical Engineering from Periyar University, India. He works as a Data Scientist at Hubbell, and previously worked with Ford.

**Venkatachalam Ragupathy** is Lecturer in Economics at the Institute of Management Studies, Goldsmiths, University of London, UK. Ragupathy obtained his PhD in Economics from the University of Trento, Italy. His research covers economic dynamics, computable economics, history of economic thought and classical behavioural economics.

**J. Barkley Rosser Jr.** PhD from U-Wisconsin-Madison, at James Madison University since 1977, Professor of Economics and Kirby L. Cramer, Jr. Professor of Business Administration. Author of over 200 publications, he edited the *Journal of Economic Behavior and Organization* and since the *Review of Behavioral Economics*. He co-founded the Nonlinear Economics Society and is coeditor of *New Palgrave Dictionary of Economics*.

**Anwar Shaikh** is Professor of Economics, Graduate Faculty of Political and Social Science of the New School University, and an associate editor of the *Cambridge Journal of Economics*. His intellectual biography is included in the book *Eminent Economists II* (2014), and his most recent book is *Capitalism: Competition, Conflict, Crises* (2016).

**Ajit Sinha** is professor at Thapar School of Liberal Arts and Sciences, Patiala, India. He has published extensively in the area of history of economic theory. His previously published work includes *Theories of Value from Adam Smith to Piero Sraffa*, *A Revolution in Economic Theory: The Economics of Piero Sraffa* (Palgrave Macmillan, 2016) and *Essays on Theories of Value in the Classical Tradition* (Palgrave Macmillan, 2019).

**Kumaraswamy Velupillai** is a retired economist living in Stockholm, Sweden. He has been Professor of Economics at various universities in Europe, USA, India and South America. He is a graduate of Kyoto, Lund and Cambridge Universities. His main interests are in Computable Economics, Macrodynamics and History of Mathematical Economics.

# List of Figures

# List of Tables

# 1

# Introduction to the *Zambelli Festschrift*

Kumaraswamy Velupillai

## 1 Some Initial Remarks

It was in Ravenna, when we went for the wedding of Silvana Convertini and Stefano Zambelli that I had the pleasure of seeing, and experiencing a performance of *Verdi*'s poignant Opera, **La Forza del Destino** as Leonora 'sings' in this fine opera by Verdi (in Act Four), 'Ah destiny! destiny!' It is appropriate that I am able to couple the *force of destiny* that brought us together, almost forty years ago, in the lovely Tuscan region, when Stefano was an advanced student at the University of Modena and I had just moved to the European University Institute (EUI), in Fiesole (to be near my *maestro*, Richard Goodwin, who had—after retirement from Peterhouse, in Cambridge—begun a wholly new and productive academic career as Professor, in the University of Siena; not long afterward, Goodwin also became Stefano's respected teacher).

I have spent many happy hours, days, weeks and months, with Stefano Zambelli, at the many universities which were 'home' to us, in more ways

---

K. Velupillai (✉)
Solna, Sweden



K. Velupillai (ed.), *Keynesian, Sraffian, Computable and Dynamic Economics*,
https://doi.org/10.1007/978-3-030-58131-2_1

than one: Modena and EUI, of course, but also in Bologna, University of California at Los Angeles (UCLA), National University of Ireland (NUI) Galway, Aalborg and Trento. We corresponded, mostly to my intellectual benefit, from and to, Madras and New Delhi, Copenhagen and Lund, Belfast and Stockholm (in my retirement), using many of the modern means of communication (in spite of my inadequate mastery of them).

Zambelli's current *CV* and the *Scheda Attivitá* of the department of economics at the University of Trento, give an ample 'instantaneous picture' (*pace* Keynes) of his intellectual contributions as of 2020, and both documents can be accessed readily on the *Internet*. Let me add three—of the many, possible—*personal stories* that I have had the privilege to share with him.

After my resignation from the EUI, in 1985, I moved back to Sweden (initially 'unemployed') and Zambelli, after graduation from the department of economics at the University of Modena,[1] took up employment at the research department of the *Banca Commerciale Italiana* (BCI), in Milan.[2]

I went back to Italy, in 1986, to see a Mantegna exhibition in Mantova, in the company of Stefano. After seeing the fine exhibition of paintings by Mantegna, we—Stefano and I—went to have lunch at a good restaurant in the central Piazza in the town of Mantova. During the excellent lunch, we asked the waiter to show us the telephone, since I wanted to make a call (I don't remember to whom or where). The waiter asked us to wait a little. We waited—and waited; no sign of the waiter—until he was sighted again, about fifteen minutes later. We repeated our request, and were asked by the waiter, to wait—again. After a further ten minutes, or so, he turned up with what today would be called a mobile telephone! Neither of us had ever seen such a gadget, ever before—and had no idea how to operate it—and were too embarrassed to 'display our ignorance' of modern 'invention of machines' and gave it back to the waiter, politely!

[1] In July 1985 with *cum laude*.

[2] Simultaneously, he was a member of the Macroeconomics and Monetary Policy Research Group of the BCI, cooperating with Bocconi University.

After my appointment as a professor at Aalborg University, in August 1986, I was invited to be a visiting professor at UCLA from January to June 1987; Stefano, who was then still at the BCI in Milan, took study leave and joined me as a visitor to the economics department at UCLA. One day, we went to a bar in Santa Monica and I ordered a can of *root beer*; after one sip I exclaimed, giving up any further attempt to finish the can, that it tasted like 'shoe leather'! Zambelli, who had 'warned' me against ordering it, asked—simply: '*When did you last taste shoe leather?*'.

Stefano had, as a high school exchange student,[3] spent a couple of terms in Los Angeles, in the 1970s. During his absence from Ravenna, his elder brother had thought Stefano's beloved, *old*, and partially rusty, *Lambretta*,[4] was of no use and sold it for a 'song' (as we would say). His elder brother, whom Stefano liked, had acted on *Aladdin's principle* of 'new lamps for old' (except that he did not exchange the 'old' *Lambretta* for a 'new' one, for Stefano); Stefano, as even evidenced by the years of the quoted references on the title page, had great respect for the Italian manufacturing and design innovations of the early post-war years.[5] He, frequently, narrated this story, wistfully, to me, over many years of life together.

In his brilliant essay, in the *Goodwin Festschrift*, Solow (1990, p. 33), observed:

> There is always a temptation on occasions like this, to focus on personal details and remembered local colour. There is nothing wrong with yielding to that temptation—and I have done so—but there is a limit, and I shall observe it.

I shall, too!

---

[3] On an *American Field Service* (AFS) scholarship, in 1976.

[4] The story of *Lambretta* can easily be accessed via the Internet. I should add that in distant Colombo, where I grew up, the more 'popular' Italian post-war scooter was the *Vespa*.

[5] I am sure he was *not* an admirer of Marinetti's *Italian futurism*, and the *machine age* which it extolled (and supported *Mussolini's fascism*, of which Stefano was an implacable opponent—in spite of the fact that *Il Duce* was born and buried in **Predappio**, a small town in the once 'red' region of Emilia-Romagna).

Fig. 1.1 Stefano Zambelli, in October 2015, making an acceptance speech after receiving the *Fondazione Pescarabruzzo* prize for the Social Sciences

However, I should like to mention that Stefano Zambelli is the recipient of the prestigious, seventh award of the *Fondazione Pescarabruzzo*'s *NordSud* Prize in the Social Sciences in October 2015 (see Fig. 1.1). In addition, he has lectured and participated—and continues to do so—in numerous conferences, special events, and has contributed to several edited volumes (as well as himself editing some). He is—and has been—also a member of the editorial board of many prestigious journals.

Keynes, Sraffa, Goodwin and Turing were very important—though not entirely to the point of emulation—for Stefano Zambelli's extraordinary intellectual interests. So, I would like to take 'representative' observations by them which Stefano Zambelli considered important:

> But the *dynamic* development [of the **Treatise on Money**], as distinct from the instantaneous picture, was left incomplete and extremely confused. (Keynes 1936, p. vii; italics added)

> It is … the purpose of this article to … attempt to co-ordinate certain materials, separating what is still alive from what is dead in the concept of *the supply curve* and of its effects on competitive price determination. (Sraffa 1926, p. 536; italics added)

> To go from two identical markets to *n* nonidentical ones will require the prolonged services of *yet unborn calculating machines*. (Goodwin 1947, p. 204; italics added)

> It is *possible to invent* a single machine which can be used to compute *any* computable sequence. (Turing 1936–37, p. 238; italics added)

I shall concentrate—mostly, but not exclusively—on the four topics listed below; this is not because Zambelli's other contributions are unimportant or not as fundamental, but because there is (increasingly) a limit to my competence in analyzing them—in addition to the necessity of keeping this 'survey' to manageable levels. Zambelli (1995) is, if my understanding is even remotely correct, primarily a pedagogical contribution,[6] which is discussed very generally under Sect. 2, below'.

I shall, therefore, concentrate, in the next four sections, on the following four topics (as *my* vision of Zambelli's contributions):

- *Frisch*'s Rocking Horse Does *Not* Rock![7]
- Busy Beavers, the *Phillips Machine*, Differential Analyzers and Computability.
- Solving and Simulating Flexible Accelerator Coupled Dynamical Systems.
- Sraffian Economics.

The Summarizing Notes of Sect. 6 tries to tie the threads together and conclude—no doubt inadequately—the rich heritage of Zambelli's innovative and idiosyncratic approach to economic analysis (as *I* see it, in Sects. 2, 3, 4 and 5). Section 7 is a brief introduction to the essays in this book.

---

[6] Not that there is always a pedagogical element in all of Zambelli's writings!

[7] However, it is *not* Wicksell's *Rocking Horse*, many times Frisch's incorrect allusion is invoked by latter-day business cycle theorists (Zambelli 2007, fn. 4, p. 147).

I should 'confess' that I am convinced that the first three topics stand together—but the last topic subsumes his work on value and pricing theories; capital and distribution theories; measurement, productivity and technical progress leading to an admirable vision of an alternative paradigm for Macroeconomics, all informed by an understanding and an interpretation of the Sraffa *oeuvre* of over a half-a-century. For convenience, not simplicity, the above division seems to bring out the different analytical contributions of Zambelli clearly. I 'confess', also, that I have a special fondness, and immense liking, for the articles—and conclusions—by Zambelli, that resulted in the twenty-year odyssey of Sect. 2.

I must point out that there is a theme running through all of Zambelli's works; this is summarized in claims 3 and 4, p. 3, of Velupillai and Zambelli (2015)[8] to the effect that *simulation*, *computation* and *dynamics* form a triptych of concepts that are fruitful in the analysis of economic systems. This theme runs through all five of the above sub-sections of Zambelli's visions (in my interpretations). I would add to the triptych also *approximation*—for without some coherent approximation, no theory of economic systems, could be confronted with experiments on 'reality'.

Zambelli was—is—a master of investigating and studying *the approximate reality of experimenting with simulation the computational dynamics of economic systems*. It will not be incongruent to add *experiments* to the above four entities—*simulation*, *computation*, *dynamics* and *approximation*—to make it 'complete', at least *pro tempore*.

I don't think these five conceptual and methodological disciplining criteria of his research agenda came 'ready-made', so to speak; it was developed in the practice, theoretically grounded, of more than forty years of modeling, and seeking answers, to an increasingly precise series of questions about economic systems. I myself became conscious of this pentagonal disciplining criteria for research in economics only after reading Zambelli's writings, again and again, sequentially and non-sequentially (Fig. 1.2).

[8] This is an absolute exception to the rule that I will not refer to any joint work by Zambelli!

**Fig. 1.2** Stefano Zambelli and his student, N. Dharmaraj, at Maso Campbell in 2010

# 2 *Frisch*'s Rocking Horse Does *Not* Rock!

Neither 'analytical elegance' nor 'simplicity' ever seems to have diverted Zambelli's attention from his 'goal': *the dynamics of the aggregative behavior of capitalist economies give rise to unstable oscillatory profiles.* As Zambelli pointed out so many years ago (1992b, p. 56; italics added):

> How are we going to determine whether oscillations are possible? .... Analytical elegance and simplicity may have sometimes directed us far away from our goals.

It was not for 'analytical elegance' that the inevitability of unstable oscillatory profiles of capitalist economies was deduced—it was, above all, for wise *policy* purposes. To the extent that wise policy could mitigate the effects of oscillations, particularly on its impact on the underprivileged, Zambelli's research strategy also had a practical motive (Fig. 1.3).

From 1985 to 2015—a thirty-year period—his published works on *Trade Cycle Theory and Macrodynamics* are marked by, above all, the investigation of *aggregate oscillations* in key macroeconomic variables. In this thirty-year period, in addition, he refined and developed his intuition and mathematical knowledge of the *stability properties of oscillatory dynamics.*

**Fig. 1.3** Stefano Zambelli walking on the sandy shore of Los Angeles, in 1987

In 1985 Zambelli completed his University of Modena *cum laude Laurea* thesis on *Mathematical Theories of the Business Cycle*;[9] in 2015, in the memorable centennial issue of the *Cambridge Journal of Economics* for Richard Goodwin, *Dynamical Coupling, the non-linear accelerator and the persistence of business cycles*, Zambelli (2015), was published. Between them, and also before 1985 and after 2015—so far as I know—Zambelli worked on every possible aggregative model of the cycle, from Marx to the newclassicals (relatively favorably of the former, and correspondingly critically of the latter).[10]

Thus, Aftalion and Schumpeter, Frisch and Tinbergen, Kalecki and Goodwin, Kaldor and Hicks, Hansen and Samuelson—all of whose interests and works on aggregate dynamics of an oscillatory nature was only a part of their vast contributions to economic theory, particularly in the nascent mathematical mode, and 'modern' theorists like Day and Lucas, and many others, was grist to the Zambelli mill. He was also interested in, and contributed to, the theories of individuals—like Hugh Hudson and J. M. Clark—who, ostensibly, did not belong to one or the

[9] In Italian, as *Teorie Matematiche del Ciclo Economico.*

[10] I was immensely pleased to read Zambelli writing (on 24 February 2020—Richard Goodwin's birthday):

> As you surely remember, the first time .... I met you was when *you* delivered a seminar where you discussed ... Frisch's *PPIP* (*P*ropagation *P*roblems and *I*mpuls*e* *P*roblems) paper—in relation with Lucas.

other of the well-established *schools of thought* (classicals, neoclassicals, Keynesians, post-Keynesians, etc.) by interpreting them in the light of the *maestros* (like the above) of theories of aggregative cycles.

His major interests were in aggregate, deterministic,[11] oscillations and the theories underpinning them.

He was not interested in *ad hoc shockeries*[12] of any sort,[13] nor in dynamical systems theory which implied no equilibrium cycles (or stable/unstable oscillatory behavior). Zambelli never specified what kind of dynamical systems theory he was investigating; by this I mean whether it was, for example, differentiable dynamics and, hence, only of hyperbolic equilibria or the implications of the *strong transversality theorem* (*no* cycles, Abraham and Marsden 1987, pp. 539–540).

He concentrated on finding methods to *approximate* whatever economic system he was investigating, so that it could be *computed* by *simulating*, for *experimenting* its *dynamics*—that is, the dynamics of the economic system. He never forgot, or lost sight of, the nature of approximation and its effect on the conclusions. In the case of aggregative cycle theory, it was a case of investigating the dynamical properties of (ordinary) differential equations by judicious approximating algorithms.

This is most evident in his investigation of Frisch's methodology, and conclusions, in *PPIP*[14] (Frisch 1933). I deal with this fundamental contribution by Zambelli (1991, 1992a, 2007) in this section, which is crucially important in the *critical* understanding of a large part of so-called *modern* business cycle research—viz., the *Real Business Cycle* (*RBC*).

Frisch's main thesis is that a first-order differential equation system is not capable of fluctuating dynamics and, hence, he postulates a mixed (second-order) differential, (first-order) difference equation system (of

[11] Sensitiveness to initial values and therefore the need to investigate, for example, the *initial value problem* (*ivp*) of *ordinary differential equations* (*ode*) required a kind of perturbation analysis, but strictly within the framework of solutions of deterministic dynamical systems.

[12] Richard Day's felicitous description of Lucasian—or newclassical—*Real Business Cycle* (*RBC*) methodology (Day 1992, p. 180), which has its origins, unfortunately, in Frisch's *Rocking Horse* metaphor in *PPIP*, which Zambelli, with precise and incisive analysis, debunked most elegantly.

[13] I hasten to add that the exception to this 'rule' was his adherence to de Finetti's view of subjective probability with *countable additivity*.

[14] *PPIP*: *P*ropagation *P*roblems and *I*mpulse *P*roblems.

economic variable) and *assumes*, without further *ado*, that such a mixed system gives rise to oscillations.

In this process Frisch does criticize J. M. Clark for not understanding the elementary fact about determinate solutions for equation systems with variables and parameters; and those, like Kalecki, who assume values of the parameters (for a 'conservative' second-order *ode*) such that oscillatory solutions are guaranteed. He—Frisch—does add what has come to be called the 'time-to-build' assumption.

Generating the mixed differential-difference system, capable of displaying oscillatory properties, is *one* important step; investigating empirically the oscillatory properties of his 'new' (restricted) equation system is the second important step. Frisch rests satisfied with the *theoretical* possibility of oscillations of such mixed differential-difference systems.

In a highly significant series of papers, originating at UCLA in 1987, informed by Samuelson (1970, pp. 72–74, 1974, p. 10), Zambelli—initially motivated by curiosity, but gradually transformed into structured scientific query—tried to understand Frisch's numerical exercises by repeating them *exactly* (see Zambelli 2007, particularly fn. 6, 9 & 13 on pp. 147, 149 & 152)—given that *any* numerical integration (step-by-step integration, Zambelli *ibid*, p. 162) involves an *approximation*.

In spite of the fact that Zambelli tries very valiantly, and sympathetically, to understand Frisch's—or his assistants Holme and Thorbjörnsen (referring the latter two as 'computers of his [Frisch's] time', footnote. 6, but I think Zambelli means 'comput*o*rs' in the sense in which Patinkin (1956, p. 11) meant it)—efforts at numerical integration, it seems to me evident that the possibility of non-oscillatory behavior theoretically, in general, was *not* confronted experimentally (or empirically[15]).

Zambelli's conclusion is unequivocal (*ibid*, p. 152; italics added):

> The [reduced-form] equation resulting from [Frisch's] *theoretical* evaluation about the functioning of the hypothetical economy is a second-order linear differential equation and first-order linear difference equation. Being a second-order differential equation, the system can potentially account for

[15] I differentiate—as does Zambelli—*experimental* from *empirical*; the latter *approximates* '*reality*' (whatever *that* may mean) and the former is an *approximation* involved in, for example, *numerical integration*. A fairly similar distinction is made in the case of *digital* and *analogue* computation.

free oscillations,[16] but the system *may not necessarily do so*. The parameter space must be investigated and it so happens that *Frisch's model* allows, *for the set of economically relevant values of the parameters*, only for a *monotonic return* toward the equilibrium.[17]

The last two italicized items, in the quote, are extremely important to remember and understand. What Zambelli tried to do—in fact, *did do*—for more than twenty years was a classic exercise in *scientific validity*: that is, *repeatability of experiments*—in this case numerical experiments—by means of simulations. Later, in the context of the 'classic' Fermi-Pasta-Ulam (*FPU*) theoretical experiment, Zambelli structured his question of scientific validity explicitly (Zambelli 2015, p. 1615) (Fig. 1.4).

**Fig. 1.4** Stefano Zambelli with his students, Selda Kao and V. Ragupathy at a Restaurant in London, January 2020

[16] *Linear, first-order, difference* equations 'can potentially account for free oscillations', as, for example, the simplest cobweb model in economics shows.

[17] At this point the text refers to 'the appendix' in Zambelli, ibid. 'Toward the *equilibrium*' is a statement that is common in business cycle theory (of any variety)—but there are *equilibrium business cycle theories*, usually of *newclassical* persuasions, but *not* exclusively so.

## 3 Busy Beavers, the Phillips Machine, *Differential Analyzers* and Computability

I don't think a busy beaver function is computable for any well-defined function that is built up from those that are 'normally' considered in any of the pure or applied sciences. However, it must be remembered that Greenleaf (1991, p. 226; italics added) did propagate (sic!) an interesting view:

> The busy beaver function … becomes *computable* when its domain and range are *properly* defined.

In this I think I am reflecting Zambelli's thoughts about 'normal' and 'pure or applied sciences.' Of course, what one means by 'proper' or 'normal'—or even 'pure or applied sciences'—is not easy to formalize (in a meaningful way).

But Zambelli, at least since 1983, was deeply interested in the formalities of computability theory, and from about the late 1990s, in modeling important economic ideas using the (uncomputability) of the busy beaver function. He read—and *re-read*—an 'umpteen' number of times both Turing (1936–37) and Rado (1962) and, in my opinion, he was a *maestro* of computability theory (especially in its classical sense, as developed by Turing, *ibid*), and the *busy beaver function* as an encapsulation of *non-computability*.

He—and I—were particularly impressed by Rado (*op.cit*) stating, p. 884 (italics added):

> If $E$ is a non-empty, *finite* set of non-negative integers, then $E$ has a largest element.

Zambelli wrote me on 25 February 2019 that Shen, A and N. K. Vereshchagin (2003, p. 3) assert (italics added):

> *Any finite* set is *decidable*.

That such sets are decidable requires subtle definitions of computability (by Turing Machines) to be remembered, and an understanding of *constructive* vs. *non-constructive proofs*. Zambelli (2012) turned his attention to issues of constructive mathematics—but he was attuned to the power of this type of mathematics, in realistic economics (i.e., with the possibilities of computing and simulating with at most rational numbers) with his deep concern for Sraffa and de Finetti.

He mastered, quite comprehensively, the books of Davis (1958), Rogers (1967) and Odifreddi's first volume (of two, Odifreddi 1989—he came to know this author personally); in particular, the intricacies of modeling the state in the context of programming a functioning Turing Machine, with its paraphernalia of *encodings*.

We were both amused by Odifreddi's 'confession', penned on p. x (*op.cit*, italics added):

> At a time when I *did not even know how to turn a computer on*.

Zambelli had been 'turning on—and off, a computer' *at least* from the time I knew him!

*Computability Theory*, as applied to aggregative economics—but also to inter-industrial economics—is represented in Zambelli's *oeuvre* in (*at least*) Zambelli (1995, 2004b, 2005, 2010, 2012)—but also (partly) in Zambelli (2011a), which is devoted, mostly, to his interpretation (with which I readily agree) of the power of the *Phillips Machine* as regards its capability of simulating the solutions of (ordinary) non-linear differential equations.[18]

It must not be forgotten, and Zambelli never did so, that the *Phillips Machine* is an *analogue computer*, used to solve *Keynesian dynamic models*—that is, to solve ordinary (non-linear) differential equations. In this sense, it is a 'primitive' *differential analyzer* (see Fig. 1.5).

[18] Clearly, both of Zambelli's published papers of 2011 (Zambelli 2011a, b) belong to the next section on solving and simulating *coupled* dynamic models of national—that is, aggregative—economies. Whereas the paper on the Phillips Machine is more explicit on the machine's analogue computing nature, the remarks on this kind of computing are not very prevalent in the Zambelli 2011b paper (but see note 10, p. 630).

Fig. 1.5 Zambelli with the (resurrected) Cambridge *Phillips Machine*, December 2015

My personal 'all-time favorite', among these Zambelli papers dealing with issues of computability, non-computability, constructivity and non-constructivity (the latter two concepts with especial regard to *proofs*), using *simulations* to understand them in the context of economic models of aggregate growth, evolution of ideas and productivity, is his 2004 **Metroeconomica** article on *Production of Ideas by Means of Ideas*[19]*: A Turing Machine Metaphor* (Zambelli 2004b). In particular, he gave a new interpretation—in the footsteps of Nelson and Winter (1982)—to the evolution of ideas, debunked the idea (sic!) of damped cycles kept alive by random shocks and, therefore, of growth being a trend path[20] and the 'metaphor' of the 'toy chemistry set' that gave rise to one wing of so-called

[19] Not too much subtlety is required to understand the parallels with *Production of Commodities by Means of Commodities* (Sraffa 1960)! But there is no explicit reference to Sraffa's book in this article by Zambelli.

[20] A reflection of his critique of Frisch's methodological precepts as in *PPIP*!

endogenous growth theory, and much else, using an encoding[21] (in terms of natural numbers) of Turing Machine encapsulation of the generation of ideas, particularly in (non-linear) growth cycle theory.

Of course, he was aware of the way Trevor Swan had invoked (inappropriately) the *Meccano metaphor* for making sense of the substitution possibilities (there were *none*) in neoclassical growth theory. Romer invoking the toy *chemistry set metaphor* to substantiate the role of ideas, in endogenous growth theory, was equally inappropriate. All this was made 'clear', but implicitly, via the use of encoding of *ideas*, as a *metaphor* in the input tape of a Turing Machine, when viewed as a Universal Turing Machine;[22] he was meticulous in considering the 'infinite' length of input tapes as 'potential'—Turing's and Zambelli's ways of granting Brouwer his due!

Zambelli (2011a) concludes on p. 184 (italics added), first pointing out that *digital computing* requires *approximations* of (ordinary, non-linear) differential by (non-linear) difference equations:

> Moreover in order to conduct *digital computations*, the *approximated* systems are further *approximated* with *difference equations*; different *approximating algorithms*: Euler, Runge-Kutta and so on.

and, then:

---

[21] I remember vividly how, in Los Angeles in the late 1980s and early 1990s, our conversations were often in terms of *Gödel numbers* of sentences!

[22] I am reminded of the sentence in the Swedish translation (by Vibeke Emond) of *Haruki Murakami*'s Japanese original, *Kishidanchōgoroshi* (italics added):

> Det är bara att låta *metaforerna förbli metaforer*, låta det krypterade förblir krypterat och låta sållen vara såll.

My 'free' translation from the Swedish of the original Japanese is:

> It is best to leave metaphors be metaphorical, encryptions be encrypted and let sieves to sieve.

> The *computation of the dynamics* of such a system is best made with *an analogue computer* like the Phillips MONIAC or with an *analogue* electrical system like the one constructed by Strotz et al. (1953).

That digital approximations of computable solutions were possible *after* approximations of the theoretically approximated differential equations by difference equations; he was also well acquainted with the pitfalls that were possible in the latter approximations,[23] in *ibid*. He was well aware that approximations were also necessitated in the analogue computation of differential equations, as evidenced by his thoroughly knowledgeable discourse, in *ibid*, about Fisher's and Phillips' machines. Neither Fisher, nor Phillips, compromised with the solutions implied by economic theory—microeconomic in one case, macroeconomic, in the other. But they—both of them—compromised with hydraulics and hydrodynamics, electrical and mechanical theories in the actual building of the analogue machines.[24]

To contrast the accuracy of (inevitable) approximations, Zambelli could have compared analogue computation by means of the *differential analyzer* (see, again, Fig. 1.5), which directly simulates the solution of a theoretical ODE (of orders that are within the range of the models solved by algorithmic approximations in MATLAB, by Zambelli), but of course, *machine precision* is approximate and, to that extent, so is analogue computation by the differential analyzer (Hartree 1938, is excellent on the principles underpinning the mechanics of the differential analyzer).

Perhaps we can expect Zambelli's fertile 'pen', even now, exploring different kinds of approximations, machine precision, algorithmic solutions—and even eschewing the specter of Taylor series truncation to 'reduce' difference-differential equations to ordinary, non-linear, differential equations! This may revitalize the Phillips Machine, viewed as a special case of the differential analyzer, as a repository of analogue

[23] As far as I know, Potts (1982) and Stuart and Humphries (1986) are 'mainstays' in Zambelli's repertoire of approximation literature. The former is on the dangers of mindless approximations of differential to difference equations; the latter is about the more general problem of approximation, for computing with numerical methods, of dynamical systems as ODEs.

[24] I remember very well Goodwin placing buckets to collect the leaking water, when he lectured on Keynesian economic policy, using the original Cambridge *Phillips Machine*!

computing of national economic models—coupled and uncoupled (rather than viewing them as 'open' or 'closed', which distinction Zambelli chose, explicitly, to eschew).

I end this section with a *tentative* Proposition and a Remark (about the Phillips and Fisher Machines):

Proposition 1 A *differential analyzer* is a *Universal Machine* with respect to solving an ordinary differential equation, subject to efficient *machining*.

Proof *Any* ordinary differential equation, i.e., of *any finite* order, can be solved by a sufficiently constructed *differential analyzer*.

Remark 1 A *Phillips Machine* is, therefore, a special case of a *differential analyzer*; but, not the *Fisher Machine*.

## 4 Solving and Simulating Flexible Accelerator Coupled Dynamical Systems

In working out, explicitly, these novel concepts, as numerical approximating algorithms in the simulation dynamics of coupled, aggregative, national economies, Zambelli produced a series of path-breaking papers: Zambelli (2010, 2011a, b, 2012) and, above all, Zambelli (2015) (Fig. 1.6).

The most important, and most interesting, *research question*, linking Zambelli (2007) with Zambelli (2015)—that is, similar to a scientific question about *PPIP simulation*[25] with one on the *FPU experiment*—is posed, explicitly, for $n$ identical economies, coupled with the same structural parameters determining their long-term dynamic behavior, that is, attractors are limit cycles (for most parameters), as follows (*ibid*, p. 1615; italics added):

[25] See footnote 13, p. 1620, in Zambelli (2015).

**Fig. 1.6** Zambelli tasting *Sassicaia*, 2009, at Velupillai's home, in Trento, September 2012

> Will the economies like the ones described above exhibit, when *subjected to asymmetric shocks* and after a transient period, a *perfectly synchronous behaviour*?

The *surprising* answer to this question—like the empirical answer to the *FPU* theoretical question of equipartition of energy—is that asynchronous, persistent, dynamics is the 'rule', as a function of the initial conditions (of the twenty coupled economies considered).

For the richness of the analysis of coupled dynamic national economies, with macroeconomic investment functions, based on micro-behavioral postulate depending on the nonlinearity due to the distinction between desired and actual aggregate 'capital' (i.e., flexible-accelerator models), it is best to proceed from the series of papers by Zambelli from 2011 to 2015.

He would endorse his maestro, Richard Goodwin, extolling the virtues of coupling (Goodwin 1992, p. 13, italics added):

> [I] was very excited to find that Phillips had two of his magical machines in London, so I could reproduce what I had analyzed back in 1947 in my *dynamical coupling* paper [Goodwin 1947]. If I remember correctly, Phillips did not believe we could produce *erratic behavior* by *coupling* his *machines*—but we did.

Here, I would like to emphasize another kind of modeling novelty. This is the way Zambelli models the coupled economies, as arranged on a chain or string—like the way *FPU* arranged the interacting particles—with *only nearest neighbor interactions*. I want to point out that Zambelli's arrangements and interactions are very similar to Turing (1952) and Conway's LIFE (Rendell 2016).[26] It was also the way Goodwin arranged his coupled markets.

The reason for *not* referring to the more standard works for LIFE[27] is that Rendell (*ibid*) is a masterly (programming) introduction to Conway's Game of LIFE, Turing Machines, the modeling of GOPHER as a case of the Universal Turing Machine and, in general, showing the equivalence of 'Conway' and 'Turing'; my own conjecture on this equivalence is that Rendall exploits the fact that both of these rich concepts can be understood as (simple) rule-based evolution of cellular automata. It is therefore a unified approach to Zambelli's fascination with Turing, *FPU*, Goodwin, Wolfram—brought together with Conway's construction.

I end this section with two conjectures and two remarks. The first conjecture refers to 'thick lines' in Figs. 2 and 3 of Zambelli (2015); the second conjecture to the *Devil's Staircase* of Zambelli (2011b). The first remark is tied to the Universal Turing Machines of the two conjectures. The second remark is about using analogue computing machines, for example, the *differential analyzer*, to solve the non-linear ODE (of system (15) in Zambelli 2011b or equation (14) in Zambelli 2015).

[26] Of course, Zambelli knew of the parallels with Turing (ibid.), see footnote 9, p. 1615, in Zambelli (2015).

[27] In the case of Conway's LIFE, for example, chapter 25 of Berlekamp et al. (1982).

Conjecture 1 The *global average*—i.e., the 'thick lines' of Fig. 2 & Fig. 3 in Zambelli (2015)—can be generated by a *Universal Turing Machine.*

Conjecture 2 The *Devil's Staircase* of Zambelli (2011b) can be generated by a *Universal Turing Machine*.

Remark 2 The *Universal Turing Machines* of the above two conjectures encapsulate the dynamics of the aggregate of the coupled economies.

Remark 3 The *differential analyzer* is a *Universal Machine* (see Proposition 1, § 3); its actions are equivalent to analogue computation of the solution of the system of non-linear ODEs (system (15) of Zambelli 2011b, or of the non-linear ODE, equation (14), of Zambelli 2015).

In 'Remark 3', I toyed with the idea of using *direct solution*; but *machine precision* ('subject to efficient machining', as in Proposition 1), of which Zambelli is fully aware, results in an approximation that may—or may not—be equivalent to the reduction of an ODE to a difference equation to facilitate digital programming by means of algorithms. This issue, as emphasized in the previous section, can be resolved *empirically*, by means of comparing the approximations in analogue computing, with those in digital computing. It is not a *theoretical* issue, unless a *thesis*—or law, such as the laws of (phenomenological) thermodynamics—is one.

Now, I claim that *every* theory, especially mathematical theory, is built on 'theses'; *sometimes*, they are called axioms. Zambelli does accept, for example, the Church-Turing *Thesis* as a foundation for computability *theory*. He might envisage both *empirical* and *theoretical* resolution of the issue of *approximation*, in analogue and digital computation. I, as an eternal and incorrigible, doubter, would enjoy reading, or listening to, Zambelli's discourse on these thorny issues![28]

[28] Post (1936, p. 105) called a *thesis* a *natural law* (I think in the sense of the 2nd Law of *Phenomenological* Thermodynamics)—'a working hypothesis' (ibid.); he could have referred to *axioms* in the same vein! I subscribe, wholly, to Post's view—which is also Turing's and, I dare say, Zambelli's, too!

# 5 Sraffian Economics

Zambelli has been reading, pondering—reading again, and again—and wondering about Sraffa's published oeuvre, from the early 1920s till Production of Commodities by Means of Commodities (PCMC) (Sraffa 1960) and also subsequently (Sraffa 1962 and Sraffa's interchange with Newman, published in Bharadwaj 1970). I surmise that he would have agreed with the opinion expressed by Sraffa, in a letter to Joan Robinson, in October 1936 (italics added) (Fig. 1.7):

> If you are not convinced, try it on someone who has not been entirely *debauched by economics*. Tell your gardener that a farmer has 200 acres or employs 10 men—will he not have a pretty accurate idea of the quantities of land & labour? Now tell him that he employs 500 tons of capital, & he will think you are dotty—(*not more so*, however, *than Sidgwick or Marshall*).

Initially, to the best of my knowledge, it was Sraffa (1922, 1925, 1926, 1932a, b, 1960, 1961, 1962, 1970); deep interests in these Sraffa-articles meant that Zambelli's writings and thoughts became increasingly dominated by money, banking, interest rate and profit rates theory, measurement, productivity, technical progress, the Standard system, viable systems of production economics, reswitching, capital reversal, the wage-profit curve, the aggregate production function, capital intensity—in

Fig. 1.7 Zambelli visiting London (photo taken by the River Thames), March 2017

general, capital and distribution theories (in the 'old fashioned' sense). It meant also his comprehensive mastery of the classical economists—particularly Ricardo and Marx; but he was also to have a comprehensive knowledge of (aggregate) neoclassical economics and many aspects of newclassical economics, particularly real business cycle theory[29] (reflecting his 'life-long' commitment to every aspect of cyclical behavior in capitalist—or industrial—economies).

Almost all his writings, again to the best of my knowledge, from 1992 to 2017, on productivity, production-based index numbers (for *Purchasing Power Parity*, *PPP*, calculations), international comparisons of productivity, were based on a judicious interpretation of the applicability of the basic framework of *PCMC*. *Ditto* for Zambelli (2004a, 2018a).

I happen to think that Zambelli (2018a) is the 'other side of the *coin*' of Shaikh (1974)—and is as fundamental—but, then, *coin tossing* is *not* an *unbiased* activity (to the extent that the mechanics of kinematic motion is correct, when formalized mathematically), even if the coin is, itself, constructed to be '*fair*'! Therefore, I don't expect a reading, and an influence, of Zambelli's pioneering paper, comparable to the 'cult' (almost) status that Shaikh's important contribution seems to have achieved.

Zambelli[30] has always read, and developed, the method of *PCMC* with the lens of algorithmic computation—that is, machine implementation—in mind; he has mastered the use of MATLAB computation and, therefore, he is fully aware of the approximations that any algorithmic formulation entails. This is the practical side, of the theoretical endeavor, as has been emphasized a number of times, earlier. The theoretical endeavor is *exact*—especially with regard to *money*, *banking* and the *rate*

[29] I remember vividly, telling Zambelli, that Prescott (2005) had written (italics added):

> In the 1960s there was the famous Cambridge capital controversy. This controversy bears on the issue "*What is money?*" *The Cambridge capital controversy was a silly one*, as pointed out so clearly by Arrow (1989).

Stefano was visibly upset by this ignorant remark by one of the *Godfathers* of *RBC*; he subsequently, but not only as the result of this stupid remark by Prescott, tore into *RBC* with a vengeance that was truly remarkable! By the way, Arrow never, particularly in Arrow (*op.cit.*), to my knowledge said anything Prescott attributes to him in the above quote.

[30] Shaikh, too!

*of profits* (which Zambelli considers equivalent to the *rate of interest*, but I am not sure whether for 'simplicity' or 'convenience', in the analytic sense).

I should like to add that Zambelli is neither a card-carrying Neo-Ricardian, nor an adherent of the 'gravitation' theory of convergence of cross-field dynamics,[31] whether it is based on some mysterious, even religious, interpretation of *PCMC* or the classical economists. Zambelli is not a practicing theological evangelist, so he does not resort to an exegetical reading of Sraffa's published and unpublished work. He is interested in taking seriously the subtitle to *PCMC—Prelude to a Critique of Economic Theory*. This is especially so since he started reading Sraffa's unpublished material deposited in the library of Trinity College, Cambridge.

He has used this reading as a springboard to relax the *assumptions* (although I myself consider these 'assumptions' in *PCMC* as *axioms* but Sraffa, at least in this book, *never* uses the word), in *PCMC* and generalize them in such a way as to make concrete the idea of a *Prelude to a Critique of Economic Theory*, in an applicable way. It must be remembered, and Zambelli always does so, that every application, especially if it is to lead to computation, involves an approximation and there are no applicable algorithms that map *exactly* theory and empirical applications.

Given all this, and my self-imposed restriction of *not* considering Zambelli's joint works (with the exception in Sect. 1 above), the most relevant contribution to a relaxing of a crucial, widely noticed, assumption is the last of his contributions, considered in this paper, that is, Zambelli (2018b). In this path-breaking contribution he relaxes Sraffa's *assumption* of the uniform rate of profits, with special relevance to the self-replacing properties of the economic system, which is *viable* (an assumption, too?). I consider the role of the uniform rate of profits, for a viable economic system, in both a self-replacing and a surplus producing

[31] Zambelli (2018b), to which I shall devote the rest of this section, refers to Ganguli (1997). I would like to state categorically that Ganguli (1997) is *not* constructive in any sense, although he claims so (ibid., p. 534 & 541). He is also comprehensively incorrect in his statements about Steedman (1984), so-called equations, (10)–(12), ibid., p. 535. Steedman is very clear that (10) is a definitional identity—in fact he uses the symbol ≡ connecting the *l.h.s* to the *r.h.s*, apart from stating explicitly (ibid., p. 135), that 'Relation (10) is just a definitional identity'. This is not a paper pointing out the infelicities in Ganguli (*op.cit*); there will be time and place for such an exercise!

state, in single- and joint-product systems of production economies, with and without land (explicitly considered), as an *axiom* (as mentioned previously).

Zambelli, however, harnesses an impressive array of Sraffian documents and also the Bharadwaj (1963) review of *PCMC*, which received the rare approval of Sraffa, to assure us—that the rate of profits be uniform for the purpose which it is put—that is, the self-replacement of a viable economic system. In particular, he refers to the excellent Bharadwaj review of *PCMC* in footnote 8, p. 794 of Zambelli (*op.cit*) and in (almost) the same 'breadth' to Sraffa's quote of *a man falling from the moon* and observing the repeatability of the process of production (*ibid*, p. 798). In the process we are given a lesson in careful reading of the unpublished material in the Sraffa archives, especially as it pertains to the structure of the various *equation*[32] systems in *PCMC*.

It is a veritable *tour de force* of the implications of *non-uniform rate of profits*[33] for the viable economic system to replicate the production system that is at the basis of its economics. I think it is squarely in the Sraffian tradition of *Prelude to a Critique of Economic Theory*.

# 6 Summarizing Notes

Investigating the reality of economic systems, both Sraffian, Sraffa-based macroeconomics and coupled, flexible-accelerator models of aggregate cycles, by means of approximate algorithms, as dynamic computations, resulting in simulation experiments, was—and is—Stefano Zambelli's *forte*. He has little time for those who peddle parables, fairy tales and unrealistic economics, in the name of scientific experiments. He believes that all economic theories—indeed all theories—should be algorithmic,

[32] The whole of *PCMC* is in terms of *equations*—not *inequalities*, concomitant slack variables, assumptions (or axioms) of satiability, and the like.

[33] In the case of the uniformity assumption, it may well be justified to refer to *rate of profits*; but with non-uniformity, perhaps Zambelli's modification to *rates of profit* may be more suitable!

and could, therefore, be approximated *precisely*,[34] for computable purposes.

Thus, even as late as a couple of years ago (Zambelli 2018a, p. 419; italics added), he was to say:

> The dominant macroeconomic *fairy tales* are just *fairy tales* and they might have nothing or very little to do with the *reality* of the economic system.

I remember very well how excited he was with Allen (1983) and the possibility of computing, with appropriate—that is, known (at least to him)—algorithms, the (approximate) *Devil's Staircase* and *mode locking* in business cycle models. For him, knowledgeable approximation of uncomputable entities was important—as shown by his fascination with *Kolmogorov complexity* as a foundation for uncertainty. He was never in doubt that uncertainty, in economics, was uncomputable. It was the obverse side of knowledge as uncomputable, best modeled in terms of the busy beaver function, as done in Zambelli (2004b).

It was, for him, a *credo—we will never know, we can never know*! We *must*, however, *try to know*.

He has, over the almost forty years I have known him, honed the method of scientific investigation, almost entirely in the noble sense of *learning by doing*. By exact simulation of the numerical experiment of Frisch, in PPIP, he learnt that possibility of repetition was one wing of acceptable scientific methodology. The other wing of scientific practice was the generation of surprise, so that conjectures could be, either tentatively accepted or refuted decisively. This was evident in the way he posed the *FPU* problem, but in the context of coupled flexible-accelerator models of aggregate national economies.

There was, of course, a *surprise* element also in repeating Frisch's *PPIP* exercise: the *surprise* that the famed Rocking Horse did *not* Rock!

This is the hallmark of Stefano Zambelli's way of doing economics—apart from basing his framework of analysis on the works of a few

[34] I have used *precisely* and *exactly* interchangeably; I mean it in the sense in which Aberth (2007) uses *precise*; Zambelli uses *precise*, coupled (sic!) to *numerical methods*. In this sense it is more in line with the title of Aberth's book, which I have seen, well-thumbed, on the shelf in his study (see Fig. 1.8).

**Fig. 1.8** Zambelli in his Office-Study, Economics Department, Trento University, February 2017

*maestros*, Hicks and Goodwin, Sraffa and Keynes, in economics; in the sciences—he never distinguished between *pure* and *applied*, nor between *closed* and *open*—it was de Finetti and Turing.

## 7 Brief Notes on the Contributions to *the Zambelli Festschrift*

The seventeen chapters by seventeen contributors are made up of Zambelli's (former) teachers, friends and (past) students. Many others, in one or another of these categories could—should—have contributed, but their absence is a reflection of my limitations. It is a heartening experience for me, as Editor, to report that almost all who were invited to contribute did so with warmth and immediate willingness; of course, it is a reflection of the esteem with which they hold the man and intellectual that Stefano Zambelli is.

I must, however, express my gratitude and extreme appreciation of Dr Silvana Convertini, who happens to be the beloved and lovely wife of Stefano Zambelli; she willingly cooperated when she had to, without interfering in any way the editorial process. This applies also to the two daughters of Zambelli and Convertini, Sofia and Martina Lucia. I am sure that all the contributors join me in thanking her for her unselfish attitude to this project.

The different distinguished contributors have been arranged, in this book, alphabetically, even though there would have been a case for grouping them thematically, particularly reflecting the subject matter as described by the title. Above all, each of the contributions reflects issues which have been, or are currently, of interest—even intense interest—for the work, life and profile of Stefano Zambelli. All the contributions were written with this in mind.

Each of the distinguished contributors made a special effort to make their chapters especially pedagogical, even at the expense of making the essays slightly 'light-hearted'; it was my request that they trade-off pedagogy and clarity at the expense of some originality—even though each chapter is both absolutely innovative in origin and clear in conception.

I don't have to display my 'prejudices' by trying to interpret what I have read in the different essays; I will let the reader savor that pleasure.

I have, finally, to thank the initial economics editor at Palgrave/Macmillan, Rachel Sangster, for making this book to honor Stefano Zambelli possible; she is no longer with Palgrave/Macmillan, having decided to seek 'greener' pastures elsewhere. She left her unfinished work in the capable hands of Wyndham-Hacket Pain and his editorial assistant, Srishti Gupta. Both of them have been very supportive and have helped my editorial work with advice, extensions (due to the difficult times we face) and experience. Again, I think these words of gratitude and appreciation for all they have done are shared by all the distinguished contributors.

## References

Aberth, O. (2007). *Introduction to Precise Numerical Methods* (2nd ed.). Amsterdam: Elsevier.

Abraham, R., & Marsden, J. E. (1987). *Foundations of Mechanics* (2nd ed., Revised, enlarged, and reset), with the assistance of T. Ratiu & R. Cushman. Reading, MA: Addison-Wesley Publishing Company, Inc.

Allen, T. (1983). On the Arithmetic of Phase Locking: Coupled Neurons as a Lattice on $R^2$. *Physica 6D, 6*(3, Apr.), 305–320.

Arrow, K. J. (1989). Joan Robinson and Modern Economic Theory: An Interview. In G. R. Feiwel (Ed.), *Joan Robinson and Modern Economic Theory* (Chap. 3, pp. 147–185). New York: New York University Press.

Berlekamp, E. R., Conway, J. H., & Guy, R. K. (1982). *Winning Ways for Your Mathematical Plays* (Volume 2: Games in Particular). London: Academic Press.

Bharadwaj, K. R. (1963, August 24). Value Through Exogenous Distribution. *Economic Weekly*.

Bharadwaj, K. (1970, December). On the Maximum Number of Switches Between Two Production Systems. *Schweizerische Zeitschrift für Volkswirtschaft und Statistik*, Nr. 4 106. Jahrgang.

Davis, M. (1958). *Computability and Unsolvability*. New York: McGraw-Hill Book Company.

Day, R. (1992). Models of Business Cycles: A Review Article. *Structural Change and Economic Dynamics, 3*(1, June), 177–182.

Frisch, R. (1933). Propagation Problems and Impulse Problems in Dynamic Economics. In *Essays in Honour of Gustav Cassel* (pp. 171–205). London: George Allen & Unwin, Ltd.

Ganguli, P. (1997). Differential Profit Rates and Convergence to the Natural State. *The Manchester School, LXV*(5, Dec.), 534–567.

Goodwin, R. M. (1947). Dynamical Coupling with Especial Reference to Markets Having Production Lags. *Econometrica, 15*(3, July), 181–204.

Goodwin, R. M. (1992, April). Foreseeing Chaos. *Royal Economic Society Newsletter*, no. 77.

Greenleaf, N. (1991). Algorithmic Languages and the Computability of Functions. In J. H. Johnson & M. J. Loomes (Eds.), *The Mathematical Revolution Inspired by Computing* (pp. 221–232). Oxford: Clarendon Press.

Hartree, D. R. (1938). The Mechanical Integration of Differential Equations. *The Mathematical Gazette, 22*(251, Oct.), 342–364.

Keynes, J. M. (1936). *The General Theory If Employment, Interest and Money*. London: Macmillan and Co., Ltd.

Nelson, R. R., & Winter, S. G. (1982). *An Evolutionary Theory of Economic Change*. Cambridge, MA: Harvard University Press.

Odifreddi, P. (1989). *Classical Recursion Theory: The Theory of Functions and Sets of Natural Numbers*. Amsterdam: North-Holland.

Patinkin, D. (1956). *Money, Interest, and Prices: An Integration of Monetary and Value Theory*. Evanston, IL: Row, Peterson and Company.
Post, E. (1936). Finite Combinatory Processes—Formulation I. *The Journal of Symbolic Logic, 1*(3, Sep.), 103–105.
Potts, R. B. (1982). Nonlinear Difference Equations. *Nonlinear Analysis: Theory, Methods and Applications, 6*(7), 659–665.
Prescott, E. C. (2005). Comments on "Inflation, Output, and Welfare" by Ricardo Lagos and Guillaume. *International Economic Review, 46*(2, May), 523–531.
Rado, T. (1962). On Non-Computable Functions. *Bell System Technical Journal, 41*(3, May), 877–884.
Rendell, P. (2016). *Turing Machine Universality of the Game of Life*. Springer International Publishing, AG Switzerland.
Rogers, H., Jr. (1967). *Theory of Recursive Functions and Effective Computability*. New York: McGraw-Hill Book Company.
Samuelson, P. A. (1970). Maximum, Principles in Analytical Economics. *Les Prix Nobel en 1970*, pp. 62–77. The Nobel Foundation.
Samuelson, P. A. (1974). Remembrances of Frisch. *European Economic Review, 5*(1), 7–23.
Shaikh, A. (1974). Laws of Production and Laws of Algebra: The Humbug Production Function. *The Review of Economics and Statistics, 56*(1, Feb.), 115–120.
Shen, A., & Vereshchagin, N. K. (2003). *Computable Functions*. Providence, RI: American Mathematical Society.
Solow, R. M. (1990). Goodwin's Growth Cycle: Reminiscence and Rumination. In *Nonlinear and Multisectoral Macrodynamics—Essays in Honour of Richard Goodwin* (Chap. 4, pp. 31–41). Basingstoke and London: The Macmillan Press Ltd.
Sraffa, P. (1922). The Bank Crisis in Italy. *The Economic Journal, 32*(126, June), 178–191.
Sraffa, P. (1925). Sulle relazioni fra costo e quantità prodotta. *Annali di economia, II*, 277–328.
Sraffa, P. (1926). The Laws of Returns under Competitive Conditions. *The Economic Journal, 36*(144, Dec.), 535–550.
Sraffa, P. (1932a). Dr. Hayek on Money and Capital. *The Economic Journal, 42*(165, Mar.), 42–53.
Sraffa, P. (1932b). [Money and Capital]: A Rejoinder. *The Economic Journal, 42*(166, June), 249–251.

Sraffa, P. (1960). *Production of Commodities by Means of Commodities—Prelude to a Critique of Economic Theory*. Cambridge: Cambridge University Press.

Sraffa, P. (1961). Comments on Hicks. In *The Theory of Capital: Proceedings of a Conference held by the International Economic Association* (in Corfu) (pp. 305–306). London: Macmillan & Co., Ltd.

Sraffa, P. (1962). Production of Commodities: A Comment. *The Economic Journal, 72*(286, June), 477–479.

Sraffa, P. (1970). Letters to Peter Newman, pp. 425–428, in the *Appendix* of Bharadwaj (1970).

Steedman, I. (1984). Natural Prices, Differential Profit Rates and the Classical Competitive Process. *The Manchester School, 52*(2), 123–140.

Strotz, R. H., McAnulty, J. C., & Naines, J. B. (1953). Goodwin's Nonlinear Theory of the Business Cycle: An Electro-Analog Solution. *Econometrica, 21*(3), 390–411.

Stuart, A. M., & Humphries, A. R. (1986). *Dynamical Systems and Numerical Analysis*. Cambridge: Cambridge University Press.

Turing, A. M. (1936–37). On Computable Numbers with an Application to the Entscheidungsproblem. *Proceedings of the London Mathematical Society*, Ser. 2, *42*, 230–265.

Turing, A. M. (1952). The Chemical Basis of Morphogenesis. *Philosophical Transactions of the Royal Society of London, Series B, Biological Sciences, 237*(641, Aug.), 37–72.

Zambelli, S. (1991). The Wooden Horse that Wouldn't Rock: Reconsidering Frisch. *UCLA Economics Working Papers, # 623*. UCLA Department of Economics.

Zambelli, S. (1992a). The Wooden Horse That Wouldn't Rock: Reconsidering Frisch. In K. Velupillai (Ed.), *Nonlinearities, Disequilibria and Simulation—Essays in Honour of Björn Thalberg* (Chap. 4, pp. 27–54). Basingstoke, Hampshire: The Macmillan Press Ltd.

Zambelli, S. (1992b). Response (to Björn Thalberg's Discussion). In K. Velupillai (Ed.), *Nonlinearities, Disequilibria and Simulation—Quantitative Methods in the Stabilization of Macrodynamic Systems, Essays in Honour of Björn Thalberg* (p. 56). Basingstoke, Hampshire: The Macmillan Press Ltd.

Zambelli, S. (1995). Logica della calcolabilità ed applicazioni economiche. *Note Economiche, XXV*(1), 191–216.

Zambelli, S. (2004a). The 40% Neoclassical Aggregate Theory of Production. *Cambridge Journal of Production, 28*(1, Jan.), 99–120.

Zambelli, S. (2004b). Production of Ideas by Means of Ideas: A Turing Machine Metaphor. *Metroeconomica, 55*(2 & 3, May/Sep.), 155–179.
Zambelli, S. (2005). Computable Knowledge and Undecidability: A Turing Machine Metaphor Applied to Endogenous Growth Models. In K. V. Velupillai (Ed.), *Computability, Complexity and Constructivity in Economic Analysis* (Chap. X, pp. 233–263). Oxford: Blackwell Publishing.
Zambelli, S. (2007). A Rocking Horse That Never Rocked: Frisch's "Propagation Problems and Impulse Problems". *History of Political Economy, 39*(1, Spring), 145–166.
Zambelli, S. (2010), Computable and Constructive Economics, Undecidable Dynamics and Algorithmic Rationality. In S. Zambelli (Ed.), *Computable, Constructive and Behavioural Economic Dynamics* (Chap. 1, pp. 15–45). London: Routledge and Taylor & Francis Group.
Zambelli, S. (2011a). Coupled Dynamics in a Phillips Machine Model of the Macroeconomy. *Economia Politica,* Special Issue, *XXVIII*(Dec.), 171–186.
Zambelli, S. (2011b). Flexible Accelerator Economic Systems as Coupled Oscillators. *Journal of Economic Surveys, 25*(3), 608–633.
Zambelli, S. (2012). Computable Economics: Reconstructing the Nonconstructive. *New Mathematics and Natural Computation, 8*(1), 113–122.
Zambelli, S. (2015). Dynamical Coupling, the Non-linear Accelerator and the Persistence of Business Cycles. *Cambridge Journal of Economics, 39*(6, Nov.), 1607–1628.
Zambelli, S. (2018a). The Aggregate Production Function is NOT Neoclassical. *Cambridge Journal of Economics, 42*(2, Mar.), 383–426.
Zambelli, S. (2018b). Production of Commodities by Means of Commodities and Non-Uniform Rates of Profits. *Metroeconomica, 69*(4, Nov.), 791–819.

# 2

# Intuitions About Welfare—Under the Constraint of Computability

Charlotte Bruun

## 1 Introduction

I've had the pleasure of both being a student of Stefano and a colleague during his years in Denmark. He has been a great inspiration for me and has had a big impact on my perspective on economics and life in general. We both grew up in the countryside, which I believe puts its mark on your values. I always admired Stefano's undaunted approach to academia and his almost *altmodisch* sense of decency and justice. We also share the fact that our parents had difficulties relating to our career choices—as Stefano expressed his father's feeling; *What a waste of a perfectly good body.* I hope his father came to appreciate that it was not a waste of a perfectly good mind.

I want to express my gratitude to Carsten Heyn-Johnsen and Thomas Fredholm (both former colleagues of Stefano Zambelli), and to Francesco Luna, who were all patient with me in going over some of the arguments presented here. However, they should not be held responsible, but they do send their greetings.

C. Bruun (✉)
University College of Northern Denmark, Aalborg, Denmark



K. Velupillai (ed.), *Keynesian, Sraffian, Computable and Dynamic Economics*,
https://doi.org/10.1007/978-3-030-58131-2_2

I had the pleasure of visiting Stefano and his family in 2018, where I took the opportunity to discuss with him an idea I had for conceptualizing the Danish, rural and *altmodisch* expression *godt købmandskab* ("the good merchant", also related to the German *Ehrbarer Kaufmann*). Being employed at a business department, my purpose was to understand what needs to be considered in evaluating the sustainability of businesses under the UN sustainable development goals, where social as well as environmental impact must be taken into account.

Here I shall employ the very same conceptualization on neoclassical welfare theory. My purpose is to put into perspective some of the critiques Stefano and Vela Velupillai have dedicated their lives to. I do not have the capacity to add to their work or to refine it. Instead my hope is that, by presenting some of their arguments in a new setting, I may encourage more people to discover the potential of computable economics. Thus, I'll merely provide some intuitions about the consequences for how we think about welfare.

## 2 The Good Merchant

In a Danish context the good merchant (*godt købmandskab*) is a concept that can be traced back at least to the middle ages, where merchants played a fatherly role to local communities as not only a merchant but also a risk bearer and a lender. The good merchant did not pursue short-term profits but had a goal of a decent living in harmony with the community. In a Danish textbook on economics from the 1920s by L.V. Birck, you still find many of the moral standards related to the good merchant—just as you find references to morals in the work of Marshall (1920), while it is deliberately absent in Samuelson's writings. Opposite to Marshall, who tends to write about morals in very general terms, Birck is specific when it comes to morally acceptable behaviour of business men: *The good merchant should not try to sell goods to people that they do not really need*, he *should aim for large turnover with small mark-ups rather than smaller turnover with large mark-ups, and he should not reward his staff with bonuses since it might encourage a less moral behaviour* (Birck 1928 (my translation)).

## 2.1 Behaviour of Merchants and Customers

Today many of the ideals related to the good merchant can be re-found in discussions concerning maximizing shareholder versus stakeholder value, corporate social responsibility, expectations for businesses in promoting the UN sustainable development goals, etc. There are many signs that more is expected of businesses today than a narrow profit optimization. But there is not much to guide businesses in the endeavour—no theoretical foundation and no clear goal to fulfil. The main message from society is for businesses to be good—they are then left to define good.[1]

As economists we know that being good depends on human behaviour. If human agents are atomic and rational utility optimizers, it is almost impossible for businesses *not* to be good. You can nudge and persuade, collect online data to learn about your customer—it will all just be a service to your customer—making their collection of information easier. Rational agents cannot be persuaded to buy something that doesn't give them at least as much utility as what they give up to get it. Therefore, economics needs no morals, as Samuelson (1983) states several times in "Foundations". But if economic agents are not atomic, and if they are not rational optimizers—a merchant may persuade them to buy things they don't really need or make them pay an overprice for caramelized and carbonated sugar water.

## 2.2 Governing the Merchants

A firm or a merchant is subjected to governance by the state and the market—for example, a merchant cannot charge an overprice since that will leave the market to competitors—it is held. Medieval merchants were also subjected to governance by guilds emerging from the merchants themselves, but in some cases empowered by state or church (de Moor et al. 2008).

But any firm is also responsible for its own internal governance. How are employees rewarded and directed towards the behaviour desired by

[1] Of course an industry has arisen with consultants wanting to help businesses be good—and a lot of frameworks with metrics have been developed. The overall goal, however, remains vague.

the firm? In particular within retail banking this has received a lot of attention since the financial crisis. There is also the question of how exchanges are handled within in conglomerates. With the centralization in firm structure, a growing part of exchanges take place outside markets. With digitalization, marketing is now able to address customers on a one-to-one basis—this we should probably also think of as transactions outside the market. This possibility increases the ability of the firm to reduce consumer surplus and should also be dealt with within the external or internal governance structure.

## 2.3 Merchants' Ability to Create Value

Governance and behaviour are also related to the way value is created. Societies consisting of hunter-gatherers are different from societies of farmers, and again different from societies relying mainly on industrial production or creation of intangible services. The moral standards of the good merchant were adapted to a period where farming and international commerce dominated value creation. Different modes of value creation promote different behaviour and need different governance. Farming and, in particular, industrial production need investment—and investment require people to abstain from consuming everything they produce today. Under feudalism power gave nobility an obligation to make investments on behalf of the population—under industrial capitalism that obligation was assigned to those that received profits—the capitalists, who got their power, not from the state but from the market. Today industrial production is responsible for a decreasing part of world value creation, just as century ago we witnessed agricultural production being responsible for a decreasing part of the value of production. We should be aware that a growing part of value creation is not operating under increasing marginal costs. This change means that our governance structure is probably in need of some updating since increasing marginal costs is an important part of the market mechanism. We should expect that changing value creation will require changing governance and may even induce behavioural changes.

## 2.4 The Good Merchant—Where Value, Behaviour and Governance Meet

We argue that the good merchant can be conceptualized by reference to *value creation*, *governance* and *behaviour* (Fig. 2.1). The good merchant adapts value creation and internal governance to human behaviour as it is observed in the market, and does that in such a way that the overall contribution to society is at a minimum positive. The good merchant does not use power to appropriate consumer surplus and pays for the public investments that benefits value creation (infrastructure, research, education) and patents are not used to optimize profit, but only to cover expenses.

The question to be posed here is whether this conceptualization of the good merchant, inspired by studies of economic history and history of economic thought, can be transferred to societal level, that is, whether we can identify *good societies*, societies providing members with the highest level of welfare, through the way value creation, governance and behaviour interact.

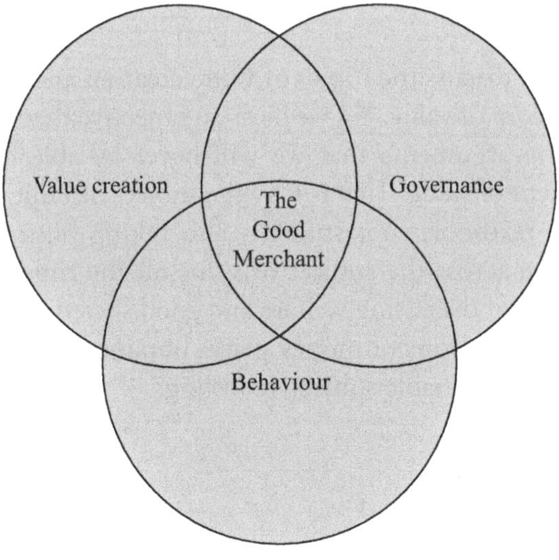


**Fig. 2.1** The good merchant—adjusting internal governance and value creation to observed behaviour, with the purpose of contributing to society as well as making an acceptable profit. (Source: Own collection)

# 3 Economics Is About Welfare

Students in Econ 101 are usually told that economics is about *efficient allocation of scarce resources*. But today, where intangibles play an increasing role in value creation—what is scarce in the economy? Intangible goods are produced by labour—but labour does not appear to be particularly scarce on a worldwide scale. Maybe the scarcity is of human imagination or human creative resources, but clearly that is not what economists think of when they refer to scarce resources.

This indicates that we need another way of thinking about our main subject. When we say allocation of scarce resources, what we really mean is how resources are employed to create human welfare. The purpose of economics must be to discuss how human welfare is created and distributed. Following the logic of *the good merchant* as described above, we need to discuss how value is created, how access to valuables is governed and what characterizes human behaviour when we interact to create and distribute value.

## 3.1 Value

It is very hard to discuss the topics of value creation and welfare without an objective theory of value. Yet we have no objective theory of value, and there are strong arguments that we will never be able to agree on an objective concept of value. That is why the subject of value does not enter the Econ 101 textbooks. Yet students also taking business classes like marketing come across the subject of value all the time. We must ask, with the purpose of discussing welfare and good societies, is it sound only to think of value in terms of money prices obtained at markets by reference to some unmeasurable subjective feeling?

## 3.2 Governance

Governance is any mechanism that governs relations between constituents in a system. Since it is somewhat disguised in most economic theory, it is important to note that it is within the sphere of governance that it is decided who has and who has not, that is, the issue of distribution is a question of governance.

For the last century discussions on governance at a societal level have concentrated on state versus market. The market comes in different forms. The theoretical argument for the superiority of markets as opposed to state is based on a top-down mechanism (the auctioneer) and the idea of methodological individualism, but these theoretical markets appear to be very different from real markets. The state was regarded as a governor with great potential in the first half of the twentieth century, but with globalization, lack of international governance and the breakdown of the Soviet Union, not much confidence is placed with the state as the dominant governor today. With Elinor Ostrom receiving the Nobel prize, a third governance form is getting more and more attention, namely governance of commons based on morals and ethics, or just on the concepts of sharing—governance without sticks or carrots (Ostrom 2010).

The governance structure of any society or organization consists of different weights of the three pure forms of governance: state, market and commons (Fig. 2.2).

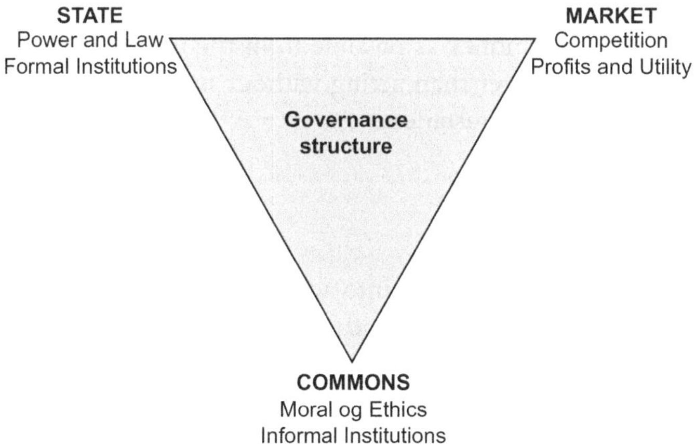


**Fig. 2.2** The three pure forms of governance. Any governance structure relies on a combination of the pure forms. (Source: Own collection)

## 3.3 Behaviour

To understand what motivates us to create (or extract) and exchange valuables we need some idea of what guides and limits human behaviour. We need to consider behaviour when we discuss value creation since only humans can tell what is valuable to them, and we need to consider behaviour when we discuss governance since it is human behaviour that is governed. Thus, any governance structure must relate to what motivates human behaviour.

Behaviour should not be seen as static—there need not be *one truth* about human nature. Behaviour should decide what value is created and how distribution is governed—but changes in technology and organization may also change human behaviour. There is a difference between the morals of the pre-industrial *good merchant* and the morals of modern financiers. Hodgson (2013, 2014) argues that moral standards and empathy is part of human nature—but that does not mean that we cannot have different moral standards. The group of people involved in the recent financial trading scandal CumEx-Files, robbing European states for billions of Euros, had a copy of Ayn Rand's "Capitalism: The Unknown Ideal" circulating among them, teaching them that their moral obligation was to free as much money as possible from the unproductive hands of the public sector. Rather than acting without moral they adapted their moral standards to circumstances.

## 3.4 Welfare

Any theory of welfare must take into account all three aspects: how value is created, how it is governed, and what motivates and limits human behaviour. Furthermore, it must concentrate on how the three play together to promote welfare—to create *the good society*. Requiring businesses to *be good* need not make society better, just as leaving governance to markets need not leave society at a social optimum—it all depends on what goes on in the other spheres. *Value creation*, *governance* and *behaviour* must confluence in a welfare promoting way to create the *good society*.

## 4 Neoclassical Welfare Theory

In neoclassical welfare theory the interrelation between value creation, governance and behaviour is also essential—you cannot explain one element without relating to the other two. Since value created is subjective it cannot be discussed without discussing human behaviour and governance. In essence, value is created in an exchange process where resources, primarily in the form of capital and labour, are transformed to commodities that are valued by consumers. The (relative) values of capital and labour, as well as commodities, are determined by a Walrasian market mechanism. The market equilibrium, defined as a vector of relative prices, ensures an optimal allocation of given resources, defined by Pareto optimality.

There are many ways of representing production within the neoclassical tradition—even if we only consider a static situation with fixed technology. In Fig. 2.3 we choose the production function to represent

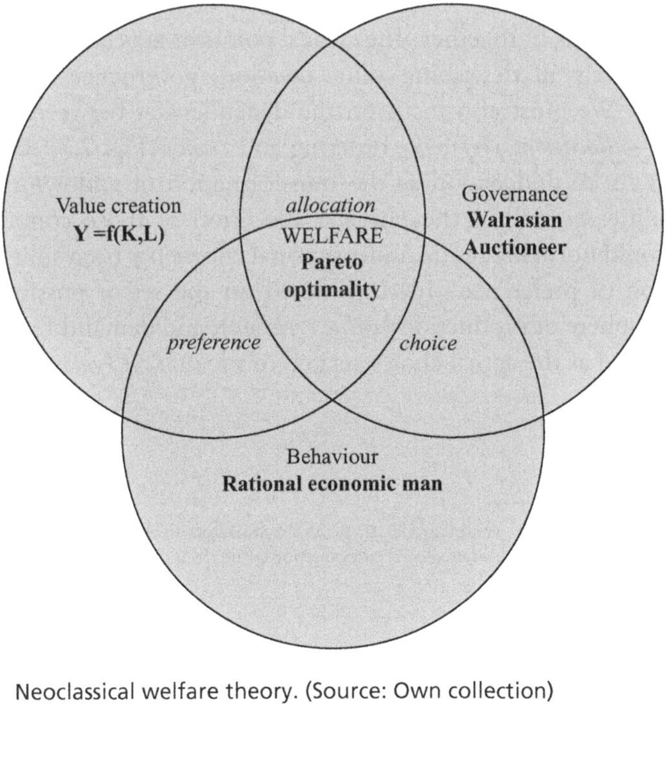


**Fig. 2.3** Neoclassical welfare theory. (Source: Own collection)

value creation, since this is the standard textbook version. As we shall see later, value creation is a rather void box—best described as an organizational structure (the firm), owned by households, that transforms endowments of capital and labour into commodities.

Behaviour is represented as rational economic man—an agent that is born with a set of preferences over all possible goods, a set of endowments and a behaviour that can be represented as maximizing utility generated from the innate preferences.

Finally, governance is represented by the Walrasian auctioneer with an implicit assumption of private property rights being somehow protected. The Walrasian auctioneer is a top-down mechanism that substitutes direct interaction between agents, to ensure that exchange only takes place at market clearing prices. We shall return to the question of equilibrating prices.

We have only shortly presented the three main ingredients: the production function, the Walrasian auctioneer and rational economic man—since the choices made in these theoretical constructs cannot be understood in isolation—most choices are made to make the three theoretical constructs fit together. The critical points of neoclassical theory are not exclusively in describing value creation, governance and human behaviour. We must also focus on the dependencies between the three subjects—*allocation*, *preference* ordering and *choice* (Fig. 2.3). Here allocation is to be understood as the transformation of endowments into commodities as well as the physical allocation of those commodities. What would normally reside under optimal choice has been split into the generation of preference orderings based on the set of possible goods from the sphere of production (*value creation*), and demand functions—here denoted as the actual choice related to the market (*governance*).[2]

[2] This option is inspired by Velupillai (2010, p. 335) who refers to Arrow (1959) for regarding orderings and demand functions as special cases of choice functions.

### 4.1 Intersection Between Value Creation and Governance—*Allocation*

In the neoclassical model it is impossible to discuss value creation outside the market. Final goods, as well as capital and labour, are not valuable until they reach the market. And at the market, their price reflects their value. This is the essence of subjective theory of value.

The market mechanism is essential in governing resources used in the creation of value—the market mechanism is what gives us fairness despite the starting point in subjective value theory that does not allow us to compare values. We cannot compare subjective values, so we can never discuss fairness in a given situation. But given our initial endowments, in the neoclassical welfare theory we can be confident that they are given a fair price. This also goes for the distribution of surplus between wages and profits—you get what you are worth, and profits reflect the value of capital used in production. The market mechanism ensures that we have an efficient allocation that is independent from distribution.

### 4.2 Intersection Between Value Creation and Behaviour—*Preferences*

An important assumption in neoclassical theory is that of methodological individualism—implying that we are born with a set of preferences over all goods. If our preferences would change during the tâtonnement process—not to mention, if there were interdependencies between agents, a vector of equilibrating prices could hardly be obtained. Furthermore, agents must have knowledge of the set of goods they may hold preferences over. That is why the ordering of preferences is placed in this intersection. As pointed out by Velupillai (2010), preference orderings are usually taken as given—but in the intersection between behaviour and value creation it seems important to emphasize that preference orderings must have as their starting point the set of possible goods determined in the sphere of value creation (or production). Preference orderings must relate to the sphere of value creation.

### 4.3 Intersection Between Governance and Behaviour—*Choice*

Finally, when the Walrasian auctioneer calls out a price vector, agents must be capable of computing the corresponding vector of supply and demand that would optimize their utility given their preference orderings, as described by choice theory. It is important to note that no actual exchanges can take place until the set of equilibrium prices are found.

Thinking of neoclassical welfare theory in terms of our three spheres (Fig. 2.3) helps us identify how its main building blocks fit together, but also allows us to identify a weak spot in the approach—agents "born with" preference orderings without knowing over what to hold preferences. We shall return to this question.

## 5 Welfare—What Prices Are For?

The neoclassical general equilibrium may also be discussed in terms of price systems, since adjustment of prices is what makes our three spheres unite in this approach. Economics tends to focus on price systems for which there is no excess demand—that is, sets of price vectors for which supply equals demand in all markets. But this equilibrium only suffices in systems without production and in systems where existence of individual balances (money) is ruled out by assumption. Walras did neither and therefore needed to consider further requirements for the existence of a general equilibrium.

As described by Schumpeter (1954) Walras could not find room for profits in his system. Even if firms are just regarded as void organizations owned by households, and thus transferring possible profits to households, he realized that in a general equilibrium there could be no room for profits.

> Let me emphasize once more that in the equilibrium of a purely competitive process, where nobody is able to exert any influence upon the prices of either services or products, every entrepreneur would in fact be an *entrepreneur ne faisant ni bénéfice ni perte*: this is neither a paradox nor a tautology

(i.e. it is not the result of a definition) but, *under Walras assumptions*, an equilibrium condition (or, if you prefer, a provable theorem). (Schumpeter 1954, p. 1011, n. 33)

Thus, we have two sets of price vectors—one set for which supply equals demand in all markets, as well as a set of price vectors for which input equals output for all firms. However, Stützel (1958) points out that we also have a third set of prices—price vectors for which receipts equals expenditure for all agents—that is, a price system for which there are no changes in monetary balances, denoted as *gleichschritt* by Stützel. It is interesting that Mirowski (1989) is uncomfortable with the fact that profits of firms are transferred to household accounts, but apparently does not object to the claim that Walras' law means that households cannot hold balances.[3]

Stützels *gleichschritt* is often confused with Walras' law—that balances must sum to zero—but that does not necessitate that individual balances must be zero. Here we touch upon the whole problem of making room for money in the neoclassical model. Walras did consider money balances, also in the case of households; *money held by consumers to finance consumers' transactions* and *monnaie d'épargne* (savings) (Schumpeter 1954, p. 1000). Furthermore, Walras did not limit behavioural equations to rule out receipts=expenditure—this is also an equilibrium condition (Schumpeter 1954, p. 1005). We thus have three different sets of price vectors or price systems (Fig. 2.4). So, in equilibrium you need a price system that, as an equilibrium condition has (1) supply=demand for every market (market balance equations), (2) receipts=expenditure for

[3] In models with households only, Walras' Law comes simply from summing the budget constraints. Firms, unlike households, have no budget constraints but do have balance sheets. Hence Walras' Law in models with firms requires us to use the fact [sic] that the profits of the firms ultimately belong to the shareholders. (Fisher 1983, p. 159)

Mirowski quotes Fisher on this matter

> The only alternative to the explicit specification of the conservation principle is the equally unwarranted assumption of constant returns to scale in all processes of production, a condition that achieves the same analytical result. (Mirowski, 1989, p. 326)

But nowhere does Mirowski comment on Fisher's first claim on Walras' law and seems to agree to the different treatment of firms and households when it comes to budget constraints.

every agent (individual balance equations) and (3) input=output for every firm (production equations).

From Fig. 2.4 it is clear what it takes to be in the lucrative position of a general equilibrium where we, according to neoclassical welfare theory, make the most of given resources. It is also evident how the requirement fits into our framework of the *good society*—the place where value creation, governance and behaviour meet in order to generate maximum welfare. We shall not even dare to ask the question whether it is likely we ever, in the real world, would end up in such a harmonic Utopia.[4] Followers of Friedman's positivism would just dismiss any suggestions of

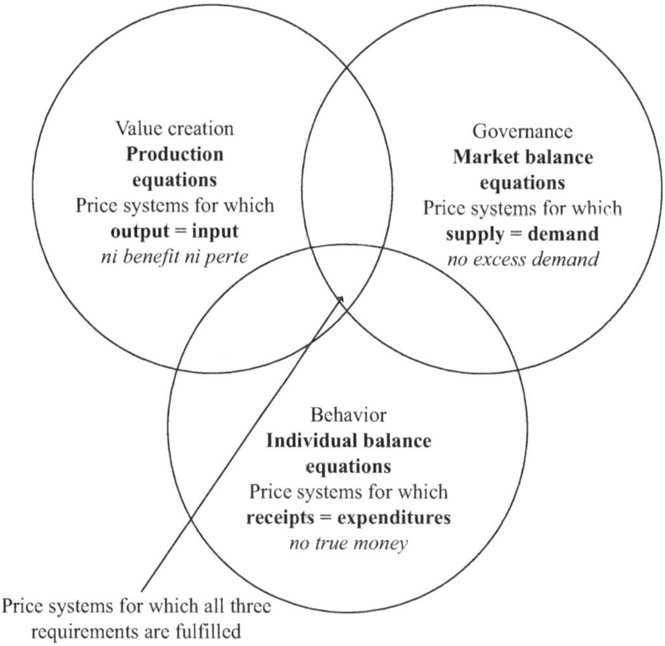


**Fig. 2.4** Three different sets of price systems representing three different requirements for an economy in general equilibrium. This figure is inspired from Stützel (1958, p. 189), although he does not include production equations. (Source: Own collection)

[4] Here, Francesco Luna reminds me, that although harmonious, it is hardly Utopia to live in a static world with no growth or development.

a negative answer to this question with the usual *as if* answer. Therefore, we pose the question from within the system of neoclassical welfare theory—and this is a question of computable economics.

## 6 Critiques Related to Computability

So far, we have discussed equilibrium requirement for the Walrasian system without discussing the problems of existence or stability—at the most foundational level we need to know whether the burden placed on the auctioneer can be lifted by a mechanism having all the computer power, memory and time in the world—can the tâtonnement process be described by an algorithm that we can be sure will stop and come up with an answer[5]?

There is fundamental critique within each of the three areas:

- The mere concept of a production function (Zambelli 2004, 2018[6]; Luna 2004; Mirowski 1989).
- The computability of the tâtonnement process. Velupillai (2010) demonstrates that Walras' existence theorem is undecidable and cannot be determined algorithmically (p. 219).[7]
- The behaviour of economic agents (behavioural economics, Simon 1978; Velupillai 2018).

Together they should render the neoclassical welfare theory useless for any practical purposes. That has not happened. Even economists true to the neoclassical vision appear to adapt behavioural economics without

[5] Velupillai (2007) describes his research on computable economics:

> My own research, since about 30 years ago has been on trying to understand the relevance of recursion theory and its applied branches for economic theory. In particular, the investigations of the computable, solvable and decidable implications of a more systematic assumption of computability in core areas of general equilibrium theory, game theory and macroeconomics.

[6] It should be noted that the primary target of Zambelli (2004) is the aggregate production function.

[7] As summed up by Zambelli we find this result in several works of K. Vela Velupillai (Zambelli, 2010, pp. 37–38).

considering the repercussions on the rest of their theoretical construct. That is why we will focus on the intersections of our three spheres. To know whether other parts of the general equilibrium constructs still hold, that is, know how far back we need to go in the arguments of general equilibrium theory before a reconstruction can begin, we shall enquire about the computability of *preferences*, *choice* and *allocation* (Fig. 2.5).

## 6.1 Critique Related to the Intersection Between Value Creation and Governance—Allocation

One of the most devastating critiques of neoclassical theory has been that of Sraffa. This critique is in the intersection of value creation and governance because it is a negative result concerning the optimal allocation of labour and capital and thus their fair remuneration. The problem is that division of the surplus into profits and wages cannot be determined in the tâtonnement process—it must be determined outside the neoclassical theoretical framework. Or put differently: prices are indeterminate unless the division between profits and wages is given outside the system (Sraffa 1926).

As argued by Velupillai (2010) the original demonstration of the problem by Sraffa is constructive and computable (p. 245). But due to computational constraints it was not possible for Sraffa to investigate the strength or the generality of his argument. What would happen if profits did not have to be uniform, and what is the empirical relevance of reswitching? Zambelli (2018) investigates these questions using brute force theoretical as well as empirical computations. In doing so he has extended the validity of Sraffa's original critique.

Sraffa's work was situated only in the sphere of production, but his results had repercussions for the sphere of governance since it demonstrates that the fair distribution of profits and wages cannot be left to the market mechanism. Zambelli (2018) takes his starting point in a distributional vector of profits and wages, maybe future work will take its starting point in other possible distributions.[8]

[8] In his work on non-uniform rates of profits, Zambelli (2018) is well aware that the *gleichschritt* (expenditures = revenues) is an assumption he makes—not a necessity:

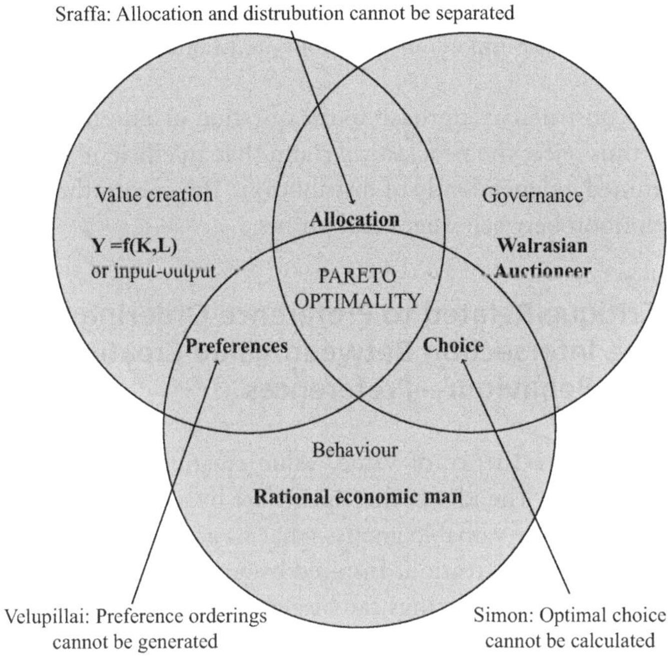


**Fig. 2.5** Neoclassical welfare theory—critiques based on computability. (Source: Own collection)

Without a complete treatment due to limitations of space, we would like to point out that the *Prelude to Critique of Economic Theory* holds and is in fact made stronger when we study the self-replacing conditions while taking distributional vector as the point of departure.

For instant the important result that the computed prices are independent of the level of activities (or demand) does not depend on whether there is a uniform rate of profits $r$ or a vector of profits rates $\mathbf{r}$. The relative prices, like the standard PCMC (production of commodities by means of commodities) case, are not a function of the quantities or level of the activ-

Here the qualification—"in general" is put to imply that the system could be in a self-replacing state if there were lending and borrowing possibilities. In that case there could be exchanges taking place at prices for which the revenues are less than the expenditures for some agents and consequently there would be other agents for which the revenues would be higher for others. (Zambelli, 2018, p. 800, n. 15)

In this quote, Zambelli indicates that a Sraffian approach may have repercussions in the sphere of behaviour as well, if the assumption of *gleichschritt* is relaxed.

> ities. Therefore, it can only be confirmed that prices depend on the set of methods and, most importantly, distribution. (Zambelli 2018, p. 26)

Using a constructive approach to the question of allocation, Sraffa and Zambelli thus reject the neoclassical claim that an efficient allocation can be determined independently of distribution. This means there is not one fair distribution between wages and profits.

## 6.2 Critique Related to Preference Orderings: The Intersection Between Value Creation and Behaviour—Preferences

Given a subjective theory of value, value creation is closely linked to human behaviour. The idea is that agents are born with preferences over the set of potentially valuable goods—that is, goods that may be created in the sphere of value creation. Inspired by Arrow (1959), Velupillai discusses how preference orderings can be generated, rather than just assuming the existence of a set of preference orderings as the standard starting point of rational choice theory (Velupillai 2000, p. 32). *Can economic agents act rationally, or choose optimally, without having access to their preference orderings, if these exists?* (Velupillai 2000, p. 37). Alas, the answer comes out negative: *There is no effective procedure to generate preference orderings* (p. 38).

## 6.3 Critique Related to the Intersection Between Behaviour and Governance—Choice

The actual choices performed by agents, the demand functions, take place in the intersection between behaviour and governance/market. Agents must respond to the price vector called out by the auctioneer. Herbert Simon puts into question whether agents have the computational capacity to calculate their optimal choices. Simon was well aware that there was a question of decidability, but, with a reference to computational complexity found it to be less important, *It really did not matter very much whether the answer to a problem would never be forthcoming, or whether it would be produced only after a hundred years* (Simon 1978, pp. 500–501). In later correspondence with Velupillai, he appears to maintain that position (Velupillai 2018). Of course Simon is right when it comes to practical matters, although one should be aware that development in physical computers has moved the boundary for what is computationally feasible.

That, however, is not the point to be made here. From a theoretical point of view, when the real world builds its actual economic and political decision-making on a combination of general equilibrium theory and Friedman's positivism, whether the assumed human behaviour is, in principle, computable, makes all the difference. On this Simon and Velupillai appear to agree:

> Many questions of economics cannot be answered simply by determining what would be the substantively rational action, but require an understanding of the procedures used to reach rational decisions. Procedural rationality takes on importance for economics in those situations where "the real world" out there cannot be equated with the world as perceived and calculated by the economic agent. [...] Nor can we rely on evolutionary arguments to conclude that natural selection will find the optimum where calculation cannot. [...]. It is much more likely [...] that the location of the objective optimum has little relevance for the decisionmakers or the situations that their decisions create. (Simon 1978, pp. 504–505)

What Velupillai adds to the argument of Simon, that we should concentrate on procedural rationality, is that the substantive solution of economic theory does not exist, thus Velupillai has demonstrated the uncomputability of choice theory—*the choice function does not necessarily single out just one alternative* (Velupillai 2010, p. 335).

## 6.4 Goodbye Walrasian Dream, Hello Moral and Ethics?

After adding the requirement of constructive proofs, not much is left of the Neoclassical dream—the dream of leaving governance to markets and relieving agents of the burden of having to take moral and ethics into consideration when interacting. We cannot think of market outcomes as being more *fair* than any other possible allocations, since they most likely have distributional effects. It is up to our moral standards, as individuals, as voters, as businesses, as wealth holders and as society, to evaluate what is a fair distribution, and act on it.

As mentioned, behaviour can hardly be regarded as a static phenomenon. What is seen as moral behaviour is not static either, and in *Economic Possibilities for our Grandchildren* Keynes envisioned a change in behaviour for his grandchildren[9]:

> I see us free, therefore, to return to some of the most sure and certain principles of religion and traditional virtue-that avarice is a vice, that the exaction of usury is a misdemeanour, and the love of money is detestable, that those walk most truly in the paths of virtue and sane wisdom who take least thought for the morrow. We shall once more value ends above means and prefer the good to the useful. We shall honour those who can teach us how to pluck the hour and the day virtuously and well, the delightful people who are capable of taking direct enjoyment in things, the lilies of the field who toil not, neither do they spin. (Keynes 1930, pp. 363–364)

A change in the way we produce (value creation) eventually will change morale standards as well as what we find valuable (behaviour) and the weighting between state, market and commons (governance). The change did not come about as soon as Keynes predicted. Maybe neoliberalism delayed the process. Maybe now is the time for the change.

## 7 A Grand Unified Theory of Economic Welfare?

For a century neoclassical welfare theory has held the status of a *grand unified theory* of economics—and maybe even social sciences. Let us for a moment return to the three different equilibrium conditions of neoclassical welfare theory—production (or input-output) equations, market balance equations and individual balance equations. Obviously these three different approaches to equilibrium prices put a lot of strain on the

[9] A thanks to Carsten Heyn-Johnsen for pointing out the relevance of Keynes in this context.

pricing mechanism meant to secure economic welfare. But how does this relate to welfare in the real world?

In his early work Sraffa (1926) realized the existence of monopolistic competition—the ability of some producers to gain market power and increase their profits. Today the relation between market prices and production costs seem even weaker, and for many of the products and, in particular, services on the market, it does not make sense to talk about increasing marginal costs, let alone prices being equal to marginal costs. Furthermore, the law of one price is challenged, for example, by sellers using consumer data to target the individual consumer (one-to-one marketing). The same commodity or service may be sold at a number of different prices with sellers attempting to rob consumers of any surplus value. The market as a governor appear to be weakened.

There are other approaches to welfare than the Neoclassical, and our three spheres can also help us identify some of them. As argued, any theory on welfare needs to consider *value creation*, *governance* and *behaviour* and it needs to consider input-output equations, market balance equations and individual balance equations. But theories may take their starting point in, or emphasize, one of the three spheres or systems of equations. Let one of the spheres rules the roost, so to speak. With the three different price systems and the apparently invincible problems of uniting them, we also see the contours of three different theoretical traditions: the Sraffian, the Neoclassical and the Keynesian (Fig. 2.6).

In developing neoclassical welfare theory, it seems that in weighing out pros and cons in developing the different theoretical elements, most weight has been given to markets as the governor. How behaviour and production is theorized has been chosen with the main aim of reaching the unified market equilibrium. Confluence with the market mechanism required production to give no surplus, and households to have no balances.

It has already been noted that Sraffa (1960) took his starting point in the sphere of production, input-output equations, or value creation in our more general terminology. Sraffa simply posed the question: what happens if we let production rule the roost with a requirement that it must at least be capable of reproduction.

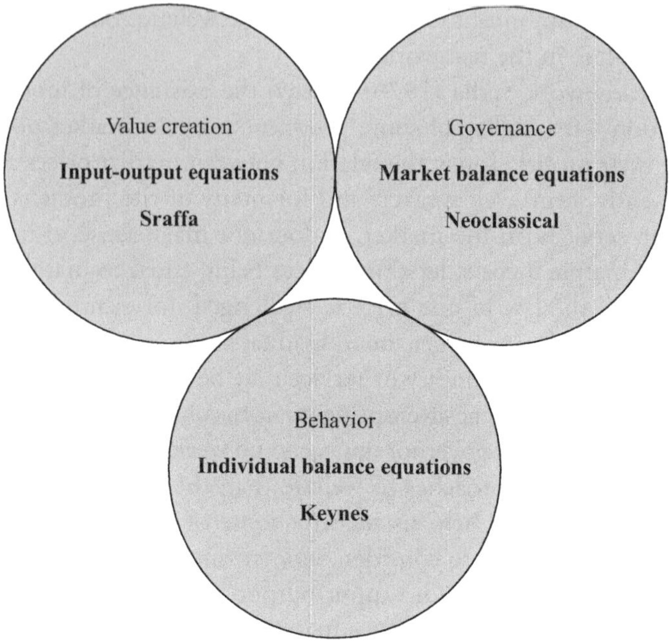


**Fig. 2.6** Three different schools of thought. (Source: Own collection)

J. M. Keynes (1936), on the other hand, can be argued to have taken his starting point in behaviour and individual balance equations. What happens if we let production adapt to demand, ignore the market equilibrium in describing behaviour, and if we treat money and credit as it appears in the real world? For some followers of Keynes, in particular the stock-flow consistent approach that has gained popularity recently, it seems to happen at the cost of making room for profits in the sphere of value creation. Their production units are just as void as those of the neoclassical approach (Bruun 2010).

Will we ever have a *grand unified theory* in economics—giving equal weight to our three spheres? Probably not—but that does not mean that we should not dream of it. The latest work by Stefano Zambelli (2019) suggests a new way forwards, allowing for individual balances in a Sraffian world. Zambelli's aim seems to be to put the behaviour approach of

Keynes on an equal footing with the production approach of Sraffa. A very interesting development that we should all follow with interest.

## 8 Intuitions on the Role of Morals in Creating Welfare

The purpose of sharing my intuitions about welfare has not been to make a complete exposition of welfare theory, of the computability critiques related to it, or to come up with new ways of thinking about value creation, governance and behaviour. My purpose has been to take a first step away from the dilemma of modern economics—its increasing irrelevance to the problems people talk about. Economics maintains that utilities cannot be compared, that incomes are fair and that governance by markets is the best we can do.

My main purpose is to suggest that we need to consider three theoretical constructs to discuss economic welfare. Based on an insight on human behaviour we need to theorize on how value is created and how it is governed. But in doing so we should be aware that human beings are reflexive creatures that may change their behaviour in search for economic benefits—but also in search for social acceptance.

*Altmodisch* concepts as moral and ethics, which have been banned from economics, may have to come back into our theories. Not because theories themselves need be judgemental or contain their own moral standards—but because economic man is a moral creature unless taught otherwise. Evolution left us with empathy—maybe we are meant to use it, also when engaging in economic transactions. As long as Neoclassical welfare theory cannot demonstrate how their claimed equilibria come about, let us at least use our common sense when evaluating the impact individuals and businesses have on sustainability in the sense defined by UN's sustainable development goals. Maybe economics was wrong in telling the individual just to mind his/her own business. Maybe being *altmodisch* holds the future.

## References

Arrow, K. J. (1959, May). Rational Choice Functions and Orderings. *Economica, 26*(102), 121–127. New Series.

Birck, L. V. (1928). *Den Økonomiske Virksomhed—Bind 1–2.* G.E.C. København: Gads Forlag.

Bruun, C. (2010). The Economics of Keynes in an Almost Stock-Flow Consistent Agent-Based Setting. In S. Zambelli (Ed.), *Computable, Constructive and Behavioural Economic Dynamics—Essays in Honour of Kumaraswamy (Vela) Velupillai.* Oxon: Routledge Frontiers of Political Economy.

de Moor, T., Lucassen, J., & van Zanden, J. L. (2008). The Return of the Guilds. *International Review of Social History, 53*, 197–233.

Fisher, F. M. (1983). *Disequilibrium Foundations of Equilibrium Economics.* Cambridge: Cambridge University Press.

Hodgson, G. M. (2013). *From Pleasure Machines to Moral Communities: An Evolutionary Economics Without Homo Economicus.* Chicago and London: University of Chicago Press.

Hodgson, G. M. (2014). The Evolution of Morality and the End of Economic Man. *Journal of Evolutionary Economics, 24*(1), 83–106.

Keynes, J. M. (1930). Economic Possibilities for our Grandchildren. In *Essays in Persuasion.* New York: W.W. Norton & Co, 1963.

Keynes, J. M. (1936). *The General Theory of Employment, Interest and Money.* London: Palgrave Macmillan.

Luna, F. (2004). Research and Development in Computable Production Functions. *Metronomica, 55*(2–3), 180–194.

Marshall, A. (1920). *Principles of Economics* (8th ed.). Hong Kong: Macmillan, reprinted 1994.

Mirowski, P. (1989). *More Heat than Light—Economics as Social Physics, Physics as Nature's Economics.* Cambridge—Historical Perspectives on Modern Economics, reprinted 1995, USA.

Ostrom, E. (2010, June). Beyond Markets and States: Polycentric Governance of Complex Economic Systems. *The American Economic Review, 100*(3), 641–672.

Samuelson, P. A. (1983). *Foundations of Economic Analysis.* Cambridge, MA: Harvard University Press.

Schumpeter, J. A. (1954). *History of Economic Analysis.* New York: Oxford University Press, reprinted 1986.

Simon, H. (1978). On How to Decide on What To Do. *The Bell Journal of Economics, 9*(2), 494–507.

Sraffa, P. (1926). The Laws of Returns under Competitive Conditions. *The Economic Journal, 36*, 535–550.

Sraffa, P. (1960). *Production of Commodities by Means of Commodities. Prelude to a Critique of Economic Theory*. London: Cambridge University Press.

Stützel, W. (1958). *Volkswirtschaftliche Saldenmechanik* (2nd ed.). Tübigen: Mohr Siebeck, reprinted 2011.

Velupillai, K. (2000). *Computable Economics* (The Arne Ryde Memorial Lectures Series). Oxford: Oxford University Press.

Velupillai, K. V. (2007). *Taming the Incomputable, Reconstructing the Nonconstructive and Deciding the Undecidable in Mathematical Economics*. Working Paper No. 0128, Department of Economics, National University of Ireland, Galway.

Velupillai, K. V. (2010). *Computable Foundations for Economics*. Oxon: Routledge.

Velupillai, K. V. (2018). *Models of Simon*. Oxon: Routledge.

Zambelli, S. (2004). The 40% Neoclassical Aggregate Theory of Production. *Cambridge Journal of Economics, 28*(1), 99–120.

Zambelli, S. (2010). Computable and Constructive Economics, Undecidable Dynamics and Algorithmic Rationality: An Essay in Honour of Professor Kumaraswamy (Vela) Velupillai. In S. Zambelli (Ed.), *Computable, Constructive and Behavioural Economic Dynamics—Essays in Honour of Kumaraswamy (Vela) Velupillai*. Routledge Frontiers of Political Economy.

Zambelli, S. (2018). Production of Commodities by Means of Commodities and Non-Uniform Rates of Profits. *Metroeconomica, 69*(4), 791–819.

Zambelli, S. (2019). *Sraffa on the Monetary Theory of Distribution and Inequality*. Work in progress. Unpublished, May 19.

# 3

# Recasting Stefano Zambelli: Notes on the Foundations of Mathematics for a Post-Neoclassical Age in Economics

Edgardo Bucciarelli and Nicola Mattoscio

## 1 Introduction: An Epistemological Rumination

Over the past decades, the logic of computability has achieved significant progress in economic theory that might eventually be able to solve any kind of limitation and constraint with respect to the applicability of standard techniques, and extend the theory to several other possibilities as is the case for mature sciences. According to Hausman (1992), and Parisi (2006), a scientific discipline can be considered as 'mature' when the dialogue between its theories and observations becomes a core element leading to knowledge development. Indeed, a theory can aspire to be represented as scientific—and not purely as speculative—when it is possible to derive rigorously, that is, without ambiguity or inaccuracies, as well as consistently, that is, without internal inconsistencies, a large

E. Bucciarelli (✉) • N. Mattoscio
Department of PPEQS, Section of Economics and Quantitative Methods, University of Chieti-Pescara, Pescara, Italy
e-mail: edgardo.bucciarelli@unich.it



K. Velupillai (ed.), *Keynesian, Sraffian, Computable and Dynamic Economics*,
https://doi.org/10.1007/978-3-030-58131-2_3

number of precise predictions that can be made in direct comparison with the observed facts. In this regard, mathematical methods are very useful, even for the economics profession, certainly the most effective in terms of rigour and consistency (e.g., see Schwartz 1966). However, when human and social sciences are involved mathematical methods are very frequently misused, mathematical models are very frequently in error, and undue reliance is placed in these models due to a basic lack of understanding of the actual underlying problem at hand. Looking at state of the art on this issue, not surprisingly, the application of mathematics—for example, *formalism*-based mathematics—to the human sciences (hereafter, we will refer only to human sciences to mean the entire set of human and social sciences), and among these in particular to economics, may prove to be not entirely effective in its results as well as questionable in its foundations, if not actually devoid of scientific significance—if mathematics aspires to build theories and models that have an acceptable foundation and are not proposed as a mere attempt to replicate theories and models of classical, Newtonian physics (among others, see Mirowski 1989; Sutton 2000; Velupillai 2005[1]). There are sciences, such as economics and formal linguistics, which, unlike what happens in the natural sciences, place restrictions on the type of empirical data that they take into consideration. Standard economics, for instance, formulates many theories in the form of mathematical language, although the theoretical tools it employs differ significantly from natural sciences, being inconsistent—*de facto*—both to describe and understand economic phenomena in their entirety. This forces the economic science to narrow the set of real phenomena it deals with (e.g., aggregate economic variables, see Brock and Durlauf 2006) by limiting itself only to those phenomena that are treatable with the inadequacy of those theoretical tools. For standard economics, therefore, and this is the drama, the phenomena that cannot be studied with the available theoretical tools do not exist (e.g., see D'Autume and Cartelier 1997; Boehm et al. 2002).

[1] It is worth noting the valuable contribution written by K. Vela Velupillai (2005) entitled *The Unreasonable Ineffectiveness of Mathematics in Economics*, whose discussion so much recalls the famous title of a seminal paper published in 1960 by the theoretical physicist Eugene Wigner (1960) titled *The Unreasonable Effectiveness of Mathematics in the Natural Sciences* and is framed therein.

Correspondingly, if economic science should be treated in terms similar to those of classical physics, it would be reduced to studying only easily identifiable cause-and-effect bonds that make it possible to make predictions. Beyond its well-traversed path, classical physics, also known as physics that developed from its origins until around the early twentieth century, was overcome by subsequent developments in new physics, in particular by the two main new branches opened in the first twenty years of the twentieth century: quantum and relativistic physics. In the new framework that is being formed, classical physics becomes a borderline case in which the descriptions of quantum and relativistic physics flow. Although it may appear paradoxical, the general scientific approach borrowed from classical physics that neoclassical economists have taken as the reference methodological model for the nascent economic science and its contemporary developments has evolved greatly during the twentieth century, opening up completely new horizons. While, instead, standard economics has been maintaining nineteenth-century classical physics as its original, primary reference—specifically, rational mechanics—focused on the study of equilibrium. Considering that it is neither undisputed nor obvious (let alone definitive) that economic theory should draw its subjects and modes from the mathematics and the related theories of physics, once it has been admitted that there may be any connections and analogies between the two macro disciplines (i.e., physics and economics), it must be stressed that the new theoretical and methodological horizons opened by the twentieth-century physics have remained completely unrelated to the developments of standard economics in the twentieth century and beyond as if it were a foreign body of thought and quantitative methods opposed to the dominant culture in economics (among others, see Mirowski 1991; Weintraub 2002). Recent coverage of this debate helped illustrate how the current phase of the development of contemporary economic theory seems to be still characterised by the predominance of theoretical approaches that identify the maximising economic behaviour as an essential element from which to start in order to develop an effective analysis of the functioning of economic systems or national economies. Especially from the second half of the twentieth century, a common feature of these approaches is the overt need to provide microeconomic foundations for macroeconomics. This suggests that the main methodological implication is to assume that the general economic equilibrium always occurs and that—in order to understand the dynamics of the economic system as a whole or aggregate—it is sufficient to study the decision-making process of a single, ideal maximising agent, namely, the representative agent, as if an isomorphism existed. It is worth mentioning a general point here: this isomorphism between the aggregate economy and the representative agent is considered by many neoclassical economists as a necessary and sufficient condition (i.e., materially equivalent) to satisfy the need to provide microeconomic foundations for macroeconomics. In any case, all types of research and all branches of knowledge—unfortunately except for most of the economic theory—describe the phenomena they try to explain by differentiating between a lower level (i.e., comparable to the micro dimension) and a higher level (i.e., comparable to the macro) prudently: the macro dimension analyses aggregates and is normally not isomorphic to the micro (among many, see Simon and Ando 1961; Anderson 1972). Therefore, if the above methodological implication was probably missing in the macroeconomic models developed up to the early seventies—thus providing them with a presumed groundlessness—the same could be demonstrated with regard to those theoretical constructions based on the presumed (representative) agent's ability to make purely rational decisions, that is, more formally, to determine the global maximum (or minimum) in mathematical terms. In the wake of these latter considerations and supported by Velupillai's seminal contributions from 1997 to 2010 (see references), in the next section we sketch out the conceptual groundwork behind the initiative that links the notion of computable with economics that Stefano Zambelli helped develop as far back as 1994, when he launched a research project in the Department of Economics of the University of Aalborg entitled *Computability and Economic Applications: The Research Program 'Computable Economics'*. Later we describe some expository notes on the main interpretations of the foundations of mathematics for a post-neoclassical age in economic theory. The last section concludes with reflections on the challenges to implement computable economics in the formation of economic hypotheses.

## 2 Zambelli Reloaded: Summing up the Logic of Computability

The alleged perfect rationality of individuals has been widely criticised, as is known, by Herbert A. Simon (1955, 1997a [1945]), who stressed that they—as a matter of fact—do not behave like maximising decision-makers being limited by contingent factors in their actual ability to make decisions. Starting from this fact, Simon argued that the analysis of the decision-making process could not take place 'as if' individuals maximised their utility functions (i.e., consumers) or their production functions (i.e., entrepreneurs or firms) but it can only occur following the specification of behavioural rules of individuals themselves (see also Mäki 2009; Lehtinen 2013). By so doing, Simon proposed the fundamental, emerging patterns of *bounded rationality* and *satisficing* not only with regard to cognitive constraints but also in relation to ontological and interdisciplinary grounds. In that regard, Simon (1976) suggested that decision-making should deal not only with the outcomes of decisions (i.e., substantial rationality) but also with the procedures by which people make decisions (i.e., procedural rationality). Not only that, but Simon (1997b) believed that "*a theory of bounded rationality is necessarily a theory of procedural rationality.*" (Simon 1997b, p. 19). On the other hand, some opponents of these patterns identify a certain indeterminacy and a lack of foundational theorising in them (e.g., see Sims 1980; Sargent 1993). Indeed, while it is assumed that everyone knows what it means to find the global maximum (or minimum) point of a function—therefore the optimum—it would not be as well known what reference point can be when trying to describe individuals' behaviour through a set of decision rules that may appear arbitrary. Nevertheless, if the knowledgeability of the optimum was not questioned, this criticism could be accepted as the limitation of the rationality of the individuals is however measurable, at least in theory, as a deviation from the optimal decision. From this point of view, the theoretical analysis should develop using the optimal solution of the decision-making process, thereby it can be compared with any sub-optimal solution as the result of the limited decisions of individuals (e.g., see Bray 1982; Conlisk 1996). Most certainly, Zambelli (1994,

2010) brought into question the ability of individuals to assess, albeit theoretically, whether any formal optimisation problem is solvable or not. Making use of fundamental theorems developed in the field of metamathematics as well as of the logic of computability, both approaches to rationality—substantial and procedural—lend themselves to being criticised on the basis that the optimal solution to decision problems can not only be very complicated to identify, but even indeterminable. This unknowability is not due to the limited abilities of individuals but derives from an intrinsic difficulty in mathematical systems whose incompleteness has been actually demonstrated by Gödel (1986 [1931]). Because of this unknowability, the parallelism between optimisation and rationality loses all meaning since it is not possible to indicate, if not for very elementary cases, whether and how important optimisation problems can be solved. From this, it follows that the optimal solutions are not always knowable, indeed these solutions are rarely known so that the neoclassical approach of the globally maximising individual can be considered neither as a starting point nor as a general reference. According to Bridges (1982), for example, in the case of neoclassical economic models, the decision problem can be identified in the determination of the set of optimal choices by the consumer: in this case, the standard approach allows taking as 'given' a subset of the Euclidean space expressed as a subset of the possible baskets of consumption. In this space, a binary relationship hypothesised as transitive, reflective, and complete is subsequently defined. This relationship expresses a typically weak preference, from which, though it is always possible to derive relationships of close preference and indifference. In the neoclassical framework, ultimately, the decision problem becomes that of determining whether there is actually a process (i.e., a procedure) capable of verifying whether an element belonging to the initial set is also belonging to the set of optimal choices or not. In this regard, the neoclassical methodological approach is to postulate that the maximising individual owns this procedure. In the absence of this postulate, not surprisingly, many theorems—thus the theories—developed in the context of modern microeconomics become completely unfounded. According to Zambelli (1994, 2005), however, the logic of calculability helps to describe decision-making in terms of algorithmic procedure, whereby 'algorithm' is meant both a calculation rule and a logical instruction to solve a problem. It is assumed, specifically, that a countable (i.e., numerable) set and a subset of the first are given. The decision-making concerning the subset provides an algorithm, conceived as a list of instructions, which allows to effectively decide whether, for each element of the set, it belongs to the subset. As far as the subset is concerned, therefore, the decision problem is to determine this procedure (in this case, the subset is said to be decidable and, as a result, solvable) or to prove that it does not exist (in this second case, the subset is undecidable and, as a result, unsolvable). Coupled with the above background and challenge, a logical addition would be to briefly mention the work of Gödel and Turing who did far more than just shake the confidence and certainty of mathematicians to its foundations and, correspondingly, also those of economists and scientists in general. This is in line with the present work, which provides some expository notes on the foundations of mathematics (see next section) although many neoclassical economists are still unaware of the following contents. More specifically, Gödel proved that arithmetic is a consistent but incomplete logical system, known as the formal proof of incompleteness: it is consistent because its theorems cannot be simultaneously true and false; nonetheless, it is incomplete because it cannot be determined for all possible theorems (considered within the countable starting set above) whether they are true or false, that is to say, belonging to the subset of the first or to its complement. This proof, which attempted to demonstrate the epistemological foundations of mathematics, too, led the scientific community to reject Hilbert's formalist program[2] coinciding with providing a complete axiomatic description of mathematics—thus, also of those sciences that

[2] During the twenties of the last century, Hilbert attempted a single rigorous formalisation of all of mathematics, named Hilbert's program, on an axiomatic basis. He was particularly concerned with the following three questions: (i) is mathematics complete in the sense that its every statement can be proved or disproved?; (ii) is mathematics consistent meaning that no statement can be proved both true and false?; and (iii) is mathematics decidable in the sense that there exists a formal method to determine the truth or falsity of any mathematical statement? Hilbert believed that the answer to the previous questions was affirmative. On the other hand, thanks to Gödel's (1986 [1931]) incompleteness theorem and the undecidability of first-order logic demonstrated by Church and Turing, we know nowadys that Hilbert's aspiration will never be fully realised (i.e., Church's and Turing's theses or, in other words, the so-called Church–Turing thesis, also known as computability thesis). This makes it an endless task of finding 'possible' partial answers to Hilbert's questions (for insights, see Gandy 1988).

use mathematics, such as standard economic theory, moreover finalising sets of axioms to the 'claim' of describing human behaviour by idealising it in the abstract—from which any statement could be decided through the use of a finite number of logical steps (see Smorynski 1991; see also Giusti 1999). One of the cornerstones on which Gödel based his proof is represented by primitive recursive functions: these functions satisfy an intuitive notion of algorithm and, for this reason, they can also be used in order to address the decision problem (specifically, see Gödel 1986 [1931]). In order to be easily implemented, an algorithm must be executed by some mechanism, be it biological or mechanical: insofar as economic theory is concerned with, it is a question of assessing whether a formal mechanism exists—which for the neoclassical approach is the *homo oeconomicus* of the microeconomics together with its close relative, the *representative agent*, an artefact for micro-founding the macroeconomics—and is deemed adequate to solve any formal problem, thus, even the so-called optimisation problems. In this regard, a straightforward and effective calculation mechanism is represented by the Turing machine (1937 [1936]). The latter represents an abstraction that, yet still, can be simulated by a real physical system, becoming an extremely powerful calculation mechanism. It can be shown that for each recursive function, there is a Turing machine that is able to calculate it. Simplifying as much as possible, we can argue that every function computable by a Turing machine is also recursive as well as each rule can be expressed in terms of recursive functions. It follows that any theory that is rigorously developed has a recursive equivalent and could, therefore, be replicable by a Turing machine (for insights, see Herbrand 1932; Gödel 1934). The relevance of the Turing machine is also due to the fact that the first Gödel's incompleteness theorem has been reformulated through Turing's specific formalism: this reformulation, known as the undecidability of the halting problem (see Turing 1937 [1936]), shows that it is not possible to determine a priori whether a Turing machine will provide an output or not, that is, whether it will halt or not. In other words, accordingly, no algorithm which could determine whether an arbitrary relation is well-founded. Indeed, if the incompleteness theorem and the halting problem represent clear breaking elements concerning the formalistic approach, particularly with respect to the axiomatic approach of mathematics, even more so, they should lead to a substantial and profound revision of the neoclassical approach to economic theory. Thus, intuitively, it is no accident that the best-known applications of these breaking elements to microeconomics may affect the different decision problems addressed in the consumer theory and business theory—the same applies to game theory—having by their very nature a structure that requires an analysis in terms of computability. This passage can be understood by reading Zambelli (2004) where, for example, the knowledge production is modelled in terms of Turing machines, or even Zambelli (2012) where he elaborated a case for Velupillai's computable economics, claiming that the methodological approach and theorems of classical recursion theory as well as constructive mathematics should be at the foundation of theorising in economics (an idea reiterated in Velupillai and Zambelli 2013, 2015; Zambelli 2010, 2015, whereby the logic of computability is fostered and applied mutatis mutandis). Quite simply, it is a question of assessing whether, whenever the consumer utility function or the producer profit function is aimed at maximisation, there is a calculable procedure—at least theoretically—and effectively implementable which describes how this occurs. If one proceeds in this way, one may find that not everything can be computable and, for that reason, not everything can be optimised (see also Kenneth Arrow's confirmation about this, 1986; see also, Velupillai 2002, 2010; Rustem and Velupillai 1990). This idea has the agreement of what is stated as being the "logic of computability" in the following quotation: "*Nevertheless systems of Turing machines [...] are very powerful systems able to simulate, following the Church–Turing thesis, any other computable system and hence also any formal aspect of decision-making [...].*" (Zambelli 2004, p. 175). In the next section, we provide some remarks underlying the logic of computability that consistently articulate Zambelli's discussions on computable economics and its research potential. We wonder, indeed, what the next future of computable economics will be. The question is much less than rhetoric, especially since it presupposes a thorough knowledge of the foundations of mathematics.

# 3 Remarks on the Foundations of Mathematics

Studying the foundations of mathematics may be used, too, to investigate such things as the nature of science in general and, particularly, of social sciences. Studying these foundations, consequently, leads to the investigation of constructive processes, where the latter incorporate both calculation rules and logical processes. Admittedly, if an algorithm is the outcome of a constructive process and the economic phenomena—for example, individuals' decisions both on the demand side and supply side, the aggregations moving from micro to macroeconomics, and so on—can be assimilated to constructive processes, then, these phenomena can be described and studied starting from algorithmic representations. Such ruminations are every bit as epistemological as they are mathematical, perhaps even more so epistemological since the fundamental question is actually one of a meta-mathematical nature. In this regard, and drawing on Agazzi (1974) and Bertuglia and Vaio (2003), it could be argued that science exists insofar as reality appears to be represented in an algorithmic form, that is to say, capable of being read and interpreted in such a form that its description can be expressed abstractly and synthetically, formulating a series of general laws that describes facts and phenomena expressed in a more reduced and compressed scale than would be necessary if one described them individually, explicitly, one after the other. Nevertheless, the underlying determinism, namely, the series of synthetic laws that describes phenomena in a deterministic way, is not establishable by a priori calculation: it is challenging if not complicated, truthfully, to identify in real phenomena—such as economic phenomena—those basic laws that generate them, of course, unless we already know them. However, if we interpret science as an attempt to algorithmically reduce the phenomena of the real world and if, at the same time, the entire universe appears to us as a single entity, then the whole universe is expected to be representable (therefore 'compressible') in an algorithmic form. Without resorting to transcendental supra-structures or hidden cognitive or social forces which would determine social phenomena and in order to develop a more conceptual understanding of mathematics, and thus of economics, one could claim to concentrate in a series of algorithmic representations the description of all the sequences of all the real phenomena, what in the past has been called, perhaps improperly, the *theory of everything*. Just as a myth, the latter is the specific expression that formerly indicated all those theories that aimed to unify the four fundamental interactions of physical phenomena, only apparently distant from social phenomena: (i) gravitational interaction; (ii) electromagnetic interaction; (iii) strong interaction (i.e., macroscopic events); and, finally, (iv) weak interaction (i.e., microscopic events, whose range of action is limited to subatomic dimensions). In the original context, the word 'everything' refers only to the description of the elementary particles and their interactions and does not indicate a theory of everything that is really knowable. The relation between the dynamics or behaviour of elementary particles and the real phenomena that can be known is too weak and indirect for a theory of everything to be useful, for example, to explain or predict consumers' or entrepreneurs' behaviours as well as to analyse the trend of some markets at an aggregate level. Following Cohen and Stewart (1994), "*Scientists often object to the concept of God on the grounds that it explains the universe too easily: You can't see how it "works." God is a contextual Theory of Everything. But a reductionist Theory of Everything suffers from the same problem. The physicist's belief that the mathematical laws of a Theory of Everything really do govern every aspect of the universe is very like a priest's belief that God's laws do. The main difference is that the priest is looking outward while the physicist looks inward. Both are offering an interpretation of nature; neither can tell you how it works.*" (Cohen and Stewart 1994, pp. 364–365). One can, therefore, conclude that there are several classes of phenomena that cannot be reducible: irreducible phenomena are encountered whenever a phenomenon is qualified as 'random' without regard to epistemological and methodological implications. As a matter of fact, randomness is a concept of convenience that translates ignorance of the laws of one or more phenomena or the inability to observe any recurrences or the emergence of underlying laws in them. As stated by Maddy (1990), and Shapiro (2000), on the one hand, the method of making reductions and expressing them in a mathematical form, that is, the application of mathematics to the sciences of both nature and society is imperfect: sometimes, in some contexts, this method is effective; at another time, as, for example, in some areas of social sciences, it is powerless. On the other side, instead, mathematics arises as a useful analytical tool even when the reductions appear extremely difficult or when data are not even numerical. A partial conclusion that can be drawn from the above is that the human mind has developed a powerful tool of thought over the millennia, mathematics, which can be applied to interpret real behaviours and phenomena. For this reason, mathematics ceases to be grounded in real phenomena, giving rise to the school of *formalism* in mathematical thought, around which standard economics began to gravitate. In that regard, as Giusti (1999) notes, "*[i]f mathematics can no longer find its raison d'etre in nature, it will find it in freedom [...] The need for mathematics goes back to the innermost regions of demonstrations which, however, can begin their route only after the free choice of definitions and axioms has been completely accomplished.*" (Giusti 1999, p. 19, authors' trans., square brackets added). Serving as the basis for the *formalism*, the concept of 'truth' refers to the postulates assumed and is purely limited to the formal consistency with these postulates, specifically, 'truth' coincides with 'consistency.' It is precisely from this identification between 'truth' and 'consistency' that the criticism of the *formalism* originates, adequately described by Smullyan (1992): "*The formalist position really strikes me as most strange! Physicists and engineers certainly don't think like that. Suppose a corps of engineers has a bridge built and the next day the army is going to march over it. The engineers want to know whether the bridge will support the weight or whether it will collapse. It certainly won't do them one bit of good to be told: «Well, in some axiom systems it can be proved that the bridge will hold, and in other axiom systems it can be proven that the bridge will fall.» The engineers want to know whether the bridge will really hold or not! And to me (and other Platonists) the situation is the same with the continuum hypothesis: is there a set intermediate in size between N and P(N) or isn't there? If the formalist is going to tell me that in one axiom system there is and in another there isn't, I would reply that that does me no good unless I know which of those two axiom systems is the correct one! But to the formalist, the very notion of correctness, other than mere consistency, is either meaningless or is itself dependent on which axiom system is taken. Thus the deadlock between the formalist and the Platonist is pretty hopeless! I don't think that either side can budge the other on iota!*" (Smullyan

1992, p. 249). As mentioned in Sect. 2 above, the ambitions of the *formalism* to rewrite mathematics within a complete and consistent system of postulates, to which to apply logical-deductive laws, underwent a downsizing with respect to the claim to formalise 'everything' in number theory—following the proof of the two famous theorems of formal incompleteness by Gödel (1986 [1931]), who basically proved that mathematics is not verifiable as 'true' from within by its rules.[3] In this vein, the collapse of the idea of mathematics as a synonym of 'truth' is summarised, even humorously, by Barrow (1992): "*[...] it has been suggested that if we were to define a religion to be a system of thought which contains unprovable statements, so it contains an element of faith, then Gödel has taught us that not only is mathematics a religion but it is the only religion able to prove itself to be one.*" (Barrow 1992, p. 19). In any case, the *formalist* approach pushed the mathematicians to a profound revision of the axiomatic system and the rigorous development of formal and logical techniques. It was also as a result of this revision that Turing, starting from the thirties, highlighted the fundamental question concerning the concept of computability for the real number system, that is to say, the question of whether the decimal representation—or in any other basis—of a number can be operationalised by an algorithm (see Turing 1937 [1936]). It was even realised that the non-computable numbers, that is, the numbers for which there is no algorithm for calculating the sequence of digits, constitute the vast majority of real numbers: they are called an uncountable infinity in the continuum of real numbers. From this, it follows that computable numbers as mere exceptions within the continuum of real numbers. The awareness of the existence of non-computable numbers, that is, of calculation procedures that do not lead to a result in a finite time, constitutes, alongside Gödel's theorems, the negative answer to Hilbert's tenth problem, the well-known *Entscheidungsproblem*, or rather, the problem of decidability. This problem explores the existence of a

[3] The fulcrum of Gödel's incompleteness theorems that brought down Hilbert's program on which *formalism* in mathematics was grounded, lies in the self-referentiality of the problem, most notably the arithmetic that aims to find its foundation in itself, even justifying itself in arithmetic form. Broadly speaking, one can encounter situations of self-referentiality whenever the symbol of an object is confused with the object itself, that is, blurring the difference between the 'use' of a word and the 'mention' of the word. In cases like this, logic inevitably brings out elements of undecidability.

general algorithmic procedure that can—at least theoretically—decide on the 'truth' or 'falsity' of any mathematical proposition. Since any mathematical problem results in a series of propositions, the *Entscheidungsproblem* resulted in the issue of whether there could be a general algorithmic procedure capable of solving any mathematical problem. In addressing this issue, it was a matter of discovering the existence of a procedure that once started its execution on an appropriately defined abstract calculation machine—precisely the Turing machine—returned a result in a finite time. A clearly negative response to this issue, suggested by the existence of non-computable numbers, introduced the awareness that not all mathematical problems can be solved in a finite time (e.g., see Giusti 1999). Coupled with the question concerning the meaning of non-computable real numbers highlighted by Turing is the central message of the *constructivist* approach in mathematics, precisely, that undecidable propositions will always exist. In line with the *constructivist* math approach, at present, science is not yet capable of knowing whether the nature of the phenomena of the world in which we are involved is such as to include non-computable elements. In other words, science is not yet capable of knowing if the laws of nature (even of social systems) are all computable, that is, if they provide a result in finite time or if they contain elements that cannot be computed. In the first case, science would be capable of managing the results (i.e., numbers) obtained; in the second case, however, it would be unable to deal with non-computable numbers that escape an algorithmic definition and, as a consequence, an understanding in terms of logical processes, which would make any *theory of everything* impossible. As mentioned in footnote 4 above, situations without a logical outlet—that self-referentiality entails—represent a consequence of an intrinsic limitation of the human mind and the way of thinking, which intersects mathematics with cognitive sciences, highlighting the complexity of behavioural decision processes (among others, see Simon 1978; Velupillai 2018). Since self-referentiality implies that there are always sources of undecidability and, therefore, non-computable operations, it follows that by adopting the *constructivist* mathematical approach it is not possible to reach complete knowledge and effective description of all the phenomena in the world. And this is true if the time required for the calculation tends to infinite, but even if the time required is finite but exceedingly long, for instance, likely longer than the life of the universe: in this case, basically, no difference would emerge since neither case would allow us to reach a result. The constructivist approach, accordingly, provides its fundamental contribution every time it warns us against a hasty and superficial use of 'certain' concepts and definitions, attributing an indispensable meaning to the methods and processes. This was also figuratively underlined by de Finetti (1963) when he pointed out that "*the ivory tower of the 'end in itself' is fraught with pitfalls. Wouldn't it be an aberration—just to make analogies—if a linguist to purify the language by suppressing what is aimed at uses and purposes outside of itself, intended to restrict it to the only words and structures necessary and sufficient to express only the rules of its own grammar and syntax? Or [wouldn't it be an aberration] if one placed the red triangle in the middle of the road for the sole purpose of signalling the stumbling block made up of the presence of the red triangle itself?*" (de Finetti 1963, p. 5, authors' trans., square brackets added).

## 4 Concluding Notes: Some Research Directions in Economic Theory

In recasting the work of Zambelli on the logic of computability and computable economics, we began this chapter by noting several lines of research in Stefano Zambelli's work, which might, at first glance, appear to be ontologically distinct from one another or even incompatible. Running through his research experience, indeed, it is easy to deduce that technological change, economic dynamics, computational economics, epistemology, micro and macroeconomics, social science algorithmic research, nonlinearity, complexity, and others are some of the major themes that he has dealt with throughout his professional activity. Over the years, we have increasingly come to believe that Zambelli saw—and sees—the fundamental importance of each theme in the logic of computability and the related computable economics. This modest chapter aims to raise awareness on Zambelli's efforts concerning the fact that, as demonstrated by Gödel's theorems, it is not possible to enumerate all the truths of arithmetic without also enumerating all the falsehoods, which poses very great theoretical limitations to the decision-making capacity of the well-known *homo oeconomicus*. Referring to the *formalist* math approach that describes it, the latter portrayal of economic 'man' will obviously find itself having to deal with intrinsically undecidable problems. This impossibility to decide—namely, to construct an algorithm that may lead to a correct yes-or-no answer—is easily understood if one accepts the fact that any formalisable decision-making process has an algorithmic description. Therefore, for Gödel's incompleteness theorem and the undecidability of the halting problem, for any given problem it is not always possible to arrive at a solution and, even less, to an optimal solution. In this regard, Rustem and Velupillai (1990) have shown the existence of undecidable propositions intrinsic to the context of the axiomatic approach of the theory of choice, describing the situation just outlined above in this way: "*Since we are assured that REMs are not 'Buridan's Asses', the implications of [quantitative undecidability results] as far as rational behaviour is concerned, are that there are inherent elements of unpredictability—but for that reason not necessarily irrational in any sense whatsoever. It only means that some aspects of behaviour cannot be encapsulated by any formalism at all. It can, so to speak, be studied only as it unfolds. The connection with the implications of Gödel's theorem for the formalists' programme enunciated by Hilbert is immediate. Since the predictable part can be formulated by Turing Machines, any assumption about intrinsic preferences are irrelevant. We can, not only do without any vestigial traces of the utility concept, but also without any vestigial traces of the preference concept! All we need to study are the decision rules—or the computable functions.*" (Rustem and Velupillai 1990, p. 431, square brackets added). As far as the theory of decision or rational choice is concerned, if one assumes that the economic decision-maker always makes a decision—and thus the system is by definition or construction as 'complete'—then the same system will necessarily be inconsistent. For this reason, the neoclassical approach to preferences can no longer be taken into consideration to found the paradigm of the decision-making process of individuals (i.e., the *homo oeconomicus*) as it is based on the definition of consistency and completeness on the same axiomatic foundations of formal mathematical systems such as arithmetic. Not by chance, and according to Zambelli's vision on economics, the intrinsic limits to an axiomatic approach determined by the impossibility to identify general procedures suitable for solving any problem or providing a theoretical interpretation of any phenomenon represent an argument in favour of the inductive methodological approach. Contrary to what happens in other scientific disciplines, honestly, the methodology generally followed by the majority of theoretical economists in investigating mechanisms of the functioning of the economy can be defined as in the majority of cases of a deductive type. This can be identified as the methodological core of the so-called neoclassical mainstream in economic studies: so many economists actually start from a set of axioms from which then derive models and theorems aimed at analysing economic issues, attributing to them a general value. The ultimate reason for this is due to the fact that the deductive approach would be 'superior' because it is based on objective first elements, while there is no objective criterion according to which the supporters of the deductive method can affirm its general validity, as widely demonstrated by Gödel, Turing, Church, and Post. Furthermore, it is rarely recognised that Zambelli was one of the Italian economists who advocated the value of the inductive approach to economic studies in his several lines of research. In this short chapter, we can only recall his references to John M. Keynes's logical-relationist theory regarding the logical probability of propositions in his *Treatise on Probability*, to de Finetti's conception of subjective probability, to the work of Polya, to the constructive mathematics by Brouwer, and, last but not least, the more general and pervasive logic of computability. Therefore, Zambelli was and is optimistic about the future of economics (e.g., see Zambelli 2010, 2012, 2015) and, even more so, of computable economics. Zambelli's inquiry on the logic of computability has significant theoretical implications. All his critical arguments have been developed having as a basic element of reference an algorithmic procedural approach recalling, in the background, the recursive functions of Gödel and the quaternary representation of the Turing machine. This allowed Zambelli to transform his criticism into an absolutely positive contribution to the development of economic theory. A necessary reminder in this regard seems to be to follow the suggestion of Simon

(1976), that is, to describe economic agents as having procedural rationality, which Zambelli accepted and fully welcomed. Zambelli's proposal, notably, can be interpreted as that of developing algorithmic descriptions that can be implemented through software, capable of capturing the procedural aspects of economic agents' behaviour. Hence, how can we not fully recognise that and justify his efforts on that regard? How not to fully agree with this proposal? By the way, this proposal also includes the work of many experimental economists since a description of economic agents in algorithmic procedural terms can always be subjected to experimental verification, both analogically and through mainly intelligent field devices. This proposal may have guided his astonishingly fertile scientific works, especially in the last quarter of a century. In his own words of a few years ago, also referring to Federico Caffè during the award ceremony of the NordSud 2015 Prize for social sciences in his honour, he clearly stated: "*The textbooks, either of microeconomics or macroeconomics, make no mention of these theoretical and methodological difficulties. Rather, the capital controversy is no longer on the economic agenda and the problem is still unsolved today. This is my contemporaneity. On the one hand there is the [bitter] realisation that in front of everyone's eyes there are very serious economic problems; on the other hand, there is a kind of unique thought of economists that tends to introduce simplifying hypotheses that lead to very little knowledge of real economic processes but impose strong prescriptions and guide the choices made by policymakers. I believe it is a duty of economists to try to understand real economic processes while avoiding harmful simplifications.*" (Zambelli 2015, p. 81, authors' trans., square brackets added).

**Acknowledgements** The authors are indebted to their colleague Ragupathy Venkatachalam for help in interpretations and analysis. Furthermore, the authors are both very grateful to Shu-Heng Chen for many really enjoyable and enlightening conversations, as well as intellectually and ethically challenging thoughts and ideas that they have benefited from. Out of any rhetoric and stereotypes, finally, the authors are deeply obliged to Stefano Zambelli whose very special encouragements and magnanimity in the last two decades have allowed them—above all—to deepen the knowledge of a brotherly friend and a praeternatural scientist. Needless to say none of them are responsible for any remaining infelicities.

## References


Agazzi, A. (1974). The Rise of Foundational Research in Mathematics. *Synthese, 27*(1/2), 7–26.

Anderson, P. W. (1972). More is Different. *Science, 177*(4047), 393–396.

Arrow, K. J. (1986). Rationality of Self and Others in an Economic System. *The Journal of Business, 59*(4), S385–S399.

Barrow, J. D. (1992). *Pi in the Sky. Counting, Thinking and Being*. Oxford: Oxford University Press.

Bertuglia, C. S., & Vaio, F. (2003). *Non Linearità, Caos, Complessità*. Torino: Bollati Boringhieri.

Boehm, S., Gehrke, C., Kurz, H. D., & Sturn, R. (Eds.). (2002). *Is There Progress in Economics? Knowledge, Truth and the History of Economic Thought*. Cheltenham (UK): Edward Elgar.

Bray, M. (1982). Learning, Estimation and Stability of Rational Expectations. *Journal of Economic Theory, 26*(2), 318–339.

Bridges, D. S. (1982). Preference and Utility: A Constructive Development. *Journal of Mathematical Economics, 9*(1–2), 165–185.

Brock, W. A., & Durlauf, S. N. (2006). Macroeconomics and Model Uncertainty. In D. Colander (Ed.), *Post Walrasian Macroeconomics. Beyond the Dynamic Stochastic General Equilibrium Model* (pp. 27–45). New York: Cambridge University Press.

Cohen, J., & Stewart, I. (1994). *The Collapse of Chaos*. New York: Penguin Books.

Conlisk, J. (1996). Why Bounded Rationality? *Journal of Economic Literature, 34*(2), 669–700.

D'Autume, A., & Cartelier, J. (Eds.). (1997). *Is Economics Becoming a Hard Science?* Cheltenham (UK): Edward Elgar.

de Finetti, B. (1963). *L'apporto della Matematica nell'Evoluzione del Pensiero Economico*. (Atti del VII Congresso dell'Unione Matematica Italiana 1963), Cremonese, Roma, 1965, pp. 238–277.

Gandy, R. O. (1988). The Confluence of Ideas in 1936. In R. Herken (Ed.), *The Universal Turing Machine: A Half-Century Survey* (2nd ed., pp. 51–102). Wien: Springer-Verlag.

Giusti, E. (1999). *Ipotesi sulla Natura degli Oggetti Matematici*. Torino: Bollati Boringhieri.

Gödel, K. (1934). *On Undecidable Propositions of Formal Mathematical Systems*. Lecture notes taken by S. C. Kleene & J. B. Rosser at the Institute for Advanced Study. Reprinted in M. Davis (Ed.). (1965). The Undecidable:

Basic Papers on Undecidable Propositions, Unsolvable Problems and Computable Functions, Raven, New York, pp. 39–74.
Gödel, K. (1986) [1931]. On Formally Undecidable Propositions of Principia Mathematica and Related Systems I. In S. Feferman et al. (Ed.), *Kurt Gödel—Collected Works* (Vol. I, pp. 145–195). Publications 1929–1936. New York: Oxford University Press.
Hausman, D. M. (1992). *Essays on Philosophy and Economic Methodology*. New York: Cambridge University Press.
Herbrand, J. (1932). Sur la Non-contradiction de l'Arithmétique. *Journal fur die reine und angewandte Mathematik, 166*, 1–8.
Lehtinen, A. (2013). Three Kinds of 'As–If' Claims. *The Journal of Economic Methodology, 20*(2), 184–205.
Maddy, P. (1990). *Realism in Mathematics*. Oxford (UK): Oxford University Press.
Mäki, U. (Ed.). (2009). *The Methodology of Positive Economics. Reflections on the Milton Friedman Legacy*. New York: Cambridge University Press.
Mirowski, P. (1989). *More Heat Than Light: Economics as Social Physics, Physics as Nature's Economics*. New York: Cambridge University Press.
Mirowski, P. (1991). The When, the How and the Why of Mathematical Expression in the History of Economic Analysis. *Journal of Economic Perspectives, 5*(1), 145–157.
Parisi, D. (2006). Introduzione «dall'Esterno della Disciplina Economica». In P. Terna, R. Boero, M. Morini, & M. Sonnessa (Eds.), *Modelli per la Complessità* (pp. 1–16). Bologna: Il Mulino.
Rustem, B., & Velupillai, K. (1990). Rationality, Computability, and Complexity. *Journal of Economic Dynamics and Control, 14*(2), 419–432.
Sargent, T. J. (1993). *Bounded Rationality in Macroeconomics. The Arne Ryde Memorial Lectures*. Oxford (UK): Oxford University Press.
Schwartz, J. T. (1966). The Pernicious Influence of Mathematics on Science. *Studies in Logic and the Foundations of Mathematics, 44*, 356–360.
Shapiro, S. (2000). *Thinking about Mathematics*. Oxford (UK): Oxford University Press.
Simon, H. A. (1955). A Behavioral Model of Rational Choice. *The Quarterly Journal of Economics, 69*(1), 99–118.
Simon, H. A. (1976). From Substantive to Procedural Rationality. In S. J. Latsis (Ed.), *Method and Appraisal in Economics* (pp. 129–148). Cambridge (UK): Cambridge University Press.
Simon, H. A. (1978). The Uses of Mathematics in the Social Sciences. *Mathematics and Computers in Simulation, 20*(3), 159–166.

Simon, H. A. (1997a) [1945]. *Administrative Behavior: A Study of Decision-Making Processes in Administrative Organizations*, (4th ed.). Free Press, New York.

Simon, H. A. (1997b). *An Empirically Based Microeconomics*. Cambridge (UK): Cambridge University Press.

Simon, H. A., & Ando, A. (1961). Aggregation of Variables in Dynamic Systems. *Econometrica, 29*(2), 111–138.

Sims, C. A. (1980). Macroeconomics and Reality. *Econometrica, 48*(1), 1–48.

Smorynski, C. (1991). *Logical Number Theory I. An Introduction*. Heidelberg: Springer-Verlag.

Smullyan, R. M. (1992). *Satan, Cantor, and Infinity. And Other Mind-boggling Puzzles*. New York: Knopf.

Sutton, J. (2000). *Marshall Tendencies. What Can Economists Know?* Cambridge (MA): MIT Press.

Turing, A. M. (1937) [1936]. On Computable Numbers, with an Application to the Entscheidungsproblem. *Proceedings of the London Mathematical Society*, s2-42(1), 230–265 (delivered to the Society in 1936). Ibid: A correction (1938), s2-43(1), 544–546.

Velupillai, K. V. (1997). Expository Notes on Computability and Complexity in (Arithmetical) Games. *Journal of Economic Dynamics and Control, 21*(6), 955–979.

Velupillai, K. V. (2000). *Computable Economics*. Oxford (UK): Oxford University Press.

Velupillai, K. V. (2002). Effectivity and Constructivity in Economic Theory. *Journal of Economic Behaviour and Organization, 49*(3), 307–325.

Velupillai, K. V. (2005). The Unreasonable Ineffectiveness of Mathematics in Economics. *Cambridge Journal of Economics, 29*(6), 849–872.

Velupillai, K. V. (2010). *Computable Foundations for Economics*. London: Routledge.

Velupillai, K. V. (2018). *Models of Simons*. London: Routledge.

Velupillai, K. V., & Zambelli, S. (2013). Computability and Algorithmic Complexity in Economics. In H. Zenil (Ed.), *A Computable Universe. Understanding and Exploring Nature as Computation* (pp. 303–331). Singapore: World Scientific.

Velupillai, K. V., & Zambelli, S. (2015). Simulation, Computation and Dynamics in Economics. *The Journal of Economic Methodology, 22*(1), 1–27.

Weintraub, E. R. (2002). *How Economics Became a Mathematical Science*. Durham (UK): Duke University Press.

Wigner, E. (1960). The Unreasonable Effectiveness of Mathematics in the Natural Sciences. *Communications in Pure and Applied Mathematics, 13*(1), 1–14.

Zambelli, S. (1994). *Computability and Economic Applications: The Research Program 'Computable Economics'*. Working Paper, Department of Economics, Aalborg University Press, Aalborg, pp. 31. Retrieved from https://vbn.aau.dk/da/publications/computability-and-economic-applications-the-research-program-comp

Zambelli, S. (2004). Production of Ideas by Means of Ideas: A Turing Machine Metaphor. *Metroeconomica, 55*(2–3), 155–179.

Zambelli, S. (2005). Computable Knowledge and Undecidability: A Turing Machine Metaphor applied to Endogenous Growth Theory. In K. Velupillai (Ed.), *Computability, Complexity and Constructivity in Economic Analysis* (pp. 233–263). Oxford (UK): Blackwell.

Zambelli, S. (2010). Computable and Constructive Economics, Undecidable Dynamics and Algorithmic Rationality. An Essay in Honour of Professor Kumaraswamy (Vela) Velupillai. In S. Zambelli (Ed.), *Computable, Constructive and Behavioural Economic Dynamics. Essays in Honour of Kumaraswamy (Vela) Velupillai* (pp. 15–45). London: Routledge.

Zambelli, S. (2012). Computable Economics: Reconstructing the Nonconstructive. *New Mathematics and Natural Computation, 8*(1), 113–122.

Zambelli, S. (2015). On Subjectivity and Contemporaneity of an Economist. *Il Risparmio Review, LXII*(3–4), 73–82.

# 4

# Sraffa, Keynes and a New Paradigm

Sara Casagrande

## 1 Introduction

The Cambridge school included economists and scholars such as John M. Keynes, Joan Robinson, Piero Sraffa, Nicholas Kaldor, Richard Goodwin and Richard Kahn. Neoclassical theory has been questioned by them in different ways, but surely a key role has been played by Keynes and Sraffa. In 1936, after the Great Depression, Keynes's *General Theory* claimed the centrality of underemployment and disequilibrium revolutionizing macroeconomics and political economy. In 1960, Sraffa wrote a short and cryptic book, *Production of Commodities by Means of Commodities* (PCC). Sraffa's PCC is an "amazingly concise little book" (Pasinetti 2012b, p. 1303), based on strict logical reasoning and dense "mathematical and methodological elixirs" (Velupillai 2008, p. 275), with profound consequences for economic theory. PCC had the fundamental aim of criticizing the marginal method, indeed its subtitle is

S. Casagrande (✉)
University of Trento, Trento, Italy
e-mail: sara.casagrande@unitn.it



K. Velupillai (ed.), *Keynesian, Sraffian, Computable and Dynamic Economics*,
https://doi.org/10.1007/978-3-030-58131-2_4

*Prelude to a critique of economic theory*, and rehabilitated the forgotten classical theory through the resolution of the Ricardian problem of an invariable measure of value (i.e., the Standard commodity). Sraffa interpreted the economy as a circular flow, demonstrating how it is possible to determine prices, wages and profits. The fundamental result is that distribution, independently of value theory, depends not only on production conditions, but also on sociological patterns, realizing the conflict between wages and profits. The PCC became the milestone of the *Cambridge capital controversy*. This controversy challenged the neoclassical interpretation of production and distribution at a strictly logical and mathematical level. The debate was between some economists at the University of Cambridge and other economists at MIT (such as Paul Samuelson and Robert Solow). Even though the value of this criticism has been confirmed by Samuelson (1966), neoclassical theory has been able, substantially, to incorporate some Keynesian results and ignore Sraffa's critique. Nowadays the controversy is simply considered as an episode, or a *curiosum* (Lunghini 1975, p. xiii). Probably, some concrete methodological and theoretical issues, related to the relationship between Keynesian and Sraffian economics, prevented the construction of an alternative paradigm, favouring the success of neoclassical arguments.

In this contribution, the controversial issues at the base of this *state of the art* will be investigated, from the compatibility between Keynes and Sraffa to their relationship with neoclassical theory. It will be claimed, together with other heterodox economists, that the construction of a real alternative to neoclassical theory will be possible considering both the findings of Keynes and those of Sraffa. After a summary of the attempts made in order to develop a Sraffian-Keynesian synthesis within heterodox economics, the further steps needed in order to develop a new paradigm will be analysed. It will be claimed that it is possible to develop Keynes's monetary theory of production through Sraffian economics for the construction of models able to analyse the dynamics of money-wage entrepreneur economies.

This contribution is organized as follows. In Sect. 2, the issues and the attempts related to the development of a Sraffian-Keynesian synthesis will be summarised. In Sect. 3, the further elements that would allow to develop a new paradigm will be commented. In Sect. 4, the possibility of developing a Sraffian-Keynesian monetary theory of production that could allow the construction of models grounded on bookkeeping principles and computable methods and able to simulate the dynamics of out-of-equilibrium monetary-entrepreneur economies will be explained. Section 5 concludes.

## 2 Towards a Keynesian-Sraffian Synthesis

### 2.1 The Controversial Issues After the Cambridge Capital Controversy

Nowadays, despite the *Cambridge capital controversy* has been recognized to be destructive for Wicksellian capital theory (Samuelson 1966), the original capital theory of Walras (in particular the intertemporal Arrow-Debreu version) has been claimed not to be touched by the controversy (see Bliss 1975; Malinvaud 1953; Mandler 2002; Bidard 1990). Indeed, while Walras developed a model of general economic equilibrium based on the assumption of heterogeneous capital goods available in arbitrary given initial quantities, Wicksell built on the notion of aggregate capital measured in value terms in order to overcome the logical contradictions in the Walrasian construction once capital is introduced (Tosato 2013, p. 106). As said, Sraffa's analysis has been recognized by the neoclassical side to be destructive for Wicksellian capital theory but not for the Arrow-Debreu version of the general equilibrium theory. One criticism to this line of defence has been that in the Arrow-Debreu version "the issues concerning the production of new capital goods are, to some extent, 'concealed' inside an extremely general formulation of the production sets which sidesteps the distinction between fixed capital goods and other factors of production and of consumers' choices, which obscures the aspects concerning the saving decision" (Tosato 2013, p. 106). Garegnani tried to demonstrate that Sraffian critique applies as much to general equilibrium as to aggregative models (see also the contribution of Schefold 1989). He accused the mainstream to solve Walras's contradictions simply by abandoning the traditional Walrasian concept of equilibrium in favour of short-run equilibrium models that allow an arbitrary initial physical condition for the capital stock (see Garegnani 1976) where the concept of capital as a single quantity reappears necessarily in the market of savings and investments inside intertemporal equilibrium (see Garegnani 2012, p. 1431). This debate remains open but without significant effects on the mainstream.

Beyond this debate, the grade of compatibility of Sraffa's analysis with neoclassical theory has been also questioned. Some researchers have tried to interpret PCC as a special case inside neoclassical theory (e.g., Hahn 1975, 1982) or as a non-destructive critique to neoclassical theory (e.g., Sen 2003). It is worth underlining how these positions are questionable especially because it could be demonstrated "that Sraffa's analysis is entirely incompatible with marginal economic theory" (Pasinetti 2012a, p. 1436). A position confirmed in particular by Garegnani (2003), who engaged in a detailed demonstration of the fallacy, in particular, of Hahn's position (Hahn 1975, 1982).

Also the grade of compatibility of Keynes's analysis with neoclassical theory has been object of debate. Indeed, Keynes's silences, ambiguities and contradictions on the real consequences of his *General Theory* for the orthodox framework (Robinson 1963, p. 78) "were to be reflected, and often magnified, in the subsequent debates" (King 1994, p. 5). Some Keynesians, in the attempt to reveal the *true Keynes*, arrived to "extract from Keynes's classic more than it actually contains"; at the end "all that appears to have been established is that Keynes's General Theory was 'revolution-making' but not 'revolutionary'" (Clower 1997, p. 47). This *doctrinal fog* (as called by Blaug 1980, p. 221) has been probably determined by more substantial problems related to Keynes's troubles with orthodox theory. Indeed, Keynes never denied the notion of substitution between labour and capital and this ambiguity had dramatic consequences for the long-run validity of his principle of effective demand. Indeed, "except for brief unsystematic statements we do not find in his work any alternative to the orthodox long-period theory of the level of aggregate output" (see Garegnani 1983, pp. 75–76). As a matter of fact, with the neoclassical synthesis "those who have tried to re-absorb [Keynes's] analysis into traditional theory have been careful not to mention the principle [of effective demand] at all" (Pasinetti 1997, p. 93).

The alleged lack of microfoundations in Keynes's theoretical construction has reinforced mainstream economists' arguments. Indeed, "to argue that Keynes's theory is grounded on microeconomic analysis is not difficult, but more complex is the problem concerning the fundamental characteristics of his microeconomics and, in particular, the relationship with neoclassical microeconomics" (Sardoni 2002, p. 7). Despite this, there are good reasons to sustain, at least, that the Keynesian and the neoclassical visions of individual behaviour are not compatible because "Keynes's notion of uncertainty is incompatible with the neoclassical analysis of individual behaviour" (Sardoni 2002, p. 7). However, there is widespread agreement that Keynesian Revolution needs to be accomplished (Pasinetti 2007).

These debates seem to suggest that it will be hard for Sraffian and Keynesian economics to develop a non-neoclassical approach autonomously. This is also Kurz's impression: he claimed that "those who seek to develop an alternative to the conventional neoclassical theory are well advised to take into account both the findings of Keynes and those of Sraffa" (Kurz 1995, p. 84). As claimed by Roncaglia, among others:

> The integration of Sraffa's and Keynes's analyses could constitute the core of *non-neoclassical economics*. However, this integration requires that Sraffa's analysis of relative prices and their relationship with income distribution should not contradict basic elements of the Keynesian paradigm. (Roncaglia 1995, p. 120, emphasis added)

One should not forget that "both Keynes and Sraffa rejected Say's Law, although for different reasons" (Kurz 2013, p. 9), and that "despite claims to the contrary, there is a strong bond uniting post-Keynesians of various brands and Sraffa: it is their opposition to the marginalist or neoclassical theory" (Kurz 2013, p. 1).

However, it is not clear how to proceed because surely Keynes and Sraffa have followed different methodologies and the difficulty of using production theory and Keynes's economics as an alternative microeconomic foundation for constructing satisfactory macro-dynamic models is a matter of fact (see Pasinetti 1975). The strictness of the Sraffian methodology could be one of the reasons for the difficulties in finding a synthesis with Keynes's approach. Indeed, Sraffa's approach was based on the "reliance on observable measurable quantities alone, to the exclusion of all 'subjectivist' concepts" (D3/12/7: 46, notation of Sraffa's unpublished manuscripts, quoted in Davis 2012, p. 1342). For Sraffa, value was a sort of "physical or chemical quality" (D3/12/12: 7, quoted in Kurz 2012, p. 1548), and he elaborated his equations like a chemist who presents "chemical reactions first as a balance sheet and then as an algebraic equation" (Kurz 2012, p. 1547). Even those economists that found some connections between Keynes and Sraffa possible have found difficult to imagine how to merge Keynes's unstable short-run approach with the widespread vision of Sraffian production prices as long-run centres of gravitation.

## 2.2 Sraffians, Keynesians and the Search of a Synthesis: An Overview

Both Sraffian and Keynesian economics have experienced significant developments over the decades, giving rise to new currents of thought and various research programs. Keynesian economics has been developed mainly by new Keynesians and post Keynesians, even though deep differences exist among them. Indeed, new Keynesians, starting from the Lucas Critique, try to reconcile Keynesian economics inside the mainstream orthodox framework. Gregory Mankiw and David Romer can be recognized as pioneers of this approach, which accepts the neoclassical microfoundations, the rational expectation hypothesis, but supposes the presence of market failures and stickiness of prices and wages that require a fiscal and monetary policy intervention (see Mankiw and Romer 1991). The extreme development of this school of thought is the construction of Dynamic Stochastic General Equilibrium (DSGE) models with Keynesian features (see Galí 2008, pp. 4–6). The post Keynesians decisively disapprove the interpretations of Keynes's thought of the neoclassical synthesis and of the new Keynesians. They try to demonstrate the total incompatibility between the real Keynes and the neoclassical approach. Starting in particular from Keynes's *General Theory*, the post Keynesians attempt to develop a Keynesian framework that rejects methodological individualism and focuses upon the role of money and effective demand (Fontana and Realfonzo 2005, pp. 9–10).

Sraffian analysis has not generated a real Sraffian school (Aspromourgos 2004, p. 181), but rather contradictory interpretations (Blankenburg et al. 2012). According to some scholars, this was probably also a consequence of the lack of detailed explanations in PCC (Newman 1972). Interesting debates about PCC have been raised because Sraffa's model is not closed; its simultaneous equation system leaves one degree of freedom—that is, one distributional parameter has to be exogenously defined. As a consequence, Sraffa's model is open to different closures (see Blankenburg et al. 2012). Sraffa's reference to a closure of the model inside financial markets, through the definition of "money rates of interest" (Sraffa 1960, p. 33), is a foundation "of a theory of income distribution" (Pasinetti 1988, p. 135). The so-called monetary theory of distribution developed in the 1980s closes Sraffa's price system considering a nominal interest rate set exogenously by the central bank and a structure of monetary assets with their own interest rates. While some researchers are convinced that Sraffa's price system is the result of a gravitational process through free competition (Caminati 1990), others focus instead upon the interdependence between societal configurations and the "surplus product" (Garegnani 1979b). Another debate focuses upon the relationship between Sraffa and Marx (Steedman 1977). The claim that Sraffa has solved the transformation problem invalidating at the same time Marx's analysis should consider that while Marx's analysis is an historical-sociological-philosophical interpretation of capitalism's dynamics, Sraffa's PCC is a logical-mathematical analysis of a production system. Few results have come from attempts to insert the typical features of Marxian (and Keynesian) economics inside Sraffian schemes, such as money, institutions, technology or dynamics (e.g. see Hodgson (1981), who introduced money as a good). Pasinetti noted that researchers have been unable to elaborate satisfactory dynamic production models (Pasinetti 1975). The only result has been the elaboration of quasi-dynamic models, with population as the only dynamic variable (i.e., no disequilibrium or sociological-behavioural patterns can be considered).

Despite this, Aspromourgos (2004) claims that there have been important points of contact between Sraffians and Keynesians for the development of a synthesis. A line of research, in particular, commonly known as the Classical-Keynesian approach, aims to combine the Sraffian long-period approach to prices and distribution with Keynes's principle of effective demand extended to the long period. Garegnani (1978, 1979a) is certainly one of the pioneers of this line of research. Relevant are also the contributions of Pasinetti (1979), Eatwell (1979) and Kurz (1985). Another line of research focuses on the classical process of gravitation of market prices around normal prices. In the models of this line of research, relative prices interact with sectoral output proportions through a cross-dual dynamics (see for example Boggio (1985), Caminati (1990), Garegnani (1990) and the recent contributions of Fratini and Naccarato (2016) and Bellino and Serrano (2017)).

Another connection between Keynes and Sraffa has been constructed starting from the monetary theory of production. Indeed, especially after 1984, a strong debate started among heterodox economists around the monetary theory of production (see Graziani 2003). Whereas most of these heterodox economists share a critical view of the Walrasian approach to money, they have not been able to share a common view for the construction of an alternative theory of money; for these reasons there are different schools of thought (e.g., the circuitist school). Edward Nell found some interesting connections between the theory of the monetary circuit and the classical theory of production as revived by Sraffa (see Nell 1992, 1998, 2004). These connections seem important for the construction of a monetary theory of production based on Keynes's and Sraffa's contributions (see for example Febrero and Alfares 2006). Indeed, these contributions present models that try to explain the role of money and credit for the circulation of the commodities in a dynamical framework where real and financial magnitudes coexist. It is important to remember that in these models, in order to harmonize the supposed Sraffian long-period approach with Keynes's short-period view, a benchmark equilibrium methodology (Febrero and Alfares 2006, p. 2) is assumed, in which benchmark prices are "guideline for current behaviour" (Nell 1998, p. 467). In these models it is not assumed that the economic system fluctuates around a centre of gravity; nevertheless, short-period analysis is framed into a long-period approach.

# 3 Looking for a New Paradigm: Some Comments

It is clear that it was both Sraffa's and Keynes's wish that their contributions could give birth to a new paradigm, capable of undermining the mainstream. Sraffa was hoping that his fundamental contribution could represent the foundation for an alternative to the marginal theory: "if the foundation holds, the critique may be attempt later, either by the writer or by someone younger or better equipped for the task" (Sraffa 1960, p. vi). It is hard to believe that, despite his ambiguities and *silences*, also Keynes was not hoping that his precious and fundamental contributions could once break free from the neoclassical theory. This appears clear in this Keynes's oft-quoted letter to Harrod: "I am frightfully afraid of the tendency, of which I see some signs in you to appear, to accept my constructive part and to find some accommodation between this and deeply cherished views which would in fact only be possible if my constructive part has been partially misunderstood" (letter dated 27 August 1935 from Keynes to Harrod cited in Pasinetti 2007, pp. 31–32). Probably, it will be extremely difficult to develop a new non-neoclassical paradigm based on a Keynesian-Sraffian synthesis without going beyond some traditional and fundamentalist interpretations of their thinking. Indeed, it is hard to believe that Sraffa's *critique* could be carried out without the study of disequilibrium dynamics, complexity and human behaviour; things that pure objectiveness does not allow to investigate. Sraffa's unpublished manuscripts, which have been available since the opening in 1993 of the Sraffa Archive kept in the Wren Library at Trinity College (Cambridge), seem precious for "revisiting and placing PCMC in the wider context of ongoing debates on economic philosophy, economic theory and economic policy" (Blankenburg et al. 2012, p. 1267), especially because "Sraffa is reported to have called his notes and papers an iceberg, the tip of which is his published work" (Kurz 2012, p. 1539). At the same time, it is difficult to think of being able to carry on Keynes's thought without facing the problem of the lack of a long-term theory of the aggregate level of production.

The creation of a new economic paradigm requires not only to engage for the development of a new theoretical framework (i.e., a theoretical apparatus able to give an explanation and a modelling of the economic phenomena, both considering the micro- and macro-dimensions), but also a series of philosophical, social and political factors that make it capable of replacing the mainstream (see Casagrande 2018). Despite this, a deeper development of the Sraffian-Keynesian synthesis would allow to finally create a complete and coherent theoretical framework, a necessary but not sufficient condition for the creation of a new paradigm capable of replacing the mainstream.

The literature on the Sraffian-Keynesian synthesis shows various attempts to contribute in this sense. It is worth remembering some factors that should be considered with more care for a further development towards a new non-neoclassical paradigm: the role of demand, institutions and society, the role of the complexity of real economies and the importance of accounting, computability and constructiveness.

## 3.1 The Role of Demand, Institutions and Society

The importance of demand, institutions and society for Keynes is well known. The role of these factors in Sraffian economics is more controversial. It is well known that the role of demand inside Sraffian Schemes is debated. Salvadori (2000) confirms that Sraffa considered demand rarely in his writings. Despite this, "Sraffa never stated that prices can be conceived independently from demand" (Bellino 2008, p. 24) so it is not possible to declare that demand plays no role in Sraffa's opinion. Famous and instructive is Sraffa's letter to Arun Bose:

> […] Your opening sentence is for me an obstacle which I am unable to get over. You write: "It is a basic proposition of the Sraffa theory that prices are determined exclusively by the physical requirements of production and the social wage-profit division with consumers demand playing a purely passive role." Never have I said this: certainly not in the two places to which you refer in your note 2. Nothing, in my view, could be more suicidal than to make such a statement. You are asking me to put my head on the block so that the first fool who comes along can cut it of neatly. Whatever you do,

> please do not represent me as saying such a thing. (C32/3, the letter is reproduced in Bellino 2008, p. 39)

Sraffa recognized the importance of institutions and society for the determination of the surplus. Thanks to his unpublished manuscripts, which have become the object of a growing literature, it has been emphasized how Sraffa realized, at some point of his intellectual journey (Kurz and Salvadori 2005, p. 431), that the surplus could not be explained only in terms of real costs, but depends also on the behaviour of capitalists and institutions. As Sraffa observes:

> When we have defined our "economic field", there are still outside causes which operate in it; and its effects go beyond the boundary [...]. The surplus may be the effect of the outside causes; and the effects of the distribution of the surplus may lie outside. (D3/12/7: 161(3–5) cited in Davis 2012, p. 1348)

Sraffa never explored these 'outside causes', nor other potential subjective factors. Nevertheless, Sraffa admitted the importance of "systemic inducement", a concept not far from Smithian "forces" or the Marxian "coercive law of competition" (Kurz 2012, p. 1559). His relationship with Gramsci permitted him to develop a 'social point of view' that marginalism denied. As claimed by Sraffa:

> [The] chief objection to utility is that it makes of value an *individual* conception: it implies that problems of Rob[inson] Crusoe and those of an economic man living in the City are exactly the same. Now, value is a *social* phenomenon: it would not exist outside society: *all* our utilities are derived from social conventions and therefore dependent upon social conditions and standard. (D1/16: 1, Sraffa's emphasis. Cited in Signorino 2001, p. 758)

In addition to this, Sraffa's concern with the consequences of the relationship between policy issues and social conflict for distribution is confirmed by his writings on banking systems and monetary policy (Blankenburg et al. 2012, p. 1276).

## 3.2 The Complexity of the Real Economies

Both Keynes and Sraffa were aware of the complexity of real economies. Keynes's claim that the causal relationship runs from investment to saving starts from the recognition that it is micro-level behaviour which generates the non-isomorphic macro-level aggregate (i.e., the *fallacy of composition*). Each agent's behaviour is subject to uncertainty and it is influenced by other people (i.e., the *beauty contest*). The failure of coordination is intrinsic in the mechanism of economic system, because different agents take different decisions according to their social role in a highly unstable, complex and interconnected environment. Also Sraffa was aware of this complexity that led him to recognize that "the surplus may be the effect of the outside causes" (D3/12/7: 161(3–5)).

It is well known that one of the most fundamental purposes of Keynes's analysis was the study of "the trading that actually occurs at non-market-clearing prices and [...] the possibility it generates of violating Walras's Law" (Bharadwaj 1983, pp. 5–7). But this type of investigation implies somehow overcoming Walras's auctioneer through the development of a non-neoclassical alternative. Despite the habit to identify general equilibrium models with the neoclassical ones, there are also *classical* versions which focus on the "accumulation and allocation of the surplus output" instead of the "allocation of given resources among alternative uses" (Walsh and Gram 1980, p. 3). Keynes never considered these alternative models while it is interesting to note that "some economists who are favourable to Sraffa's theses have interpreted *PCC* as the basis for a theory of general equilibrium to rival those which were constructed by Walras and Pareto and strengthened, in the modern period, by Debreu" (Arena 2014, p. 54). Sraffa as "the architect of a dissident theory of general equilibrium" is a thesis that met "certain sympathies among the so-called neo-Ricardians although it never became predominant among them" (Arena 2014, p. 56). Indeed, it is doubtful that the real interest of Sraffa laid in the development of an alternative to neoclassical general equilibrium theory. It is well known that Sraffa, in order to overcome the intrinsic problems of the Marshallian theory of competition, claimed that the examination of the conditions of simultaneous equilibrium becomes necessary: "a well-known conception, whose complexity, however, prevents it from bearing fruit, at least in the present state of our knowledge, which does not permit of even much simpler schemata being applied to the study of real conditions" (Sraffa 1926, p. 541). This means that Sraffa considered the general equilibrium alternative useful but intractable. This is even more clear in a comment on the problem of indeterminacy inside Walrasian equations:

> [T]he economists have gone too far in making their abstractions, they have simplified too much: in trying to make it simple, they have gone so far as to ignore some condition which is essential to the determination of the problem. Therefore the proof of indeterminateness only can prove the inadequacy of the assumptions made. (Sraffa, *SA*, D 2/4, p. 28, notation of Sraffa's unpublished manuscripts, quoted in Arena 2014, p. 64)

The "excess of abstraction" and the "lack of practical applicability" are at the basis of Sraffa's refusal of a general equilibrium model as an instrument for the explanation of the "observable phenomena in real capitalist market economies" (Arena 2014, p. 64). Sraffa refused to investigate complexity with non-objective instruments: his abandonment of the idea to develop an alternative to the general equilibrium theory has been determined basically by this "lack of instruments". Keynes, despite his interest in out-of-equilibrium market behaviour, never engaged in the development of a model able to generate violations of Walras's law.

## 3.3 The Role of Accounting, Computability and Constructiveness

The limits of the Walrasian general equilibrium theory in coping with complexity have been partly recognized by the same neoclassical economists. Indeed, the emergence of the new mainstream research field of the Computable General Equilibrium (CGE) theory (i.e., models in the Herbert Scarf tradition) and the agent-based computational models testify the need to develop models able to simulate the dynamics of the exchange process. The purpose of these fashionable mainstream models is to cope with the self-organizing properties of real economies and with the bounded rationality of their heterogeneous agents. But this is only a part of the story. Indeed, these models do not represent attempts to displace the preeminence of neoclassical theory, but a questionable attempt to make the model more realistic, a "complement not a substitute" of modelling approaches (Tesfatsion and Judd 2006, p. 864). The result has been basically a further concealment of the limitations and the ambiguities of the Arrow-Debreu model.

Anyway, similar simulation techniques have been applied to Keynesian economics with the different purpose to investigate what happens in real economies where agents trade at non-market-clearing prices and where money plays an essential role. The fundamental idea is that "Keynesian macrotheory was allegedly dismissed because of its lack of microfoundation, but it could not be microfounded with the tools available at the time of its dismissal. Using agent-based computational techniques, Keynesian macrotheory may be microfounded without loosing its sting" (Bruun 1999, p. 2). In these agent-based Keynesian models the macrofoundation of their microfoundations in terms of behavioural and accounting consistency is in general considered with more care with respect to mainstream economics (see for example Godley and Lavoie 2012). This is coherent with Keynes's *General Theory* which "set the stage for national income accounting [while] his recognition of the equality of saving and investment provided the basis for an accounting approach" (Ruggles and Ruggles 1999, p. 135).

Accounting was fundamental also for Sraffa whose equation systems are based on the equality between costs and revenues. But Sraffa accounting consistency implied also computability and constructiveness. Most researchers probably underestimate the relation between accountability, constructiveness and computability for the development of non-neoclassical models. Indeed, few heterodox theorists emphasize that algorithms utilized in Computable General Equilibrium (CGE) theory, or Applied Computable General Equilibrium (ACGE) analysis and Dynamic Stochastic General Equilibrium (DSGE) modelling "are effectively meaningless from computable and constructive points of view" (Velupillai 2015, p. 187). Since "the fixed-point theorem is the most common method in general equilibrium theory" (Marion 2005, p. 390), most neoclassical models (such as CGE models) have no value from a mathematical point of view, that is, they are non-constructive. The reason is that Brouwer's fixed-point theorem is not valid (it is non-constructive and uncomputable) because it invokes in its proof the Bolzano-Weierstrass theorem that can be proven to be undecidable (see Velupillai 2006, 2015). Sraffa's schemes are mathematically constructive (see on the constructiveness of Sraffa's schemes Velupillai 1989) and for this reason the accounting approach must be accompanied by a strong attention to computability and constructiveness. The aim towards accountability, constructiveness and computability requires that models are developed in terms of algorithms able to be transformed into equations. In other words, a simulation model should be represented by mathematical equations that can be computed theoretically also *by hand*.

## 4 A Keynesian-Sraffian Monetary Theory of Production

The topics discussed previously (i.e., the role of demand, institutions and society, the awareness of the complexity of real economies and the importance of accounting, computability and constructiveness) are factors that can contribute to the development of an alternative to the general equilibrium theory; an alternative complete and coherent theoretical framework in which Keynesian theory, and in particular his monetary theory of production, can be integrated by a theory of production compatible with Sraffian economics. This could represent a starting point for the development of computable models able to analyse the out-of-equilibrium micro- and macro-dynamics of a monetary entrepreneur economy.

### 4.1 From a Real to a Money-Wage Economy

The idea of a monetary theory of production is traced back to Keynes (1973), even though some researchers claim that the monetary theory of production has a longer tradition (see for example Fontana and Realfonzo 2005). The fundamental idea is that a monetary economy is "an economy in which money plays a part of its own and affects motives and decisions" (Keynes 1973, p. 408). It is instructive to consider carefully not only Keynes's original monetary theory of production (as in Keynes 1973, pp. 408–411) but also his discussion about how to distinguish between a *real-wage*, a *neutral* and a *money-wage* economy:

> The first type of society we will call a *real-wage* or *co-operative economy*. The second type, in which the factors are hired by entrepreneurs for money but there is a mechanism of some kind to ensure that the exchange value of the money incomes of the factors is always equal in the aggregate to the proportion of current output which would have been the factors' share in a co-operative economy, we will call a *neutral entrepreneur economy*, or a *neutral economy* for short. The third type, of which the second is a limiting case, in which the entrepreneurs hire the factors for money but without such a mechanism above, we will call a *money wage* or *entrepreneur economy*. (Keynes 1979, pp. 77–78)

According to Keynes, a *real-wage cooperative economy* is a barter economy in which factors of production are "rewarded by allocating in agreed proportions the actual outcome of their cooperative effort" (Fontana and Realfonzo 2005, p. 2). In the *neutral entrepreneur economy* money is a simple means of exchange that does not change the "barter nature" of an economy, in which "sale proceeds exceed variable cost by a determinate amount" (Keynes 1979, p. 80). The fundamental feature of a *money wage* or *entrepreneur economy* can be traced back, ultimately, to the fluctuations of effective demand:

> In a co-operative or in a neutral economy, in which sale proceeds exceed variable costs by a determinate amount, effective demand cannot fluctuate [...]. But in an entrepreneur economy the fluctuations of effective demand may be the dominating factor in determining the volume of employment. (Keynes 1979, p. 80)

According to Keynes "fluctuations in employment will primarily depend on fluctuations in aggregate expenditure relatively to aggregate costs. This is the essential feature of an entrepreneur economy in which it differs from a co-operative economy" (Keynes 1979, p. 91). It is clear that

Keynes seeks the fundamental factor that characterizes a money-wage entrepreneur economy and his research leads him to share Marx's intuition:

> The distinction between a co-operative economy and an entrepreneur economy bears some relation to a pregnant observation made by Karl Marx, [...] the nature of production in the actual world is not, as economists seem often to suppose, a case of C-M-C', i.e., of exchanging commodity (or effort) for money in order to obtain another commodity (or effort). That may be the standpoint of the private consumer. But it is not the attitude of *business*, which is a case of M-C-M', i.e. of parting with money for commodity (or effort) in order to obtain more money (Keynes 1979, p. 81).

It is interesting to note that Keynes asks himself explicitly "could then such an entrepreneur economy exist without money?" (Keynes 1979, p. 85). Keynes answers as follows:

> Money is *par excellence* the means of remuneration in an entrepreneur economy which lends itself to fluctuations in effective demand. But if employers were to remunerate their workers in terms of plots of land or obsolete postage stamps, the same difficulties could arise. Perhaps anything in terms of which the factors of production contract to be remunerated, which is not and cannot be a part of current output and it is capable of being used otherwise that to purchase current output, is, in a sense, money. If so, but not otherwise, the use of money is a necessary condition for fluctuations in effective demand. (Keynes 1979, p. 86)

Keynes seems to point out that what it is really important is the possibility to have fluctuations of effective demand.

> [F]luctuations in employment will primarily depend on fluctuations in aggregate expenditure relatively to aggregate costs. This is the essential feature of an entrepreneur economy in which it differs from a co-operative economy. (Keynes 1979, p. 91)

Probably, the simplest device for exchanges able to make possible these fluctuations is the IOU (*I owe you*). The IOU is a contract, a deferred payment of an exchange which is taking place now. The connection between IOUs and money is strong, indeed: "money today is a type of IOU, but one that is special because everyone in the economy trusts that it will be accepted by other people in exchange for goods and services" (McLeay et al. 2014, p. 4). We should not forget that in principle money is not necessary for exchanges "[e]veryone in the economy could instead create their own financial assets and liabilities by giving out IOUs every time they wanted to purchase something, and then mark down in a ledger whether they were in debt or credit in IOUs overall" (McLeay et al. 2014, p. 7). This is exactly what happened in medieval Europe, where "merchant houses would periodically settle their claims on one another at fairs, largely by cancelling out debts. But such systems rely on everyone being confident that everyone else is completely trustworthy" (McLeay et al. 2014, p. 7). So, it is only the lack of trust that requires necessarily the presence of money. But money, as a social institution, requires the presence of a monetary institution.

The advantage of IOUs is that they do not imply necessarily the presence of a monetary institution or a banking system, and this allows one to construct a very minimal model of monetary entrepreneur economy. Remember that, while monetary institutions, financial systems and banking systems are important inside post-Keynesian economics, they have not been mentioned by Keynes in the definition of a monetary entrepreneur economy. Keynes overlooks the banking system and bank money inside the *General Theory*, where he explicitly assumes that the money supply is fully controlled by the central bank. It is also a matter of fact that Keynes's *liquidity preference theory* "overlooks the presence of banks and bank money" (Bertocco 2011, p. 8), an aspect that Keynes underlines also in his debate with the supporters of the *loanable funds theory*. This does not mean that Keynes's liquidity preference theory was unambiguous: it is well known that Kaldor was critical of some aspects of Keynes's theory of money and interest rate (see also Sardoni 2007) while Sraffa underlined his perplexities about Keynes's liquidity preference theory, that he called *Keynes's system* (Kurz 2013, pp. 11–12). This should reinforce the idea that, in order to overcome Keynes's ambiguities about monetary phenomena, it is advisable to start with a very simple framework. Despite this, it is out of discussion that complex institutions will become fundamental when a complex, modern and developed monetary entrepreneur economy is considered.

## 4.2 Modelling a Monetary Entrepreneur Economy: From Keynes to Sraffa

At this point, it is possible to clarify what it is really essential in order to identify a money-wage entrepreneur economy. This exercise has been performed by Keynes himself in a section titled *the characteristics of an entrepreneur economy* (Keynes 1979, p. 87) oriented to "an analysis which is endeavouring to keep as close as it can to the actual facts of business calculation" (Keynes 1979, p. 88). If we simplify Keynes's description in order to focus on the strictly necessary conditions for a money-wage entrepreneur economy and we add some important elements of Sraffian economics for a characterization of the production phase, the following elements should be stressed: production is carried out by producers in order to earn profits; workers sell their labour in order to earn the wage; producers produce and hire workers according to expected demand (without a profit expectation based on expected demand, producers do not hire new workers so that unemployment can emerge); production is heterogeneous, it is conceived as a circular process with methods of the fixed proportion type (joint production or fixed capital can be excluded in a simple model); workers and producers buy commodities according to their preferences and disposable income; there can be cases of excess demand or excess supply; any exchange (commodities or labour) is associated to the underwriting of an IOU denominated in a socially accepted unit of account; debt and credit relations can emerge in order to carry on production and consumption.

The introduction of Sraffian schemes into Keynes's monetary theory of production or, put it differently, the introduction of debt and credit relations into Sraffian schemes represents the starting point for modelling a money-wage entrepreneur economy. Indeed, constructing a Keynesian-Sraffian synthesis through the monetary theory of production implies an important development both for the Sraffian and the Keynesian side. The Sraffian side can start to consider disequilibrium and dynamics, the Keynesian side can start to incorporate concretely an appropriate theory of production.

With reference to the introduction of debt and credit relations into Sraffian schemes, Stefano Zambelli is certainly a pioneer of this fascinating topic. After having extended the Sraffian schemes to the general case where the rates of profits are not uniform (Zambelli 2018), he is working at extending Sraffian schemes to the cases in which commodities can be exchanged thanks to the issuing of new loans, which implies the generation of credit and debt relations and transfers of fiat money (i.e., money is not treated as a commodity produced inside the system). This extension of Sraffian schemes is carried out without the assumption of uniform rates of profits and self-replacing, which imply the abandonment of the hypothesis of Sraffian production prices as long-run centres of gravitation and the exploration of disequilibrium within the Sraffian schemes without any benchmark equilibrium methodology.

All this represents a true novelty and a source of inspiration for economic modelling. Indeed, on the basis of this theoretical framework, it is possible to develop digital simulation models, grounded on bookkeeping principles and computable methods, in which virtual economic agents interact and organize their production and consumption decisions. In these models of monetary-entrepreneur economies, production is heterogeneous and conceived as a circular process and deferred means of payments (i.e., IOUs) are generated and used for the exchanges, so that credit and debt are endogenous and the complexity of out-of-equilibrium market behaviour can be investigated. A model of this type has been proposed, for example, by Casagrande (2017) on the basis of Zambelli's research. However, further research is needed in order to carry out simulations. For the moment, these theoretical premises give us hope that soon other new remarkable results will be achieved.

# 5 Conclusions

The purpose of the present contribution was the demonstration of the importance of Keynes and Sraffa for the development of a new paradigm. Even though different heterodox economists have recognized the importance both of Keynes and Sraffa, unfortunately, some concrete methodological and theoretical issues prevented the construction of an alternative paradigm able to replace the mainstream.

Some controversial issues related to the compatibility between Keynes and Sraffa and their relationship with neoclassical theory have been analysed. In particular, the apparent incompatibility between the strictness of Sraffian methodology and the behavioural and psychological features of Keynesian economics and the ambiguous relationship between Keynes and orthodox theory.

The analysis of Keynes's and Sraffa's writings allowed us to emphasize how the problem is not the compatibility between Keynesian and Sraffian economics but how to integrate them. From our analysis, some points of connection between Keynes and Sraffa are particularly important and should be emphasized: the role of demand, institutions and society, the recognition of the complexity of real economies and the importance of accounting, computability and constructiveness.

These factors are premises for the development of a complete and coherent theoretical Keynesian-Sraffian framework that can represent an alternative to the general equilibrium theory. The development of a similar framework is a necessary but not sufficient condition for the creation of an alternative paradigm. In this framework, Keynesian theory, and in particular his monetary theory of production, should be integrated by a theory of production compatible with Sraffian economics. The introduction of Sraffian schemes into Keynes's monetary theory of production or, in other words, the introduction of debt and credit relations into Sraffian schemes represents the starting point for modelling a money-wage entrepreneur economy. This implies an important development for the Sraffian side that can start to consider disequilibrium and dynamics, while the Keynesian side can start to incorporate concretely an appropriate theory of production.

Stefano Zambelli is certainly a pioneer of the introduction of debt and credit relations into Sraffian schemes, the abandonment of the hypothesis of Sraffian production prices as long-run centres of gravitation and the exploration of disequilibrium within the Sraffian schemes without any benchmark equilibrium methodology.

His research is a source of inspiration for the development of digital simulation models, grounded on bookkeeping principles and computable methods, in which the complexity of out-of-equilibrium market behaviour can be investigated. The further development of his theoretical findings gives us hope that soon other new remarkable results able to challenge the mainstream will be achieved.

## References


Arena, R. (2014). Sraffa without Walras? In R. Baranzini & F. Allisson (Eds.), *Economics and Other Branches—In the Shade of the Oak Tree: Essays in Honour of Pascal Bridel* (pp. 53–67). London: Pickering and Chatto Publishers.

Aspromourgos, T. (2004). Sraffian Research Programmes and Unorthodox Economics. *Review of Political Economy, 16*(2), 179–206.

Bellino, E. (2008). Book Reviews on Production of Commodities by Means of Commodities. In G. Chiodi & L. Ditta (Eds.), *Sraffa or An Alternative Economics* (pp. 23–41). London: Palgrave Macmillan.

Bellino, E., & Serrano, F. (2017). Gravitation of Market Prices towards Normal Prices: Some New Results. *Centro Sraffa Working Paper 25.*

Bertocco, G. (2011). On the Monetary Nature of the Interest Rate in Keynes's Thought. *Working Paper 2.* Department of Economics, University of Insubria.

Bharadwaj, K. (1983). On Effective Demand: Certain Recent Critiques. In J. Kregel (Ed.), *Distribution, Effective Demand and International Economic Relations* (Chap. 1, pp. 3–27). London: Palgrave Macmillan.

Bidard, C. (1990). From Arrow-Debreu to Sraffa. *Political Economy: Studies in the Surplus Approach, 6*(1–2), 125–138.

Blankenburg, S., Arena, R., & Wilkinson, F. (2012). Piero Sraffa and the True Object of Economics: The Role of the Unpublished Manuscripts. *Cambridge Journal of Economics, 36*(6), 1267–1290.

Blaug, M. (1980). *The Methodology of Economics: Or, How Economists Explain.* Cambridge: Cambridge University Press.

Bliss, C. J. (1975). *Capital Theory and the Distribution of Income*. Oxford: North-Holland.

Boggio, L. (1985). On the Stability of Production Prices. *Metroeconomica, 37*(3), 241–267.

Bruun, C. (1999). *Agent-Based Keynesian Economics: Simulating a Monetary Production System Bottom-Up*. University of Aaborg: Department of Economics, Politics and Public Administration.

Caminati, M. (1990). Gravitation: An Introduction. *Political Economy: Studies in the Surplus Approach, 6*(1–2), 11–44.

Casagrande, S. (2017). A Digital Simulation Model of Out-of-Equilibrium Market Behaviour. *ASSRU Discussion Paper, No. 9-2017/I*. Algorithmic Social Sciences Research Unit.

Casagrande, S. (2018). The Nature and Dynamics of Socio-Economic Paradigms. In R. Roni (Ed.), *Mantua Humanistic Studies* (Vol. II, pp. 145–189). Mantova, Italy: Universitas Studiorum.

Clower, R. W. (1997). Effective Demand Revisited. In G. Harcourt & P. Riach (Eds.), *A 'Second Edition' of the General Theory: Volume 1* (Chap. 3, pp. 28–51). New York: Routledge.

Davis, J. B. (2012). The Change in Sraffa's Philosophical Thinking. *Cambridge Journal of Economics, 36*(6), 1341–1356.

Eatwell, J. (1979). Theories of Value, Output and Employment. In J. Eatwell & M. Milgate (Eds.), *Keynes's Economics and the Theory of Value and Distribution* (pp. 93–128). London: Gerald Duckworth & Co Ltd.

Febrero, E., & Alfares, A. (2006). *Monetary Theory of Production: A Classical-Circuitist Alternative Interpretation*. Paper presented at X Jornadas de Economía Crítica in Barcelona, 23–25 May 2006.

Fontana, G., & Realfonzo, R. (2005). *The Monetary Theory of Production: Tradition and Perspectives*. New York: Palgrave Macmillan.

Fratini, S. M., & Naccarato, A. (2016). The Gravitation of Market Prices as a Stochastic Process. *Metroeconomica, 67*(4), 698–716.

Galí, J. (2008). *Monetary Policy, Inflation, and the Business Cycle: An Introduction to the New Keynesian Framework and Its Applications*. Princeton, NJ: Princeton University Press.

Garegnani, P. (1976). On a Change in the Notion of Equilibrium in Recent Work on Value and Distribution. In M. Brown, K. Sato, & P. Zarembka (Eds.), *Essays in Modern Capital Theory* (pp. 25–45). Amsterdam: North-Holland.

Garegnani, P. (1978). Notes on Consumption, Investment and Effective Demand: I. *Cambridge Journal of Economics, 2*(4), 335–353.
Garegnani, P. (1979a). Notes on Consumption, Investment and Effective Demand: II: Monetary Analysis. *Cambridge Journal of Economics, 3*(1), 63–82.
Garegnani, P. (1979b). *Valore e Domanda Effettiva*. Turin: Einaudi.
Garegnani, P. (1983). Two Routes to Effective Demand: Comment on Kregel. In J. Kregel (Ed.), *Distribution, Effective Demand and International Economic Relations* (pp. 69–80). London: Macmillan.
Garegnani, P. (1990). On Some Supposed Obstacles to the Tendency of Market Prices towards Natural Prices. *Political Economy-Studies in the Surplus Approach, 6*(1–2), 329–359.
Garegnani, P. (2003). Savings, Investment and Capital in a System of General Intertemporal Equilibrium. In F. Hahn & F. Petri (Eds.), *General Equilibrium: Problems and Prospects*. London: Routledge.
Garegnani, P. (2012). On the Present State of the Capital Controversy. *Cambridge Journal of Economics, 36*(6), 1417–1432.
Godley, W., & Lavoie, M. (2012). *Monetary Economics: An Integrated Approach to Credit, Money, Income, Production and Wealth* (2nd ed.). New York: Palgrave Macmillan.
Graziani, A. (2003). *The Monetary Theory of Production*. Cambridge: Cambridge University Press.
Hahn, F. (1975). Revival of Political Economy: The Wrong Issues and the Wrong Arguments. *Economic Record, 51*(3), 360–364.
Hahn, F. (1982). The Neo-ricardians. *Cambridge Journal of Economics, 6*(4), 353–374.
Hodgson, G. (1981). Money and the Sraffa System. *Australian Economic Papers, 20*(36), 83–95.
Keynes, J. M. ([1933] 1973). A Monetary Theory of Production. In D. Moggridge (Ed.), *Collected Writings of John Maynard Keynes, Vol. XIII—The General Theory and After, Part I—Presentation* (pp. 408–411). London: Macmillan.
Keynes, J. M. (1979). *The Collected Writings of John Maynard Keynes: Towards the General Theory* (D. Moggridge, Ed., Vol. 24). London: Macmillan.
King, J. E. (1994). Aggregate Supply and Demand Analysis since Keynes: A Partial History. *Journal of Post Keynesian Economics, 17*(1), 3–31.
Kurz, H. D. (1985). Effective Demand in a Classical Model of Value and Distribution: The Multiplier in a Sraffian Framework. *The Manchester School, 53*(2), 121–137.

Kurz, H. D. (1995). The Keynesian Project: Tom Asimakopulos and 'The Other Point of View'. In G. Harcourt, A. Roncaglia, & R. Rowley (Eds.), *Income and Employment in Theory and Practice. Essays in Memory of Athanasios Asimakopulos* (pp. 83–110). London: Macmillan.
Kurz, H. D. (2012). Don't Treat Too Ill My Piero! Interpreting Sraffa's Papers. *Cambridge Journal of Economics, 36*(6), 1535–1569.
Kurz, H. D. (2013). Sraffa, Keynes, and Post-Keynesianism. In G. Harcourt & P. Kriesler (Eds.), *The Oxford Handbook of Post-Keynesian Economics, Volume 1: Theory and Origins*. New York: Oxford University Press.
Kurz, H. D., & Salvadori, N. (2005). Representing the Production and Circulation of Commodities in Material Terms: On Sraffa's Objectivism. *Review of Political Economy, 17*(3), 413–441.
Lunghini, G. (1975). Teoria Economica ed Economia Politica: Note su Sraffa. In G. Lunghini (Ed.), *Produzione, Capitale e Distribuzione* (pp. xi–xxviii). Milan: ISEDI.
Malinvaud, E. (1953). Capital Accumulation and Efficient Allocation of Resources. *Econometrica, 21*(2), 233–268.
Mandler, M. (2002). Classical and Neoclassical Indeterminacy in One-Shot versus Ongoing Equilibria. *Metroeconomica, 53*(3), 203–222.
Mankiw, N. G., & Romer, D. (1991). *New Keynesian Economics. Vol. 1: Imperfect Competition and Sticky Prices. Vol. 2: Coordination Failures and Real Rigidities*. Cambridge, MA: MIT Press.
Marion, M. (2005). Sraffa and Wittgenstein: Physicalism and Constructivism. *Review of Political Economy, 17*(3), 381–406.
McLeay, M., Radia, A., & Thomas, R. (2014). Money Creation in the Modern Economy: An Introduction. *Bank of England Quarterly Bulletin Q1*, 4–13.
Nell, E. J. (1992). *Transformational Growth and Effective Demand. Economics after the Capital Critique*. London: Macmillan.
Nell, E. J. (1998). *The General Theory of Transformational Growth: Keynes After Sraffa*. Cambridge: Cambridge University Press.
Nell, E. J. (2004). Monetising the Classical Equations: A Theory of Circulation. *Cambridge Journal of Economics, 28*(2), 173–203.
Newman, P. (1972). Produzione di merci a mezzo merci. In G. Lunghini (Ed.), *Produzione, Capitale e Distribuzione* (pp. 3–20). Milan: ISEDI.
Pasinetti, L. (1975). *Lezioni di Teoria della Produzione*. Bologna: Il Mulino.
Pasinetti, L. (1979). *Growth and Income Distribution: Essays in Economic Theory*. Cambridge: Cambridge University Press.

Pasinetti, L. (1988). Sraffa on Income Distribution. *Cambridge Journal of Economics, 12*(1), 135–138.
Pasinetti, L. (1997). The Principle of Effective Demand. In G. Harcourt & P. Riach (Eds.), *A 'Second Edition' of the General Theory: Volume 1* (Chap. 6, pp. 93–104). New York: Routledge.
Pasinetti, L. (2007). *Keynes and the Cambridge Keynesians: A Revolution in Economics to be Accomplished.* Cambridge: Cambridge University Press.
Pasinetti, L. (2012a). A Few Counter-factual Hypotheses on the Current Economic Crisis. *Cambridge Journal of Economics, 36*(6), 1433–1453.
Pasinetti, L. (2012b). Piero Sraffa and the Future of Economics. *Cambridge Journal of Economics, 36*(6), 1303–1314.
Robinson, J. (1963). *Economic Philosophy.* Chicago: Aldine.
Roncaglia, A. (1995). On the Compatibility between Keynes's and Sraffa's Viewpoints on Output Levels. In G. Harcourt, A. Roncaglia, & R. Rowley (Eds.), *Income and Employment in Theory and Practice. Essays in Memory of Athanasios Asimakopulos* (pp. 111–125). London: Macmillan.
Ruggles, N. D., & Ruggles, R. (1999). *National Accounting and Economic Policy: The United States and UN Systems.* Northampton, MA: Elgar.
Salvadori, N. (2000). Sraffa on Demand: A Textual Analysis. In H. D. Kurz (Ed.), *Critical Essays on Piero Sraffa's Legacy in Economics* (pp. 181–197). Cambridge: Cambridge University Press.
Samuelson, P. A. (1966). A Summing Up. *Quarterly Journal of Economics, 88*(4), 568–583.
Sardoni, C. (2002). On the Microeconomic Foundations of Macroeconomics: A Keynesian Perspective. In P. Arestis, M. Desai, & S. Dow (Eds.), *Methodology, Microeconomics and Keynes. Essays in Honour of Victoria Chick* (Vol. 2, pp. 4–14). London: Routledge.
Sardoni, C. (2007). Kaldor's Monetary Thought. A Contribution to a Modern Theory of Money. In M. Forstater, G. Mongiovi, & S. Pressman (Eds.), *Post-Keynesian Macroeconomics: Essays in Honour of Ingrid Rima* (Chap. 8, pp. 129–146). New York: Routledge.
Schefold, B. (1989). *Mr Sraffa on Joint Production and Other Essays.* London: Unwin Hyman.
Sen, A. K. (2003). Sraffa, Wittgenstein, and Gramsci. *Journal of Economic Literature, 41*(4), 1240–1255.
Signorino, R. (2001). Piero Sraffa on Utility and the 'Subjective Method' in the 1920s: A Tentative Appraisal of Sraffa's Unpublished Manuscripts. *Cambridge Journal of Economics, 25*(6), 749–763.

Sraffa, P. (1926). The Laws of Returns under Competitive Conditions. *The Economic Journal, 36*(144), 535–550.
Sraffa, P. (1960). *Production of Commodities by Means of Commodities*. Cambridge: Cambridge University Press.
Steedman, I. (1977). *Marx after Sraffa*. London: NLB.
Tesfatsion, L., & Judd, K. L. (Eds.). (2006). *Handbook of Computational Economics: Agent-Based Computational Economics* (Vol. 2). Amsterdam: North-Holland.
Tosato, D. (2013). Determinacy of Equilibria in a Model of Intertemporal Equilibrium with Capital Goods. In R. Ciccone, C. Gehrke, & G. Mongiovi (Eds.), *Sraffa and Modern Economics* (Vol. 1). New York: Routledge.
Velupillai, K. V. (1989). The Existence of the Standard System: Sraffa's Constructive Proof. *Political Economy-Studies in the Surplus Approach, 5*(1), 3–12.
Velupillai, K. V. (2006). Algorithmic Foundations of Computable General Equilibrium Theory. *Applied Mathematics and Computation, 179*(1), 360–369.
Velupillai, K. V. (2008). Sraffa's Economics in Non-Classical Mathematical Modes. In G. Chiodi & L. Ditta (Eds.), *Sraffa or An Alternative Economics* (Chap. 14, pp. 275–294). New York: Palgrave Macmillan.
Velupillai, K. V. (2015). Negishi's Theorem and Method: Computable and Constructive Considerations. *Computational Economics, 45*(2), 183–193.
Walsh, V. C., & Gram, H. (1980). *Classical and Neoclassical Theories of General Equilibrium: Historical Origins and Mathematical Structure*. Oxford, NY: Oxford University Press.
Zambelli, S. (2018). Production of Commodities by Means of Commodities and Non-uniform Rates of Profits. *Metroeconomica, 69*(4), 791–819.

# 5

# On the Meaning Maximization Doctrine: An Alternative to the Utilitarian Doctrine

Shu-Heng Chen

## 1 Motivation and Introduction

This chapter proposes an alternative doctrine to utilitarianism upon which modern economics is built. The doctrine is christened as the *meaning maximization doctrine* as opposed to the utility maximization doctrine. Since the latter has a historically long position, it is imperative to make it clear how this research positions itself in front of this huge volume of literature.

First, while much has already been said on this subject (Barbera, Hammond, and Seidl 1999, 2004; Eggleston and Miller 2014), utility theory continues to stand in a core position of economic polemics, such as the polemic between expected utility versus non-expected utility, or hyperbolic discount rates versus alternative choice heuristics, not to mention the highly controversial and sometimes repugnant "*De gustibus non est disputandum*" (Stigler and Becker 1977). We make no attempt to

S.-H. Chen (✉)
AI-ECON Research Center, Department of Economics, National Chengchi University, Taipei, Taiwan



K. Velupillai (ed.), *Keynesian, Sraffian, Computable and Dynamic Economics*,
https://doi.org/10.1007/978-3-030-58131-2_5

address these long-standing problems; instead, we hope that our proposed alternative, if it is accepted, may make some of the long-standing problems less palpable.

Second, this chapter will not be positioned as another contribution to the historically long debates on what happiness is and its proper measurement. The reader who is interested in the general historical background of British Utilitarianism, the Science of Happiness, Hedonics, or Subjective Well-Being is referred to the splendid survey given by McMahon (2006). That stream of the literature may continue as it is now, but this chapter is not part of that extension.

Third, this chapter could be positioned as a contribution to the literature pioneered by Viktor Frankl (1905–1997) and many of his followers (Frankl 1964; Smith 2017). In this regard, we provide a formalism for meaning. While we do not get involved in the essential ingredients of meaning, our formalism may be used to justify whatever has been offered, for example, the four pillars as given by Smith (2017).[1] For this reason, our proposed formalism is also expected to shed some light on the relationship between happiness and meaning. Are the meaning-pursuing or maximizing people necessarily happy? This question is intriguing since we have in the past asked to compare a satisfied fool with a dissatisfied Socrates. While one can say that meaningfulness and happiness are, to some extent, correlated, they are not identical; neither is the necessary or sufficient condition for each of them. As we have learned from the maxim given by George Mallory (1886–1924), "because it is there" (Loewenstein 1999), it may be inappropriate to ask mountaineers or adventurers or scientists, who put their lives at risk, "Are you happy?," even though they will certainly be unhappy if their expeditions have to be called off. We shall come back to this point in Sect. 4.

Fourth, we also understand that the subject, the meaning of meaning, cannot be rigorously treated without invoking the history of philosophical underpinnings. It will, then, not surprise us that the meaning discussed in this chapter could be constrained by some historically intellectual roots. For example, one can always ask whether the notion of meaning proposed

[1] According to Smith (2017), the four pillars of meaning are belonging, purpose, storytelling, and transcendence.

in this chapter is mainly a product after the Enlightenment, and not universal over time and history. That is, we have to allow for such a possibility. Nevertheless, this chapter should not be read as a chapter on a philosophic treatment on meaning, but rather as an alternative to the orthodox formalization under the influence of Jeremy Bentham (1748–1832).

These four remarks delineate the realm of this chapter given its very dense surrounding. With this landscape in mind, we now look at the motivation behind this work. This chapter is motivated by a fundamental quest: Is *lifetime utility maximization*,[2] a cornerstone in modern economics, a proper characterization of the life of a rational individual?[3] The lifetime utility maximization assumption plays a critical role in the development of modern macroeconomics accompanied by the device of the representative agents (Deaton 1992; Hall 1978; Hartley 1997), and has even been tested at the microeconomic level using laboratory experiments (Duffy 2016; Hey and Dardanoni 1988). However, the life of a man, say, with a span of 75 years, and that of a woman, say, a span of 80 years, is long enough to evoke *fundamental* or *radical uncertainty*, characterized by a set of *unknown unknowns* or what Stuart Kauffman has christened as *unprestatable adjacent possibilities* (Kauffman 2016, 2019). Kauffman's main assertion is that the development of life is *not causal* but *enabling*. One stage of development *enables* the next stage, but does not directly cause it to happen. Each stage is *enabled* or made possible by what went before, but is not solely determined by it. Unlike physical change, which is completely determined, what will come out of the adjacent possibilities is unprestatable.

Basically, unknown unknowns are synonymous with the unprestatable adjacent possibilities, while the latter are closely attached with an organizing or development process. A good example is technology. The development of Web 2.0 and 3.0 *enables* one of their adjacent possibilities,

[2] Different terms also exist, such as "intertemporal optimization," "stochastic dynamic optimization," and "infinite-time horizon optimization under uncertainty."

[3] As we shall see below, we have a holistic view of man, that is, a view of the whole man, not just fragmentally on some slices of their decisions, such as saving and consumption, or leisure, education, and employment, those dimensions that have been well formulated using the lifetime utility maximization framework. Alternatively put, by proposing an alternative doctrine, we question the *external validity* of the lifetime utility maximization formulation.

namely *user-supplied contents*, which in turn enable the subsequent adjacent possibilities, including a participatory culture and open-source and peer production economy (Dolgin 2012). Similarly, the invention of the distributed storage and management systems, like Hadoop or Spark, enables its adjacent possibilities, namely the storage and the use of big data; likewise, the breakthrough in search engines, such as Google Search and Elastic Search, enables its adjacent possibilities, such as the sharing economy or the gig economy (Kessler 2018; Munger 2018; Prassl 2018; Sundararajan 2016). In fact, many modern information and communication technologies, ranging from smart phones, wearable devices, the Internet of Things, and cloud computing, to blockchains, are all enabled by others, and they further enable their own adjacent possibilities. They, nonetheless, were largely unknown in the last century; in fact, before their predecessors were sucked into their becoming, their status had remained as unknown unknowns.

Events associated with these unknown unknowns cannot even be derived and defined in the first place; in the parlance of measure theory, they (unknown unknowns) are simply nonmeasurable, or in plain English, inconceivable or unimaginable. Thanks to Taleb (2007), these events are now popularly referred to as *Black Swans*. In a parallel line, Elie Ayache (Ayache 2010), drawing from a lengthy review of the philosophy of probability, contingency and events, contributed by Henri Bergson (1859–1941), Martin Heidegger (1889–1976), Gilles Deleuze (1925–1995), Alain Badiou, and Quentin Meillassoux, proposed the term *history-changing events*. The occurrence of these events will change the way or the context in which we can imagine the future and hence gain access to a new set of imaginable events, which can be dramatically different from the old ones, and might further drive us to gain a different retrospect to identify a cause of the event. Essentially, this process is very hermeneutical (subjective) and, to some extent, Shacklian (Shackle 1979).[4]

[4] This is the place where we can see the role of science fiction: it enriches our capacity to imagine or expand the set of imaginable events. Regardless of whether these inspired events or epiphanies can be properly clothed with a probabilistic calculation, economists, except for a very few (Beckert 2016; Boulding 1956; Bronk 2009; Shackle 1979), ignore the significance of imagination in economic theorizing and its potential channels to other disciplines, ranging from philosophy and psychology to the humanities.

Evaluating the likelihood of these events is beyond what the standard probability theory can handle, and hence they cannot be incorporated into the Arrow-Debreu Economy, which was forged in the spirit of *Laplacian determinism*, named after Pierre-Simon de Laplace (1749–1827). Nevertheless, both the theoretical and experimental environments used to test lifetime utility maximization are not sufficiently complex to accommodate radical uncertainty, which either substantially reduces its "external validity" or simply obtains a right answer for a practically irrelevant question.

The effort made in relation to this new formalism can be considered to be a continuation of the recent *humanistic turn* in economics, which is also known as humanomics, narrative economics, and so on (Bookstaber 2017; McCloskey 2016; Morson and Schapiro 2017; Roy and Zeckhauser 2016; Shiller 2017, 2019; Smith and Wilson 2019; Watts 2003). Of course, humanomics has already been advocated by Deirdre McCloskey in the last century, but the recent progress in information, communication and digital technology (ICDT) has substantially reshaped the "data" that can be used to revitalize this project. Basically, the humanistic turn refers to the awareness of the relevancy of the humanities to economics. It has both ontological and methodological implications. Ontologically, it facilitates economic reorientation to the social reality fraught with radical uncertainty, as long advocated by Tony Lawson (Lawson 2003). Methodologically, it entices economists to work with a fundamentally different kind of data, including narratives, stories, newspapers, novels, epics, prose, biographies, poems, and, generally, big data (Chen and Venkatachalam 2017), by using tools from natural language processing, artificial intelligence, and machine learning (Moretti 2005, 2013). This way of describing humanomics distinguishes the old-fashioned, "low-tech" version in the 1990s, as depicted by Deirdre McCloskey and Vernon Smith, from the newly fashioned, "high-tech" version as now advocated by Robert Shiller; this "upgarade" is well expected since, from the 1990s to the 2020s, we have envisioned huge progress in ICDT.

The rest of the chapter is organized as follows. Partially inspired by Simon (1996), we begin with a discussion on *the model of life* in Sect. 2, because this is the subject which makes it easier to see our departure from the lifetime utility maximization (LUM, hereafter) doctrine toward the alternative, the meaning maximization (MM, hereafter) doctrine. We first argue that the LUM doctrine cannot properly formulate a model of life, since the latter is much more complex than any LUM model that has ever existed or has been known to us. Then in Sect. 3 we propose a framework based on the philosophy of Schopenhauer (Schopenhauer 1969) to answer our inquisitiveness for models of life. The answer involves a kind of *data*, namely *biographies*, which can hardly rivet the eyes of economists. Using biographies as a theoretic construct, in Sect. 4, we then apply algorithmic information theory to biographies and argue that the meaning of life can ideally be measured by the Kolmogorov complexity of the corresponding canonical biography. This enables us to have a new interpretation of the economic agent as an information-processing agent when maximal information can be regarded as maximal meaning. The core of the meaning maximization doctrine is to maximize meaning, but we have not had the maturity to formalize this part. Obviously, the familiar stochastic dynamic programming may be irrelevant. Hence, in Sect. 5, we present three genres that are employed in reality to create meaning. These three genres enable us to better see the relationship between meaning and information and to pinpoint the routine trap as a fundamental threat to meaning maximization. The established MM doctrine can be applied to economic theory and practice, and may collaborate or compete with the LUM doctrine. Section 6 shows a number of applications of the MM doctrine, and is followed by some concluding remarks in Sect. 7. In the appendix, we suggest that agent-based modeling can be an insightful toolbox that provides a panoramic view of the meaning maximization doctrine. Here, it serves as a biography generator, and is not limited to the biographies of a single person, but rather to many others in parallel.

## 2 Model of a Complex Life

Depending on the dimension of the decision space for a life, there are different versions of the formulation of lifetime utility maximization. Two familiar examples are given below. The first example, as in Eqs. (5.1) and (5.2), is one-dimensional and deals with the decision regarding consumption (saving) only.

$$\max_{\{c_t\}_{t=1}^{\infty}} U(\{c_t\}_{t=1}^{\infty}), \tag{5.1}$$

$$\sum_{i=1}^{\infty} c_t = \sum_{i=1}^{\infty} y_t, \tag{5.2}$$

where $c_t$ and $y_t$ denote the consumption and income in period $t$. $c_t$ is the control variable, to be determined, and $y_t$ is exogenously given. The decision problem facing an individual, given a sequence, deterministic or stochastic, of exogenous income, $\{y_t\}_{t=1}^{\infty}$, is to decide a sequence of consumption $\{c_t\}_{t=1}^{\infty}$ that can maximize the lifetime utility of the agent, as shown in (5.1), subject to (5.2).

The second example is two-dimensional and deals with the decisions for both consumption and leisure, Eqs. (5.3) to (5.5).

$$\max_{\{c_t\}_{t=1}^{\infty},\{l_t\}_{t=1}^{\infty}} U(\{c_t\}_{t=1}^{\infty},\{l_t\}_{t=1}^{\infty}) \tag{5.3}$$

$$\sum_{i=1}^{\infty} c_t = \sum_{i=1}^{\infty} y_t(n_t) \tag{5.4}$$

$$l_t + n_t = L_t, \ \forall t \tag{5.5}$$

Here, the exogenous variable $L_t$ is the time resource exogenously given to an individual in period $t$, that should be allocated to labor $n_t$ and leisure $l_t$, as shown in Eq. (5.5). Now, differing from the previous example, income is no longer given, but has to be earned through $n_t$. Then the rest is the same; the agent, given a sequence of time endowment $\{L_t\}_{t=1}^{\infty}$, needs to decide a sequence of consumption and leisure $\{c_t,l_t\}_{t=1}^{\infty}$ such that his/her lifetime utility will be maximized subject to (5.4) and (5.5).

Notice that the decisions in both cases are a stream of decisions, $\{c_t\}_{t=1}^{\infty}$ or $\{c_t,l_t\}_{t=1}^{\infty}$ made from the beginning of life ($t = 1$) to the end of it ($t = \infty$). Life does not have an infinite duration; one can replace the symbol $\infty$ with $T$, which can be exogenously given or endogenously determined, and can be deterministic or stochastic. The stream can be reviewed and revised as time goes on, so long as the constraints are not violated; in this case, the decision-maker can learn over time about the exogenous states in the future, based on his/her expectations and learning. In addition, his/her utility function, $U(\cdot)$, may change over time in some more realistic settings.

Without giving further mathematical details for both examples, we shall point out that, while it is possible to scale up the dimension and granularity of the decision space, almost down to the details of how each single unit of resources (time, money, physical energy, etc.) is allocated among many piecemeal competing ends, no one ever tries to swim very far away from the beach, not to mention any remote island in the center of a grand ocean. Models with five or more dimensions are rarely seen, not to mention double-digits, because practically it is very difficult to do so. The lifetime utility maximization model does not have enough capacity to handle the complexity of life, fraught with a long list of unknown unknowns, turns, and twists.

One additional source of complexity is that the dimension of the decision space itself is not fixed but can change when life unfolds itself, just as in a story named "*The Apple*" brilliantly given by Herbert Simon (1916–2001) in his biography (Simon 1996). This makes the mathematical formulation of the problem even more formidable, which basically indicates that the lifetime utility maximization model is no more than a puppet, which may be useful for some pedagogical purposes, but is hard to apply to keep track of or understand the life of any flesh. In fact, an experiment is to cordially invite one to find a single person in the world, whose trace of life, according to his/her repertoires or biographies, can be manifested as the consequence of lifetime utility maximization. For example, one can select any mathematician reviewed by Young (1981), any psychologist reviewed by Sheehy (2004), any economists collected in Szenberg and Ramrattan (2014) or simply Simon (1996) to see how a story based on the plot of lifetime utility maximization can be informatively constructed. If such efforts are doomed to fail, then what is a model of life, if lifetime utility maximization is not the answer? What is *a model of life* for Simon's "Models of My Life"?

# 3 Schopenhauer Mapping

Simon's "Models of My Life" or, generally, biographies provides a natural representation of the trace of life. In fact, an autobiography, such as Simon (1996), can be regarded as an inner representation of the "footprints" left by the protagonist in the world external to him/her. In other words, an autobiography can be understood as a mapping from the external world as perceived by the protagonist to his/her own inner representation. In the mapping referred to here, the protagonist and his/her autobiographies (codes of life) are depicted as in Fig. 5.1. For convenience, we shall denote the external world, the protagonist, the inner representation, and the codes of life (autobiography) by four upper cases, $W$ (world), $P$ (protagonist), $R$ (representation), $C$ (codes), respectively, and then call it the WPRC framework as shown in Fig. 5.1.

The mapping from the space of $W$, $\mathbf{W}$, to the space of $R$, $\mathbf{R}$, is subjectively determined by the protagonist, $P$, in question. In this part, we are inspired or influenced by the philosophy of the German philosopher, Arthur Schopenhauer (1788–1860), "The World as Will and Representation":

> Everything that in any way belongs and can belong to the world is inevitably associated with this being-conditioned by the subject, and it exists only for the subject. The world is representation. (Schopenhauer 1969, Vol. 1, p. 3)

We take $W$ as the *things-in-themselves*, $P$ as the subject, and $R$ as the perception constructed by the *being-in-itself* or *will* of the subject.

As to what we have shown in the two subfigures of Fig. 5.1, the same $W$ can be mapped into two different $R$s. One can say that the two subfigures correspond to two different protagonists, $P_1$ (Fig. 5.1a) and $P_2$ (Fig. 5.1b), with the same surrounding. The specific $W$ shown in Fig. 5.1a, in plain English, is pretty monotone or boring. For example, one could imagine that the $W$ could refer to a life in the camp as described in Frankl (1964); nevertheless, as also described in Frankl (1964), the protagonists $P_1$ and $P_2$ have come up with different inner representations even though they are identically situated. Now, the essential observation which

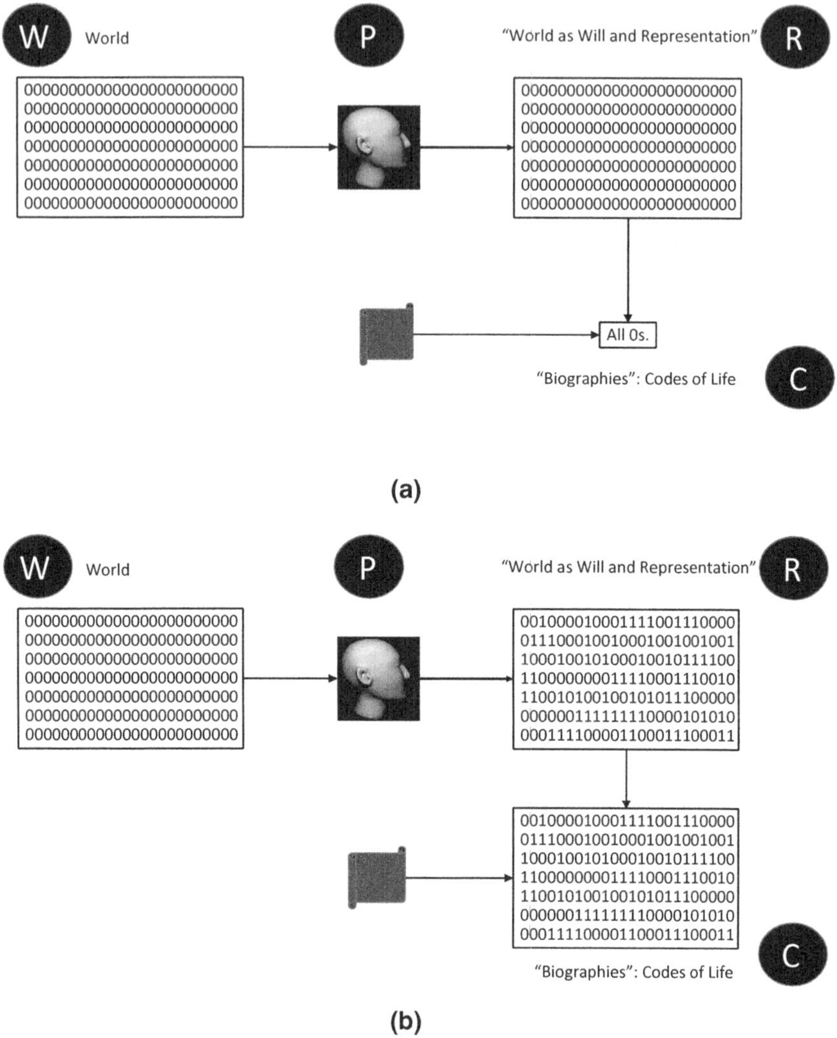


**Fig. 5.1** The WPRC framework

interests Victor Frankl is that, even though with the surrounding like $W$, people can still get meaning from it as shown by $R_2$, Fig. 5.1b. Frankl believed that getting meaning or not, that is, $R_1$ versus $R_2$, may become a matter of life or death. If Frankl's finding on the relation between lifespan and the underpinned meaning is convincing, then it is pertinent to know whether $P_1$ can be channeled to embrace the internal representation $R_2$. Here, the age-old question, "*De gustibus non est disputandum*," is evoked again.

In Fig. 5.1, we use the bit representation for *W*, *R* and *C*, in other words, computer languages. This usage has become quite typical. To justify this usage, one could delve into the situation by replacing the human protagonist with an intelligent robot, which has all sensory capabilities to deal with data and information received from the world reconfigured by bits. In this way, Fig. 5.1, despite its high abstraction, seems to be "natural" from the viewpoint of theoretical computer science. We, however, have no intention of derailing ourselves in a long pile of literature on artificial intelligence and the philosophy of intelligence, and the bit representation used here is mainly for pedagogical purposes and is not pertinent to the formation of doctrine. After all, technically, various representations can be discussed, but the utmost quest for the transformation from the external world into the inner representation of the protagonist has already been championed by Schopenhauer (Schopenhauer 1969), as he is often cited by "the world is my representation." With this clarifying remark, we shall stick with the binary representation of Fig. 5.1 in the following discussion.

Now, we have already discussed the Schopenhauer mapping, from the external world to the inner representation, that is conditioned on a subject (a protagonist). The next step is the *biographical mapping* from the space of representations to the space of biographies or autobiographies.[5] Of course, biographies are not just ordinary records of the streams of life down to its every detail, such as what Frank Ramsey did on January 1, 1920, what John von Neumann did on January 1, 1944, what Herbert Simon did on November 20, 1978, and so on and so forth. Neither is the way in which each of their biographies or autobiographies has been prepared (Macrae 1992; Paul 2012; Simon 1996). Instead, biographies give a *structure* of the life of the protagonist, and arrange the stories of events

[5] At this point, we shall not further distinguish the fine difference between biographies and autobiographies, although to be strictly consistent with the Schopenhauer mapping, only the latter can be considered. We, however, will assume that all biographies are or can be "endorsed" by their protagonist.

in different phases to substantiate the structure. It is this writing style that cannot accommodate redundancies, trivialities, and irrelevancies. In other words, biographies can be regarded as a condensed representation of life as it was. In this spirit they can be taken as the *codes* of life. *Ideally*, by "codes of life," we mean that by inputting these codes into a computer, then the "life as it was" will be replicated. If one is content with this view of biographies, then biographies can be formally treated by theoretical computer science, more specifically, by *algorithmic information theory* (Li and Vitanyi 2008; Shen 2016).

# 4 Algorithmic Information Theory of Meaning

In algorithmic information theory, the information of an object can be measured by *the size of the algorithm* operating in a Universal Turing Machine that can output the given object. In this way, unlike the earlier Shannon information theory, by which information is narrowly applied only to probabilistic objects (random variables), and, inevitably, in the probabilistic context (Cover and Thomas 1991), in algorithmic information theory, every object, including any physical, biological, and social entity, can be asked for its amount of information. In principle, one can ask the information amount of the life of Frank Ramsey, John von Neumann, or Herbert Simon based on the algorithms, descriptions, or biographies of them. In addition, to enable the measurement to properly perform and to avoid inflated information, redundancies have to be removed; in other words, everything in the description is deemed necessary, and is referred to as the *minimal description* or the *maximally condensed program*. The length of the minimum description of the object is also known as its *Kolmogorov complexity* or *algorithmic complexity*.

In relation to Fig. 5.1, we see that both $P_1$ and $P_2$ have the same size of inner representation, that is, the same length of the bit string ($|R_1| = |R_2|$), but the former has a lot of redundancies and can be further condensed. Therefore, the minimum description length of the former is much smaller than that of the latter. The publishers are probably not interested in the biography of $P_1$, since it has too much repetition and too little to offer, whereas the biographies of $P_2$ are very publishable since each of his/her single days (pages) contributes to the stories of his/her life and hence cannot be skipped (i.e., there is no redundancy).

With this little background on algorithmic information theory, we are ready to *quantify* the meaning of life used in this chapter. Ideally, the meaning of a life can be measured by the *minimum description length of a life or the minimum description length of R as indicated in the WPRC framework*. Furthermore, the minimum description is called the *canonical biography* of the subject in question, that is, the *C* in the WPRC framework. Intuitively, this way of quantifying the meaning of life is motivated by taking the biographies as the algorithm of a life, followed by redundancy-removal editing. Hence, technically, the WPRC framework requires the canonical biography, which is to be distinguished from the usual biographies. A caveat is that we should not take the word "biographies" too literally in the sense of the historical format of biographies; instead, we advocate a modern version, which may involve materials known as the digital trace, digital identity, digital footprint, or cyber shadow. After all, we only use biographies to concretize the model of a life.

Measured in this way, meaning refers to *the amount of information on a life*, and a meaningful life, essentially, is an *informative life*. The meaning maximization doctrine states that the subject has a natural tendency to maximize the meaning of his/her life in the sense of gaining as much *information about this life*. If a subject has a very informative life, such as Frank Ramsey, John von Neumann, Herbert Simon, and many others, then he/she must have plenty to say about his/her life, which implies a large amount of information about his/her life, and likewise for the people whose life is meaning impoverished. A conventional characterization of the economic agent, as characterized by Hayek or Simon, is an *information processor*. The meaning maximization principle or the information-maximization principle or, on the other side of the same coin, the entropy maximization principle may serve as a consistent interpretation of this information-processing agent, in the sense that what the information-processing agent does is to "process" the information that he/she acquired in his/her lifetime by removing redundancies and keeping the remaining ingredients as much as possible. We believe that this doctrine will serve us better to understand the nature of human agency than with the lifetime utility maximization doctrine.

Here, we come to the subtle difference between the biography and the autobiography. The Schopenhauer mapping is about the inner representation of the subject, not the subject in somebody else's inner representation. In this sense, the meaning of life has to be experienced by the subject, and not to be *interpreted* by others. If Marcel Proust (1871–1922) considered that a taste of madeleine and a drink of tea can be so much inspiringly associated with much of his *Lost Time* and pleasant memories, then he certainly could enjoy this afternoon tea and declare the meaning of savoring a cake, even though most people would have failed to experience such meaning with their usual diet. The essence is that, just like utility, $R$ is subjective, and so is $C$; if the subject cannot feel the way and experience how people describe his/her life, then it is simply not his/hers.

Notice that, by our definition, whether a life is meaningful does not depend on the life span, wealth, health, power, fame (vanity), and other elements that one may expect to be crucial for the subjective or objective well-being. The pursuit of money, power, and fame itself does not guarantee anything up to meaning unless they can be translated into information.[6] John Keats (1795–1821) and Frank Ramsey both died young. Karl Marx (1818–1883) was not rich. William Kermack (1898–1970) had been blind since 26, not to mention the health condition of Stephen Hawking (1942–2018). Antonio Gramsci (1891–1937) was in prison for his last few years, was deprived of political power and was poor and unhealthy after a long time in prison. Yet, for us as bystanders, their lives seem so meaningful, while not necessarily happy in the sense of lifetime utility or utilitarianism. Here, we, once again, touch on the difference between meaningfulness and happiness.

One may argue that all the exemplars above are *famous*. Can the rank and file also be on a par with those celebrities? Is fame an indispensable element. The use of the canonical biography has an advantage: it does not require a person to have one or more biographies *literally*. Many people

[6] Herbert Simon, once, said "[l]eaders should exercise power, but enjoying it is another, and more dangerous, matter" (Simon 1996, pp. 248–249). In addition, food, no matter how much we eat, does not automatically bring in meaning unless the energy which we gain from food helps us gain a lot of information about our life.

did not formally have a biography or autobiography, but that does not imply that their lives were stuffy. In fact, the market and technology in the past could not support each person to formally own his/her biography; nevertheless, in this digital society with the user-supplied contents, stories of an individual can be generated, coauthored, and distributed among different corners of digital space.[7] As long as everything said about the protagonist can be accepted by the protagonist and can be verified, they can contribute to his/her canonical biography, *C*, in the sense of the WPRC framework. Although active social interactions and friends may help one gain a richer canonical biography, as Smith (2017) suggested, for us it is not necessary. Based on our definition, we believe that there are many ordinary people whom few people know or have ever read their "canonical biographies" but who still have a very meaningful life. For example, one may not spend most of one's life quietly and remotely in Thoreau's Lake Walden (Thoreau 2004) but one can still have a quite informative and hence meaningful life as Henry David Thoreau (1817–1862) had.

Our formulation of meaning based on algorithmic information theory also does not exclude those highly controversial people. Meaning, like utility, is subjective and there is no moral or ethical ground for it. It may seem unfair, but the sun also shines on the wicked. The lives of both Maximilien Robespierre (1758–1794) and Charles Ponzi (1882–1949) could be informative and meaningful; if they could "endorse" McPhee (2012) and Zuckoff (2006) as the description of their life, from the viewpoint of Kolmogorov complexity, their life could be meaningful, too.

## 5 Meaning-Creation Genres

Once meaning can be quantified, the next step for the meaning maximization doctrine is to maximize meaning, but in this part we are not so much blessed with the maturity that neoclassical mathematical economics has. In fact, it is still not clear to us on the *right mathematics* or *right*

[7] As to a review of the evolution of the economy of authorship since the Enlightenment, the interested reader is referred to Woodmansee and Osteen (2005).

*formulation* for meaning maximization, given everything that we have said about meaning up to this point. Hence, instead of pretending to know how the problem can be formulated and solved analytically, we search for the "numerical solutions," that is, *empirically* how people tried to maximize the meaning of their life. Since these are "numerical recipes," which have no guarantee of succeeding, a more practical term is *meaning creation*. However, we have no intention of reiterating the rhetoric that philosophers (Schopenhauer 1901) or psychologists (Frankl 1964; Smith 2017) usually maintained. Instead, given the information-theoretic notion of meaning, in this section we shall examine meaning creation also from the algorithmic perspective. The rhetoric used here does not consist of the usual expressions that we often find in biographies or similar kinds of narratives. In fact, what we would like to propose is the *algorithmic structures* of the *genres* or the *kinds of plots* that generate the narratives of meaning. In this manner, we are working on something very similar to Booker (2004) or Tobias (2011). How many genres ("numerical recipes") are there: 7, 20, or more? We do not know; here we only give the three that we consider the most prevalent. The point is to show what these meaning-creation genres look like; once the idea is made clear, interested readers may find their own way to organize these and other genres.

## 5.1 Genre One: Halting Problems

One typical genre to generate meaning and hence to contribute to the algorithmic complexity of life is to embark on a *halting problem*, that is, roughly speaking, the problem with the property that we cannot know (decide) in advance whether we will ever stop and when.[8] Man's desire to conquer the universe, be it outer space, oceans, mountains, scientific projects, and everything that can test the limits of our will, and

[8] Here, we do not make an attempt to give a rigorous treatment of the halting problem and its significant role in the history and the philosophy of mathematics. The interested reader is referred to Sommerhalder and van Westrhenen (1988) and Enderton (2011). For a concrete metaphor of a real problem which a meaningful life is grappled with, one can think of the *Hilbert tenth problem*, that is, the solvability of the *Diophantine equation* (Matiyasevich 2008).

intellectual and physical capability, gives the examples of halting problems. Once after a halting problem is taken, each step ahead does add meaning to life, but how well or how badly we did in the past tells us in a very limited way whether we will get to the end and, if so, when. The essence of the navigation on a halting problem is the presence of fundamental uncertainty, that is, we know little about the future from our past.

The degree of uncertainty encapsulated in the halting problem is the source of meaning (information); in this regard, the relationship between meaning and uncertainty is the same as the relationship between information and uncertainty in the standard Shannon information theory (Cover and Thomas 1991). When we cannot find a halting problem to embark on or when the problems on our hands are not the kind of halting problems, uncertainty diminishes and so does meaning.

In this way, even though *routines* may have important implications in the behavioral economics of decision-making, a life fully occupied by routines cannot generate much meaning to life since it becomes too predictable. Consider an extreme case. If life can be known right from the beginning based on the subject having perfect foresight, then that is equivalent to saying that, relative to the whole lifespan, we can have a much shorter program to narrate the entire life all the way to the end, as the solution for a differential equation or the life of the familiar neoclassical (Arrow-Debreu) economic agent. Hence, the degree of the algorithmic complexity of a life in this case can be low, and thus its meaning, too.

Nevertheless, we should also take this opportunity to address a subtle point regarding routines. From a technical viewpoint, say, algorithmic information theory, routines refer to redundancy, repetitions, or condensability. However, as a conceptual framework applied to real life, say, biographies, attention should be paid to the nuanced difference between the mechanical life per se and the *will* behind it. The latter involves a will to fulfill a goal set at the beginning of a journey and to be carried out at its every single step; therefore, the will becomes an example of Genre One, that is, to embark on a halting problem, where no one can foreknow whether it will be fulfilled at the outset. Considering all the possible interruptions in the middle and all the efforts made to circumvent them, it may be worth a lengthy description and hence be characterized by a high degree of algorithmic complexity for this scenario of life. Once again, it is not about the routines per se, but about the will to keep the life seemingly mechanical. One example, *arguably*, to be given here is the afternoon walk of Immanuel Kant (1724–1804), precisely set at three-thirty every day.[9]

In sum, embracing a halting problem is probably one of the most common genres by which meaning can be generated; basically, it is a fundamental inquiry into the limit or the possible range of the life. Meaning then stems from the *undecidable* nature of life during our exploration of the unknown lifespan. Given its undesirability, one has to falter through most of the journey to see the arrival at the destination. Hence, everywhere we go, we continue to wonder what the next thing is and the next thing after the next, as what are coined as the unprestatable adjacent possibilities by Stuart Kauffman. The key is that the engaging meaning-pursuing agents can only imagine but not see through the whole agenda from where they are currently standing, while the agents in the Arrow-Debreu economy require no imagination regarding the future (Athreya 2013).

## 5.2 Genre Two: Space Filling

Genre One applies well to the class of subjects entitled *entrepreneurs*; however, no matter how broadly or how inclusive this term is defined (Braun 2015), only a limited number of people can be qualified as entrepreneurs. Fortunately, "voyage and return" is only one of the seven plots that can tell stories (Booker 2004), and we still have other genres for meaning creation. The second genre to be introduced here can apply to many *ordinary people*.

The second genre for meaning creation is called *space filling*. The protagonist in this genre is given a space that is real or imaginary and the map of the space. The space, as indicated by the map, is organized into many regions, each of which is further organized into many subregions, and that hierarchy can be extended further down into many levels,

[9] Kant is intentionally chosen here because his will regarding self-control has been described by some biographers as turning himself into a machine (Kuehn 2001).

depending on the *granularity* of the map. Given this structure (map) of the space, meaning is created each time when the protagonist has an ice-breaking step over any of the unvisited or unexperienced places. For example, the familiar expression under this genre is "I have never been to Latin America, but tomorrow I will leave for Buenos Aires," or "I have never dated before, but tonight is going to be my first romance," and so on. Sometimes, we also coin this action as a *milestone* in life; for example, "I finally passed my oral exam and got my PhD degree," or "I finally had my first peer-review article accepted," and so on and so forth. More proactively, one may perceive the protagonist as taking a *space-filling algorithm* to arrange his/her life such that the space can be filled as much as he/she can.

The required description length and hence the algorithmic complexity of a life can then depend on the granularity of the accompanying map and the actual explorations. A life with a simple map and/or limited explorations of the space, such as "through all of his life, he did not go anywhere outside the town, not even crossing a street," may lead to a life with a rather thin canonical biography.

With this general understanding, it is crucial to add two remarks regarding the map. First, the map is individually and socially constructed. The map is acquired by the protagonist in his/her interactions with his/her surroundings. While part of the map can be created by the protagonist himself/herself, a substantial part of the map is socially, culturally, or institutionally constructed. The latter is particularly true for the hierarchical structure of the map, and that can be clearly exemplified in various curricula vitae or resumés, mentioning academic degrees, career positions, honors, and so on. Here, the aforementioned space-filling algorithms show a property of *enumeration*, that is, a mapping from the well-established hierarchical structure to a sequence of well-ordered natural numbers, such as $\{1, 2, 3, \ldots, N\}$ (usually, the range is finite). The protagonist then proceeds from 1, 2, ..., to $N$ sequentially, say, from a PhD to a postdoc and finally to a Noble laureate.

This kind of enumeration provides the most common genre for meaning creation, although for different protagonists the sequence of numbers may point to very different things. Since counting the well-recognized objects only requires very elementary skills, the socially constructed enumeration does not require much talent to learn. While agents may not be able to perform dynamic optimization throughout their entire life, one thing that may comfort neoclassical economists is that they may act *as if* they are lifetime optimizers, since even before getting to high school they could already have embraced a kind of socially constructed enumeration, by which a whole life is agendized.

Second, the map for each individual is constantly evolving with social changes and individual adaptions, as well described by Herbert Simon in his *Apple* (Simon 1996). In this vein, the map is the sketch of the *model of a life*. A key parameter is the *granularity of the map*. We may expect that a protagonist may begin with a coarser resolution, when he/she is young, and evolve gradually toward finer and finer resolutions, when he/she gets older. This change in granularity can help meaning creation since it helps identify those regions long unseen, thinking of Kauffman's unprestatable adjacent possibilities. With the increasingly finer map, the protagonist may seemingly revisit the same old region, but in fact he is visiting a novel place that could never have been discovered using the old maps. This remark, properly placed in business, may echo well with the essence of the *experience economy* as advocated by Pine and Gilmore (2011).

## 5.3 Genre Three: Gram-Schmidt Orthogonalization Process

In the space-filling genre, it is obvious that a protagonist with poor creativity or imagination, thinking of Kenneth Boulding's *image* (Boulding 1956), further situated in a monolithic culture, may have difficulties experiencing a colorful life. In addition, in some either socially or individually adverse situations, it is likely that a well-drawn map and a well-established enumeration are not available. It is especially difficult for people who were born and/or grew up in chaos to obtain a clear map and enumeration; see, for example, Frankl (1964) and Ninh (2012). Nevertheless, instead of having a map *ex ante*, they can construct the map *ex post*, as if Christopher Columbus (1451–1506) discovered the islands in the Caribbean Sea one by one essentially without a map. In this case, the question to be asked by the protagonist is *what is new*. To answer the question, the protagonist needs to *project* his/her most recent encountering against the background constituted (spanned) by what he/she had experienced and *extract out* the novel element. This process is familiarly known in linear algebra or functional analysis as the *Gram-Schmidt Orthogonalization Process*, originally named after the Danish mathematician Jørgen Pedersen Gram (1850–1916) and the German mathematician Erhard Schmidt (1876–1959). Here, we also name our third genre by this term.

The *Gram-Schmidt Orthogonalization Process* is well used in macroeconomics and econometrics as a way to characterize an innovation process or a process of news, surprises, and the unanticipated (Ljungqvist and Sargent 2004). Given a sequence of vectors, say $f_1$, $f_2$, ..., in a Hilbert space, the process will lead us to extract a sequence of orthogonal bases as $g_1$, $g_2$, ..., in such a way that

$$f_1 = g_1, \tag{5.6a}$$

$$g_2 = f_2 - \frac{\langle f_1, f_2 \rangle}{\langle f_1, f_1 \rangle} f_1, \tag{5.6b}$$

$$g_n = f_n - \sum_{n-1}^{j=1} \frac{\langle g_j, f_n \rangle}{\langle g_j, g_j \rangle} g_j, \tag{5.6c}$$

where <·, ·> is the inner product operator.[10]

Obviously, we do not mean to take the mathematical operation above literally; we use (5.6) as an aspiration. Nevertheless, to have a good understanding of Genre Three, the role of the Gram-Schmidt orthogonalization process is not just a metaphor. We use it to visualize how such a process can be possible and can be articulated and then, based on that articulation, used to get access to the metaphysics of mind and its

[10] For a more formal introduction to the Gram-Schmidt orthogonalization process in function analysis, the interested reader is referred to Sasane (2017).

mentally new constructs. Basically, as portrayed by this orthogonalization process, every single step of the path of our life may have something novel, something never experienced before, or something orthogonal to the past; because of that, every single step of life may drive us away from the same dimensional space (the same world) in which we were situated before. The beauty of Eqs. (5.6a) to (5.6c) is that they point to a way to organize our canonical biography: on the one hand, we are trying to make sense of what happens now in terms of our past, that is, searching for connections (the projected vector), and, in the meantime, we discover the uniqueness of each encounter, that is, extensions (the orthogonal basis). Hence, even without a map and a well-arranged enumeration, we constantly attempt to extend our space in life while keeping its emergent structure in sight.

Meaning generated by this genre shows that life is potentially complex, and it could defy any attempt to compress it. The only way to understand it is to live it, and not to theorize it as the lifetime utility maximization doctrine tends to do. In a nutshell, meaningful life is *computationally irreducible* (Wolfram 2002). In the seemingly insipid life, a life filled with routines or repetitions, Genre Three provides a very important way to make life meaningful and interesting (see more discussions in Sect. 6).

While the formalism of the orthogonalization process may not be explicitly known, the ideas emanating from it have been circulated with different emblems. For example, similar ideas have been introduced as *mindfulness* or *mediation* in Buddhism (Hanh 1987). Thich Nhat Hanh, a Vietnamese Buddhist monk, has long encouraged people to practice mindfulness, which essentially can be regarded as a pragmatic reification of the orthogonalization process.

> When you are walking along a path leading into a village, ...if you practice mindfulness you will *experience that path*, ...You practice by keeping this one thought alive: "I'm walking along the path leading into the village." ...you keep that one thought, but *not just repeating it like a machine*, over and over again. *Machine thinking is the opposite of mindfulness.* If we're really engaged in mindfulness while walking along the path to the village, then we will consider the act of *each step we take* as *an infinite wonder*, .... (Ibid, p. 12; Italics added)

Reading the above notation, one notices that *Hanh's path to a village* can be prosaic and routinary if we just do it *over and over again*. However, our mind has the power to make us experience the same path differently with an infinite wonder and that, according to Hanh, distinguishes men from machines, or human thinking from machine thinking.

## 5.4 A Corroborative Remark

Before we move on, an additional remark about the three genres is given here. As we mentioned earlier, the three genres proposed are suggestive; in fact, so far, there exists no such kind of taxonomy known to us, not to mention the one germane to algorithmic information theory. However, general understandings of different genres for portraying the meaning of life are often seen. Among them, the one proposed by Pearce (2014) fits our three genres quite well.[11]

> One way of looking at a lifetime's career is to see it as *a set of steps to Parnassus*, progressing steadily – or by revelations – to the present exalted position. Another is to look at events, and to see how they have contributed towards *the amalgam of experiences* that one has accumulated up to that point. (Ibid, p. 95; Italics added.)

In the quotation above, *the set of steps to Parnassus* or even *Mount Everest* can be perceived as a microcosm of Genre One, the embarkation of a halting problem. However, a less-ambitious interpretation is to picture *the set of steps* as a map or a ladder mentioned in Genre Two, the space-filling enumeration. The use in Pearce (2014) is closer to Genre One. As to *the amalgam of experiences accumulated*, depending on our characterization of experiences, it has two interpretations as well. If the experiences refer to something new in an incremental or marginal sense, that is, experiences gained from a rather ordinal life, such as Proust's madeleine or Hanh's path to a village, then it points to Genre Three. However, if the

[11] Richard Pearce wrote a book review (Pearce 2014) for an autobiography of George Walker, director general of the International Baccalaureate from 1994 to 2006, specifically about his devotion to education.

experiences refer to something new by being situated in different locations of the map or altitudes of the ladder, then it is akin to Genre Two. The use as Pearce (2014) reviews the biography of George Walker is veritably Genre Two. If so, then what is missing in Pearce (2014) is Genre Three, Proust's madeleine or Hanh's path. As we shall see in the next section, for ordinal people or even elites, Genre Three plays a substantial role in the meaning maximization doctrine.

# 6 Applications

The established MM doctrine can be applied to economic theory and practice, and may collaborate or compete with the LUM doctrine. In this section, we show a number of applications of the MM doctrine, which include applications to mainstream utility theory (Sects. 6.2 and 6.8), motivation (Sects. 6.3 and 6.8), the theory of labor (Sect. 6.3), economic development (Sect. 6.4), management science and public administration (Sect. 6.6), ideology and political economy (Sect. 6.7), and humanomics (Sects. 6.1 and 6.5).

## 6.1 Corpus Linguistics

From our observations of children's behavior and their playing, it is rather persuasive that we human beings are constantly searching for things that are *interesting* and, as a whole, an *interesting life*. Our formulation of meaning based on the algorithmic description of life is consistent with every intuitive notion of "interesting," which nicely corresponds to *information* in its essential elementary from, namely, *coding*. Hence, on this ground, our doctrine can also be called the *information maximization doctrine* (see also Sect. 4). On the way to growing up, what interests us may keep on evolving, but their essence in terms of coding, information, and algorithmic complexity remains unchanged.[12] It is unlikely that peo-

[12] Quite the opposite, algorithmic information theory has a different interpretation and tends to consider the objects which can be substantially compressed, relative to their original size as interesting. This idea has been exemplified by *numbers* where interesting numbers, also termed as "simple

ple will evoke the term "expected lifetime utility" in their usual conversations, but the term "a meaningful life" is heavily engaged in various kinds of communication. Therefore, from the viewpoint of the language used by ordinary people, the meaning maximization doctrine seems to be more *natural* than the utility maximization doctrine.

## 6.2 Law of Diminishing Marginal Utility

The meaning maximization doctrine is not necessarily in contradiction to the utility maximization doctrine. In fact, the meaning maximization doctrine can provide an alternative and probably even better interpretation of some familiar economic laws which were initially formed under the utilitarianism principle. Here, we give one example, and another one will be given in Sect. 6.8. The example provided here is the famous *law of diminishing marginal utility*, established by W. Stanley Jevons (1835–1882), Carl Menger (1840–1921), Leon Walras (1834–1910), and their predecessors (Black, Coats, and Goodwin 1973). "We may state as a general law, that the degree of utility varies with the quantity of commodity, and *ultimately* decreases as that *quantity increases*"(Jevons 1879, p. 57; italics added.). Here, we shall reinterpret this law in light of algorithmic information theory and use of *routines*, mentioned in Sect. 5.1, as a general characterization of the state of the *increased quantity*.

By algorithmic information theory, the law of diminishing marginal utility can be restated as follows: the algorithmic complexity of actions undertaken over a series of identical events will not grow linearly with the series. With this interpretation, we may christen the law as *the law of diminishing marginal complexity*. This newly christened law remains as a law in relation to the meaning maximization doctrine, since the same path after being repeatedly followed gradually becomes a fossilized routine. It is increasingly difficult to extract something new from routines; hence, the complexity (description length) of undertaking the routine an additional time *ultimately* decreases. Nevertheless, the law of diminishing marginal complexity (utility) can be violated as long as we can keep on

numbers," are to be distinguished from uninteresting numbers, also termed as "random numbers." The subtle difference between AIT's and our notion of "interesting" itself is an interesting issue.

experiencing something new even when walking along the same path (Hanh 1987) (Sect. 5.3).

Consider an example which we may borrow from the *experience economy* (Pine and Gilmore 2011), say, the experience of consuming apples. If we have a *capability* to endow each apple with a different context (narrative, story, imagination) so that we can constantly enjoy eating them even though they are identically the same, then the law can be violated.[13] In this case, the first apple gives us juice to quench our thirst, the second one give us sweetness to satisfy our hunger, the third one enables us to visualize the authentic redness, the fourth one reminds us about the encapsulated nutrients, the fifth one drives us to search for lost time as Marcel Proust did, and so on and so forth, ending with an *infinite wonder* (Hanh 1987).

This apple example also exemplifies how the operation of the Gram-Schmidt Orthogonalization Process, that is, Genre Three, provides us with an escape out of the *routine trap* that Jevons predicted will *ultimately* occur and prevents us from feeling bored from repeating the same thing, which is manifested by a short description (coding) of life. This spirit of *a constantly fresh start in life* is part of the inculcation of the Confucian tradition. Tang (1675–1646 BC), the founding King of the Shang Dynasty, inscribed on his bathtub the following inscription: "If you renew yourself for one day, you can renew yourself daily, and continue to do so." The quoted text has been documented in Chapter 2, *The Great Learning*, one of the *Four Books* in Confucianism. In the same chapter, the text continues as follows: "So monarchs of high morality do their utmost to make themselves and the masses endeavor for fresh starts." When Eastern civilization meets Western civilization, it is marvelous to see how the deep ancient Chinese philosophy, after 3500 years, can be palpably interpreted by the Gram-Schmidt Orthogonalization Process.[14]

[13] We particularly choose the word *"capability"*, mainly due to Amartya Sen, as we shall see in Sect. 6.4.

[14] For the English translations of the Great Learning used in this paragraph, the reader should consult Muller (1992) and the website https://www.en84.com/dianji/jingshu/201008/00003960.html.

## 6.3 Intrinsic Motivation

While the marginalists did not explicitly acknowledge the term *routine trap*, they may have implicitly noticed the role that it plays in their operation of the law of diminishing marginal utility. This is particularly evident from Jevons's famous graphical representation of the theory of labor. In this graph, when the *x*-axis reads the quantity of labor and the *y*-axis reads the degree of pleasure or pain (Jevons 1879, p. 187), the depicted disutility function of labor shows a segment that labor is not considered as a pain but as a source of pleasure. Jevons used the term *spontaneous energy* to indicate the possibility that man can have pleasure from labor, even though in the end no one can escape from what we consider to be the routine trap.

We understand that Jevons's consideration is more physiologically oriented, as influenced by Richard Jennings (1814–1891) (Jennings 1855), whereas our consideration is based on *will-to-meaning*. For us, the main source of spontaneous energy is the *context* in which the meanings of work are generated, which has long been well-acknowledged by economists. Since this chapter is also prepared for a book referring to John Maynard Keynes (1883–1946), we have two quotations from the anthology *Rethinking Keynes*, edited by Pecchi and Piga (2008):

> *Many people go to work for reasons beyond money*, and might prefer to work longer than Keynes's fifteen hours a week *under almost any situation*. Workplaces are social settings where people meet and interact. On the order of 40 to 60 percent of American workers have dated someone from their office. (Freeman 2008, p. 140; Italics added)

> The most basic of these is that nowhere does Keynes recognize the wisdom of the pragmatist school – from James to Dewey to Rawls and on to Sen – that *people need to exercise their minds with novel challenges – new problems to solve, new talents to develop*. (Phelps 2008, p. 102; Italics added)

The quotation above makes us reminiscent of the affirmative view of human nature expounded by Thorstein Veblen (1857–1929) in his *Instinct of Workmanship* (Veblen 1914). The *instinct of workmanship* is the human proclivity to explore new and better ways of doing things, to be both efficient and creative, for the betterment of humanity; it is, in spirit, similar to the Gram-Schmidt Orthogonalization Process (Genre Three), which makes routines look like kaleidoscopes as we have seen in the aforementioned apple example.

The observations above, therefore, allude to the relationship between our meaning maximization doctrine and what economists are now familiarized with, namely, the *intrinsic motivation*, to be distinguished from the early overwhelming beacons of the extrinsic motivation (Frey 1997; Romaniuc 2017; Scitovsky 1976). Meaning-making can serve as a source for the intrinsic motivation. With Genre Three, the derived inherent meaning from routines enables us to escape from the routine trap and the subsequent pains; in this way, work itself provides a source of pleasure rather than of pain.

## 6.4 Capability Approach

The meaning maximization doctrine, as opposed to the utility maximization doctrine, may stand closer in spirit to the *capability approach* advocated by Amartya Sen over the decades. In Sen (1999), the term *education* was mentioned a total of 141 times; it and health care are the key premises for human beings owning the capability to pursue what Sen considers the paramount end for development, namely *freedom*, that is, to choose and to lead lives that we have reason to value. Sen, unlike mainstream economists, does not narrowly restrict his interest to the conventional operational metrics, such as income per capita, since these metrics can be "rather *poor indicators* of important components of well-being and quality of life that people have reason to value" (Ibid, p. 80; Italics added).

For us, the presence of the routine trap, as described above, can also adversely influence humans' well-being, but may not be well encapsulated in those operational metrics. It is phenomenal, from recent studies, to see that income did not generate happiness in the way that we may have anticipated (Layard 2005). Hence, we may work hard and get paid well, but still fail to value much of life. Here, we argue that if education is solely targeted for increasing national output rather than to cultivate the capability, a mental power, to escape from the routine trap, then this result is inexorable.

There is no unique determination of the routine trap, and Jevons noticed two of them. First, it is determined by the nature of the routine. For example, one may suppose that the blue-collar kinds of routines may trap *ordinary people* more easily or faster than the white-collar kinds of routines, since it seems more difficult for ordinary people to have incessant serendipities of the former than the latter.

> A man of lower race,..., enjoys possession less, and loathes labour more; his exertions, therefore, soon stop. A poor savage would be content to gather the almost gratuitous fruits of nature, if they were sufficient to give sustenance; it is only physical want which drives him to exertion. The rich man in modern society is supplied apparently with all he can desire, and yet he often *labours unceasingly for more*. (Jevons 1879, p. 198; Italics added)

In fact, despite the savage criticism it has received, one advantage of the *gig economy*, is that it could make the otherwise highly routinary jobs a little more protean (Kessler 2018; Prassl 2018). As we shall see in the next quotation of him, Jevons specifically mentioned the "*highest kinds of labour*." In our parlance, it is equivalent to saying that routines have high kinds and low kinds, and Genre Three can be applied more easily to the former, but not the latter.

The second determination of the routine trap is education or training, which is related to Sen's *capability approach* to economics as depicted above.

> It may be added that in the *highest kinds of labour*, such as those of the *philosopher, scientific discoverer, artist*, etc., it is questionable how far great success is compatible with ease; the mental powers must be *kept in perfect training* by constant exertion, just as a racehorse or an oarsman needs to be constantly exercised. (Jevons 1879, pp. 197–198; Italics added)

Training or education can elevate men's mental power or imagination or *the instinct of workmanship* so as to find an otherwise irksome routine "interesting and stimulating" (Ibid, p. 197). Hence, if a person is becoming polymathic, he/she can stand on high ground to see the world surrounding him/her, and to appreciate the maxim of Nietzsche, "[i]f we have our own *why* of life, we shall get along with almost any *how*" (Nietzsche 1912, in Maxims and Arrows; Italics added), as an epiphany to help him/her escape the trap, as a myriad of stories narrated in Robinson and Aronica (2009), Ballard (2011), and many others.

Of course, one could not expect that our current education and schooling systems, often criticized as built upon the antiquated factory model (Robinson and Aronica 2009), can help children and youth find their *capability* to be richly inspired with great revelations even in a routinary *madeleine moment* as Proust enjoyed. However, when young talents' answers for Nietzsche's *why* are only limited to GPA, the Ivy League, and careers, then the capability to create alternatives to grapple with routine traps is undermined. When this happens, development and freedom, in the sense of Sen, is disentangled. The consequence is not just in relation to employment, productivity and creativity, but without capability of imagination, the democratic and social operation can be threatened as well. We shall come to this point in the next few subsections.

## 6.5 Humanomics

The maximizing meaning doctrine that we propose clearly paves a road to the humanities and can be part of what is now recognized as *humanomics*. Indeed, it is the great literature, novels, stories, history, philosophy, and religion that provide humans with "programs" to generate the meaning of their life and make it "interesting" in the algorithmic manner.

As we have already seen in the previous subsection (Sect. 6.4), Genre Three, when applied to a substantial degree, requires extraordinary capability for *imagination*, or in our parlance the capability to find the hidden codes of life. This is not easy for ordinary people in their daily life that is occupied with various routines. In Sect. 6.4, we mention the role of education; while education may help people gain such a capability, just school education is not enough. Education is generally referred to as continuing education or lifetime learning, and it is definitely not just about science or technical matters, but also on the humanities. As Peter Salovey, the President of Yale, once said at the 2017 World Economic Forum,[15]

> In our complex and interconnected world, we need leaders of imagination, understanding, and emotional intelligence–men and women who will move beyond polarizing debates and tackle the challenges we face. ...Art, literature, history, and other branches of the humanities are vital for developing our emotional intelligence–essential to understanding ourselves and others. ...We develop our emotional intelligence–and learn skills of empathy, imagination, and understanding–through the humanities.

To have enough materials for lifetime learning, a society needs to have sufficient numbers of quality humanists, including artists, painters, poets, novelists, musicians, and philosophers, and so on. One of the most important writers in modern Chinese literature, Zhou Shuren (1881–1936), more familiarly known by his pseudonym Lu Xun, is an example; he gave up his original pursuit to be a medical doctor and became a literary scholar since he felt that the Chinese nation at his time suffered from a huge void in spirituality. Humanists help inspire ordinary people to constantly make sense of their work especially in great adversity.

## 6.6 Leadership and Governance

The meaning maximization doctrine also has implications for governance and politics. Ordinary people may not have the capability to maximize the algorithmic complexity of their life; not all of them are able to receive a decent education and may not have the chance to nurture their habitual reading. So, they need philosophers and scholars to help them out (Sect. 6.4); in addition to that, most people spend most of their time in the *workplace*. The meaning of the work that they can get out of this workplace depends on the culture or the ethos to which they are subsumed. Since, among many things, the culture or ethos is shaped by the leaders of the organization, bosses or supervisors or employers or capitalists play

[15] https://www.weforum.org/agenda/2017/03/the-key-to-responsible-and-responsive-leadership-the-humanities/.

an important role in helping ordinary people to escape routine traps, because they, either partially or wholly, hold the hermeneutic power of the routines derived from the workplace. When great humanists are largely reticent to them, employees can still constantly meet serendipities to evade routine traps if their employer aspires to clothe their work with meaning. Details of these go beyond the realm of mainstream economics, but constitute very pragmatic issue in management. There we can see some revolutionary changes or paradigm shifts in the theory of organization and leadership, which can be regarded as the companion to the meaning maximization doctrine (Laloux 2014; Sinek 2019).

Among many possible avenues, Laloux (2014) presents a historical review of the evolution of organization, and identifies seven distinct phases along this evolution and even colors each phase differently. While the framework proposed by Laloux (2014) is about organizations and the meaning maximization doctrine is about individuals, it seems entirely pertinent to address how organizations have evolved in a way to facilitate the meaning-maximizing individuals in light of Laloux (2014). This issue itself is also related to radical political economy, considering that, exactly 200 years before the publication of Laloux (2014), the series of *Luddite revolts* of workers had just come to an end (Binfield 2004; Jones 2006; Thompson 1963).

## 6.7 Meaning Crisis

When a routine trap is so adhesive that it is difficult to get away with it, then a prolonged routine trap will lead to the familiar *meaning crisis*, that is, a general frustration with the void regarding meaning in life, a subject already well addressed in philosophy, psychology, and the humanities. None of the three genres can prevent the meaning crisis from happening, since each genre has its limitations. Earlier, we mentioned how ordinary people can suffer from their meaning crisis if Genre Three fails to help them discover novelties from the seemingly insipid life. Maybe one way to reinterpret what happened to Nora Helmer, the protagonist of the play *A Doll's House* by the Norwegian playwright Henrik Ibsen (1828–1906), is that Nora finally gave up her long dependence on the algorithm of Genre Three, that is, loving her husband, and got an epiphany with an algorithm of Genre One, that is, to be more than a plaything in her whole life. She then "successfully" escaped from her routine trap.[16]

Here, let us take a closer look at Genre Two (Sect. 5.2). Genre Two, a space-filling enumeration of a map, is another accessible form for meaning creation. However, unlike Genre Three, this genre may have a property of *exclusiveness*, that is, the success of one protagonist implies the failures of many others who use the same algorithm. This is because for those enumerations, hierarchically organized as a pyramid, to enumerate further up one needs to constantly stand out from a sequence of increasingly feverous competition. Therefore, the competition among those who employ a similar space-filling algorithm will inevitably generate many losers, who just have no luck in filling such a precipitous space in their map of life, and, very reluctantly, get stymied somewhere on the ladder.

Without being able to find another space-filling algorithm or another genre to create meaning, the stymied protagonists are plagued by constantly staying in the doldrums. To reduce the pain, some of them may be driven to misconduct and to employ illegitimate, illegal, immoral, and unethical alternatives, which correspond to various kinds of *corruption*. Even though some of them remain honest and do not evoke anything unlawful, those who are unable to sustain suffocation could develop a self-destruction tendency and resort to drugs, alcohol, or even suicide. Hence, the meaning crisis is a crisis, because it could lead to various kinds of corrupting and ruinous behavior and incur ethical concerns.

In economics, we have dealt with various failures, from market failures, government failures, coordination failures, organization failures, and, also, in this digital society, platform failures, but what has been left largely unfinished is the implications of these failures for *individuals*, which we may term *individual failures*, specifically characterized by the meaning crisis. This inquiry can be generally extended to unemployment, poverty, inflation, financial crises, economic miracles, globalization, inequality, immigration, universal basic income, war and peace, and all major economic and social episodes. The general question is how the algorithmic complexity of a life is determined by the temporal-spatial milieu that accommodates it. Probably, literal scholars know more about

---

[16] Of course, Ibsen did not tell us what actually happened after Nora left the house. It is up to the pleasure of the feminists' imagination.

the answer than economists.[17] Maybe what humanomics tries to fill is exactly this lacuna (also see Sect. 6.5).

> Ignoring the burden of art and literature and philosophy in thinking about the economy is bizarrely unscientific: it throws away ...a good deal of the evidence of our human lives. I mean that the exploration of human meaning from the Greeks and Confucians down to Wittgenstein and *Citizen Kane* casts light on profane affairs, too. ...And so (the hypothesis goes) economics without meaning is incapable of understanding economic growth, business cycles, or many other of our profane mysteries. (McCloskey 2016, p. 508; Italics, original)

The meaning maximization doctrine also provides us with a new perspective to examine the role of *ideology*, that is, the totality of ideas, beliefs, and values common to a society or to a group of people in general. As we mentioned in Sect. 5, genres of meaning creation, to a large extent, are socially constructed, while ideologies, explicitly or implicitly, shape the use of various genres. In that sense, ideologies are competing with each other based on how well they facilitate meaning creation. There was a time when communism was promoted as a kind of Genre One for directing people to have their meaning of life; indeed, people were given a passion for building a new society, such as a "New China," with a full regard for human dignity via the realization of egalitarianism. Nevertheless, pragmatically, this ideology failed badly in meaning creation for people; on the contrary, it generated a meaning crisis for billions of people (Butterfield 1982). The ensuing large-scale meaning crises called for the transformation toward capitalism (Qian 2017). In this transformation, meaning creation is more channeled through Genre Two, the space-filling enumeration for self-fulfillment.[18] However, probably because of its

[17] As professors of economics, we often wonder how students who are originally trained in economics can better immerse themselves in the study of poverty if, in addition to Samuelson and Nordhaus (2009), they also read *Les Miserables* by Victor Hugo (1802–1885), *La Dame aux Camelias* by Alexandre Dumas (1824–1895), *Oliver Twist* by Charles Dickens (1812–1870), and many more novels included in Marsh (2011).

[18] This is the time in which many narratives have been developed on how ordinary people become economically independent, rich, famous, knowledgeable, and so on. For example, one may refer to Chang (2009) to see how factory girls find their ladder to become a *modern Nora*.

overwhelming reliance on Genre Two plus, as mentioned above, the exclusiveness property of the socially constructed ladders, the transformation has gradually been exposed to another wave of meaning crises when many people faltered along the ladder. Corruption, in various forms, turns out to be the "solution" for this second wave of meaning crises. Dishonest and misconduct behaviors are prevalently seen in various spheres, even including academic communities (Kwong 1997). The use of Genre Three to support meaning creation or the use of imagination to make novel sense of routines seems to be lacking during China's current transition to the *political capitalism* or the so-called socialist market economy with Chinese characteristics (Milanovic 2019).[19]

## 6.8 Money and Power

In Sect. 6.2, we show the connection between the MM doctrine and the second-order derivative of the utility function; in this subsection, this connection is further extended to the functional form per se and its first-order derivative. Specifically, we want to comment on the single-variate utility function, namely $U(W)$, where $W$ denotes *wealth* or, simply, *money*. Needless to say, $U(W)$ plays a substantial role in the LUM doctrine. In economics and, in particular, in finance, it is assumed that $U$ is monotonically increasing in $W$, denoted by its positive first-order derivative $U'(W) > 0$. However, mainstream economics generally does not seriously address *why being wealthier makes people happier*, that is, how to "process" the increment in wealth such that the degree of pleasure or happiness experienced by a tycoon, say, John Rockefeller (1839–1937), can be enhanced. Directly equating wealth with consumption ($W = C$) is the vernacular provided by mainstream economics; despite its convenience, this argument is too simple to clothe the enigmatic life of Rockefeller, as narrated by Chernow (1998).

[19] The lack of using Genre Three is manifested by the society failing to spiritually enrich those who happen to get stymied on the ladder, by leaving them, consciously or unconsciously, to accept "losers" as their name. What may be hard to observe is that the other side of this "society of wolves," expressed in a vernacular way, is a colossal flock of sheep. They constitute a new version of *Doll's House*.

From the viewpoint of the MM doctrine, the transformation of wealth into consumption is less pertinent than its use to create meaning. As a matter of fact, not everyone could have the capability to carry out the philanthropic plans that Rockefeller had done, had they been endowed identically wealthy. Having said that, we notice that the wealth-consumption equivalence ($W = C$) can sweep away many non-trivial details of the realization of wealth in the form of consumption, no matter how broadly the latter is defined. Hence, without knowing what agents will do after they get wealthier, the function $U(W)$ and the inequality $U'(W) > 0$ are problematic.

One of the reasons that the wealth-consumption equivalence ($W = C$) has been long espoused by economists is due to the legacy of Jevons (1879); over a century and a half ago, he said:

> The calculus of utility aims at supplying *the ordinary wants of man* at the least cost of labour. Each labourer, *in the absence of other motives*, is supposed to devote his energy to the accumulation of wealth. A *higher calculus of moral* right and wrong would be *needed to show* how he may best employ that wealth for the good of others as well as himself. But when that higher calculus gives no prohibition, we need the *lower calculus* to gain us the utmost good in matters of moral indifference. (Ibid, p. 29; Italics added)

Following this legacy, and ignoring the "economy chivalry" of Alfred Marshall (1842–1924), one tends to accept that there are two levels of calculus and the lower one can be carried out irrespective of the higher one.[20] In this light, mainstream economics seems to be the economics of *ordinary wants* or *low needs*, if we borrow the term from Maslow's

---

[20] In the preface to his first edition of the *Principles of Economics*, Marshall says the following:

> But ethical forces are among those of which the economist has to take account. Attempts have indeed been made to construct an abstract science with regard to the actions of an "economic man,".... But they have not been successful, .... For they have never really treated the economic man as perfectly selfish: no one could be relied on better to endure toil and sacrifice with the unselfish desire to make provision for his family; and his normal motives have always been tacitly assumed to include the family affections. But if they include these, why should they not include all other altruistic motives the action of which is so far uniform in any class at any time and place, that it can be reduced to general rule! ...in the present book *no attempt is made to exclude the influence of any motives*, the action of which is regular, merely because they are altruistic. (Marshall 1920, p. vi; Italics added.)

hierarchy of needs (Maslow 1954). If so, is there an economics of *high needs*? What happens to those people who have climbed to the higher level of the Maslow pyramid and have a demand for esteem or self-actualization or transcendence? For those people, is $U'(W) > 0$ still valid? If that additional wealth, $\Delta W$, cannot help people gain meaning in life, for example, avoiding a routine trap, or, worse, driving their life into the doldrums, does that golden-emblemized inequality, $U'(W) > 0$, still hold?

In addition, in the quotation from Jevons above, we empathetically highlight *the absence of other motives*. As already discussed in Sect. 6.3, one should ask what changes it could make *when other motives appear and have to be considered together*. In this regard, the mainstream economics built upon the legacy of Jevons is incomplete and fragmental. The MM doctrine, on the other hand, suggests an integration rather than separation or fragmentalization, and in this assertion we are in line with the spirit of Alfred Marshall as we quote in footnote 20. For the MM doctrine, money or wealth is desirable because it is an apparatus for getting meaning in life, namely a tool for helping us in getting freedom, independence, and vision, and hence to avoid being a slave of anything or routine traps. To achieve the aforementioned pursuits, we need to begin with adequate nutrition, education, and health maintenance, and money is absolutely indispensable for us to be granted these *ordinary wants*. However, as advocated by Amartya Sen, the capability approach urges us not to stay here but to gain the capabilities compatible with the freedom that we have acquired. In fact, from the series of studies done by Abhijit Banerjee and Esther Duflo (Banerjee and Duflo 2011), we realized that the poor have their kinds of routine traps, and what may surprise those field experimenters is that aid originally designed for supporting their low needs has been used for other purposes to escape their routine traps. In fact, if we can understand that the poor may have their own perception of meaning and their way to search for meaning, then we can build our "salvation" plan to extend along their way, their narratives, their storytelling, and their perception of meaning construction.

To sum up, our main point is that, by the MM doctrine, wealth is desirable because it enhances our capacity to escape routine traps and overcome meaning crises, but unless that happens *just getting wealthier* can eventually suffer from the so-called *treadmill effect* and can even be deleterious to meaning creation.[21] The way that we treat money also applies to power. Hebert Simon once said, "[l]eaders should exercise power, but enjoying it is another, and more dangerous, matter"(Simon 1996, pp. 248–249). To us, people try to gain power to escape an otherwise routine trap, but the same warrant of the treadmill effect also applies here; in fact, the power-pursuing game often ends up with corruption. Maybe, the quotation of Simon can be rephrased as follows: power is used for discovering or creating meaning, and not for indulging ourselves in a delusional narcissism.

## 7 Concluding Remarks

In this chapter, we propose an alternative doctrine to the long-held lifetime utility maximization (LUM) doctrine. We touch a very familiar subject that has long been dealt with in philosophy, psychology, and religion; however, we have a completely different formulation, underpinned by a unique theoretical origin, which articulates what meaning is and how meaning can be generated. In light of algorithmic information theory, we formalize meaning as being identical to the minimum description length or Kolmogorov complexity of the algorithm of life. By this formulation, meaning is to be discovered from life; we, therefore, focus on its elementary form, the algorithm of life, as the counterpart of the utility function in neoclassical economics. The algorithm, after being decoded, may refer to a life with love, responsibility, sacrifices, power, or money, but these

---

[21] In their classic article on adaptation, Brickman and Campbell (1971) argued that people are confined to a *hedonic treadmill* as, on an exercise treadmill, one can increase the speed by as much as one wants, although always remaining in the same place. The treadmill effect has already been known since Adam Smith (Smith 1759).

> Happiness consists in tranquillity and enjoyment. Without tranquillity there can be no enjoyment; and where there is perfect tranquillity there is scarce any thing which is not capable of amusing. But in every permanent situation, where there is no expectation of change, the mind of every man, in a longer or shorter time, returns to its natural and usual state of tranquillity. In prosperity, after a certain time, it falls back to that state; in adversity, after a certain time, it rises up to it. (Ibid, p. 172)

The recent rise of the Economics of Happiness makes the treadmill effect popular.

particularities are not what we are primarily concerned with. Instead, it is the length of the algorithm; hence, the content of life, that matters to us.

The accompanying agent-based modeling (Appendix) further expounds that the path of the life of an agent is dependent on the epoch and the ambience by which he/she was dictated and with which he/she interacted. If an agent was born in a communist country and grew up during the Vietnam War, his/her life may have some of the characteristics as portrayed in Ninh (2012); in this case, the Bellman equation may not be a useful tool to shed light on the organization and the evolution of his/her life. Likewise, if an agent was born in historical India, his/her main character will be determined by *Homo hierarchicus* as well as documented in Dumont (1980); again, dynamic programming may help us only a little to "code" his/her life.

Hence, in contrast to the MM doctrine, the LUM doctrine does not offer us much insight into most real life in the real world. By reading the biography of Frank Ramsey (Paul 2012), we could not find a single page addressing his saving behavior, not to mention the celebrated permanent income hypothesis. What we did find was his search for meaning and his uneasiness with his sexual orientation. This does not mean that saving, consumption, labor supply, and portfolio management are not important issues for us. They are, but their significance can only be shown in their wider context. What, therefore, is substantially missing in the current economics is exactly these contexts, pointing to the pursuit of a meaningful life. So, the question to ask is: To what meaningful life is optimal saving important? Would Alan Turing (1912–1954) care about it? Would Kurt Godel (1906–1978) care about it?

It is hoped that readers can see our attempt to bring in some fresh air and thinking to economics. This chapter is just the beginning. Du Bois (1868–1963) once said, "I insist that the object of all true education is not to make men carpenters, it is to make carpenters men" (Du Bois 2002, p.88). Having served as a professor of economics for more than 25 years, I share Du Bois's view, but worry that the education of mainstream economics is exactly to make men carpenters. Nevertheless, this worry is not my own, but is generally shared by a large group of economists. In fact, if we offer a course, say, a humanistic concern for economics, the syllabus will be long. This chapter could distinguish itself from many others in the list, but, I believe, their commonalities would be greater than the differences.

**Epilogue** This epilogue, in fact, could also be considered as a prologue of this chapter or, at least, appear as a footnote on the title page of the chapter. However, since the size of a normal footnote cannot accommodate it, it is written separately as an epilogue of the chapter. When I was invited by Prof. Vela Velupillai to contribute a piece of work in honor of Prof. Stefano Zambelli, a respectable scholar with whom I spent some time together both at UCLA and at Trento, I had a great passion to do so. Zambelli is a very versatile scholar; his contribution to economics, needless to say, is manifold. When I was a graduate student, his work on the *rocking horse* (Zambelli 2007; Zambelli and Thalberg 1992) had already been introduced to my class on business cycles. That was probably my first step toward the economics of Zambelli. In 2006 and the following few years, the time that I became a frequent visitor to Trento University, I had the opportunity to be impressed by his profound work on the *aggregate production function* (Zambelli 2004, 2018). This work can be considered to be my second course in the economics of Zambelli. In addition to these two direct influences, Stefano and I are intellectually genealogically related. Being both pupils of Prof. Velupillai, we share general interests in economics studied as a dynamic system, understood as Turing universal computation and the associated properties of computability and complexity (Velupillai 2000, 2010; Velupillai, Zambelli and Kinsella 2012). I have prepared this chapter in the vein of the legacy of the economics of Zambelli with these highlights.

In this chapter, I join Stefano by also taking a stand to criticize neoclassical economic theory, this time not the aggregate production function, but the utility function. In a tone parallel to his one, I argue that lifetime utility maximization, in any technical form known to us, describes no one's actual life path and does not hint at what most biographies will tell us. Ironically, it is almost irrelevant to understand a person's life. I then go on an adventure to propose an alternative doctrine, namely the meaning maximization principle, and argue that the human nature to pursue an interesting (meaningful), but not necessarily, happier, life can be formulated using algorithmic information theory.

Unlike many of his works, this chapter does not have an empirical counterpart. I, somehow, have the confidence that one day when a biography of Prof. Stefano Zambelli is prepared, he would prefer the book to be written in a style of meaning maximization rather than in a style of lifetime utility maximization. In fact, based on my understanding, he hardly knows his utility function, not to mention its risk curvature, showing no interest to estimate it, regardless of its being differentiable or not; however, in everything that he deems right or just, he has no hesitation to get involved with little calculation of the expected costs. Obviously, neoclassical economic theory cannot give a decent portrait of this "empirical fact," I, therefore, have written this chapter to meet this deficiency.

In addition to the shared intellectual roots, there is another commonality between Stefano and me, that is, administration experience. Being pupils of Prof. Velupillai, both of us were trained and threaded by the ideas of Herbert Simon, following his legacy on decision-making and administration (Simon 1997; Velupillai 2018). We have both devoted a substantial amount of time to what Prof. Velupillai has called *institutional building* in our life. He had been the head of the Department of Economics at the University of Trento, and I had been the dean and the vice president of National Chengchi University. Our common experience of serving and shaping an academic community is another driver for choosing the subject *meaning maximization* so as to resonate the legacy of the savant, from whom I learned a great deal about the virtues mentioned in Adam Smith's *Theory of Moral Sentiments* (Smith 1759). That is why part of the chapter can be read as the microcosm of that public service.

**Acknowledgment** The author is grateful for the support this research received from the Taiwan Ministry of Science and Technology (MOST) [grant number MOST 108-2410-H-004-016-MY2].

## Appendix: Epochs and Biographies: Agent-Based Modeling

If *it takes a village to raise a child*, then it may take the entire society to prepare a biography or a set of biographies. A biography documents how the protagonist interacted with the people and the ethos of a society during some specific epochs, but that same milieu has also shaped the biographies of many others. These biographies are strongly intertwined with each other if their protagonists had substantial interactions. Hence, instead of treating them individually, there is a system-wise approach to threading and reading them together. In fact, a similar idea has been pursued by humanistic scholars when they try to have a macroscopic view of the microscopic behavior of each character in a play; a term has been introduced for this, called *character path walks* (Kokensparger 2018). Chen and Venkatachalam (2017) have argued that agent-based modeling is the only kind of method that can generate and simulate *big data*, which is a collection of what people said, did, and thought during their interactions, both *beings and time*. This unique feature enables us to have a panoramic view or *distant reading* of biographies (Moretti 2013). In this section, we show how we can *visualize* this possibility through agent-based modeling.

Without losing generality, we only employ the simplest model, that is, *elementary cellular automata* as championed by Stephen Wolfram (Wolfram 2002). Wolfram's elementary cellular automata is a one-dimensional lattice arrayed with $N$ individuals, each one only interacting with two neighbors (one on the left and one on the right). Furthermore, each individual is characterized by only a binary state, either 0 or 1. The interaction (behavioral) rule is to dictate the state of an individual, say, $i$, at his immediate next step given his current state (0 or 1) and that of his neighbors, say, $i-1$ (the left one) and $i+1$ (the right one), as shown in Eq. (5.7).

$$S_i(t+1) = f(S_{i-1}(t), S_i(t), S_{i+1}(t)); \;\; S_j(t) \in \{0,1\}, \;\; \forall j,t, \;\; \forall i. \quad (5.7)$$

Since the transition function, $f$, can only take three binary values, there are only eight ($2^3$) possible scenarios, and a rule, say, $f_u$ can differ from the other rule, say, $f_v$, if they behave differently in at least one of the eight scenarios. Accordingly, there are a total of 256 ($2^8$) rules. Wolfram further assumed that individuals are homogeneous in the employed rule, as already indicated in Eq. (5.7), and numbered these rules and studied them systematically.

Let us consider one of these 256 rules, Rule 110, as shown in Eq. (5.8) below. In Eq. (5.8), the eight possible scenarios are fully listed, and the corresponding transition is indicated below, respectively.

$$f_{110}: \underbrace{000}_{1}, \underbrace{001}_{1}, \underbrace{010}_{1}, \underbrace{011}_{1}, \underbrace{100}_{1}, \underbrace{101}_{1}, \underbrace{110}_{1}, \underbrace{111}_{1}, \tag{5.8}$$

Hence, once the initial condition, that is, the initial state of each individual, is given, the $1 \times N$ array can have its dynamics. If we stack up the dynamics from its initial period all the way up to the most recent one, say, $T$, then we can have a $T \times N$ binary matrix $M(t)$. $M(t)$ gives the history of the entire society since the first day or the collection of all biographies of the society up to the present time $t$.

An example is given in Fig. 5.2a. Figure 5.2a shows a theater of 257 (=128 + 1 + 128) characters ($N$= 257),[22] each, with a state of either 0 (black) or 1 (green), occupying a grid, as indicated on the horizontal axis. They entered and exited the stage at the same time, with a duration of 129 periods ($T$= 129), as indicated by the vertical axis. Hence, what is shown in Fig. 5.2a is, in effect, a binary matrix with 129 rows (periods) by 257 columns (characters).

As in Fig. 5.1, the *life path* of each of these 257 agents has been represented by a 129-bit string, that is, each single column of the matrix $M(129)$. To proceed further, let $B_{i,T}$ ($i$= −128, −127, …, 0, …, 127, 128) be the biography of an individual $i$, which is the continuous record of the path of the individual $i$ traversing through his/her life up to the period $T$. For example,

$$B_{0,129} = \{11111111001111111001111001111100\ldots1100010110\} \tag{5.9}$$

In addition to $B_{0,129}$, Fig. 5.2b also gives $B_{-128,129}$ (L-128, the 128th grid left of the origin), $B_{-64,129}$ (L-64), $B_{64,129}$ (R-64), and $B_{128,129}$ (R-128). Without evoking some technical details, one can take these five strings as

[22] This is just about half of the number of characters appearing in Leo Tolstoy's *War and Peace*.

the biographies (codes of life) of these five agents, equivalent to the character path walks obtained from a play (Kokensparger 2018).

Instead of a play, let us take the biography of Frank Ramsey as an example (Paul 2012). By supposing that we are dealing with the digital version of Paul (2012), then the entire biography can be perceived as a sequence of binary digits, such as the one in (5.9). Obviously, this sequence can be rather long.[23] Once it is conceivable that the life path of an individual can be represented by his/her digital trace $B_{i,t}$, a key issue related to our further discussion is the generation or simulation of the sequence of $B_{i,t}$. Obviously, Ramsey was not situated on a remote island or lived a solitary life like Robinson Crusoe. Instead, Ramsey received a good education at Cambridge, and that further enabled him to have fascinating interactions with many contemporary celebrities, such as George Moore (1873–1958), Bertrand Russell (1872–1970), John Maynard Keynes (1883–1946), Peiro Sraffa (1898–1983), and Ludwig Wittgenstein (1889–1951), to name a few.[24] Therefore, as already revealed in Fig. 5.2a, $B_i$[25] could overlap with $B_j$ as if the former (the protagonist) is played out against the background containing part of $B_j$.[26]

Hence, after the agent-based simulation of the interactions of a society of people in a specific period of time (history), one can then project the entire obtained matrix $M$ into a specific individual $i$, as the cutting of a slice of cake, to derive $B_i$; if Ramsey is taken as the protagonist $i$, then the biographies of everyone else, $B_{-i}$, become his background. This shows that agent-based modeling can first give us a panoramic view of an epoch (Fig. 5.2a), the big data, within which the details (path walks) of each character can be derived (Fig. 5.2b). This resonates well with the main argument of Chen and Venkatachalam (2017), that is, agent-based modeling is the only method that can generate and simulate big data. In the

[23] Despite his unfortunately short span of life, one can still be amazed by Ramsey's long list of academic contributions as reviewed by Misak (2020).

[24] Unlike the elementary cellular automata, different characters, say, $i$ and $j$, could only have some overlaps, but their *time of being* can hardly be identical. However, it is not hard to introduce the heterogeneous entry and exit time for the characters in a nonelementary model of cellular automata.

[25] Since in a non-elementary model of cellular automata (see footnote 24), each character has a different time of being, without causing any confusion, we have removed the time index.

[26] Hence, one can introduce an idea of the *closure* of $B_i$ by including all materials related to $i$ from all $B_j$, $(j \neq i)$.

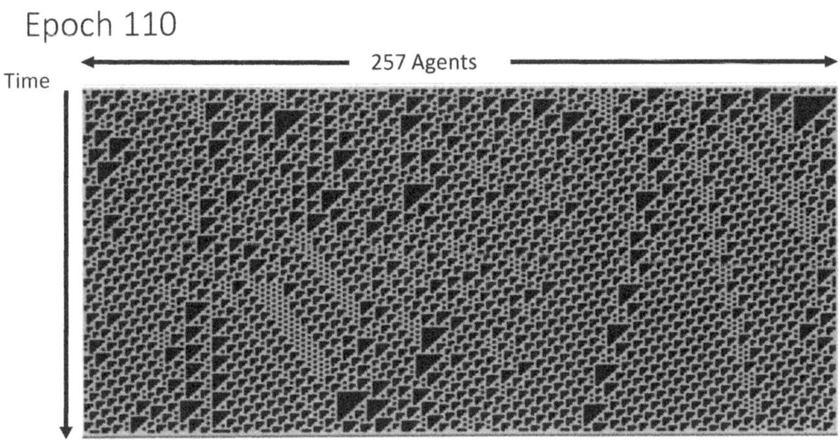


(a)

Epoch 110

Agent L-128

[0 1 1 1 1 1 1 1 1 1 1 1 1 1 1 1 1 1 0 0 0 1 0 1 1 0 1 1 0 1 1 1 1 1 0 0 1 1 1 1 1 1 1 1 0 0 1 1 1 1 1 0 0 1 1 1 1 1 0
0 1 1 1 1 1 1 0 0 1 1 1 1 1 0 0 0 1 1 1 1 1 1 1 0 0 1 1 1 1 1 1 1 1 1 1 0 0 1 0 1 0 1 1 0 0 0 1 0 1 1 0 1 0 0 0 1 0 1
1 0 1 0 0 0 1 0 1 1 0 0 0 1]

Agent L-64

[0 1 0 1 1 0 0 0 1 1 0 1 0 1 1 0 1 0 1 1 0 0 0 1 0 1 1 0 1 0 0 0 1 0 1 1 0 1 0 0 0 1 0 1 1 0 0 0 1 0 1 1 0 1 0 1 0
1 1 1 1 1 0 0 0 1 0 1 1 0 0 0 1 1 1 1 1 1 1 1 1 1 1 1 1 1 1 0 0 1 1 1 1 1 0 0 1 1 1 1 1 1 1 0 0 1 1 1 1 1 0 0 1 1 1
1 1 0 0 1 1 1 1 1 0 0 1 1 1]

Agent 0

[1 1 1 1 1 1 1 1 1 0 0 1 1 1 1 1 1 1 0 0 1 1 1 1 1 0 0 1 1 1 1 1 0 0 1 1 1 1 1 0 0 1 1 1 1 1 0 0 1 1 1 1 1 0 0 0 1
1 1 1 1 1 1 1 1 1 1 0 0 1 1 0 1 1 0 1 0 1 1 0 0 0 1 0 1 1 0 0 0 1 1 0 1 0 0 0 1 0 1 1 0 0 0 1 1 0 1 0 0 0 1 0 1 1 0
0 0 1 0 1 1 0 0 0 1 0 1 1 0]

Agent R-64

[1 1 1 1 1 1 1 0 0 1 1 1 1 1 0 0 1 1 1 1 1 1 1 1 1 1 1 1 1 1 1 1 1 1 1 1 1 1 0 0 0 0 0 1 1 0 0 0 0 0 1 0 1 0 1 1
0 0 0 1 0 1 1 0 1 0 0 0 1 1 0 1 0 0 0 1 0 1 1 0 0 0 1 0 1 1 0 0 0 1 0 1 1 0 0 0 1 0 1 1 0 0 0 1 0 1 1 0 0 0 1 0 1 1
0 0 0 1 0 1 1 0 0 0 1 0 1 1]

Agent R-128

[0 0 1 0 1 1 0 1 0 1 1 0 1 0 1 0 1 1 1 1 1 0 0 1 0 0 1 0 0 1 1 0 1 0 0 0 1 1 0 1 0 1 0 0 0 1 1 0 1 0 0 0 1 0 1 1 0
0 0 1 1 0 1 1 0 0 0 1 0 1 1 0 0 0 0 1 0 1 0 1 1 0 0 0 1 0 1 1 0 1 0 1 1 1 1 1 1 0 0 1 1 1 1 1 0 0 1 1 1 1 1 1 1 1 0 0
1 1 1 1 1 1 1 0 0 1 1 1 1 1]

(b)

**Fig. 5.2** Epoch 110: a panoramic view with selected samples of biographies

same vein, it also serves those historians who do research following the paradigm of the *bottom-up history* (Lynd 2014).

In general, $B_i$ is determined by the particularities of the epoch and the ambience by which the protagonist $i$ was dictated and with which he/she interacted. While these given premises can be rather sophisticated, in the elementary cellular automata they have been simplified to an extreme, namely a transition rule, for example Rule 110, and the initial configuration. If we change the rule or the initial configuration, we may be able to have a different history $M$ with different $B_i$, for some or all $i$. To see this, Fig. 5.3 shows a run using Rule 108, fully expressed in Eq. (5.10).

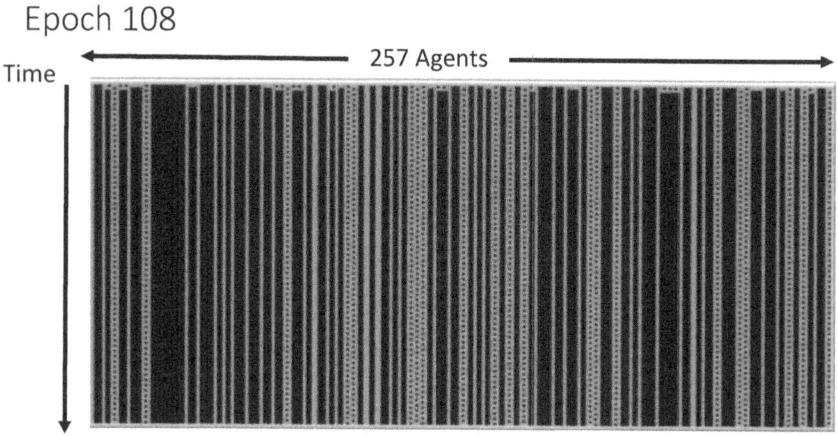


**(a)**

Epoch 108

Agent L-128

[1 1 1 1 1 1 1 1 1 1 1 1 1 1 1 1 1 1 1 1 1 1 1 1 1 1 1 1 1 1 1 1 1 1 1 1 1 1 1 1 1 1 1 1 1 1 1 1 1 1 1 1 1 1 1 1 1
1 1 1 1 1 1 1 1 1 1 1 1 1 1 1 1 1 1 1 1 1 1 1 1 1 1 1 1 1 1 1 1 1 1 1 1 1 1 1 1 1 1 1 1 1 1 1 1 1 1 1 1 1 1 1 1 1 1
1 1 1 1 1 1 1 1 1 1 1 1 1 1]

Agent L-64

[0 1 0 0 0 0 0 0 0 0 0 0 0 0 0 0 0 0 0 0 0 0 0 0 0 0 0 0 0 0 0 0 0 0 0 0 0 0 0 0 0 0 0 0 0 0 0 0 0 0 0 0 0 0 0 0 0
0 0 0 0 0 0 0 0 0 0 0 0 0 0 0 0 0 0 0 0 0 0 0 0 0 0 0 0 0 0 0 0 0 0 0 0 0 0 0 0 0 0 0 0 0 0 0 0 0 0 0 0 0 0 0 0 0 0
0 0 0 0 0 0 0 0 0 0 0 0 0 0]

Agent 0

[1 1 1 1 1 1 1 1 1 1 1 1 1 1 1 1 1 1 1 1 1 1 1 1 1 1 1 1 1 1 1 1 1 1 1 1 1 1 1 1 1 1 1 1 1 1 1 1 1 1 1 1 1 1 1 1 1
1 1 1 1 1 1 1 1 1 1 1 1 1 1 1 1 1 1 1 1 1 1 1 1 1 1 1 1 1 1 1 1 1 1 1 1 1 1 1 1 1 1 1 1 1 1 1 1 1 1 1 1 1 1 1 1 1 1
1 1 1 1 1 1 1 1 1 1 1 1 1 1]

Agent R-64

[0 0 0 0 0 0 0 0 0 0 0 0 0 0 0 0 0 0 0 0 0 0 0 0 0 0 0 0 0 0 0 0 0 0 0 0 0 0 0 0 0 0 0 0 0 0 0 0 0 0 0 0 0 0 0 0 0
0 0 0 0 0 0 0 0 0 0 0 0 0 0 0 0 0 0 0 0 0 0 0 0 0 0 0 0 0 0 0 0 0 0 0 0 0 0 0 0 0 0 0 0 0 0 0 0 0 0 0 0 0 0 0 0 0 0
0 0 0 0 0 0 0 0 0 0 0 0 0 0]

Agent R-128

[1 0 1 0 1 0 1 0 1 0 1 0 1 0 1 0 1 0 1 0 1 0 1 0 1 0 1 0 1 0 1 0 1 0 1 0 1 0 1 0 1 0 1 0 1 0 1 0 1 0 1 0 1 0 1 0 1
0 1 0 1 0 1 0 1 0 1 0 1 0 1 0 1 0 1 0 1 0 1 0 1 0 1 0 1 0 1 0 1 0 1 0 1 0 1 0 1 0 1 0 1 0 1 0 1 0 1 0 1 0 1 0 1 0 1
0 1 0 1 0 1 0 1 0 1 0 1 0 1]

**(b)**

**Fig. 5.3** Epoch 108: a panoramic view with selected samples of biographies

$$f_{108} : \underbrace{000}_{1}, \underbrace{001}_{1}, \underbrace{010}_{1}, \underbrace{011}_{1}, \underbrace{100}_{1}, \underbrace{101}_{1}, \underbrace{110}_{1}, \underbrace{111}_{1}, \tag{5.10}$$

$M_{108}$ is in stark contrast to $M_{110}$. From both Fig. 5.3a and b, one can see that the life paths of all these 257 characters are much simpler (prosaic) as opposed to their counterparts in the epoch characterized by Rule 110. In general, distinguishing any two epochs or historical moments, say, the Middle Ages and the Renaissance, is much onerous than distinguishing the two epochs in the computer, say, Epoch 108 and Epoch 110.

## References

Athreya, K. B. (2013). *Big ideas in macroeconomics: A nontechnical view*. Cambridge: MIT Press.

Ayache, E. (2010). *The blank swan*. Hoboken: John Wiley & Sons.

Ballard, E. (Ed.). (2011). *Epiphany: True stories of sudden insight to inspire, encourage, and transform*. Lagos: Harmony.

Banerjee, A. V., & Duflo, E. (2011). *Poor economics: A radical rethinking of the way to fight global poverty*. New York: Public Affairs.

Barbera, S., Hammond, P., & Seidl, C. (Eds.). (1999). *Handbook of utility theory* (Vol. 1). Principles. Berlin: Springer.

Barbera, S., Hammond, P. & Seidl, C. (Eds.). (2004). *Handbook of utility theory* (Vol. 2). Extensions. Berlin: Springer.

Beckert, J. (2016). *Imagined futures: Fictional expectations in the economy*. Cambridge: Harvard University Press.

Binfield, K. (Ed.). (2004). *Writings of the Luddites*. Baltimore: John Hopkins University Press.

Black, R. D., Coats, A. W., & Goodwin, C. D. (1973). *Marginal revolution in economics*. Durham: Duke University Press.

Booker, C. (2004). *The seven basic plots: Why we tell stories*. London: A & C Black.

Bookstaber, R. (2017). *The end of theory: Financial crises, the failure of economics, and the sweep of human interaction*. Princeton: Princeton University Press.

Boulding, K. E. (1956). *The image: Knowledge in life and society*. Ann Arbor: University of Michigan Press.

Braun, A. (2015). *The promise of a pencil: How an ordinary person can create extraordinary change*. New York: Simon and Schuster.

Brickman, P., & Campbell, D. T. (1971). Hedonic relativism and planning the good society. In M. H. Apley (Ed.), *Adaptation-level theory: A symposium* (pp. 287–302). New York: Academic Press.
Bronk, R. (2009). *The romantic economist: Imagination in economics*. Cambridge: Cambridge University Press.
Butterfield, F. (1982). *China: Alive in the bitter sea*. New York: Times Books.
Chang, L. T. (2009). *Factory girls: From village to city in a changing China*. New York: Random House Digital, Inc.
Chen, S. H., & Venkatachalam, R. (2017). Agent-based modelling as a foundation for big data. *Journal of Economic Methodology, 24*(4), 362–383.
Chernow, R. (1998). *Titan: The life of John D. Rockefeller*. New York: Sr. Vintage.
Cover, T. M., & Thomas, J. A. (1991). *Elements of information theory*. Hoboken: John Wiley & Sons.
Deaton, A. (1992). *Understanding consumption*. Oxford: Oxford University Press.
Dolgin, A. (2012). *Manifesto of the new economy: Institutions and business models of the digital society*. Berlin: Springer.
Du Bois, W. E. B. (2002). *Du Bois on education*. In E. F. Provenzo Jr. (Ed.). Lanham: Rowman Altamira.
Duffy, J. (2016). Macroeconomics: A survey of laboratory research. In J. Kagel, & A. Roth (Eds.), *Handbook of experimental economics* (Vol. 2, pp. 1–90). Princeton: Princeton University Press.
Dumont, L. (1980). *Homo hierarchicus: The caste system and its implications*. Chicago: University of Chicago Press.
Eggleston, B., & Miller, D. E. (Eds.). (2014). *The Cambridge companion to utilitarianism*. Cambridge: Cambridge University Press.
Enderton, H. B. (2011). *Computability theory: An introduction to recursion theory*. Cambridge: Academic Press.
Frankl, V. E. (1964). *Man's search for meaning: An introduction to logotherapy* (Rev. ed.). London: Hodder & Stoughton.
Freeman, R. B. (2008). Why do we work more than Keynes expected? In L. Pecchi, & G. Piga (Eds.). *Revisiting Keynes: Economic possibilities for our grandchildren*. Cambridge: MIT Press.
Frey, B. S. (1997). *Not just for the money: An economic theory of personal motivation*. Cheltenham: Edward Elgar.
Hall, R. (1978). Stochastic implications of the life cycle-permanent income hypothesis: theory and evidence. *Journal of Political Economy, 86*(6), 971–987.

Hanh, T. N. (1987). *The miracle of mindfulness: An introduction to the practice of meditation*. Boston: Beacon Press. (Original in Vietnamese, 1975, 1976; translated by Mobi Ho).
Hartley, J. (1997). *The representative agent in macroeconomics*. Abingdon: Routledge.
Hey, J. D., & Dardanoni, V. (1988). Optimal consumption under uncertainty: An experimental investigation. *The Economic Journal, 98*(390), 105–116.
Jennings, R. (1855). *Natural elements of political economy*. Harlow: Longman, Brown, Green, and Longmans.
Jevons, W. S. (1879). *The theory of political economy*, 2nd Edition (1st Edition, 1871). New York: Macmillan and Company.
Jones, S. E. (2006). *Against technology: From the Luddites to neo-Luddism*. Abingdon: Routledge.
Kauffman, S. A. (2016). *Humanity in a creative universe*. Oxford: Oxford University Press.
Kauffman, S. A. (2019). *A world beyond physics: The emergence and evolution of life*. Oxford: Oxford University Press.
Kessler, S. (2018). *Gigged: The end of the job and the future of work*. New York: St. Martin's Press.
Kokensparger, B. J. (2018). Navigating the forest through the trees: Visualizing character paths through Shakespeare'ss *As You Like It. Digital Archives and Digital Humanities* (2), 15–48.
Kuehn, M. (2001). *Kant: A biography*. Cambridge: Cambridge University Press.
Kwong, J. (1997). *The political economy of corruption in China*. Armonk: Sharpe.
Laloux, F. (2014). *Reinventing organizations: A guide to creating organizations inspired by the next stage in human consciousness*. Brussels: Nelson Parker.
Lawson, T. (2003). *Reorienting economics*. Abingdon: Routledge.
Layard, R. (2005). *Happiness: Lessons from a new science*. City of Westminster: Penguin UK.
Li, M., & Vitanyi, P. (2008). *An introduction to Kolmogorov complexity and its applications*, 3rd edition. New York: Springer.
Ljungqvist, L., & Sargent, T. J. (2004). *Recursive macroeconomic theory*. 2nd Edition. Cambridge: MIT press.
Loewenstein, G. (1999). Because it is there: The challenge of mountaineering ...for utility theory. *Kyklos, 52*(3), 315–343.
Lynd, S. (2014). *Doing history from the bottom up: On EP Thompson, Howard Zinn, and rebuilding the labor movement from below*. Chicago: Haymarket Books.

Macrae, N. (1992). *John von Neumann: The scientific genius who pioneered the modern computer, game theory, nuclear deterrence, and much more*. New York City: Pantheon Books.

Marsh, J. (2011). The literature of poverty, the poverty of literature classes. *College English, 73*(6), 604–627.

Marshall, A. (1920). *Principles of economics*. New York: Macmillan and Company.

Maslow, A. (1954). *Motivation and personality*. New York, NY: Harper.

Matiyasevich, Y. (2008). Computation paradigms in light of Hilbert's tenth problem. In *New computational paradigms* (pp. 59–85). New York, NY: Springer.

McCloskey, D. N. (2016). Adam Smith did Humanomics: So should We. *Eastern Economic Journal, 42*(4), 503–513.

McMahon, D. M. (2006). *Happiness: A history*. New York: Grove Press.

McPhee, P. (2012). *Robespierre: A revolutionary life*. New Haven: Yale University Press.

Milanovic, B. (2019). *Capitalism, alone: The future of the system that rules the world*. Cambridge: Harvard University Press.

Misak, C. (2020). *Frank Ramsey: A sheer excess of powers*. Oxford: Oxford University Press.

Moretti, F. (2005). *Graphs, maps, trees: Abstract models for a literary history*. Brooklyn: Verso Books.

Moretti, F. (2013). *Distant reading*. Brooklyn: Verso Books.

Morson, G. S., & Schapiro, M. (2017). *Cents and sensibility: What economics can learn from the humanities*. Princeton: Princeton University Press.

Muller, C. (1992). The great learning. http://www.acmuller.net/con-dao/greatlearning.html.

Munger, M. C. (2018). *Tomorrow 3.0: Transaction costs and the sharing economy*. Cambridge: Cambridge University Press.

Nietzsche, F. W. (1912). *Twilight of the idols*. In O. Levy (Ed.). Crows Nest: Allen & Unwin. (Original in German, 1889).

Ninh, B. (2012). *The sorrow of war*. New York City: Random House.

Paul, M. (2012). *Frank Ramsey (1903–1930): A Sister's Memoir*. Cambridgeshire: Smith-Gordon.

Pearce, R. (2014). Book review of 'Glimpses of Utopia: A lifetime's education'. *The International Schools Journal, 33*(2), 95–97.

Pecchi, L., & Piga, G. (Eds.). (2008). *Revisiting Keynes: Economic possibilities for our grandchildren*. Cambridge: MIT Press.

Phelps, E. S. (2008). Corporatism and Keynes: His philosophy of growth. In L. Pecchi, & G. Piga (Eds.). *Revisiting Keynes: Economic possibilities for our grandchildren*. Cambridge: MIT Press.
Pine, B. J., & Gilmore, J. H. (2011). *The experience economy*. Cambridge: Harvard Business Press.
Prassl, J. (2018). *Humans as a service: The promise and perils of work in the gig economy*. Oxford: Oxford University Press.
Qian, Y. (2017). *How reform worked in China: The transition from plan to market*. Cambridge: MIT Press.
Robinson, K., & Aronica, L. (2009). *The element: How finding your passion changes everything*. City of Westminster: Penguin.
Romaniuc, R. (2017). Intrinsic motivation in economics: A history. *Journal of Behavioral and Experimental Economics, 67*, 56–64.
Roy, D., & Zeckhauser, R. (2016). Ignorance: literary light on decision's dark corner. In *Routledge Handbook of Behavioral Economics* (pp. 242–261). Abingdon: Routledge.
Samuelson, P. A., & Nordhaus, W. D. (2009). Economics. In *19th International Edition*. New York: McGraw-Hill.
Sasane, A. (2017). *A friendly approach to functional analysis*. Singapore: World Scientific.
Schopenhauer, A. (1901). *The wisdom of life: And other essays*. Rochester: M. Walter Dunne (Original in German, 1851).
Schopenhauer, A. (1969). *The world as will and representation: In two volumes*. United States: Dover Publications (Originally published in 1818, 2nd expanded edition in 1844, 3rd expanded edition in 1859).
Scitovsky, T. (1976). *The joyless economy: An inquiry into human satisfaction and consumer dissatisfaction*. Oxford: Oxford University Press.
Sen, A. (1999). *Development as freedom*. Oxford: Oxford University Press.
Shackle, G. L. S. (1979). *Imagination and the nature of choice*. New York: Columbia University Press.
Sheehy, N. (2004). *Fifty key thinkers in psychology*. Abingdon: Routledge.
Shen, A. (2016). Algorithmic information theory. In *The Routledge Handbook of Philosophy of Information* (pp. 53–59). Abingdon: Routledge.
Shiller, R. J. (2017). Narrative economics. *American Economic Review, 107*(4), 967–1004.
Shiller, R. J. (2019). *Narrative economics: How stories go viral and drive major economic events*. Princeton: Princeton University Press.
Simon, H. A. (1996). *Models of my life*. Cambridge: MIT press.

Simon, H. A. (1997). *Administrative behavior: A study of decision making processes in administrative organizations*, 4th Edition. New York: Free Press.
Sinek, S. (2019). *The infinite game*. New York: Portfolio/Penguin.
Smith, A. ([1759]2002). *The theory of moral sentiments*. In K. Haakonssen (Ed.). Cambridge: Cambridge University Press.
Smith, E. E. (2017). *The power of meaning: Finding fulfillment in a world obsessed with happiness*. New York: Broadway Books.
Smith, V. L., & Wilson, B. J. (2019). *Humanomics: Moral sentiments and the wealth of nations for the twenty-first century*. Cambridge: Cambridge University Press.
Sommerhalder, R., & van Westrhenen, S. C. (1988). *The theory of computability: programs, machines, effectiveness, and feasibility*. Boston: Addison Wesley Publishing Company.
Stigler, G. J., & Becker, G. S. (1977). De gustibus non est disputandum. *The American Economic Review, 67*(2), 76–90.
Sundararajan, A. (2016). *The sharing economy: The end of employment and the rise of crowd-based capitalism*. Cambridge: MIT Press.
Szenberg, M., & Ramrattan, L. (Eds.). (2014). *Eminent economists II: Their life and work philosophies*. Cambridge: Cambridge University Press.
Taleb, N. N. (2007). *The black swan: The impact of the highly improbable*. New York: Random house.
Thompson, E. P. (1963). *The making of the English working class*. London: Victor Gollancz.
Thoreau, H. D. (2004). *Walden and civil disobedience*. New York: Simon and Schuster. (Originally, 1854)
Tobias, R. B. (2011). *20 master plots: And how to build them*. New York City: F+ W Media, Inc.
Veblen, T. (1914). *The Instinct of workmanship and the state of the industrial arts*. New York: Macmillan.
Velupillai, K. (2000). *Computable economics: the Arne Ryde memorial lectures*. Oxford: Oxford University Press.
Velupillai, K. V. (2010). *Computable foundations for economics*. Abingdon: Routledge.
Velupillai, K. V. (2018). *Models of Simon*. Abingdon: Routledge.
Velupillai, K. V., Zambelli, S., & Kinsella, S. (2012). *The Elgar Companion to computable economics*. Cheltenham: Edward Elgar.
Watts, M. (Ed.). (2003). *The literary book of economics: Including readings from literature and drama on economic concepts, issues, and themes*. Wilmington: Intercollegiate Studies Institute.

Wolfram, S. (2002). *A new kind of science*. Champaign: Wolfram media.
Woodmansee, M., & Osteen, M. (2005). *The new economic criticism: Studies at the interface of literature and economics*. Abingdon: Routledge.
Young, L. (1981). *Mathematicians and their times: History of mathematics and mathematics of history*. Amsterdam: Elsevier.
Zambelli, S. (2004). The 40% neoclassical aggregate theory of production. *Cambridge Journal of Economics, 28*(1), 99–120.
Zambelli, S. (2007). A rocking horse that never rocked: Frisch's "propagation problems and impulse problems". *History of Political Economy, 39*(1), 145–166.
Zambelli, S. (2018). The aggregate production function is NOT neoclassical. *Cambridge Journal of Economics, 42*(2), 383–426.
Zambelli, S., & Thalberg, B. (1992). The wooden horse that wouldn't rock: Reconsidering Frisch. In: Velupillai K. (Eds.), *Nonlinearities, Disequilibria and Simulation* (pp. 27–56). London: Palgrave Macmillan.
Zuckoff, M. (2006). *Ponzi's scheme: The true story of a financial legend*. New York City: Random House Trade Paperbacks.

# 6

# A Generalization of Sraffa's Notion of 'Viability' in a 'Land Grabbing' Context

Guglielmo Chiodi

## 1 Preamble

Over the past years, I had several occasions to reflect and to elaborate on Sraffa's notion of 'viability',[1] which consists—as it is stated at the very beginning of his seminal book *Production of Commodities by Means of Commodities* (*PCMC* 1960, p. 5)—in the capacity of a system *being brought* to a self-replacing state, viz. a state in which no deficit appears in any production whatsoever. A 'viable' system is thus a system *in the condition to reproduce itself.*

I am very proud on this very occasion to say that I was very lucky for having greatly benefitted, at different times and places, of the many discussions with Stefano Zambelli and Kumaraswamy (Vela) Velupillai on

[1] Chiodi (1992, 1998, 2010), Chiodi and Ditta (2013). On the notion of 'viability' cfr. also Scazzieri (2018), Cardinale (2018), which address the socio-political dimension of economic structures in a structural change framework, and Bellino (2018).

G. Chiodi (✉)
Sapienza Università di Roma, Rome, Italy
e-mail: guglielmo.chiodi@uniroma1.it


K. Velupillai (ed.), *Keynesian, Sraffian, Computable and Dynamic Economics*,
https://doi.org/10.1007/978-3-030-58131-2_6

Sraffa's thought, in general, and on the aforementioned Sraffa's notion of 'viability', in particular. To both of them I am profoundly grateful for their generous and highly stimulating suggestions, as well as for the strong intellectual stimulus and support they both gave me, which encouraged the writer to make further reflections on that topic.

## 2 Introduction

The field on which I will try to apply (and possibly to generalize) Sraffa's notion of 'viability' in this chapter will be the contemporary phenomenon of Large-Scale Land Acquisitions (LSLAs)—popularly and more appropriately referred to as 'Land Grabbing' (LG).

It essentially consists in buying or leasing abroad vast tracts of agricultural land by government and corporate firms to produce crops.

The recent phenomenon of LG came into being at a high pace and intensity over the last years, particularly since 2008, when an unusual economic and financial crisis, springing from the USA, hit soon afterwards many Western countries.

The most generally recognized factors behind the recent LG can be found in the demographic and environmental pressure, due to population growth, energy policy and climate change, which have greatly contributed in enhancing contemporary deals in LSLAs between companies and governments of some investor countries, on the one hand, and governments of the target countries, on the other. The great majority of the target countries are developing countries, whose communities heavily rely on agriculture for their own livelihood.

The motivations formally given for undertaking investment in target countries are essentially that of closing the gap between the *potential* productivity yield and the *actual* one achieved by the local smallholders through the introduction of new technologies. That would enhance agricultural production to the benefit of both the investor countries and the local population, thereby reducing poverty and alleviating the economic and social conditions of the indigenous people.

Yet, the real reason beneath the projects of the investor countries is generally recognized as that of having access to vast areas of land abroad (through leasing or to own them directly) in order to secure future food *and* water, as well as energy needs, for their own countries, paying little, and in most of the cases not at all, attention to the population of the local smallholders.

However, according to the majority of the research studies in the literature on LG—which will be briefly examined further below—the most striking and dramatic *impact* produced by the processes of LG is that of constantly and heavily putting at high risk and danger the *lives* of millions of people.

It is also worth noting from the very beginning that the phenomenon of LG seems to have not attracted any interest by theoretical economists, whereas agrarian and development economists, sociologists, politics and scientists have instead massively devoted much of their attention.

## 3 'Viability' Within the Context of 'Land Grabbing'

Quite obviously, LG invites reflections on one of the most important aims that every economy should pursue, viz. the achievement and perpetuation of its own reproduction, which means to secure, period after period, the livelihood of its own community. A system which succeeds in that achievement can be said to be 'viable'.

In the case of the LG, however, there is a complication in ascertaining whether the economy is pursuing its own 'viability'—a complication which arises from the *asymmetrical* relation which comes into being between one economy (the investor country) and another (the target country). Within this context, in fact, the analysis of 'viability' becomes far more complicated, for, obviously enough, it crucially depends on which country's viewpoint one chooses to take on. The result in each of the three possible cases (i.e. by considering, in turn, the 'viability' of the investor country, that of the target country and then the 'viability' of both countries taken together) might in general be different from one another.

As LG is a phenomenon covering *all* the continents of the world, the analysis of 'viability' of any two countries taken together would also suggest a possible extension to *the entire globe*, if it would be possible to appropriately select one set of countries as the 'investor' economy, and the remaining set as the 'target' one—by grouping the economies not necessarily on the nationality-based criterion. This further step might perhaps be seen as the ultimate generalization of the notion of 'viability', which might appear far less imaginary by simply considering the pervasive and accelerated process of globalization which has taken place in the world over the last decades.

To accomplish that task, it seems quite natural to make recourse to Sraffa's notion of 'viability', in conjunction with his treatment of 'land', which occupies the whole chapter XI of his book.

One of the reasons to follow that line of research essentially lies in the very disappointing approach, in the opinion of the writer, followed by mainstream economics in tackling with the most serious and urgent problems of contemporary societies—an approach which manifests itself in an ever increasing *restricted vision* it holds, which materializes in the purposed *exclusion* from their theories and models of too many important *human* aspects and features, of which any society is instead generally characterized.

Mainstream economics, in fact, obsessively focuses attention almost exclusively on the *market*, as the pivotal institution *anonymously* and *objectively* governing any society, by making persistent use—it should be added—of unjustified tools and models ultimately based on faulty logical foundations.[2]

Such an approach, it is much worth noticing, is patently in contrast with the richer and far more open one which characterizes, instead, the respective conceptual frameworks of the Classical economists *and* of Sraffa, both of them so abysmally distant from that of mainstream economics.

The aim of this chapter is ultimately addressed to interpreting the recent phenomenon of LG in the light of Sraffa's notion of 'viability'. In

[2] It suffices here to recall the general reviews by Harcourt (1972, 1976), the penetrating papers by Velupillai (2002, 2004, 2008) and by Zambelli (2004, 2018).

so doing, an attempt will be made (1) to *generalize* that very notion in a LG context, (2) to *enlarge* the economic perspective on 'land', a fundamental natural resource for *all* human beings, (3) to *question* the widespread tendency of today's economic profession, *in almost its entirety*, to adopt an *objective* and apparently *value-free* approach.

## 4 An Outline of the Recent Phenomenon of 'Land Grabbing'

In the issue dated May 21, 2009, *The Economist*, in highlighting the recent phenomenon of 'land grabbing'—which started to take place at a very high speed and gigantic dimension at the beginning of the twenty-first century—published an article titled 'Buying farmland abroad—Outsourcing's third wave'. The sub-title summarized in a nutshell what that phenomenon essentially consisted of, and the crucial question naturally arisen from it: 'Rich food importers are acquiring vast tracts of poor countries' farmland. Is this beneficial foreign investment or neo-colonialism?'

The term 'neo-colonialism' can originally be traced back to a statement made by a United Nations' official, Mr. Jacques Diouf, the then director-general of the Food and Agriculture Organisation, with reference to the LG phenomenon: 'The risk is of creating a *neo-colonial* pact for the provision of non-value added raw materials in the producing countries and unacceptable work conditions for agricultural'—as reported by *Financial Times*, August 20, 2008 (italics added), which makes it also evident that the recent phenomenon of LG is an 'outsourcing third wave', after that of manufacturing in the 1980s and information technology in the 1990.

The phenomenon of 'land grabbing' is not new in the history of mankind. It suffices to recall the entire history of colonialism and the enclosures taking place in England between the fifteenth and the seventeenth centuries. What is specifically new in the contemporary phenomenon is its *global* dimension (every continent except Antarctica is being involved), the impressive *vast scale* and *high speed* with which land is brought or leased over the recent years, the *causes and motivations* behind it.[3]

The great impulse which gave rise to a 'land rush' by governments and corporate firms in recent years is mainly due to the *fear* of not being able *to secure* enough supply of food and raw materials for their own countries. That fear has been caused by a multiplicity of reasons: (1) the trade bans imposed by some exporting countries, (2) the recent rises in food prices and their volatility, (3) the increase in oil price and the consequential energy policies adopted by some countries (like the USA and the European Union), which have contributed to increase the global demand of biofuel production, (4) water shortages, due to climate change.[4]

Land is a universally acknowledged *scarce* commodity. Like labour, it cannot be produced by any economic process, but, *unlike* labour, it does not possess the features of reproducibility and mobility of the latter. As a result, some countries try to cultivate their *own* land extensively or intensively, according to the circumstances (although, even in this case, having access to land *abroad* could be sometimes far more economical than cultivating domestic land); in other cases, where land is neither suitable for specific agricultural production nor being susceptible of further extensive or intensive production, some countries try to acquire property rights or leasing on land *abroad*, to meet the needs of their own population.

Usually, the acquiring countries (which can roughly be identified with the northern countries of the globe) are the richest ones, whereas the target countries (by and large the southern countries, whose governments sell property rights or leasing on tracts of land to the acquiring countries) are developing poor countries, having large areas of uncultivated or 'unproductively' cultivated land, quite often 'commons', subjected to customary tenure instead of ordinary written law.

The projects of the acquiring countries, formally intended in making land abroad more 'productive', are *virtually* of the 'win-win' type. They would in fact be highly beneficial to the target countries, to the effect of providing new technology, new seeds, new market and job opportunities,

---

[3] FAO (2009), The World Bank (2011), Rulli et al. (2013), Dell'Angelo, et al. (2016, 2017). Land Matrix (2016) has captured 1204 concluded deals which cover 42.2 million hectares of land, p. vi and 33 million people may potentially be affected by those deals, p. 37.

[4] De Schutter (2011), Akram-Lodhi (2012), Arezki, et al. (2013).

as well as construction of infrastructures, schools and health services. All of this—it should be noted—from the one-sided perspective of the investor countries.[5]

Some important international institutions, such as the World Bank (WB), the International Monetary Fund (IMF) and the World Trade Organization (WTO), have had since long the crucial role of preparing the most appropriate intellectual atmosphere to convey the 'philosophy' of the market-centred economic paradigm—witness the export-oriented policies promoted by the WB and the Structural Adjustment Programs of the IMF.[6]

In so doing, each one of them, according to the respective assigned institutional role, has indirectly but efficaciously paved the way to the transnational land deals, the latter seen as means to access to land via market mechanism, thus encouraging the development of a land market and giving support with financial and technical assistance.[7]

## 5 The Impact of 'Land Grabbing' on Populations and the Environment

The core literature on 'land grabbing' generally agrees that the impact of the recent land rush has been utterly devastating on populations and the environment.[8]

Most of the targeted countries are developing economies whose populations earn their income and make in general their livelihood by working in the agricultural sector. Food is mainly produced by small-scale farms worldwide, which use land on the basis of traditional, customary systems of common property. Moreover, part of the rural population is composed by pastoralists, to whom property rights on land turn out to be absolutely unnecessary. It should also be noted that 'land grabbing' implies at the

[5] FAO (2009).

[6] Bello (2008).

[7] The World Bank (2011), Land Matrix (2016).

[8] Land Research Action Network (2011), Oxfam (2012), Rulli, et al. (2013), Rulli and D'Odorico (2014), Davis, et al. (2014).

same time 'water grabbing' (rainwater and irrigation water), which are an essential input in the production of agricultural food.[9]

The above conditions make rural populations of the targeted countries highly vulnerable. The transition from small-scale farming to large-scale intensive production, in fact, is a quite radical and socially disruptive transformation of a system of production into another. Most of the rural population (smallholders, indigenous people, pastoralists) are dispossessed of, and displaced from, the land they were using before the grab (in many cases with coercion and with violent conflicts). As a result, they are *ipso facto* deprived of all the means necessary for their own survival.[10]

The negative impact on the rural populations of the targeted countries is explicitly admitted even by the World Bank which, with other international institutions, has constantly had a key role to play in deals for land acquisition abroad.

The 2011 report of the World Bank, in fact, having acknowledged the fact that 'although yields on smallholder farms are lower than or equal to those on large farms, often by a large margin, lower yields do not necessarily translate into lower efficiency' and 'there is no strong case to replace smallholder with large-scale cultivation on efficiency grounds', states that (p. 35):

> the new wave of investments creates risks beyond those present in more traditional investments: investors may lack the necessary experience, countries' institutional infrastructure may be ill-equipped to handle an upsurge in investor interest, and weak protection of land rights may lead to uncompensated land loss by existing land users or land being given away well below its true social value. […] In light of these deficiencies, it should not come as a surprise that many investments, not always by foreigners, failed to live up to expectations and, instead of generating sustainable benefits, contributed to asset loss and left local people worse off than they would have been without the investment.[11]

[9] Rulli, et al. (2013).

[10] Dell'Angelo, et al. (2016) have identified three categories of coercion: (a) coercion without manifested conflicts, (b) coercion with non-violent conflicts, (c) coercion with violent conflicts. Out of 27 countries taken into consideration, the first typology of coercion resulted in 34% of the cases, the second for 25% and the third one for 23%.

[11] The World Bank (2011), pp. 70–71.

Further on in that same report it is emphasized that 'even if a project is viable, social impacts need not be positive if local land rights or livelihood are disrupted, net employment generations is low, or if unequal distribution of benefits create social tensions'.[12]

In a more recent report, the World Bank focuses attention on the 'safeguards against land expropriation and the recognition of customary land rights' as 'key to ensure land tenure security'.[13]

## 6 The Notion of 'Viability' in Sraffa and in the Economic Literature

As a preliminary, let us take as a reference Sraffa's single-product industries framework, wherein every commodity is produced by one industry only.

Thus we can write:

$$\mathbf{N} \rightarrow \bar{\mathbf{Q}} \tag{6.1}$$

$\mathbf{N} = n \times n$ input matrix, $\bar{\mathbf{Q}} = n \times n$ diagonal output matrix, $\bar{Q}_{ii} > 0$, $\bar{Q}_{ij} = 0$, $i \neq j$.

It is very much worth noticing, following Sraffa, that the input matrix contains means of production *and* productive consumption mixed together, without any distinction whatsoever between the two components.[14]

The above productive representation will be called an 'economic system' if it contains at least one *basic* commodity. In this case, matrix **N** must contain an irreducible sub-matrix, which will coincide with the whole matrix if *all* products were basic.

A group of *n isolated* 'economic systems' can be assembled together so as to form the input matrix **H** of what might be called an 'economic set',

---

[12] Ibidem, p. 109.

[13] The World Bank (2019), p. 5.

[14] This is also the same feature of the von Neumann model (1937).

which is *not* an 'economic system', because, as a whole, it does *not* possess any basic product. In the case here under consideration we thus have:

$$H = \begin{pmatrix} \mathbf{N}_{11} & \cdots & \mathbf{0} \\ \vdots & \ddots & \vdots \\ \mathbf{0} & \cdots & \mathbf{N}_{nn} \end{pmatrix} \tag{6.2}$$

It is curious that a group of 'economic systems' does not constitute an 'economic system' in itself.

The Sraffa definition of 'viability' can *formally* be given in the following way: $\mathbf{N} \rightarrow \bar{\mathbf{Q}}$ will be called a *viable* 'economic system' if there exists a set of positive multipliers, given by a vector $\mathbf{x} > \mathbf{0}$, such that the net product-vector be *non-negative*, viz.

$$\left(\bar{\mathbf{Q}} - \mathbf{N}^T\right)\mathbf{x} \geqq \mathbf{0} \tag{6.3}$$

In other words, an 'economic system' will be *viable* if it is *capable* of reproducing itself, that is to say, if it is capable to reproduce each basic product in a quantity equal or greater than that employed in the whole system of production.

The above formal definition of 'viability' is quite general, because it comprises 'economic systems' both in a self- as well as in a not-self-replacing state—to use Sraffa's own terminology. The former show either no deficit in any production or a surplus in at least one industry; whereas the latter show *simultaneously* at least one deficit and at least a surplus in some industries. *Non-viable* 'economic systems' are thus those in a non-self-replacing state for which no change in the *proportions* in which the single industries appear in the system representation can possibly eliminate all the existing deficits.[15]

From the input matrix **N** we can *formally* 'detach' the means of production only, in order to compose with the quantities of these

[15] Chiodi (1992, 1998).

commodities another input matrix **M**, leaving aside, in this way, the quantities of the commodities used as productive consumption.

An alternative notion of 'viability' can then be given. The 'economic system' can formally be represented as follows:

$$\mathbf{M},\boldsymbol{\ell} \rightarrow \bar{\mathbf{Q}} \tag{6.4}$$

**M** = input of the means of production, $\boldsymbol{\ell} = n \times 1$ vector of the quantities of labour employed, and it will be 'viable' if there exists a set of positive multipliers, given by a vector $\mathbf{x} > \mathbf{0}$, such that the net product-vector be *strictly positive*, viz.

$$\left(\bar{\mathbf{Q}} - \mathbf{M}^T\right)\mathbf{x} > \mathbf{0} \tag{6.5}$$

However, the two definitions of 'viability', according to expressions (6.3) and (6.5) given above, are *not* easily comparable, for according to the second definition *no constraint is given on the dimension and composition of the subsistence/consumption bundle of the workers* and this imposes the necessity for the 'economic system' of having a surplus. From this viewpoint, therefore, the latter notion of 'viability' is of a purely 'technological' type, because it excludes the crucial social constraint of workers' subsistence, which is instead aptly captured by the Sraffa definition.[16]

The 'technological' definition of 'viability' is precisely that taken into account since its explicit appearance in Hawkins and Simon (1949), and later on in Gale (1960) and Pasinetti (1977), with the appreciable exceptions of Goodwin (1970) and Quadrio-Curzio and Pellizzari (2018).

It should also be noted that according to the 'technological' definition of 'viability' is *ispo facto* excluded an 'economic system' producing with *no surplus*—which is indeed the one contemplated by Sraffa in the first chapter of his 1960 book, in which the notion of a 'viable' system did make its first appearance.

[16] For a wider discussion on this issue cfr. Chiodi (2010).

## 7 Quantities and Prices in the Sraffian Framework

By far the most significant aspect of Sraffa's (1960, p. 3) notion of 'viability'—beyond the analytical aspect dealt with so far—rests substantially in the very circumstance that the commodities which appear as input, in the two-industry table of chapter one of *PCMC*, '[b]oth are used, in part as sustenance for those who work, and for the rest as means of production'. It is particularly worth noticing that the *first* use mentioned by Sraffa is referred to workers' subsistence and only *afterwards* referred to the means of production. Note also that until the introduction of the possibility for the workers to share with the surplus, *no quantitative separation* is being made between the two distinct uses of the input.

The relations expressed by the set of the quantities of the commodities used and produced are called by Sraffa 'the methods of production and productive consumption' (p. 3). They appear from the very beginning of *PCMC* as the *given* initial data representing the 'economic system', thereby structuring the 'inner core' of the analytical Sraffian framework.

They should be thought as a result of complex historical processes, which, over the centuries, have deeply forged the institutions, the laws, the culture, the traditions, the religious attitudes, the language of a society, as well as its specific modes of production.

This way of representing the economy marks a big and significant difference with the traditional (neoclassical) economic theory, which, since the beginning of its foundational period in the last decades of the nineteenth century, has always seen both quantities *and* prices as being essentially determined by the interplay of the anonymous market forces of demand and supply. This is not to say that in Sraffa the market does not have any role to play, but certainly it does not have the role which neoclassical economic theory attributes to it.

From a different perspective, this can be seen by briefly scrutinizing the role of production prices in the Sraffa framework. *Given* the methods of production and productive consumption and, in the presence of a surplus, *given* the existing power relations with their inherent disputes and conflicts on income distribution, the adoption of production prices makes it possible for the *reproduction* of the entire 'economic system', that is the continuation of *the life of the people*, which is *ultimately* the goal that any society should pursue.

The given quantities of the commodities used and produced tie strongly together the members of a community, and the prices of production are but the ultimate reflection of the way through which society tries to achieve its own reproduction. The attention is thus focused on what is 'best' for the *community*, as opposed to on what is 'best' for the *individual* (or a particular constituency).

It must be added that the given quantities used and produced in the production processes should not be seen as a mere devise for representing the economy in any 'objective' way. To put it other way, it should not be considered a purely 'neutral' devise. It reflects instead—in the opinion of the writer—Sraffa's 'vision' of the society and, in this sense, it should be seen as the most appropriate background for a prelude to a critique of economic theory. Indeed, what prima facie appears 'objective data', it actually embeds a strong ideological feature, and rigour and consistency—necessary ingredients in any logical construction—cannot be confused with 'neutrality'.[17]

From this perspective, Pasinetti's (2007, p. 275) 'separation theorem' does not fit well with the thesis already mentioned above. That 'theorem', in fact, 'states that we must make it possible to disengage those investigations that concern the foundational bases of economic relations [...] from those investigations that must be carried out at the level of the actual institutions'. Pasinetti has maintained that in '*Production of Commodities* he [Sraffa] does not rely on any institutional set-up, he does not make reference to any historical context' (p. 192). However, to be more precise, it would be preferable to state that Sraffa does not rely on any *specific* institutional set-up, and that he does not make reference to any *specific* historical context. For example, the 'extremely simple society' contemplated by Sraffa in chapter I of his book reflects a *general* historical context, without any further specification. The introduction of 'the rate of profits' and the class of 'capitalists' in chapter II and the 'money rates

[17] The explicit separation of any value judgment from economics is due to Robbins (1932). On this issue cfr. Chiodi (2019).

of interest' in chapter V, all reflect an institutional set-up which contemplate the recognition of property rights, class division and financial institutions, without the necessity of specifying their particular features.

Pasinetti's 'separation theorem' would have had to distinguish *two different levels of abstraction*, rather than to separate a-historical and a-institutional stages from the historical and institutional ones.

Sraffa's analytical 'core', in fact, belongs to the highest level of abstraction, wherein it is possible to state basic logical propositions; whereas the context *outside* the 'core' belongs to an inferior level of abstraction. However, what might happen *outside* the 'core' (which cannot be stated or explained in the 'logical' way as the propositions belonging to the 'core' can) is as much important as what might happen *inside* it. Sraffa in making his framework *open*, viz. by simultaneously contemplating a 'core' and an outside of it, has definitely shown how economic theory is inherently incomplete—in sharp contrast to the traditional (neoclassical) economic theory whose supporters still believe in its own 'self-sufficiency'.

## 8 The Treatment of 'Land' in the Economic Literature and in Sraffa

Land in the economic literature has generally been treated as that resource generating a rent to the benefit of its owner.

Land occupies a privileged place in the physiocratic thought, as Quesnay's *Tableau Economique* testifies.[18] It is in fact considered the only 'productive' resource because the only one capable of producing *a net product* for society as a whole, as opposed to other resources and labour working in other sectors, which were instead considered 'sterile'.

The Classical economists and Marx also devoted much attention to land as a source of rent accruing to the landowners, especially Ricardo, who laid the foundations for a consistent treatment of land in economic theory.[19]

[18] Cfr. Mirabeau (1760), Tsuru (1942), Meek (1962), Vaggi (1985).

[19] Ricardo (1951), chapter II, Marx (1972), Part VI.

Since the advent of the neoclassical era, land has been simply reduced to a 'factor of production', on the same footing of labour and 'capital'. It would generate a rent to be calculated according to the principle of 'marginal productivity', like any other factor.[20]

Sraffa devoted the entire chapter XI to the treatment of land. He firstly points out that the *scarcity* of the natural resources (like land and mineral deposits) 'enable their owners to obtain a rent' (Sraffa 1960, p. 74). Differently from Ricardo's analysis, he correctly points out that there does not exist a *natural* order of fertility, 'which is not defined independently of the rents' (ibidem, p. 75).

From a *purely analytical* point of view, land is included, in the Sraffa (1960, p.74) framework, 'in the wider definitions of non-basics' for, appearing only on one side of the production-equations, it cannot enter the standard product, neither more nor less than any other non-basic commodity. It might perhaps be added, however, that independently of the analytical position which land assumes within the Sraffa framework, its *substantial role* firmly rests on its being, directly or indirectly, the basis of *all* production processes. This position is very much similar to that of the necessary subsistence of the workers where, once wages include a share of the surplus, its value is added to the 'surplus' wage 'for not tampering with the traditional wage concept' (Sraffa 1960, p. 10). In this way the necessaries of consumption are relegated 'to the limbo of non-basic products' (ibidem). 'Necessaries however are *essentially basic* and if they are prevented from exerting their influence on prices and profits under that label, they must do so in *devious* ways' (ibidem, italics added). Here the importance of the context *outside* the 'core' comes out with great clarity.

Thus, from a wider perspective, it would be improper to attribute to land a second-class or even a marginal role in the production system. Unfortunately, this is just the point of view which Pasinetti (1981) seems

[20] In this connection, may I point out only the single but important exception of Wicksell (1935). It is true that he contributed to the refinement of the marginal productivity theory of income distribution. Nevertheless, he was perhaps the first economist in pointing out the conceptual and analytical *difference* existing between land and labour, on the one hand, and 'capital', on the other. In addition, he was always particularly insisting on the fact—in line with Böhm-Bawerk's view—that in any 'reduction' to dated quantities of the original input, land had to be taken *always* into account together with labour.

to take when, in his multi-sectoral model of economic growth, he declares not to take into considerations scarce resources to 'avoid unnecessary complications', because being included 'in the wider definitions of non-basics'—as Sraffa has stated—they 'do not affect the rest of the analysis' (pp. 23–25).

The above Pasinetti approach to land (and to natural resources in general) is rightly criticized by Quadrio-Curzio and Pellizzari (2018, p. 672), who aptly emphasize that (1) scarce resources are not an unnecessary complication in a multi-sectoral model, because they 'deeply transform the dynamics of the economy', (2) scarce resources, independently of an optimal allocation point of view, should be considered for the effects they produce on income distribution and the choice of techniques.

As will be seen presently, in fact, natural resources do have a fundamental role to play in the economy.

Let us take a single-product industries framework representing an economy producing $n + 1$ *basic* products with a surplus: $n$ non-agricultural products plus one homogeneous agricultural product $c$ (corn). Corn is produced on $k$ different qualities of land, each one with its own method of production, and $t$ is the number of qualities totally available in the economy ($t < k$).[21]

The production equations of the economy can thus be written as follows:

$$\mathbf{M}^{na}\mathbf{p}(1+r)+\boldsymbol{\ell}^{na}\, w=\bar{\mathbf{Q}}^{na}\,\mathbf{p}^{na}\ (\mathrm{A})$$

$$\mathbf{M}^{a}\mathbf{p}(1+r)+\boldsymbol{\ell}^{a}\, w+\hat{\mathbf{P}}\hat{\Lambda}=\bar{\mathbf{Q}}^{a}\, p_{n+1}\ (\mathrm{B})$$

$\mathbf{M}^{na}$= $n \times n + 1$ input matrix of non-agricultural products, $\mathbf{p} = n + 1 \times 1$ price vector, $r$ = rate of profits, $\boldsymbol{\ell}^{na} = n \times 1$ vector of labour employed in non-agricultural production, $w$ = wage rate, $\bar{\mathbf{Q}}^{na} = n \times n$ diagonal output matrix of non-agricultural products, $\mathbf{p}^{na} = n \times 1$ price vector of non-agricultural products, $\mathbf{M}^{a} = k \times n + 1$ input matrix of agricultural production, $\boldsymbol{\ell}^{a} = k \times 1$ vector of labour employed in the agricultural production, $\hat{\mathrm{P}} = k \times k$ diagonal matrix of the rents, $\hat{\Lambda} = k \times k$ diagonal

[21] Without loss of generality, the case of extensive rent only will be considered.

matrix of the $k$ qualities of land, $\bar{\mathbf{Q}}^a$ = $k \times k$ diagonal output matrix of agricultural products, $p_{n+1}$ = the price of the agricultural product.

(A) and (B) together form a system of $n + k$ equations containing $n + k + 3$ unknowns: $n + 1$ prices, $k$ rents, $w$ and $r$. The price of the agricultural product $p_{n+1}$ can be chosen as a unit of value ($p_{n+1} = 1$) and income distribution can be determined by putting $r$ equal to a known number $r'$. Having just one degree of freedom left, and assuming that the *last* of the $k$ processes takes place on the *least* productive land which does not yield any rent ($\rho_k = 0$), we can write the following equation:

$$\rho_1 \cdot \rho_2 \ldots \rho_k = 0 \, (\text{C})$$

The $n$ equations of (A) and the *last* equation of (B) can together determine the $n + 1$ prices, with no need to referring to the other agricultural processes. To determine the $k - 1$ rents, it suffices to put the prices in the first $k - 1$ equations of (B).

All the above is simply a concise presentation of Sraffa's treatment of land, on which some Sraffian-inspired economists have produced a vast literature by going many steps further, most of them consisting in valuable refinements and assessments of what Sraffa implicitly already said or left open to a subsequent enquiry.[22] In all the instances—it should be noted—the economists have been focusing only on *one single* 'economic system' and they are mainly treated the issue on essentially *analytical grounds*.

## 9 'Land' in a Wider Context

We have to turn again to matrix (6.2) of Sect. 6 representing the input matrix of an 'economic set' of 'economic systems'. To make things as simple as possible without any loss of generality, it is convenient to select just two 'economic systems', call them $S_1$ and $S_2$ respectively. The

[22] Cfr. Quadrio-Curzio (1967, 1980, 1987), Quadrio-Curzio and Pellizzari (2018), Montani (1975), Kurz (1978), Parrinello (1982), Fratini (2016).

corresponding input matrices of the two 'economic systems' are $\mathbf{N}_1$ and $\mathbf{N}_2$ which, once put both together, give rise to the input matrix $\mathbf{Z}$:

$$\mathbf{Z} = \begin{pmatrix} \mathbf{N}_1 & \mathbf{0} \\ \mathbf{0} & \mathbf{N}_2 \end{pmatrix}$$

We can imagine $S_1$ as the 'investor country' (or a set of investor countries) and $S_2$ as the 'target country' (or a set of target countries).

Before any 'land rush' takes place, we can suppose that both of them are 'viable' systems. It can be supposed that the economy of $S_1$ be represented by the set of equations (A) and (B) of Sect. 8 immediately above.

Due to the scarcity of land, and given the possibility of acquiring land more cheaply abroad than domestically, $S_1$ suddenly starts a deal for the acquisition of land in the 'economic system' $S_2$ in order to secure food to its own population. One of the effects produced by the acquisition of land abroad will be the coming into being of a rent for $S_1$, in the amount far greater than the highest rent already accruing to the owners of the most 'fertile' land in $S_1$—being the price of the agricultural product still determined by the least productive land in the mother country. This is the direct consequence, for $S_1$, of having the possibility of acquiring land at ridiculous prices, and to pay, in the case, extremely low wages to local labourers for agricultural production, compared with those which are paid at home. It should also be noted that the behaviour of the corporate firms or the government of $S_1$ might be interpreted as a practical result of the traditional (neoclassical) economic theory, characterized by market-centred 'philosophy' and maximizing behaviour of the agents, in which one of the basic rule is the *commoditization* of everything.[23]

On the other side, the effects of land grabbing produced by $S_1$ on $S_2$ are generally devastating—as they have been described in Sects. 4 and 5. The people of $S_2$ will not have their land any more to farm on and from which to get the means for their own livelihood. Hence $S_2$ will cease to be 'viable'. Far more than this, however, they are *deprived* of their land which represents not only the *material* source of their means of sustenance but,

[23] On this specific point cfr. Chiodi (2018).

above all, a strong and highly valued *symbol* of their life, of their traditions, of their culture, of their identity as a community and of the environment in which they have been living for generations.

If we tried to apply the notion of 'viability' to the 'economic set' composed by $S_1$ and $S_2$ *after* land grabbing has produced all its effects, we would be forced to admit that one system is still 'viable' whereas the other one not any more. Contemporaneous 'land grabbing', which is taking place on a *global scale*, might be represented in a similar way.

John Steinbeck, in illuminating passages of his much celebrated *The Grapes of Wrath* (a novel which captures the tragic effects on human beings of the Great Depression better than any economist has done so far), made it evident that the far more *symbolic value* which the American people, forced to abandon their own land and to emigrate to the West, attributed to their land—especially when it is contrasted with its being a purely *material* means for the production of food and non-food crops:

> The houses were left vacant on the land, and the land was vacant because of this. Only the tractor shed of corrugated iron, silver and gleaming, were alive; and they were alive with metal and gasoline and oil, the disk of the plows shining. The tractors had lights shining, for there is no day and night for a tractor and the disks turn the earth in the darkness and they glitter in the daylight. And when a horse stops work and goes into the barn there is life and vitality left, there is a breathing and a warmth, and the feet shift on the straw, and the jaws champ on the hay and the ears and the eyes are alive. There is a warmth of life in the barn, and the heat and the smell of life. But when the motor of a tractor stops it is as dead as the ore it came from. The heat goes out of it like the living heat that leaves a corpse. (Steinbeck 2002, p. 115)

> For nitrates are not the land, nor phosphates and the length of fiber in the cotton is not the land. Carbon is not a man, nor salt nor water nor calcium. He is all of these, but he is much more, much more; and the land is so much more than its analysis. That man who is more than his chemistry, walking on the earth, turning his plow point for a stone, dropping his handles to slide over an outcropping kneeling in the earth to eat his lunch; that man who is more than his elements knows the land that is more than its analysis. (Ibidem, p. 116)

> How can we live without our lives? How will we know it's us without our past? No. Leave it. Burn it.
>
> They sat and looked at it and burned it into their memories. How'll it be not to know what land's outside the door? How if you wake up in the night and know—and know the willow tree's not there? Can you live without the willow tree? Well, no, you can't. (Ibidem, pp. 89–89)

The factitious distinction between 'economic' and 'non-economic' aspects immediately reminds one Pigou's distinction between Welfare and *economic* Welfare, on which criticism has rightly been raised, though it does not seem to have left any remarkable trace in contemporary economic thought.

Hicks (1959) may perhaps be considered the economist that better than others has properly understood the *unnatural* characteristic of that distinction. With regard to Pigou's distinction, he writes the following propositions, which seem to me the best concluding remarks of the present chapter.

> The economist, as such, is still allowed, and even encouraged, to keep within his 'own' frontiers; if he has shown that a particular course of action is to be recommended, *for economic reasons*, he has done his job. I would now say that if he limits his function in that manner, he does not rise to his responsibilities. It is impossible to make 'economic' proposals that do not have 'non-economic aspects', as the Welfarist would call them; when the economist makes a recommendation, he is responsible for it in the round; all aspects of that recommendation, whether he chooses to label them economic or not, are of his concern. (Hicks 1959, p. 137)

## References

Akram-Lodhi, A. H. (2012). Contextualising Land Grabbing: Contemporary Land Deals, the Global Subsistence Crisis and the World Food System. *Canadian Journal of Development Studies, 33*(2), 119–142.

Arezki, R., Deininger, K., & Selod, H. (2013). What Drives the Global 'Land Rush'? *The World Bank Economic Review, 29*(2), 207–233.

Bellino, E. (2018). Viability, Reproducibility and Returns in Production Price Systems. *Economia Politica—Journal of Analytical and Institutional Economics, 35*(3), 845–861.

Bello, W. (2008). How to Manufacture a Global Food Crisis: The Destruction of Agriculture in Developing Countries. *The Asian-Pacific Journal, 6*(5), 1–8.

Cardinale, I. (2018). A Bridge Over Troubled Water: A Structural Political Economy of Vertical Integration. *Structural Change and Economic Dynamics, 46*, 172–179.

Chiodi, G. (1992). On Sraffa's Notion of Viability. *Studi Economici, 46*, 5–23.

Chiodi, G. (1998, February). On Non-Self-Replacing States. *Metroeconomica, 49*(1), 97–107.

Chiodi, G. (2010). The Means of Subsistence and the Notion of 'Viability' in Sraffa's Surplus Approach. In S. Zambelli (Ed.), *Computable, Constructive & Behavioural Economic Dynamics. Essays in Honour of Kumaraswamy (Vela) Velupillai* (pp. 318–330). Abingdon: Routledge.

Chiodi, G. (2018). Interpreting Global Land and Water Grabbing Through Two Rival Economic Paradigms. *Academicus International Scientific Journal*, Entrepreneurship Training Center Albania, issue 18, pp. 42–52.

Chiodi, G. (2019). Sraffa's Silenced Revival of the Classical Economists and of Marx. In A. Sinha (Ed.), *A Reflection on Sraffa's Revolution in Economic Theory*. London: Palgrave Macmillan.

Chiodi, G., & Ditta, L. (2013). Sraffa and Keynes: Two Ways of Making a Revolution in Economic Theory. In E. S. Levrero, A. Palumbo, & A. Stirati (Eds.), *Sraffa and the Reconstruction of Economic Theory* (Vol. I, pp. 218–240). Basingstoke: Palgrave Macmillan.

Davis, K. F., et al. (2014). Land Grabbing: A Preliminary Quantification of Economic Impact on Rural Livelihoods. *Population Environment, 36*, 180–192.

De Schutter, O. (2011). How Not to Think of Land-Grabbing: Three Critiques of Large-Scale Investments in Farmland. *The Journal of Peasant Studies, 38*(2), 249–279.

Dell'Angelo, J., D'Odorico, P., Rulli, M. C., & Marchand, P. (2016). The Tragedy of the Grabbed Commons: Coercion and Dispossession in the Global Land Rush. *World Development, 92*, 1–12.

Dell'Angelo, J., et al. (2017). Threats to Sustainable Development Posed by Land and Water Grabbing. *Science Direct, 26*, 120–128.

FAO. (2009, June). *From Land Grab to Win-Win*. Policy Brief 4.

Fratini, S. M. (2016). Rent as a Share of Product and Sraffa's Price Equations. *Cambridge Journal of Economics, 40*, 599–613.
Gale, D. (1960). *The Theory of Linear Economic Models*. New York: McGraw-Hill.
Goodwin, R. M. (1970). *Elementary Economics from the Higher Standpoint*. Cambridge: Cambridge University Press.
Harcourt, G. C. (1972). *Some Cambridge Controversies in the Theory of Capital*. London: Cambridge University Press.
Harcourt, G. C. (1976). The Cambridge Controversies: Old Ways and Old Horizons—Or Dead End? *Oxford Economic Papers, 28*, 25–65.
Hawkins, D., & Simon, H. A. (1949). Note: Some Conditions of Macroeconomic Stability. *Econometrica, 17*, 245–248.
Hicks, J. R. (1959). Manifesto on Welfarism. In *Essays in World Economics*, Clarendon Press, Oxford, reprinted with modifications as 'A Manifesto' in Hicks, J. R. 1981. *Wealth and Welfare, Collected Essays on Economic Theory*, vol. I, Oxford: Basil Blackwell, 135–141.
Kurz, H. D. (1978). Rent Theory in a Multisectoral Model. *Oxford Economic Papers, 30*(1), 16–37.
Land Matrix. (2016). *International Land Deals for Agriculture*. Bern: Centre for Development and Environment, University of Bern, Bern Open Publishing.
Land Research Action Network. (2011). Introduction: Global Land Grabs. Investments, Risks and Dangerous Legacies. *Development, 54*(1), 5–11.
Marx, K. (1972). *Capital*, Volume III. London: Lawrence & Wishart. (Originally published in 1894.)
Meek, R. L. (1962). *The Economics of Physiocracy—Essays and Translations*. London: George Allen and Unwin.
Mirabeau, V. R. (1760). Tableau Economique Avec Ses Explications par François Quesnay. L'Ami Des Hommes, Vol. II, Part VI.
Montani, G. (1975). Scarce Natural Resources and Income Distribution. *Metroeconomica, 27*, 68–101.
Oxfam. (2012, October). *Our Land, Our Lives*. Oxfam Briefing Note.
Parrinello, S. (1982). Terra (Introduction and Part II). In Lunghini (ed.), *Dizionario Critico di Economia Politica*. Torino: Boringhieri. (English Excerpt in ed. Kregel J., *Distribution, Effective Demand and International Economic Relations*. London: Macmillan, 186–199.)
Pasinetti, L. L. (1977). *Lectures on The Theory of Production*. London and Basingstoke: The Macmillan Press Ltd..

Pasinetti, L. L. (1981). *Structural Change and Economic Growth. A Theoretical Essay on the Dynamics of the Wealth of Nations.* Cambridge: Cambridge University Press.

Pasinetti, L. L. (2007). Keynes and the Cambridge Keynesians. In *A 'Revolution in Economics' to be Accomplished.* Cambridge: Cambridge University Press.

Quadrio-Curzio, A. (1967). *Rendita e Distribuzione in un Modello Economico Plurisettoriale.* Milano: Giuffrè.

Quadrio-Curzio, A. (1980). Rent, Income Distribution and Order of Efficiency and Rentability. In L. L. Pasinetti (Ed.), *Essays on the Theory of Joint Production* (pp. 219–240). London: Macmillan.

Quadrio-Curzio, A. (1987). Land Rent. In J. Eatwell, M. Milgate, & P. Newman (Eds.), *The New Palgrave Dictionary of Economics.* London: Macmillan.

Quadrio-Curzio, A., & Pellizzari, F. (2018). Political Economy of Resources, Technologies, and Rent. In I. Cardinale & R. Scazzieri (Eds.), *The Palgrave Handbook of Political Economy* (pp. 657–704). London: Macmillan.

Ricardo, D. (1951). *On the Principles of Political Economy and Taxation,* Vol. I. *The Works and Correspondence of David Ricardo,* ed. Piero Sraffa with the Collaboration of M. H. Dobb. Cambridge: Cambridge University Press. (Originally Published in 1817.)

Robbins, L. (1932). *An Essay on the Nature and Significance of Economic Science.* London: Macmillan and Co., Ltd, 2nd ed. 1935.

Rulli, M. C., & D'Odorico, P. (2014). Food Appropriation Through Large Scale Land Acquisitions. *Environmental Research Letters, 9*(6), 1–8.

Rulli, M. C., Saviori, A., & D'Odorico, P. (2013). Global Land and Water Grabbing. *Proceedings of the National Academy of Sciences, 110*(3), 892–897.

Scazzieri, R. (2018). Political Economy of Economic Theory. In I. Cardinale & R. Scazzieri (Eds.), *The Palgrave Handbook of Political Economy* (pp. 193–233). London: Macmillan.

Sraffa, P. (1960). *Production of Commodities by Means of Commodities. Prelude to a Critique of Economic Theory.* Cambridge: Cambridge University Press.

Steinbeck, J. (2002). *The Grapes of Wrath.* New York: Penguin Books. (Originally Published in 1939.)

The Economist. (2009, May 21). Buying Farmaland Abroad.

The Financial Times. (2008, August 20). UN Warns of Food 'Neo-Colonialism'.

The World Bank. (2011). *Rising Global Interest in Farmland.* Washington, DC.

The World Bank. (2019). *Enabling the Business of Agriculture 2019.* Washington, DC.

Tsuru, S. (1942). On Reproduction Schemes. In P. M. Sweezy (Ed.), *The Theory of Capitalist Development* (pp. 365–374). New York: Oxford University Press.
Vaggi, G. (1985, December). A Physiocratic Model of Relative Prices and Income Distribution. *The Economic Journal, 95*(380), 928–947.
Velupillai, K. (2002). Effectivity and Constructivity in Economic Theory. *Journal of Economic Behavior and Organization, 49*, 307–325.
Velupillai, K. (2004). Rational Expectations Equilibria: A Recursion Theoretic Tutorial. In K. Velupillai (Ed.), *Macroeconomic Theory and Economic Policy: Essays in Honour of Jean-Paul Fitoussi* (pp. 167–188). London: Routledge.
Velupillai, K. (2008). Sraffa's Economics in Non-Classical Mathematical Modes. In G. Chiodi & L. Ditta (Eds.), *Sraffa or An Alternative Economics* (pp. 275–294). Basingstoke: Palgrave Macmillan.
von Neumann, J. (1937). Über ein ökonomisches Gleichungssystem und eine Verallgemeinerung des Brouwerschen Fixpunktsatzes. In K. Menger (Ed.), *Ergebnisse eines mathematischen Kolloquiums* (1935–1936), Heft 8. Leipzig und Wien: Franz Deuticke, pp. 73–83. English Translation 1945 in *The Review of Economic Studies*, Vol. 13, 1–9.
Wicksell, K. (1935 [1901]). Föreläsningar i Nationalekonomi, Första delen: Teoritisk Nationalekonomi, Lund. English Edition 1935: *Lectures on Political Economy*, Translated from the Swedish by E. Classen and Edited with an Introduction by Lionel Robbins, Vol. I. New York: The Macmillan Company.
Zambelli, S. (2004). The 40% Neoclassical Aggregate Theory of Production. *Cambridge Journal of Economics, 28*, 99–120.
Zambelli, S. (2018). The Aggregate Production Function is NOT Neoclassical. *Cambridge Journal of Economics, 42*, 383–426.

# 7

# The Sea Battle Tomorrow: The Identity of Reflexive Economic Agents

John B. Davis

## 1 The Identity of Reflexive Economic Agents

Zambelli in many important contributions demonstrates that economic systems function in an intrinsically dynamical way. This raises the question: what sort of economic agents inhabit such systems? This chapter proposes we understand such agents as reflexive and self-adjusting.[1] Reflexive economic agents continually revise their expectations of the

Modified for this volume
Originally presented as a plenary paper presented at the Third International Economic Philosophy Conference, Aix-en-Provence, France, June 2016.

[1] The chapter is intended as a contribution to the Zambelli Festschrift honoring his many important scholarly contributions.

J. B. Davis (✉)
Marquette University, Milwaukee, WI, USA

University of Amsterdam, Amsterdam, Netherlands
e-mail: John.davis@mu.edu; john.davis@marquette.edu



K. Velupillai (ed.), *Keynesian, Sraffian, Computable and Dynamic Economics*,
https://doi.org/10.1007/978-3-030-58131-2_7

future and continually adjust their behavior to those changing expectations. This chapter develops a conception of reflexive economic agents as an alternative to the standard utility conception of economic agents and explains their individual identity terms of how they adjust to change, rather than in terms of fixed preferences. The idea that identity might lie in change rather than fixity may at first appear paradoxical, but I draw on Herbert Simon and the idea of self-organization to motivate it. Simon dismissed the exogenous preferences utility function representation of agents as inadequate to the task of explaining behavior in complex, changing environments (Simon 1956, p. 138), and recommended we replace it with a conception of endogenous agents whose "behavior is shaped by a scissors whose blades are the structure of task environments and the computational capabilities of the actor" (Simon 1990, p. 7). I use this idea to extend Simon's idea of self-organizing systems to agents, reasoning that just as he thought we ought to explain the behavior of complex systems "in terms of the concepts of feedback and homeostasis" (Simon 1962, p. 467), so we should also explain the nature of economic agents "in terms of the concepts of feedback and homeostasis." Indeed, I argue that treating complex economic processes as reflexive and self-organizing entails we also should explain agents and their behavior as reflexive and self-organizing.

Needless to say, the identity focus of this chapter departs from the main concern with Simon's thinking associated with his idea of bounded rationality (cf. Grüne-Yanoff et al. 2014).[2] I agree that explaining bounded rationality is important to economics, but my view is that a bounded rationality and a bounded individuality are two sides of one issue (Davis 2015). Since the utility function representation of individual identity is formally derived from the axiomatic representation of preferences, behavioral anomalies associated with the latter imply we lack an adequate definition of what individuals are. Indeed, how boundedly rational individuals can or should be explained is precisely the issue in a recent symposium and exchange in *Journal of Economic Methodology* between Gerardo Infante, Guilhem Lecouteux, and Robert Sugden and Daniel Hausman

[2] See the special December 2014 issue of the *Journal of Economic Methodology* on bounded rationality and the Grüne-Yanoff, Marchionni, and Moscati introduction to the issue.

regarding 'preference purification'—or how we might "reconstruct individuals' underlying or *latent* preferences by simulating what they would have chosen, had they not been subject to reasoning imperfections" (Infante et al. 2016a, p. 6; cf. Hausman 2016; cf. Infante et al. 2016b).[3] The symposium debates whether bounded rationality implies a dualistic view of the self and focuses on the idea that agents weigh their options rather than simply respond to them. In my view, this asks, in Simon's terms, whether boundedly rational individuals are self-organizing, and this is the issue I consequently investigate in this chapter, if in a different connection than the symposium.

The argument of this chapter, however, does not start with individual agents but with discussion of two characterizations of the economy as a whole—the standard static equilibrium conception and an alternative dynamic economic process conception. My view is that the problematic character of the utility conception and the advantages of a reflexive agent conception are respectively tied to the problematic character of the standard static equilibrium conception and the advantages of the dynamic process conception. I thus begin in Sect. 2 with a critical review of standard equilibrium thinking using Aristotle's classic sea battle tomorrow problem and argue that the standard view employs an equilibrium-shock model that cannot explain time in a before-and-after sense because it employs a closed systems view of the economy. In Sect. 3, I turn to the idea of a reflexive economic process and use the truth-reversing properties of self-fulfilling prophecies as a special kind of reflexive judgment to show how reflexive economic systems are open process systems in which behavior has a before-and-after character. I provide a causal model of how a reflexive economic system operates through feedback channels, characterize open systems as non-ergodic on reflexivity grounds, and finally return to Aristotle's sea battle problem.

Section 4 discusses the utility conception of the agent and argues that if we say that the economy functions as an open, reflexive process, then it is misguided to think preferences should be complete, unless agents construct them as such themselves. Alternatively, it seems we should rather

[3] The expression 'preference purification' is Hausman's (2012), though see his many caveats, especially in Hausman (2016).

ask what sort of choice behavior is consistent with how we understand action and time. I characterize this behavior as adjustment behavior, which introduces the following section's treatment of reflexive economic agents. In Sect. 5, following Simon, I first explain adjustment behavior in terms of its moving to stopping points. I then advance a general account of individual agent identity in which an endogenous shock event disrupts an existing basis on which agents' individual identities operate, and their adjustment involves them self-organizing themselves on some new basis on which their individual identities subsequently operate. I give four examples from the literature to show how different models of behavior emphasize change in the sub-personal and/or supra-personal dimensions of identity, and then use the idea of self-defeating prophecies to characterize agents' own orientation on their identities. Section 6 comments briefly on the chapter's arguments.

## 2 Standard Theory's Equilibrium-Shock Model and Time

The standard Nash definition of equilibrium in economics is defined as a state of affairs fully at 'rest,' meaning no agent has an interest in deviating from the allocation of resources and strategies associated with that state. That is, it is a state of perfect coordination of all agents' plans and the idea of a perfectly static state of affairs. Consider the application of this conception to the Walrasian understanding of a general equilibrium of markets, the dominant framework employed by economists to explain the market economy. Equilibrium is then a perfectly static state of affairs in the infrequently appreciated sense that, according to the Sonnenschein-Mantel-Debreu results regarding multi-market general equilibria, equilibria generally cannot be shown to be stable (Rizvi 2006). This means that the standard equilibrium conception cannot explain movements from out-of-equilibrium to equilibrium, or how an economy gets into equilibrium, and thus refers to a perfectly static state of affairs in the further sense that it lacks any *internal* principle of motion. An equilibrium just is, full stop, as shown by the fact that only existence (and even not the uniqueness) of equilibrium can be shown. This renders comparative static analysis, the work-horse of standard theory, essentially meaningless, because comparative static analysis is about getting into a new equilibrium given a 'shock' to an old equilibrium. But if the theory lacks any *internal* principle of motion associated with how an economy gets into equilibrium, does the idea of shocks suggest a theory of *externally* caused motion associated with how an economy can get *out* of equilibrium?

My hypothesis is that the standard view of equilibrium as a perfectly static state of affairs with no internal principle of motion renders the 'equilibrium-shock' model of external motion philosophically problematic. To argue this, I claim that the 'equilibrium-shock' model of motion cannot address an ancient philosophical problem associated with the relation of truth claims to time, which first emerged as the problem of future contingents advanced by Aristotle in his famous sea battle tomorrow example (Aristotle 1963). Future contingents are statements about future states of affairs that are neither necessarily true nor false today. For Aristotle, that a sea battle will not be fought tomorrow is neither necessarily true nor false today. Suppose, then, that a sea battle will not be fought tomorrow. If a sea battle will not be fought tomorrow, then it was true yesterday that it will not be fought tomorrow. Yet since all past truths are necessary truths, it must also be necessarily true today that a sea battle will not be fought tomorrow. However, this conclusion is fatalistic and runs counter to our intuitions about the future being open. Thus any theory that employs future contingents needs an answer to Aristotle.

Consider the standard 'equilibrium-shock' model of external motion regarding how an economy can get out of equilibrium. A shock is an event in time because it differentiates before and after. On the one hand, then, from the perspective of a given equilibrium, a shock event is a future contingent state of affairs, something that could occur, and as such its occurrence should be neither necessarily true nor false. On the other hand, given that an equilibrium is a perfectly static state of affairs, shocks are fully external to any given equilibrium configuration. Thus from the perspective of any given equilibrium configuration, shocks necessarily do not occur. Equilibrium is forever. But then without shocks there is no differentiation of time into before and after, so the 'equilibrium-shock' model fails as a theory of externally caused motion. Note also that the failure of this conception is due to the lack of any internal principle of motion in the standard equilibrium conception, which as a fully complete, static representation of the economy closes off any role for external causal factors. Just as necessarily there can be no sea battle tomorrow, so there can never be equilibrium shocks tomorrow.

Aristotle, in fact, similarly diagnosed the problem of future contingents as a problem of completeness, specifically, completeness with respect to the scope of application of the logical principle of bivalence—the idea that every statement must be either true or false—to any and all statements irrespective of their temporal dimensions. His solution to the problem and escape from fatalism were to say that the principle of bivalence applies to the future differently than it applies to the past and the present, though what he meant by this and what philosophers have argued this could mean is much disputed in the history of logic and philosophy (see Rice 2014), and will not detain me here. Instead, in the next section I will discuss why we cannot always say that a statement about the future is true or false when we operate with an open process conception of the economy, and here only comment on why it may seem odd for me to have used the problem of future contingents to comment on standard equilibrium theory.

That oddness, I believe, comes from combining a discussion of how truth is determined with the mathematics of equilibrium determination. A Nash representation of a set of equilibrium strategies models a mathematical solution to a set of behavioral functions. That it 'models' that solution and its attendant representation of 'behavior' tells us that the empirical truth or falsity of the propositions involved is of no particular importance, and indeed can even be set aside. Rather, the main thing that is important about that representation of agents' behavior is that it be mathematically consistent in the sense of producing a solution to a set of equations.[4] Indeed, the mathematical utility function representation of agent behavior is not meant to be evaluated according to how well it describes people's behavior, but according to its mathematical tractability,

[4] Hausman makes essentially this same point in connection with his distinction between theories and models (1992, pp. 70–82). Boumans does as well in discussion of models (2015). Lawson makes the point in relation to the goals of consistency and realisticness (2013).

so the common complaint that this representation of agents is unrealistic basically aims at the wrong target, at least according to its proponents.

The problem that Aristotle's sea battle problem points us toward, then, is the sharp divorce in mainstream economics between the logic of truth and the mathematics of equilibrium determination. What I conclude from this, however, is not that we ought to abandon mathematical representations, nor certainly that claims about the realism of economic theory are of no philosophical importance, but rather that realism and a concern with how truth is determined ought to constrain and determine the nature of mathematical reasoning in economics. In particular, then, I recommend that we abandon mathematical representations of the economy that preclude employing before-and-after treatments of time in favor of mathematical representations that allow for this.[5]

However, I leave the task of advancing alternative mathematical representations of the economy to others, and in the following section give a philosophical characterization of the economy as an open or endogenous process rather than as the closed system such as standard equilibrium theory employs. There of course exists considerable philosophical and methodological literature regarding the distinction between open and closed types of systems in economics, much of which emphasizes uncertainty, but I adopt a somewhat different entry point on the subject from many others by developing the open-closed distinction in terms of the idea of reflexive economic processes driven by the behavior of reflexive economic agents. This will in turn introduce my discussion of reflexive economic agents in Sect. 5. In the following section, then, I will emphasize how an open reflexive economic process conception makes action and time central to the explanation of economic systems, and offers one way of addressing Aristotle's problem of future contingents.

---

[5] In my opinion (and it is just an opinion), an alternative mathematical representation of the economic process that accommodates a before-and-after treatment of time involves an algorithmic type of mathematics (cf. e.g., Velupillai 2011).

## 3 The Reflexive Economic Process Conception and Time

A reflexive economic process is one in which agents form expectations and beliefs about the future based on their understanding of the world, and this influences their actions in the present, which in turn influences future states of the world. The conception of the world as a reflexive economics process is thus a conception of action framed in before-and-after terms. All economics, then, is in principle concerned explaining the world as a reflexive economic process, since economic agents are assumed to form expectations and beliefs about the future that affect their actions in the present.

At the same time, the standard rationality theory treatment of equilibrium as a state of affairs ultimately at 'rest' negates this before-and-after temporal dimension of action, both in macroeconomics via the idea of rational expectations and in microeconomics via the idea of optimal or Bayesian (and least-square) learning. In the macro case of rational expectations agents' expectations regarding the future are on average consistent with the correct model of the world. In the micro case of optimal or Bayesian learning agents' rational beliefs about the future smoothly converge on the correct model of the world. When agents' expectations and beliefs regarding the future are rational or on average consistent with the correct model of the world, and when agents converge smoothly on the correct model of the world, then the economy simply achieves the equilibrium values inherent in agents' model of the world as if time did not matter. Nominally agents' expectations of the future still influence their actions in the present, but this occurs in such a benign way that one can ignore it and proceed as if there were no temporal dimension to behavior.

This standard view, then, can nonetheless be represented in causal terms so as to distinguish the direct effects of people's actions on the world associated with agents' models of the world and a feedback channel associated with how agents' expectations/learning affect their models of the world. Agents' actions $a$ can then be said to have direct effects on the world $b$, or $a \rightarrow b$:

$$a \rightarrow b \tag{7.1}$$

Thus, (7.1) represents agents' model of the world. When agents form rational expectations or optimally learn about this causal relation $a \rightarrow b$, and act on this basis, then the $a \rightarrow b$ relation acts reflexively on itself, and makes that model of the world self-confirming:

$$a \rightarrow b \rightarrow (a \rightarrow b) \tag{7.2}$$

Then the combined overall effects (=>) of the direct causal model (7.1) and the reflexive feedback channel (7.2) produce both $b$ and ($a \rightarrow b$):

$$a \text{ and } a \rightarrow b \text{ and } a \rightarrow b \rightarrow (a \rightarrow b) \Rightarrow b \text{ and } (a \rightarrow b) \tag{7.3}$$

Consequently, since $a \rightarrow b$ and ($a \rightarrow b$) exhibit the same direct effect of $a$ on $b$, the feedback channel only plays a nominal role that can be ignored, the process is closed, and the passage of time is effectively negated.

Contrast this with the case of an open, endogenous economic process where expectations are not rational and learning is not optimal. Agents' actions $a$ have direct effects on $b$, but since agents' expectations and learning do not confirm (7.1), the feedback channel changes the nature of the relation between $a$ and $b$ such that (7.2) is replaced as follows:

$$a \rightarrow b \rightarrow (a \rightarrow b)' \tag{7.4}$$

Replacing the $a \rightarrow b$ relation by the ($a \rightarrow b$)' relation, (7.3) is then replaced as follows:

$$a \text{ and } a \rightarrow b \text{ and } a \rightarrow b \rightarrow (a \rightarrow b)' \Rightarrow b \text{ and } (a \rightarrow b)' \tag{7.5}$$

In this case, time operates in a substantial, before-and-after way on account of the changed feedback channel. Were (7.5) to be the general case, and (7.3) a limiting case, then across a sequence of periods in time agents would need to constantly adjust their causal models of the economy: $(a \rightarrow b)'$, $(a \rightarrow b)''$, and so on.[6]

The world in this second case, then, is open in the sense of being nonergodic and path-dependent due to how reflexive agents' changing expectations and consequent actions alter the relation between *a* and *b* in time.[7] The limiting case rational expectations/optimal learning view produces a closed systems approach because the allowed operation of reflexivity only confirms the existing model of the economy. It also allows the $a \rightarrow b$ causal model of the economy to be reduced to a type of mathematical expression which omits any real incorporation of time. All other types of expectations and non-optimal learning are open systems approaches in that the operation of reflexivity requires dynamic representations of the economy in before-and-after time via how agents' expectations and models of the economy are continually revised in terms of one another. The principle of motion that these dynamic pathways exhibit is an endogenous one in that the operation of reflexivity ensures that what occurs at one point in time influences what occurs at a later point in time. Time is not an unconnected sequence of independent states, as it must be represented in the equilibrium-shock model according to the mathematical treatment of 'shock' as an 'event' outside the model, but rather a connected process appropriate to our before-and-after representation of time. What is principally different, then, about a reflexivity-based treatment of the open-closed systems distinction is that it makes action and time central. That is, a reflexivity-based treatment of the open-closed distinction is both an ontological treatment of that distinction, because of the role of action, and also an epistemological one, because action is predicated on agents' state of knowledge.

---

[6] Simon's two blades process analysis is richer than (7.5) since he allows for the case in which a change in the environment occurs independently of the effects of the feedback channel. I leave this additional layer of complexity aside in order to emphasize the role of the feedback channel in order to focus on the behavior of reflexive agents in Sect. 5.

[7] In Paul Davidson's terms, the world is 'transmutable' (Davidson 1996). At the same time, the world is only 'evolutionary' in the loosest sense of the term. Evolutionary processes, at least in the classical Darwinian sense, basically occur 'behind the backs' of agents, whereas reflexive systems depend on how agents' actions influence the economy's time path. See Barkley Rosser's careful discussion of the meaning and interpretation of the concept of nonergodicity in Post Keynesian economics emphasizing its relation to the concepts of non-stationarity and non-homogeneity (cf. Rosser 2015).

But this causal analysis leaves unexplained just how 'open' an economic process understood as endogenous and reflexive can be. Action influences the world and its time path. Yet it could still be the case that the economy is an endogenous process due to less than rational expectations, is a nonergodic system because action causes the phenomena to be less than stationary, and yet the effects of agents' behavior through the feedback channel in the expectations-models adjustment process are sufficiently modest that it still largely appears as if the world is an ergodic system in which time does not matter. After all, as we know, in a large number of respects the world works pretty much the same way day-in-day-out.

This then calls for closer attention to the nature of the expectations feedback channel, and to do this I emphasize its agency-social structure character (Archer 1995; Lawson 1997), and illustrate this with a special case, the now classic, highly stylized example of how a feedback channel has significant effects on an economy's time path, namely, Robert Merton's (1948) treatment of a bank run as a self-fulfilling prophecy (SFP). In his famous Depression bank run example, a bank examiner mistakenly judges a bank will become insolvent (an endogenous 'shock'[8]), people act in conformity with this judgment causing a bank run, and the bank becomes insolvent, thus fulfilling the examiner's prediction or prophecy. Rather, then, than explain the feedback channel in a purely epistemological way in terms of only changes in beliefs or expectations, Merton characterizes the situation in agency-social structural terms involving the agency interaction relationship between the bank examiner's actions and depositors' actions which is embedded in and acts on the social-institutional structure that determines how the banking system works. All this, then, is what underlies the bank causal model $a \rightarrow b$ that agents work with and the expectations feedback channel $a \rightarrow b \rightarrow (a \rightarrow b)'$ that agents exercise when that causal model is called into question.

If, then, a causal analysis of the economy as an open, endogenous process leaves unexplained how 'open' an economic process might be, what an SFP does is provide a clear measure of openness in the form of a truth reversal of agents' judgments, where this reversal in turn is the product of

[8] It is endogenous because it arises from a judgment internal to the system as compared to an exogenous shock brought about by an event outside that system.

a whole set of changes in the attendant agency-social structure relationships. The bank examiner mistakenly judges the bank to be insolvent when it is solvent, and this causes the bank to become insolvent on account of the nature of the interaction between the examiner and depositors in the context of how the banking system works. What was false is taken by depositors to be true, and then after the bank run it is indeed true that the bank is insolvent because this agency-structure interaction has changed what is true.

Of course the Merton bank run example is highly simplified case that exaggerates how clearly agents' interaction affects what is true. More often than not changes in what is taken to be are not clear since our views about what is the case in the world with complex social structures involves many claims and assumptions whose interconnected nature makes it difficult to evaluate individual truth claims. But it would be a mistake to infer that this Merton's extreme truth reversal case is therefore unlikely to occur or that when it does it is only on a small scale. As everyone now knows, the recent financial crisis was essentially a banking crisis quite parallel to Merton's bank run example in which banks were judged solvent until they were successfully shorted and indeed became insolvent. Those who shorted the banks, that is, played the role of Merton's bank examiner,[9] and the crash in the overnight lending market played the role of Merton's depositors.

So openness should be characterized not only in truth-functional terms but also in terms of the social stability of beliefs. Depending on the domain, people's beliefs are more or less secure, and thus more or less subject to, or vulnerable to, a revision process in which agents search for causal models $a \rightarrow b$ and investigate possible feedback channels $a \rightarrow b \rightarrow (a \rightarrow b)'$ regarding their strategies for revising those models. This makes just how 'open' an economic process is depend on the way in which the agency-structure relationships are embedded in social institutions—obviously still a quite 'open' matter. But this, I suggest, is what one should expect when one takes the economy to be an open, endogenous, and path-dependent process.[10]

[9] The nature of a 'short' is to bet against the consensus view, or what is taken to be true, and a successful short changes that view.

[10] How much lock-in, then, economic processes exhibit (David 1985) would seem to depend in part on how durable the social-institutional foundations of social interaction are.

This analysis, then, also points to one advantage of an open systems, agency-structure approach to the economy over a mathematical representation of the economy. A mathematical representation of the economy as a complex dynamic process can map changes in variables and explain how an economy works in unexpected ways in terms of the idea of phase transitions. But when do mathematically described phase transitions count as the economy working in an unexpected way, and when do they count as it working in pretty much the same way? In thermodynamics, a phase transition involves a clear qualitative change since it involves a change from one state of matter to another, which clearly marks out a before-and-after sequence. What counts as a change from one 'state of matter' to another in the economic world? In social science changes in 'states of matter' are subject to judgments regarding what differences those changes make to agents. Thus agents' judgments about what is true or false ultimately determine what counts as a phase transition, as when we say the characteristics of the economy after the financial crisis are not true of the characteristics of an economy before the crisis.

From this vantage point, it seems a rather straightforward interpretation of Aristotle's sea battle tomorrow problem is as follows. Whether there is a sea battle tomorrow affects many people, and thus many people would form expectations about this possibility. Agents' expectations of possible sea battle tomorrow, then, are likely to influence other agents' actions. Should these actions fulfill or defeat the expectation of a sea battle tomorrow would then determine whether a sea battle occurs tomorrow. Thus the fatalism paradox that Aristotle suggested fails since whether a sea battle occurs tomorrow is not inevitable but depends on the actions people undertake. Indeed, Aristotle likely posed the fatalist view as a *reduction ad absurdum* argument to show that the claim a sea battle would or would not occur as inevitable was false and the paradox is not a paradox. Accordingly, the key assumption the paradox makes that Aristotle likely believed to be false was that action and truth are independent. If they are not, then action can change what is true, and the future is open, not inevitable.

## 4 The Utility Conception of the Economic Agent and the Completeness Assumption

I have claimed that rational choice theory's standard utility function conception of the economic agent goes hand-in-hand with standard theory's equilibrium-shock model of the economy. Rational choice theory is a normative theory of choice in that the utility conception of the agent depends on axiomatic foundations which discipline what choices agents ought to make. The axioms were originally taken to be self-evidently true, but the consistency in choice they produce is as much a matter of consistency with the equilibrium-efficiency properties of the standard equilibrium theory. The purpose of the axioms governing utility functions, that is, is not just to prescribe consistent choices, but to prescribe equilibrium-efficient consistent choices. But if standard equilibrium theory is questionable in regard to our understanding of action and time, then searching for axiomatic foundations for utility functions and rational choice seems misguided—the project aptly dubbed the 'preference purification approach.'[11] Rather, one ought to ask what behavior is consistent with how we understand action and time, and then explain the foundations for that behavior with an appropriate understanding of the agent.

Consider the important completeness axiom, which says that the agent must be able to compare any two imaginable states of the world, *x* and *y*, by a relation of preference *R*. If the axiom does not hold, and individuals' preferences are incomplete, much of standard theory is called into question, including welfare analysis and the weak axiom of revealed preference (WARP) axiom of revealed preference theory. Why then might it fail? The most widely held answer is vagueness, or that agents may be unable to clearly determine their preferences regarding vaguely specified alternatives (Broome 2004). How, then, ought researchers understand vagueness? The dominant response seems to be to investigate how though preferences might be vague, but the completeness axiom can still be retained, or at least some correlate assumption about preferences holds

[11] See footnote 2.

that largely serves the same purpose so that agents' choices are still effectively rational. But I believe this strategy gets things backward. Rather it would seem to make more sense to address incompleteness straight on, and explain decision-making behavior on that basis, as does much of behavioral economics, which has unmoored itself from rational choice.

The motivations of behavioral economists, however, differ from mine. They largely set aside the issue of how the economy as a whole should be represented in the interest of achieving greater ground-up realism regarding choice. In contrast, if how we explain behavior depends on how we explain the economy as a whole—in equilibrium terms or process terms—then we ought to investigate vagueness and incompleteness as reflective of agent behavior when we operate with a process conception of the economy. This is indeed what the causal model analysis of the last section implies. Since the feedback channel,

$$a \to b \to (a \to b)' \tag{7.4}$$

alters the $a \to b$ relation, there is good reason to suppose that the $b$ terms in $a \to b$ and $(a \to b)'$ are not comparable or perhaps only vaguely comparable. If the world has not changed too much, then the completeness axiom might be retained not as an axiom but as an observed relationship. Its basis, that is, would not be the requirements of equilibrium theory, but an assessment of how open or closed the world is in particular circumstances when we explain the economy as an open reflexive process. That assessment would also entail giving attention to the agency-structure background of the change in question, since how inertial change is, and how complete preferences might be, depends on how robust institutions governing social interaction are in making tomorrow more or less like today. So in contrast to behavioral economists, I give the issue of completeness reflexivity foundations, not psychological ones.

However, the general caution regarding the nature of preferences that behavioral economists have advanced, that preferences are often not stable for a whole variety of reasons, is still worth attention. Menu dependence, for example, tells us that a given set of preferences need not be stable when events occur that alter menus. However, in my view the more difficult issue here concerns preference formation. If the world is non-ergodic, then new states of the world regularly appear. To suppose that options in new states of the world can always be compared based on sets of preferences used to compare options in past states of the world is heroic at best, since completeness has to then be defined as an unknown ability individuals have that is everywhere and always versatile and competent. This mystery flies in the face of clear, every day evidence that some market participants actively work to manipulate other market participants' preferences (by often exploiting menu dependence). Of course the idea that preferences are not just formed but are actually constructed by social forces has been around for a long time, and indeed has also been off the agenda of mainstream economics for a long time. Why is this when the world outside of economics does not regard preference manipulation as controversial? Why do most economists neglect it? One answer is that questioning preference autonomy undermines the independence of supply and demand and the supply-and-demand balance on which standard economics relies. But that balance is premised on the equilibrium-shock model being a correct since it is that balance which mathematically 'closes' the model. Doubts on this score consequently unravel all that depends on it right back to how we should interpret the completeness assumption.[12]

An alternative view of completeness is John Searle's view that complete preferences are "the product of practical reasoning" and not given characteristics of the individual (Searle 2001, p. 253). I comment further on the identity implications of this idea below, and here only connect it to the idea of a reflexive economic process. If we regard a reflexive economic process as one that continually changes the world, then essentially preferences are continually being made incomplete, so that the issue is rather how and whether they might become complete through the actions of

[12] Questioning preference autonomy, clearly, also jeopardizes the basis on which individual identity operates in the utility conception—in a circular way I have argued (e.g., Davis 2011, pp. 6ff). If individuals' sets of preferences are what constitute their individual identities, and their preferences are influenced by others, what kind of 'individuals' are they? The problematic 'inner self' view is one strategy to respond to this.

agents. This then makes adjustment behavior central to our characterization of economic agents, and consequently I now go on to how such agents can be understood both in terms of adjustment behavior and in terms of identity.

## 5 The Behavior and Identity of Reflexive Economic Agents

I argued at the outset that explaining complex economic processes as reflexive and self-organizing entails explaining agents in such processes as reflexive and self-organizing. My goal in this section of the chapter, then, is link my Sect. 3 account of reflexive economic processes to an explanation of the behavior and identity of reflexive economic agents in terms of their ability to adjust the grounds for their behavior in a self-organizing way in response to change in their environments. I see two steps involved in doing this. First, I need to explain agents' adjustment behavior in terms of how it continues to a stopping point. Adjustment processes are not open-ended, as Simon made clear with his satisficing idea. They involve a response to an event that initiates them, and they run their course when agents have adjusted to that event. Second, I need to explain how agents' adjustment behavior causes them to self-organize their identities as individual economic agents at such stopping points. To explain the idea of agents' identities as self-organizing, I argue that reflexive processes can disrupt agents' individual identities, and their adjustment and self-organization come about through their re-organization of these identities. I illustrate this first using Merton's bank run example, and then generalize that explanation to three additional examples.

First, to explain adjustment behavior, I follow Simon's explanation in terms of satisficing, which he understood to be a matter of reaching an aspiration level. The two questions Simon's explanation naturally raises are, how are aspiration levels set, and how does one know when they are achieved? His 'two blades of the scissors' answer was that agents' aspiration levels depend on the type of process in which the agent is involved, and their achievement depends on how the agent adjusts within that process (Simon 1955, pp. 111–113).[13] Consider, then, the reflexive economic process that I outlined above in connection with Merton's SFP bank run example. There the bank examiner's evaluation of the bank affects depositors' view of the bank's solvency, this feeds back on and changes their causal model of the bank and also their behavior, and this produces the bank run. Depositors' adjustment behavior is thus caused by the reversal in judgment about the bank's solvency. This then tells us both how aspiration levels are set and how one knows when they are achieved. The new judgment that the bank is insolvent when it was previously believed solvent sets depositors' new aspiration levels (to withdraw all their deposits) and also drives their adjustment behavior (withdrawing their deposits) to the stopping point (full withdrawal of deposits) at which they achieve their aspiration level.

We can increase the realism of this account by explaining how this reflexive process works in agency-structure terms. At the outset, the bank examiner and depositors interact in a socially structured way determined according to how banking laws work, monetary systems, and financial markets are organized. The basis on which they interact is then disrupted by the agency of the bank examiner (agency affecting social structure). The ensuing withdrawal adjustment process on the part of depositors reflects the effects of their re-aligning their judgments about the bank to the bank examiner's judgment. In effect, then, the bank examiner sets an aspiration level inconsistent with the existing basis on which the examiner-depositor relationship operates, so depositors' withdrawals must proceed until the results of their actions conform to this new aspiration level, and thereby establish the new basis on which the examiner-depositor relationship operates. At the same time, the banking system and how markets are organized has been affected by the bank's failure. In agency-structure terms, the agency of the bank examiner has influenced social structure, and the consequent adjustment within that structure has changed the basis on which this agency-structure relationship will subsequently operate.

[13] In terms of process, Simon argued that decision makers' aspiration levels rise or fall as the alternatives they face are respectively easy or difficult to discover.

Second, then, to explain how agents' adjustment behavior leads them to self-organize themselves as individual economic agents, note how in Merton's example the bank examiner's evaluation affects depositors' identities. Before the evaluation becomes known depositors' identities are tied to their individual interests alone, since the earnings on their deposits accrue to them individually. However, when that evaluation becomes known, depositors recognize they then also have social identities as depositors since each has the same interest as every other depositor, and each acts on the same basis as every other depositor in withdrawing their funds. That is, all depositors now see themselves as representative agents of the group of depositors, and act as a representative depositor would act. Yet at the same time, though depositors adopt this depositor social identity, they nonetheless still retain and are still motivated by their individual identities, since they know that if they fail to withdraw their own funds when others are withdrawing theirs, that they will lose their funds individually in the bank failure, and put their individual identities at risk. They thus act on both identities, in social identity terms as representative agent depositors and in individual identity terms as independent agents. However, when the bank run has run its course, their social identity as depositors ceases to be relevant, their individual self-interested identities fully occupy them. That is, they have self-organized themselves in terms of those individual identities. In Simon's terms, then, the stopping point in his satisficing-aspiration level explanation of an adjustment process is also a stopping point in agents' self-organizing identity adjustment.

The general view, then, is that an endogenous shock event disrupts an existing basis on which agents' individual identities operate, and their adjustment involves them self-organizing themselves on some new basis on which their individual identities subsequently operate. Below, I further explain the two sides of this analysis in reflexivity terms, the disruption side and the self-organizing side, by demonstrating the complementarity between SFPs on the disruption side and self-defeating prophecies (SDPs) on the self-organizing side. But to better prepare the ground for this I first give three more examples to generalize from the Merton example.

Consider, then, Don Ross's neurocellular account of individual identity. Ross argues that individuals are made up of collections of sub-personal neural agents or neurons, their sub-personal multiple selves, which interact in coordination games internal to the individual to produce individual identity (Ross 2005, 2006, 2007). These sub-personal neural agents each act in their own interest and compete for bodily resources as relatively independent agents and individual identities. The human body, of course, is regularly affected by any number of psychophysical events that influence how these sub-personal agents interact and coordinate in order to serve their own individual identity interests. I characterize these events as endogenous shocks that disrupt an existing neural agent coordination, and the adjustment to a new neural agent coordination as the self-organization of a new individual identity. Ross's explanation is more sophisticated than this outline because he also discusses at length how the interaction between individuals compels each individual's sub-personal neural agents' coordination.[14] Nonetheless, his model illustrates the general one suggested above: an endogenous shock to an existing identity basis followed by self-organizing adjustment to a new identity basis. The main difference from the Merton example is in the forms of identity involved. If Merton's process goes from individual identity to individual identity with social identity to individual identity,

$$\mathrm{I} \rightarrow \mathrm{I} / \mathrm{SD} \rightarrow \mathrm{I}'$$

Ross's process,

$$\mathrm{I} / \mathrm{MS} \rightarrow \mathrm{I}' / \mathrm{MS}'$$

goes from one individual identity with multiple selves to a differently organized individual identity with multiple selves.

For a related individual identity/multiple selves case, consider the Santa Fe artificial stock market model developed by complexity researchers under Brian Arthur's leadership (Arthur 1995; Arthur et al. 1997). Profit-maximizing agents have the task of investing in a single asset, and form multiple subjective expectation models regarding what moves the market price of that asset. Different agents prioritize different models,

[14] For example, see his discussion of language (Ross 2007).

and in a trading day the price of that asset moves to a value that reflects the distribution of these different expectation models across agents. How well agents do in terms of profits with their respective prioritizing at each stage of the process then causes them to re-order their expectation models to improve performance in subsequent rounds. Seen in evolutionary terms, agents' models take on a life of their own as they effectively compete with one another through the intermediary of investors. These models effectively 'inhabit' investors and are thus like Ross's sub-personal agents or neural multiple selves. One difference is that investors are ordered collections of such models whereas the ordering principle for Ross's whole individuals is a coordination equilibrium. In identity terms, however, the analysis is formally parallel—I/MS → I′/MS'—though rules or expectation models are not internal to investors in the way neural selves are internal to people. The Santa Fe artificial stock market model of course does not work as a coordination game, but rather as an evolving complex dynamic system. Its periodization through successive trading rounds nonetheless lends it a disruption-adjustment pattern that works through identity change in self-organizing investors' constant re-ordering of their expectation models.[15]

Last, moving away from multiple selves approaches and back to social identity approaches like Merton's, consider the Marseille fish market analysis developed by Alan Kirman and his colleagues (Kirman 2011, pp. 72–109). In the late 1980s the Marseille market was reorganized in such a way as to allow it to function as an open, arms-length auction type process as in standard competitive theory. What was observed, however, is that buyers and sellers instead formed close contacts, interacted directly rather than indirectly with one another, and developed preferences regarding partnering with some people versus others. That is, rather than a typical competitive auction process, trading networks emerged which segregated buyers and sellers into different loyalty relationships. These loyalty relationships, then, are a partnership type of social identity (rather than social group type social identity as in Merton's example) that

[15] More fully, since the market continually evolves, the expectation models that individuals are made up of also continually evolve. Thus the analysis allows that new expectation models may emerge as combinations of old ones, and the identity scheme is better represented as I/MS → I′/MS' → ....

individual buyers and sellers adopt alongside their individual identities. Thus, since buyers and sellers came to the market as individual identities under the disruption associated with the market's reorganization as an auction, their adjustment to the new market organization involves them layering these new loyalty social identities onto their individual identities,

$$I \rightarrow I / SD$$

and self-organizing themselves on that basis, unlike in Merton's example where they move back to individual identities alone. Later, this analysis was extended in a different context to the social group type of social identity, such as individuals joining groups that function like clubs (Horst et al. 2007).[16]

What is the general form of the explanation, then, across these four examples? Turning to the two sides of the analysis, the disruption side and the self-organizing side, I argue that as reflexive processes they exhibit a complementarity which can be explained in terms of the complementarity between SFPs on the disruption side and self-defeating prophecies (SDPs) on the self-organizing side. An SFP, as in Merton's example, makes something false become true due to how people react to some event, whereas an SDP makes something true become false due to how people react to some event. The now classic stylized example in this case is the failure of the Y2K prophecy that computers would all fail at the beginning of the year 2000. It seems that this would indeed have happened, but the prediction that it would lead computer engineers to reappraise their existing $a \rightarrow b$ model of computers, and act in such a way as to instantiate a new $(a \rightarrow b)'$ model that secured computer systems against breakdown. Rather than the disruption that SFPs involve, SDPs thus deliver systems from disruption by making the undesirable, imminent, true states of affairs they involve false states of affairs through the actions agents undertake on their view of those undesirable state of affairs. In agency-structure terms, SDPs exhibit the tendency of social structures to re-stabilize themselves in response to endogenous agency shocks.

[16] Clubs exhibit high excludability and low rivalry. Horst et al. argue that adding new members changes the character of the club. Thus the social identity character of that club evolves as new individuals join it, just as the identity of individuals change when they become club members.

In identity terms, SDPs are an adjustment response to an identity disruption, whatever its origin, that precludes what would be the case from becoming the case. For Merton, depositors see their individual identities as linked to their social identities, and act so as to avoid losing their funds. For Ross, the appearance of new coordination equilibria for an individual's neural selves prevents the individual from being incapacitated. For Arthur and his colleagues, investors re-order their expectation models of the asset price to prevent themselves from losing money. For Kirman and his colleagues, buyers and sellers form loyalty relationships to forestall undesirable atomistic trading outcomes.

Seen in this way, however, there is an asymmetry between SFPs and SDP behaviors. Adjustment in the case of an SFP is reactive and backward-looking whereas adjustment in the case of an SDP is prospective and forward-looking. At the same time, the asymmetry between SFP and SDP behaviors goes beyond different orientations toward time because SDP behavior also involves individuals taking a position in regard to their own identities framed by the goal of self-organization. This is where the debate in the *Journal of Economic Methodology* between Infante, Lecouteux, and Sugden and Hausman in my view comes into play. They ask whether there is some kind of option weighing activity in which individuals engage, the effect of which would be to remove the possibility that individuals are dual selves. Implicitly, then, they ask whether individuals can effectively 'step outside of themselves' to take positions on their own identities framed by the goal of self-organization.

What it consequently seems they are addressing is the need for some sort of hierarchical or multi-level conception of individuals with a reflexive capacity to manage their behavior based on the goal of individual self-organization. In SFP behavior, individuals' organization of their sub-personal and/or supra-personal identities is disrupted, but in SDP behavior individuals take a position toward this disruption of themselves, where that position involves setting out a behavioral course of action meant to re-organize their sub-personal and/or supra-personal identities.

My argument in terms of SFPs and SDPs, then, may seem unduly labored. However, its ultimate rationale is simply to argue that individual behavior and identity need to be understood in terms of some sort of capacity to reflexively orient on that behavior and identity, a type of idea which has had little place in the theory of decision-making in economics, with a few exceptions. Most notable in this latter regard is Amartya Sen's representation of agents' overall identities that distinguishes on one level three different types of 'privateness' or kinds of individual identities that need to be managed (self-centered welfare, self-welfare goal, and self-goal choice) and on another level altogether a 'fourth aspect of self' associated with being able to engage in 'reasoning and self-scrutiny' and "examine of one's values and objectives and choose in the light of those values and objectives" associated with those types of privateness (Sen 2002, pp. 33–36; cf. Davis 2007, 2011).[17] Searle, I suggested, reasons in a related in way in his emphasis on practical reasoning, arguing that it is a mistake to think that complete "preferences are given *prior* to practical reasoning" when they are instead "the product of practical reasoning" (Searle 2001, p. 253). In relation to individual identity, practical reasoning then involves taking a stance on one's identity in a self-organizing way.

My argument here, however, avoids claims about practical reasoning capacities, because it is framed only in terms of what we need to say about agents if we suppose the economy is a reflexive process. What I claim we need to say is that their adjustment behavior is self-organizing, and this involves not only their revising their behavior in light of their expectations of the future, but also revising it in such a way as to function as individuals.

## 6 A Sea Battle Tomorrow?

My goal in this chapter was to explain how the behavior and identity of individual reflexive economic agents might be understood as an alternative to the standard utility conception of agents. My explanation depends on understanding the economic process as reflexive, and I explain reflexive economic processes in terms of the adjustment behavior of reflexive economic agents. What I say about this process and agent conception is

[17] Self-centered welfare concerns one's own self-interest, self-welfare goal concerns one's own welfare, which may include own-welfare enhancing sympathy for others, and self-goal choice concerns one's own non-welfare goals. See Hedoin (2016) for a discussion of the relation of Sen's different levels of the self to revealed preference theory.

that they are both open in the sense that action affects the world, and thus occur in before-and-after time, so that what is the case in the world depends on action in a non-fatalistic way. So my assumption—one it seems not held by many economists—is that explanations in economics need to be adequate to our most basic views about the relationship between time and action. An implication of these views is that the future is not determined. Whether, as Aristotle asked, there will be the equivalent of a sea battle tomorrow depends on the actions people undertake in advance of tomorrow. This can be seen in how our judgments about what is true or false are susceptible to reversal according to what we do, as demonstrated, albeit in a highly stylized and simplified way, by SFPs and SDPs. Of course, many of our beliefs about what is true and false about the world are unstable and contested, so some might say this explanatory strategy is overly ambitious. One might then be tempted to despair about making time central to economics, and retreat to the discourse of mathematical equilibrium models that set time and realism aside. However, such a retreat, I suggest, only confirms the openness of the economy since its object is to close our explanations, and one can only close something that is open.

What can we then accomplish in this uncertain scientific environment? I have tried to argue that agents' pursuit of individual identity remains one relatively certain phenomenon. My argument for this turns on whether we believe agents are self-organizing and engage in an adjustment behavior in which they act upon themselves. The motivation for this view was the bounded individuality idea. If individuality in what different forms it takes is the product of action, then it is bounded in a reflexive way by that action, just as in behavioral explanations rationality is bounded in a reflexive way by its own mechanisms. Simon was the original proponent of the bounded rationality idea. But his self-organizing systems idea, once applied to individual agents, allows us to extend the bounded rationality idea to the idea of bounded individuality. This chapter aimed to develop that account by framing it explicitly in identity terms on the assumption that any systematic account of economic agents needs to be framed in those terms.

## References


Archer, M. (1995). *Realist Social Theory: The Morphogenetic Approach*. Cambridge: Cambridge University Press.

Aristotle. (1963). *Categories* and *De Interpretatione* (J. H. Ackrill, Trans.). Oxford: Clarendon Press.

Arthur, W. B. (1995). Complexity in Economic and Financial Markets. *Complexity, 1*(1), 20–25.

Arthur, W. B., Holland, J., LeBaron, B., Palmer, R., & Tayler, P. (1997). Asset Pricing under Endogenous Expectations in an Artificial Stock Market. In W. B. Arthur, S. Durlauf, & D. Lane (Eds.), *The Economy as an Evolving Complex System II* (pp. 15–44). Reading, MA: Addison-Wesley.

Boumans, M. (2015). *Science Outside the Laboratory*. New York: Oxford University Press.

Broome, J. (2004). *Weighing Lives*. Oxford: Oxford University Press.

David, P. (1985). Clio and the Economics of QWERTY. *American Economic Review, 75*, 332–337.

Davidson, P. (1996). Economic Theory and Reality. *Journal of Post Keynesian Economics, 18*, 479–508.

Davis, J. (2007). Identity and Commitment: Sen's Fourth Aspect of the Self. In F. Peter & H. B. Schmid (Eds.), *Rationality and Commitment* (pp. 313–335). Oxford: Oxford University Press.

Davis, J. (2011). *Individuals and Identity in Economics*. Cambridge: Cambridge University Press.

Davis, J. (2015). Bounded Rationality and Bounded Individuality. *Research in the History of Economics and Methodology, 33*, 75–93.

Grüne-Yanoff, T., Marchionni, C., & Moscati, I. (2014). Introduction: Methodologies of Bounded Rationality. *Journal of Economic Methodology, 21*(4), 325–342.

Hausman, D. (1992). *The Inexact and Separate Science of Economics*. Cambridge: Cambridge University Press.

Hausman, D. (2012). *Preference, Value, Choice, and Welfare*. Cambridge: Cambridge University Press.

Hausman, D. (2016). On the Econ Within. *Journal of Economic Methodology, 23*(1), 26–32.

Hedoin, C. (2016). Sen's Critique of Revealed Preference Theory and Its 'Neo-Samuelsonian' Critique: A Methodological and Theoretical Assessment. *Journal of Economic Methodology, 23*(4), 349–373.
Horst, U., Kirman, A., & Teschl, M. (2007). *Changing Identity: The Emergence of Social Groups.* Princeton, NJ: Institute for Advanced Study, School of Social Science, Economics Working Papers: 1–30.
Infante, G., Lecouteux, G., & Sugden, R. (2016a). Preference Purification and the Inner Rational Agent: A Critique of the Conventional Wisdom of Behavioral Welfare Economics. *Journal of Economic Methodology, 23*(1), 1–25.
Infante, G., Lecouteux, G., & Sugden, R. (2016b). On the Econ Within: A Reply to Daniel Hausman. *Journal of Economic Methodology, 23*(1), 33–37.
Kirman, A. (2011). *Complex Economics: Individual and Collective Rationality.* London: Routledge.
Lawson, T. (1997). *Economics and Reality.* London: Routledge.
Lawson, T. (2013). Soros's Theory of Reflexivity: A Critical Comment. *Revue de Philosophie Économique, 14*(1), 29–48.
Merton, R. K. (1948). The Self Fulfilling Prophecy. *Antioch Review, 2*, 193–210.
Rice, H. (2014). Fatalism. In E. N. Zalta (Ed.), *The Stanford Encyclopedia of Philosophy* (Summer Edition). Retrieved March 9, 2016, from http://plato.stanford.edu/archives/sum2015/entries/fatalism/.
Rizvi, S. A. T. (2006). The Sonnenschein-Mantel-Debreu Results after Thirty Years. *History of Political Economy, 38*(Annual Supplement), 228–245.
Ross, D. (2005). *Economic Theory and Cognitive Science.* Cambridge, MA: MIT Press.
Ross, D. (2006). The Economic and Evolutionary Basis of Selves. *Cognitive Systems Research, 7*, 246–258.
Ross, D. (2007). *H. sapiens* as Ecologically Special: What Does Language Contribute? *Language Sciences, 29.5*(7), 10–731.
Rosser, B. (2015). Reconsidering Ergodicity and Fundamental Uncertainty. *Journal of Post Keynesian Economics, 38*, 331–354.
Searle, J. (2001). *Rationality in Action.* Cambridge, MA: MIT Press.
Sen, A. (2002). *Rationality and Freedom.* Cambridge, MA: Harvard University Press.
Simon, H. (1955). A Behavioral Model of Rational Choice. *Quarterly Journal of Economics, 69*, 99–118.

Simon, H. (1956). Rational Choice and the Structure of the Environment. *Psychological Review, 63*, 129–138.

Simon, H. (1962). The Architecture of Complexity. *Proceedings of the American Philosophical Society, 106*(6), 467–482.

Simon, H. (1990). Invariants of Human Behavior. *Annual Review of Psychology, 41*, 1–19.

Velupillai, K. V. (2011). Towards an Algorithmic Revolution in Economic Theory. *Journal of Economic Surveys, 25*(3), 401–430; Republished in *Nonlinearity, Complexity and Randomness in Economics*, S. Zambelli & D. George (Eds.). Hoboken, NJ: Wiley-Blackwell, 2012; 7–35.

# 8

# Production, Innovation, and Disequilibrium

Dharmaraj Navaneethakrishnan

## 1 Trento Days: From Engineering to Economics ...

To discover and learn something that opens up, lights up, and expands one's curious mind is always an enchanting experience. For me, like most of us, the PhD research was one such experience; it left a deep and ever-lasting mark in my life. Having come from an engineering background, when I joined the doctoral program at CIFREM (Interdepartemental Centre for Research Training in Economics and Management), in the fall of 2007, I had originally planned to work on technology management—in the *management* stream. During the first-year coursework I was introduced to advanced economic theory, and for a person who had only

Special thanks to Vela Velupillai and Stefano Zambelli for taming, inspiring, educating, and letting us explore and follow our passion. This chapter is an extension of the PhD thesis written under their supervision in 2011 (see Dharmaraj 2011). Though all the ideas and themes of this chapter originated out of their work, any misinterpretation or remaining infelicities remain mine.

D. Navaneethakrishnan (✉)
Data Science and Analytics Team, Hubbell India, Chennai, India



K. Velupillai (ed.), *Keynesian, Sraffian, Computable and Dynamic Economics*,
https://doi.org/10.1007/978-3-030-58131-2_8

taken two courses in economics (first, engineering economics in the *undergraduate* degree, and then managerial economics during the *post-graduate* degree), it was a challenge to start thinking like an economist. I had to unlearn and learn to think like an economist, but my engineering training always kept me on track to look at economic theory from an engineer's point of view.

By the time I completed my first year, I was convinced that I needed to pursue research in economic growth, building upon the rich tradition in economic theory. On 30 May 2008, I first met Prof. Stefano Zambelli, at his via Rosmini Office,[1] to discuss about my research interests. He patiently listened through and encouraged me to pursue the research interests. When I requested if he could take me as his student, he said, "Yes, but before that you have to meet my supervisor Prof. Kumaraswamy (Vela) Velupillai, who is also here; let us go meet him and get his thoughts!" Vela's office was just across Stefano's office, so we both went to his office and by the time the meeting ended, I got an outline on how to proceed with the doctoral research and soon embarked on *traverse* analysis. Stefano agreed to be my first supervisor and, his supervisor, Vela, became my second supervisor.

Stefano's teaching style is a very unique and his thinking process might look more like M.C. Escher's art; at first his originality will strike you, it will give you a new perspective, and when you start to catch his train of thoughts, you will appreciate even more and realize how creative and innovative his thoughts/ideas are. Robert Solow (1990, p. 33) once remarked that Richard Goodwin's intellectual style was special: "The unspoken message was that if a thing is worth doing it is worth doing playfully. Do not misunderstand me: 'playful' does not mean 'frivolous' or 'unserious'. It means, rather, that one should follow a trail the way a puppy does, sniffing the ground, wagging one's tail, and barking a lot, because it smells interesting and it would be fun to see where it goes." I wonder Stefano, during his Modena days, meeting and attending Goodwin's lectures—who then was in Siena—and Vela's lectures at Florence had left an everlasting impression on him. Why I say that is, one just has to ask a curious question and he will become a think-tank starts

[1] Stefano, by spring of 2008, had moved to Trento, Italy, from Aalborg, Denmark.

exploring the answers with you, giving its history and references, and why he thinks that that answer is complete or not complete or convincing, and goes further in explaining why and so on. By the end of the lecture Stefano would have given so many tips and directions for research that students would not need to search anywhere else.

Logic and problem-solving comes naturally to Stefano, which also probably explains why it is not surprising that he was a master in chess. He is also a MATLAB wizard and I consider him *tech-savvy*. Because when I was working on the third chapter of my thesis, we were developing a complex model that needed extensive computing resources—because the algorithm was to build several Turing Machines (TM) in a larger search space, and due to the *halting problem*, one doesn't know when a TM will halt producing a result—so Stefano connected with the university's Computer Science department and got access to the Cluster to run the algorithm. We could have done the simulations in an abstract manner, but Stefano encouraged me to harness the available computing power and the results were something very interesting (see Dharmaraj 2011).

In 2010, a decade ago, Vela and Stefano founded the Algorithmic Social Sciences Research Unit (ASSRU) and we (Selda, Ragupathy, and I) were fortunate to be a part of it. ASSRU's spiritual patrons include Alan Turing (Computable Economics), Herbert Simon (Classical Behavioural Economics), Maynard Keynes (Adaptive Monetary Macrodynamics), Piero Sraffa (Algorithmic Production Theory), Richard Goodwin (Nonlinear Coupled Economic Dynamics), and Luitzen Brouwer (Constructive Mathematics). Works of Stefano and Vela always had deep roots in the above tradition and built upon it. In the following sections, first, I will discuss about my adventures in endogenous economic growth theories, especially modelling innovation; second, I will discuss the importance of viability creating mechanisms during traverse and, then, the next steps.

## 2 It is in the Transition That We Actually Have Our Being[2]...

Economic systems develop, innovate, and evolve in a *morphogenetic nature*,[3] so understanding economic development[4] is crucial in order to manage the resources effectively. The three main factors that cause structural change are technology, preferences, and endowment; so, any changes in these factors will cause imbalances in an economic system and move it away from its equilibrium. Of the above factors, production is a central one because it is often considered as the heart of the economic system. When innovation occurs, the structural change brings in new production techniques and, consequently, expands the possibilities of production. As Winter (2005, p. 235; italics added) emphasizes, "When the activity attempted is of a novel kind in itself, judgements about feasibility are subjected to hazards and uncertainties well beyond those that attend such transfer. The part of the knowledge territory that is near *the advancing frontiers has special importance and a special character, and requires separate attention*." Hence, in disequilibrium, the economic system should adopt

---

[2] Keynes (1936, p. 343, fn. 3).

[3] Recollecting and emphasizing the point, Richard Goodwin (1989; italics added) wrote, "Like Marx he [Joseph Schumpeter] was a student of *the morphogenetic nature of capitalism*. The economy is not a given structure like von Neumann's model, ...., *it is an organism perpetually altering its own structure, generating new forms. Unlike most organisms it does not exhibit durable structural stability: it is perhaps best thought of as a kind of hyper-Darwinian, perpetual evolution*. We are so familiar with it, we normally do not realize how remarkable it is. It is not like morphogenesis in animals and plants, where the species is programmed to generate a particular structure, and exhibits structural stability by creating the same form for thousands of years. Rather it is analogous to the much disputed problem of the generation of new species. *The economy is unsteadily generating new productive structures*. In this sense Schumpeter was profoundly right to reject the elegant new mathematical models: they are the analysis of the behaviour of a given structure. He saw that not only was the economy creatively destroying parts of its given structure, but also that one could not analyze a given structure, ignoring that this cannibalism was going on."

[4] "*By 'development,' .... we shall understand only such changes in economic life as are not forced upon it from without but arise by its own initiative, from within*. .... [T]he mere growth of the economy, as shown by the growth of population and wealth, [will not] be designated here as a process of development. .... *Development in our sense is a distinct phenomenon*, entirely foreign to what may be observed in the circular flow or in the tendency towards equilibrium. *It is spontaneous and discontinuous change in the channels of the flow, disturbance of equilibrium, which forever alters and displaces the equilibrium state previously existing*" Schumpeter ([1911] 1934, pp. 63–64; italics added).

*viable* production techniques and effectively manage both human resources and money.

Production is essentially a *process* in time; it takes *time to build* (Böhm-Bawerk 1890). A production technique is often denoted as a function (*or carry-on activity*), which is technically a blueprint of a product; it directs labourers and machineries to follow a set of steps or procedures, in time, to produce products. So, changes in technology will modify or replace the production process—in other words, the production function. The magnitude of change in the production function will determine the magnitude of change and impact on the economic system. The degree of evolution of the production function due to innovation will then classify if the innovation is a process innovation or an incremental innovation or a disruptive innovation.

As Marshall (1920, p. 115) righty points out, "Knowledge is our most powerful engine of production; it enables us to subdue Nature and forces her to satisfy our wants. Organization aids knowledge." The accumulation of ideas, knowledge, and technologies over time becomes an asset for the economic system. So, in order to understand economic growth, one needs to understand how ideas are being generated and managed within an economic system. Emphasizing the point, Romer (1993, p. 63) notes, "The key step in understanding economic growth is to think carefully about ideas. This requires careful attention to the meaning of the words that we use and to the metaphors that we invoke when we construct mathematical models of growth" (Also see Romer 1986, 1990). One such metaphor that Velupillai (2000, 2010) and Zambelli (2004, 2005) adopted was the Turing Machine (TM) metaphor because it encapsulates the intrinsic uncertainties of endogenous growth[5] in a more realistic way. TM is a mathematical model of computation that defines an abstract machine, which, with a given a set of rules and input, manipulates symbols on an input strip of tape and provides an output. The working of a TM is analogous to the production process. What makes the TM a powerful metaphor is because of the *halting problem*. That is, for a given set of

[5] Schumpeter: "[W]hat we are about to consider is that kind of change arising from within the system *which so displaces its equilibrium point that the new one cannot be reached from the old one by infinitesimal steps*" ([1911] 1934, p. 64, fn. 1; italics in the original).

rules and input, when fed into a TM, one cannot know *a priori* if the TM will halt, producing an output or not. It is only when it halts we know that a TM, with that input fed and a specific set of rules, would halt and produce an output. This then becomes knowledge. Moreover, there is a category of TM that is known as *busy beaver*; it could operate on a blank input tape but could produce a maximum number of ones (output) on its tape before halting (Zambelli 2004). The working of a busy beaver is very similar to the machines, where with little input the machine can produce a larger output. Thus, modelling the research and development process as a TM process, we could encapsulate the indeterminacies of knowledge generation and innovation in an insightful way and analyse the evolution of production functions.

## 3 Innovation: Engine of Economic Growth

In a paper written jointly with Stefano (Dharmaraj (2011; Chapter 4), Zambelli & Dharmaraj (2013)), we infused the TM metaphor within the *time-to-build* macroeconomic model (Frisch 1933; Kalecki 1935)—especially the Neo-Austrian model (see, Hicks 1973; Amendola and Gaffard 1998, 2006) to study its evolution. The Neo-Austrian model is very insightful for traverse analysis because it captures the interaction and evolution between production, labour, and money, in time.

Let's consider an economy with $n$ number of firms, producing a homogeneous product—using similar production functions, with input as labour ($l$). The period of production or time taken to produce a product in each firm is denoted by $\varepsilon_i$. A firm's production decision made at time $t - \varepsilon_i$ will be realized at time $t$:

$$Q^P(t) = \sum_{i=1}^{n} q_i^P(t) \quad \text{Aggregated actual real planned output (planned deliveries)} \tag{8.1}$$

$$O^P(t) = \sum_{i=1}^{n} o_i^P(t - \varepsilon_i) \quad \text{Aggregated real planned production (orders)} \tag{8.2}$$

At every stage of production, corresponding to the production function, each firm allocated labour, $\ell^{Z_i} = \left[\ell(0), \ell(1), \ell(2), \ldots, \ell(\varepsilon^{Z_i})\right]$. Each firm has a production possibility sequence, which is described by: $(\ell^{Z_i}, \varepsilon^{Z_i})$. Therefore, a decision of production made at time $t - \varepsilon_i^{Z_i}$ to produce a unit of the quantity $q_i^t$ would require a proportional $\omega_i^{t-\varepsilon_i^{Z_i}}$ use of labour:

$$\ell(t - \varepsilon_i^{Z_i}), \ell(t - \varepsilon_i^{Z_i} + 1), \ell(t - \varepsilon_i^{Z_i} + 2), \ldots, \ell(t) \rightarrow 1 \tag{8.3}$$

$$\omega_i^{t-\varepsilon_i^{Z_i}} \ell(t - \varepsilon_i^{Z_i}), \omega_i^{t-\varepsilon_i^{Z}} \ell(t - \varepsilon_i^{Z_i} + 1), \omega_i^{t-\varepsilon_i^{Z_i}} \ell(t - \varepsilon_i^{Z_i} + 2), \ldots, \omega_i^{t-\varepsilon_i^{Z_i}} \ell(t) \rightarrow q_i^t \tag{8.4}$$

The firm's production process remains the same as long as no process innovation takes place. Firms use labour for production and R&D. The total labour demand of firm *i* at time (*t*) is given by:

$$L_i^{tot}(t) = L_i^q(t) + L_i^{R\&D}(t) = \sum_{j=0}^{\varepsilon_i^Z} \omega_i^z (t - \varepsilon_i^Z + j) \ell_i^Z(j) + L_i^{R\&D}(t) \tag{8.5}$$

A firm's decision to produce and employ labour depends on the revenue and costs. The revenue from sales of the produced output is given by:

$$\text{Rev}_i^q(t) = p(t) q_i(t) \tag{8.6}$$

The expenditure for production purposes would be,

$$\exp_i^q(t) = w(t) L_i^{tot}(t) = w(t)\left(L_i^q(t) + L_i^{R\&D}(t)\right) \tag{8.7}$$

The total output at given time (*t*) would be,

$$Q(t) = \sum_{i=1}^{n} q_i(t) \tag{8.8}$$

The market clearing price will be determined as follows:

$$p(t) = \frac{w(t)L^D(t)}{Q(t)} \tag{8.9}$$

Within the time-to-build framework, the TM model of computation is introduced as a function of production—that is, product is encoded[6] (Chaitin 1995, 2010) as a binary bit string of *n*-digit length, that is, production blueprint of the product,

| |
|---|
| 01101001011001001011110010...10100110001010101010111100101 |

The production does '*n*' steps to produce the product; the period of production directly depends on the blueprint length. As production is a process, adopting the Church-Turing thesis (see Velupillai 2000, 2010; Zambelli 2004, 2005, 2010), we could construct a Turing Machine to produce the same output. In a *worst-case scenario* one could build a TM with '*n*' states that has halted to produce the product. The algorithmic complexity of the TM (measured by the number of states) would be '*n*'. In this context, if research and development develops/finds a TM that could produce the same output with less algorithmic complexity than the worse-case scenario, it could be categorized as a *process innovation*.

The model developed in the Zambelli and Dharmaraj (2013) paper was simulated for various initial conditions and policy parameters to study how the economic system would evolve over time. In this section

[6] Chaitin (2010): In algorithmic information theory, you measure the complexity of something by counting the number of bits in the smallest program for calculating it:

Program → *Universal Computer* → output

If the output of a program could be a physical or a biological system, then this complexity measure would give us a way to measure the difficulty of explaining how to construct or grow something, in other words, measure either traditional smokestack or newer green technological complexity:

Software → *Universal Constructor* → physical system

DNA → *Development* → biological system

I will attempt to develop the notion of innovation from process innovation to a generalized notion of innovation—namely, incremental innovation and product innovation.

We have noted that the algorithmic complexity of the product originally is '*n*' and firms research for TMs by allocating a portion of available labour for R&D in such a manner as to keep the production going. When innovation happens, that is, R&D discovers a TM which produced a segment or the whole of blueprint with lesser algorithmic complexity, the firm can decide to use it and reduce the number of production steps—in other words, innovation reduces the period of production and labour employed for production. The richness of the TM's equivalent computations and discoveries is crucial and insightful in modelling innovation. For example: if the blueprint is as follows:

| |
|---|
| 0110100101100100101111 0010...10100110001010101010111100 1011 |

and the newly discovered $TM_x$ (of states $x$) halted, producing an output string:

| |
|---|
| 11110010...101 |

the output of $TM_x$ is matched in the product blueprint,

| |
|---|
| 01101001011001001011110010...1010011000101010101011110010 1111 |

The string match is marked with blue. The new blueprint, incorporating the process innovation, will have an algorithmic complexity that is less than '*n*' (complexity reduction = length of string (11110010...101 )—no. of states in $TM_x$).

The new blueprint will look like:

| |
|---|
| 011010010110010010($TM_x$)0011000101010101010111100101111 |

The new TM's algorithmic complexity is lesser than the length of "11110010...101 ", so it is categorized as *process innovation*.

If the R&D discovers a TM whose output does not entirely match the segments in blueprint, even if it has lower algorithmic complexity, it will not be considered, and the ideas will be stored in the firm's knowledge base. What if there are cases in which a TM produces an output that is large (with lower algorithmic complexity) but matches partially (say, >50% of the matched segment in the blueprint), will the new discovery be considered?

To illustrate an example, if R&D discovers a new $TM_y$, whose output string is as follows:

| |
|---|
| 11110010...101001111 |

The segment that matches with the product blueprint is marked in blue and the mismatch is marked in green. As a major part of $TM_y$'s output string matches except the last few digits, would the firm not utilize the new idea? If the innovation is added, algorithmic complexity of the production function will be significantly reduced from the original length '*n*'. If the firm decides to adopt the new discovery, the blueprint of the product will look like:

| |
|---|
| 011010010110010010(11110010...101001111)0011000101010101011100101111 |

which is equivalent to:

| |
|---|
| 011010010110010010($TM_y$)0011000101010101011100101111 |

The economic interpretation is that this type of innovation could be considered as an incremental product innovation—like a product with added features, but one that reduces the original production time and efforts. In a competitive market, firms often differentiate their products by adding features and expanding the market. As the firms add new features over time the product takes a new form—which in some cases is disruptive and creates an entirely new market. With the proposed idea, if we can model individual firms taking different R&D and innovation policies, like exact match or even partial match (like >50% or >60%, …, or >90%), the evolution of the production function and the economic system, using simulations, will provide much richer insights into production policies, R&D policies, monetary policies, and so on.

## 4 Viably Traversing the Disequilibrium ...?

When the economic system is evolving by destroying existing productive structures and creating new productive structures, the policies and strategies should assist the system to sustain and evolve. Some firms will survive and some won't, but that is the way the economic system adapts and evolves. In such disequilibrium cases, it would be challenging, if not impossible, to know *a priori* if there indeed exists an equilibrium and the economic system is moving towards an equilibrium. So the economic system should attempt to employ *viability creating mechanisms* to create and manage, in order to *self-replace*[7] itself over time, sustain, and grow:

> Eventually in the process of simulating such a model, some of the feasibility conditions for a given "model agent" will be violated. To restore viability a mechanism must be introduced by the modeler that allows for the formation of new "model agents" to whom the resources associated with disappearing agents are transferred. Alternatively, a new organizational form can be installed that will transfer resources so as to maintain individual agent feasibility and overall systems viability as an analog of "Chapter Eleven" proceedings [which is on 'Self-Organization as a Process in Evolution of Economic Systems'], unemployment insurance, and welfare payments.
>
> Such *viability creating mechanisms* are the analog of equilibrium "existence" proofs, but in the out-of-equilibrium setting. They are required to guarantee the existence of a continuing "solution" to the system in terms of feasible actions for all of its constituent model components. When they are explicitly represented, then not only the population of production processes evolve, *but also the population of agents, organizations and institutions.* (Day 1993, pp. 38–39; italics in original)

[7] It is interesting to note that Sraffa's notion of viability is "synonymous of survival of the system as a whole" (Chiodi 2010); hence, his definition captures all the aspects of viability (see Sraffa 1960, p. 5, fn. 1).

Only through such mechanisms the system could viably traverse the desired growth paths and reach a desired state. This process of developing policies and refining them in order to reach a desired state is analogous to that for a computing system. As Goodwin (1951, p. 3; italics added) aptly puts, if "[t]he desired value is not known, but rather the difference between successive trials is taken as the error and this is successively reduced to zero—hence the name zeroing servo. At this point we have found the answer, our process repeats itself until disturbed. Thus *the economy may be regarded as slowly computing the answer to an ever-changing problem.*"

The viability creating mechanisms are vital in enabling economic systems to *traverse* the disequilibrium. What kind of viability mechanism or policies could a policymaker devise?[8] In the previous section we looked at how the TM metaphor could be used to model various types of innovation, but the R&D search space in which researchers (TMs) explore to find innovative processes (algorithms) that reduce the blueprint (information length) is unexplored. In that context, it must be noted that viability creating mechanisms should focus not only on production structures but also on R&D activities, because some of the TMs' efficient processes and product features might not be realized as innovation. The accumulation of knowledge of efficient processes (TMs) then becomes part of an organization's knowledge base—perhaps as *heuristic* (Polya 1945), leading to knowledge spillovers and technological disruptions. Economic systems must enable organizations to focus on emerging technologies and share key knowledge across organizations.

Moreover, if we expand the developed model from a homogeneous product to a heterogeneous product, and from one sector to multiple sectors, we could simulate how different coupled sectors would evolve over time. This will enable policymakers to understand how knowledge spillovers happen and analyse the disruptions that they cause to the economic system.

[8] It should be noted that "an effective theory of policy is impossible for a complex economy". See Velupillai (2007, 2010).

## 5 Traversing Beyond

Stefano's contribution to economics is original and creative; his work has deep roots in Schumpeter's notion of economic development, Goodwin's nonlinear dynamics, and Velupillai's computable foundations. Goodwin, when exhibiting his paintings (Barche 1990, p. 14; emphasis added), said, "The main thing I'm interested in is that my paintings should appeal in some way to other people as well. *It's like having children and then wanting them to go out into the world to make their own life. They are doing their work, I hope*". The same applies to *tradition*[9] as well. Stefano and Vela, first as supervisors, then as mentors, and now as friends, have helped us learn the subject and encouraged us to think freely and follow our passion. Probably that is why when I decided to build a career in the industry, both Stefano and Vela, though concerned at first, wished me well and let me explore the business world.

Over the last few years, I have been analysing how businesses and markets evolve, and what I have observed is that businesses most often—if not always—evolve due to endogenous factors. Sometimes, businesses take actions based on the limited data they have about customers, but they often engage in market research to understand how customer preferences are changing, so that their businesses could develop new products and use efficient production techniques to sustain and be relevant. The metaphors, analogies, and models that we use to explain/communicate are more relevant and useful in understanding the various dimensions of economic life.

[9] "Yet if the only form of tradition, of handing down, consisted in following the ways of the immediate generation before us in a blind or timid adherence to its successes, "tradition" should positively be discouraged. We have seen many such simple currents soon lost in the sand; and novelty is better than repetition. *Tradition is a matter of much wider significance. It cannot be inherited, and if you want it you must obtain it by great labour*" T.S. Eliot, "Tradition and the Individual Talent" (italics added).

## References


Amendola, M., & Gaffard, J. (1998). *Out of Equilibrium*. Oxford: Oxford University Press.

Amendola, M., & Gaffard, J. (2006). *The Market Way to Riches: Behind the Myth, Cheltenham*. UK: Edward Elgar Publishing.

Barche, G. (1990). *Richard M. Goodwin: Selected Paintings*. Siena: Nuova Immagine Editrice.

Böhm-Bawerk, E. (1890). *Capital and Interest* (William Smart. Trans.). London: Macmillan.

Chaitin, G. (1995). Foreword. In C. Calude (Ed.), *Information and Randomness: An Algorithmic Perspective* (pp. IX–X). Berlin: Springer.

Chaitin, G. (2010). The Information Economy. In S. Zambelli (Ed.), *Computable, Constructive and Behavioural Economic Dynamics: Essays in honour of Kumaraswamy (Vela) Velupillai*. London: Routledge.

Chiodi, G. (2010). The Means of Subsistence and the Notion of 'Viability' in Sraffa's Surplus Approach. In S. Zambelli (Ed.), *Computable, Constructive and Behavioural Economic Dynamics: Essays in Honour of Kumaraswamy (Vela) Velupillai*. London: Routledge.

Day, R. (1993). Nonlinear Dynamics and Evolutionary Economics. In R. Day & P. Chen (Eds.), *Nonlinear Dynamics and Evolutionary Economics*. Oxford: Oxford University Press.

Dharmaraj, N. (2011). *Out of Equilibrium: Modelling and Simulating Traverse*. PhD thesis, University of Trento, Italy.

Frisch, R. (1933). Propagation and Impulse Problems in Dynamic Economics. In *Economic Essays in Honour of Gustav Cassel*. London: George Allen & Unwin Ltd..

Goodwin, R. (1951). Iteration, Automatic Computers and Economic Dynamics. *Metroeconomica, 3*(1), 17.

Goodwin, R. (1989). *"Schumpeter: The Man I Knew", in Essays in Nonlinear dynamics: Collected Papers (1980–1987)*. Frankfurt-am-Main: Peter Lang.

Hicks, J. (1973). *Capital and Time: A Neo-Austrian Theory*. Oxford: Clarendon Press.

Kalecki, M. (1935, July). A Macrodynamic Theory of Business Cycles. *Econometrica, 3*(3), 327–344.

Keynes, J. (1936). *The General Theory of Employment, Interest and Money*. London: Macmillan.

Marshall, A. (1920). *Principles of Economics*. (Revised 8th ed.). London: Macmillan.

Polya, G. (1945). *How to Solve It*. Princeton, NJ: Princeton University Press.
Romer, P. (1986). Increasing Returns and Long Run Growth. *Journal of Political Economy, 94*, 1002–1037.
Romer, P. (1990). Endogenous Technological Change. *Journal of Political Economy, 98*, S71–S102.
Romer, P. (1993). Two Strategies for Economic Development: Using Ideas and Producing Ideas. In *Proceedings of the World Bank Annual Conference on Development Economics*, IBRD, World Bank, Washington, DC.
Schumpeter, J. (1934). *The Theory of Economic Development*. Cambridge: Harvard University Press. (First published in German in 1911.)
Solow, R., (1990). Goodwin's Growth Cycle: Reminiscence and Rumination", in Velupillai K. Vela, Editor. 1990. Nonlinear and Multisectorial Macrodynamics: Essays in Honour of Richard Goodwin. London: Macmillan.
Sraffa, P. (1960). *Production of Commodities by Means of Commodities*. Cambridge: Cambridge University Press.
Velupillai, K. V. (2000). *Computable Economics*. Oxford: Oxford University Press.
Velupillai, K. V. (2007). The Impossibility of an Effective Theory of Policy in a Complex Economy. In M. Salzano & D. Colander (Eds.), *Complexity Hints for Economic Policy* (pp. 273–290). Milano and Heidelberg: Springer-Verlag Italia.
Velupillai, K. V. (2010). *Computable Foundations for Economics*. London: Routledge.
Winter, S. (2005). Towards an Evolutionary Theory of Production. In K. Dopfer (Ed.), *The Evolutionary Foundations of Economics* (pp. 223–253). Cambridge: Cambridge University Press.
Zambelli, S. (2004). Production of Ideas by Means of Ideas: A Turing Machine Metaphor. *Metroeconomica, 55*(2–3), 155–179.
Zambelli, S. (2005). Computable Knowledge and Undecidability: A Turing Machine Metaphor. In K. V. Velupillai (Ed.), *Computability, Complexity and Constructivity in Economic Analysis* (pp. 233–263). Blackwell.
Zambelli, S. (2010). *Computable, Constructive & Behavioural Economic Dynamics: Essays in Honour of Kumaraswamy (Vela) Velupillai*. London: Routledge.
Zambelli, S., & Dharmaraj, N., (2013). "Carry – on – Activity" and Process innovation, ASSRU Discussion Papers: 3 – 2013/II, ASSRU - Algorithmic Social Science Research Unit. University of Trento, Italy.

# 9

# The Non-Robustness of Saddle-Point Dynamics: A Methodological Perspective

Donald A. R. George

## 1 Introduction

You will never observe an egg standing on its end. The egg may balance there for a split second, but almost instantly it will roll onto its side and come to rest there. The property "standing on its end" might reasonably be called **non-robust**. It may occur by a fluke, but small random perturbations will cause it to disappear, and so, in any meaningful sense, it is unobservable. Economists need to make observations against which to test their theories. So it would be reasonable to treat an economic model which makes non-robust predictions as empirically non-testable. In Sect. 2 I discuss the relationship between robustness and the methodology of economics. In Sect. 3 I provide a mathematical definition of robustness and show how a wide range of macroeconomic models, which rely on saddle-point dynamics, fail the test of robustness. Section 4 applies this analysis to models of

D. A. R. George (✉)
School of Economics, University of Edinburgh, Edinburgh, UK
e-mail: D.George@ed.ac.uk



K. Velupillai (ed.), *Keynesian, Sraffian, Computable and Dynamic Economics*,
https://doi.org/10.1007/978-3-030-58131-2_9

economic growth and to rational expectations models of inflation. In Sect. 5 I examine the related issue of global versus local analysis, and Sect. 6 concludes.

## 2 Robustness and Methodology

Despite appearances to the contrary, economics is (or should be) an empirical discipline. Theories should be confronted with data and, if found wanting, modified or discarded. It may be that the underlying assumptions of a theory are not themselves open to empirical test but that testable implications can be drawn from them. However, there immediately arises the problem of verisimilitude. The underlying assumptions of any theory are unlikely to be exactly true descriptions of the real world but, one hopes, are close approximations to it. Under such circumstances it is important that the implications of a scientific theory are robust with respect to small variations in the underlying assumptions. Such variations should only produce small variations in the theory's implications, not wild and dramatic ones. Without this property, empirical testing of theories becomes impossible, because of random environmental perturbations in the conditions under which observations are made. As Baumol (citing Solow) (1958) puts it:

> since our premises are always more or less false, good theorising consists to a large extent in avoiding assumptions … where a small change in what is posited will seriously affect the conclusions.

Consider, for example, a physical theory which predicts the outcome of a particular nuclear reaction in a constant magnetic field. Whatever care the experimental physicist may take, she will not be able to hold the magnetic field exactly constant; it is bound to fluctuate slightly during the course of the experiment. Suppose the outcome of the experiment is substantially different from what the theory predicted. Is the theory refuted? The theorist can always reply that the magnetic field was not exactly constant, as his theory requires, so that the experiment does not, therefore, constitute a refutation. This would not be the case if the robustness property, discussed above, had been required of the theory ab initio. Had the theory satisfied this property, the experimenter could be sure that, according to the theory, small fluctuations in the magnetic field could only generate small fluctuations in the outcome of the reaction. An experimental outcome substantially different from the theory's predictions would then constitute a genuine refutation of the theory. Non-robust theoretical predictions are, in practice, non-observable, and therefore of no scientific interest. I argue that robustness be considered a necessary (though not sufficient) condition for a theory to be scientifically valid.

## 3 Robustness in Economic Models

This kind of problem clearly arises in economics as well as physics. The theory under test is typically expressed as a model involving some parameters which are assumed to be constant. The marginal propensity to consume or the interest elasticity of the demand for money might fall into this category. Of course, no one actually believes that parameters such as these are exactly constant over time: they are bound to vary slightly, just as the magnetic field would in the physical example discussed above. It is clear then that the robustness property should be required as a necessary (though not sufficient) property of any economic theory, if that theory is to be regarded as scientifically valid. There are many economic theories which fail this robustness test (e.g. most models involving saddle-point dynamics; see Oxley and George (2007) for an elaboration of this argument) and cannot, therefore, even be considered candidates for empirical refutation.

To sharpen the analysis, I offer a more rigorous definition of robustness, relying on the fact that economic theories are typically expressed in the form of mathematical models which include some endogenous variables and some parameters. I adopt the following definition of "robustness".

**Definition 1** Any property of a model will be called **robust** if the set of parameter values for which it occurs is of strictly positive Lebesgue measure.

This definition ensures that small random perturbations of parameters will not cause the given property to disappear. A non-robust property is one which occurs for a set of parameter values of measure zero, and thus can be thought of as having a zero probability of occurring. Of course, it is a well-known conundrum of probability theory that, although an event which cannot occur has a probability of zero, the converse does not hold. An event with zero probability could occur, though I think it is appropriate to label such events as unobservable. Note that the definition has been framed in such a way as to ensure that the randomness of perturbations is appropriately captured. Suppose that a certain property $P$ occurs for given parameter values. There may be parameter values arbitrarily near the given values, which cause the property $P$ to disappear, but that does not necessarily mean that $P$ is a non-robust property. For example, the property of "having a chaotic trajectory" can easily be robust even though, in models with a chaotic attractor, there often exists a set of periodic points which is dense in that attractor. In this case, arbitrarily close to an initial state of a chaotic trajectory there are unstable periodic points. In fact, dense sets may easily have measure zero. For example, the set of rational numbers is dense in the set of reals, but is countable and therefore certainly of measure zero.

The familiar saddle-point phase portrait is depicted in Fig. 9.1. Economic models with saddle-point dynamics include Buiter and Miller (1981), Eastwood and Venables (1982) and Neary and Purvis (1982).

The textbooks often describe saddle-point phase portraits as "semi-stable", but in reality they are more unstable than stable. The robustness problem is immediately apparent. Only solution paths starting on the stable branch (shown in blue) converge to a long-run equilibrium: all other paths diverge to zero or infinity. Divergent paths are shown in red or yellow; the unstable branch is shown in brown. Moreover, even a convergent path, starting on the stable branch, is a fragile thing. Small random perturbations of the model's parameters will cause a convergent path to transmute into a divergent one. The set of parameters for which

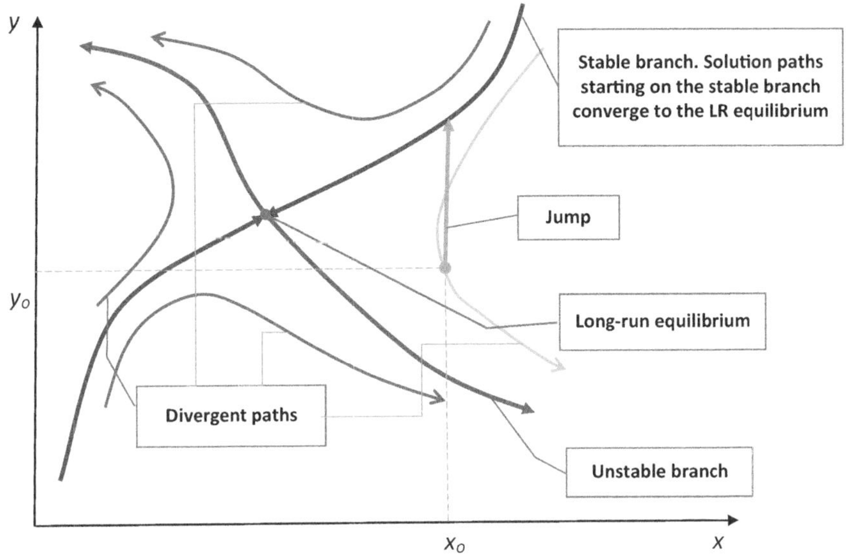


**Fig. 9.1** Two-dimensional non-linear saddle-point phase portrait

the model is convergent is of measure zero and so, from definition 1 above, we describe convergence as a **non-robust** property. Conversely, divergence is a **robust** property: small random perturbations will cause a divergent path to transmute into another divergent path close to it. This situation is problematic for economists' standard methodology, which requires the model to converge to a long-run equilibrium (see George and Oxley 1994 for a discussion). Consider the effects of a parameter shift. The standard methodology analyses such a shift by calculating the new long-run equilibrium and comparing it with the old one. This is the method of comparative dynamics, to which I return in Sect. 5. But if the model does not converge to its new long-run equilibrium this approach is bound to fail. So the model must operate on its stable branch (or stable manifold in higher dimensions), but what guarantees that this is indeed the case? At this stage the standard methodology invokes the helpful concept of a "jump variable". These are variables (often control variables) which can change discontinuously (jump) in such a way as to place the system on its stable branch. Such a jump (in the control variable *y*) is

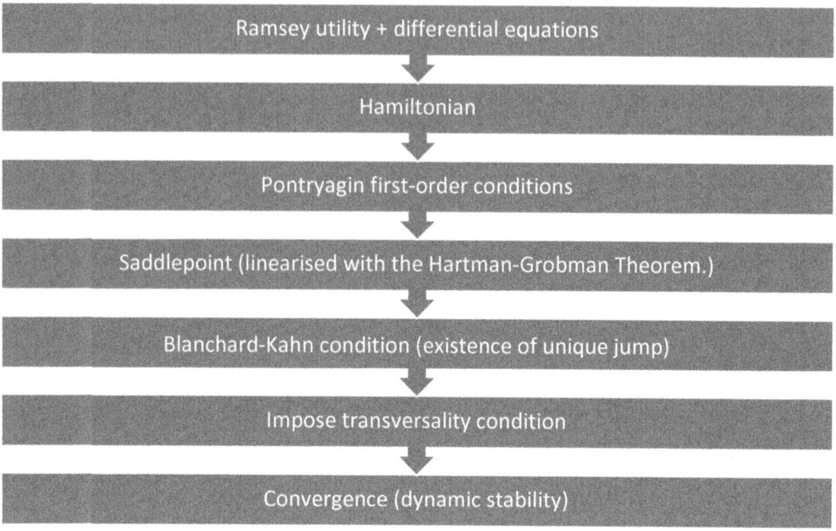


**Fig. 9.2** Dynamic stability of economic models: standard approach (flow diagram)

shown in green in Fig. 9.2. Starting at $(x_0, y_0)$ the system would diverge on the yellow path if it were not for the jump in $y$. For a model in many dimensions Blanchard and Kahn (1980) show that it is necessary and sufficient for the existence of a unique jump that the number of jump variables equals the dimension of the unstable manifold (the number of eigenvalues with positive real parts). The Blanchard/Kahn condition is satisfied in Fig. 9.2, where there is one jump variable ($y$) and the unstable manifold (branch) has dimension one. But what mechanism brings about the requisite jump? I consider the following three possibilities:

1. Divine intervention: God imposes the necessary jump.
2. A centrally planned economy: a central planning board imposes the necessary jump.
3. Mainstream economic theory: an equilibrium concept is invoked which restricts the model's solution paths to those lying in the stable branch.

The first of these (divine intervention) I deem to be beyond the scope of Economics, and I imagine the Deity is not overly concerned with validating economists' models. The second (centrally planned economy) is of little use. Most economists are interested in modelling decentralized market economies and, in any event, central economic planning has decisively gone out of fashion in the last 30 years. So that leaves the third option (mainstream economic theory). But it is not immediately obvious what kind of equilibrium is intended here. The standard approach to defining such an equilibrium is to invoke a controlling agent maximizing a Ramsey-type utility function with an infinite horizon. In macroeconomic models, such as those considered below, this maximand might be interpreted as a social welfare function or the utility function of a "representative household". Buiter (2009) refers to this controlling agent as "The Auctioneer at the end of time".

A four-step guide to the economist's standard methodology is presented below.

## 3.1 Step 1

Set up the problem as the maximization of a Ramsey-type utility (or welfare) function, such as that of Eq. (9.1), subject to some differential equation constraints, summarized in Eq. (9.2).

$$\text{Maximize } W = \int_0^\infty U(\boldsymbol{x},\boldsymbol{y})e^{-rt}\,dt \tag{9.1}$$

$$\text{subject to } \dot{\boldsymbol{x}} = G(\boldsymbol{x},\boldsymbol{y},t) \tag{9.2}$$

Where $\boldsymbol{x}$ is a vector of state variables (governed by the differential equation constraints of Eq. (9.2)), $\boldsymbol{y}$ is a vector of control variables and $r$ is the discount rate. To carry out the maximization, a Hamiltonian is formed:

$$H(\boldsymbol{x},\boldsymbol{y},\boldsymbol{p}) = U(\boldsymbol{x},\boldsymbol{y})e^{-rt} + \boldsymbol{p}.G(\boldsymbol{x},\boldsymbol{y},t) \tag{9.3}$$

The vector $\boldsymbol{p}$ consists of co-state variables, one for each state variable, each representing the discounted shadow price of the state variable to which it corresponds. In economic models the state variables are typically stocks (e.g. the stock of physical capital, human capital or "knowledge"). The control variables are typically choice variables of the "representative household" or a benign "social planner".

## 3.2 Step 2

Appealing to Pontryagin's Maximum Principle, calculate the first-order (necessary) conditions by differentiating the Hamiltonian (9.1). This yields:

$$H_y = 0 \text{ for each control variable } y \text{ and :} \tag{9.4}$$

$$H_x + \dot{p} = 0 \text{ for each state variable } x \text{ and corresponding co-state variable } p. \tag{9.5}$$

Equations (9.2), (9.4) and (9.5) together yield a non-linear dynamical system in the control variables $\boldsymbol{y}$ and the state variables $\boldsymbol{x}$.

## 3.3 Step 3

Locate the equilibria of the dynamical system (and hope there is only one): they are values of $\boldsymbol{x}$ and $\boldsymbol{y}$ such that:

$$\dot{\boldsymbol{x}} = 0, \dot{\boldsymbol{y}} = 0 \tag{9.6}$$

Appealing to the Hartman-Grobman Theorem (see Hartman 1960; Arrowsmith and Place 1992), linearize the dynamical system derived in Step 2 in the neighbourhood of an equilibrium. This procedure yields a local linear approximation to the original dynamical system in the neighbourhood of *any* given point in phase space (provided all the eigenvalues of the linearization have non-zero real parts), though in economic models it is almost always an equilibrium as defined by Eq. (9.6). It is important to note that this approximation is local, not global, and takes the form of homeomorphism. That is, there exists a local homeomorphism mapping the phase portrait of the original dynamical system to that of its approximation. By calculating the eigenvalues of the linearization, deduce that it is a saddle-point phase portrait. (Some eigenvalues have positive real parts, others have negative real parts.) By the Hartman-Grobman Theorem it follows that the original phase portrait is (locally) also a saddle-point.

## 3.4 Step 4

By definition all the solution paths of the Hamiltonian problem, including the divergent ones, satisfy the first-order conditions. So to confine attention to those solution paths lying in the stable branch (or manifold in higher dimensions) the standard procedure is to invoke the transversality condition with an infinite horizon. This condition asserts that:

$$\mathbf{p}.\mathbf{x} \to 0 \; as \; t \to \infty. \tag{9.7}$$

Or, in economic terms, the discounted shadow value of the state variables (usually stocks such as capital) tends to zero as time tends to infinity. It is easy to show that this transversality condition (9.7) can only be satisfied on the stable branch. It can be thought of as a terminal condition (at infinity) and, combined with initial conditions for the state variables, picks out a unique convergent solution path.

At first sight the transversality condition may appear plausible, if one is willing to accept the premises of the model. In a growth model in which the maximand is the discounted present value of the utility (or "welfare") of consumption, it is plausible that the shadow value of the capital stock is zero "at the end of time". If it were not, then the economy could have gained more utility (or welfare) by consuming more capital. However, there are several difficulties with step 4:

1. Transversality condition (9.7) is not always a necessary condition for the solution of the Hamiltonian problem (e.g. see Halkin 1971).
2. Transversality condition (9.7) could be imposed by invoking a "no Ponzi Games" condition or an overlapping generations model, but these would entail a suite of extra assumptions in addition to those underlying the model.
3. In a model with a finite horizon ($T$) the transversality condition becomes:

$$p(T).x(T)=0 \tag{9.8}$$

which can be satisfied on a divergent path but not a convergent one, as illustrated in Fig. 9.3. Even imposing a transversality condition with an infinite horizon (such as condition (9.7)) does not eliminate the problem raised above. Ruling out divine intervention and central planning, it is not clear what mechanism causes the necessary jump to come about. Buiter (2009) comments:

> And then a small miracle happens. An optimality criterion from a mathematical dynamic optimisation approach is transplanted, lock, stock and barrel to the behaviour of long-term price expectations in a decentralised market economy. In the mathematical programming exercise it is clear where the terminal boundary condition in question comes from. The terminal boundary condition that the influence of the infinitely distant future on asset prices today vanishes, is a 'transversality condition' that is part of the necessary and sufficient conditions for an optimum. But in a decentralised market economy there is no mathematical programmer imposing the terminal boundary conditions to make sure everything will be all right.

That is not to say that discontinuously changing (jump) variables should never appear in economic models. For example, catastrophe theory provides a means to model such variables in an illuminating way (e.g. see Rosser 1991; Poston and Stewart 1978; George 1981). Catastrophe models explicitly analyse both fast and slow speeds of adjustment. A "catastrophe", or jump, occurs when the fast flow dominates the slow flow. Such jumps are treated as endogenous to the model, and not bolted

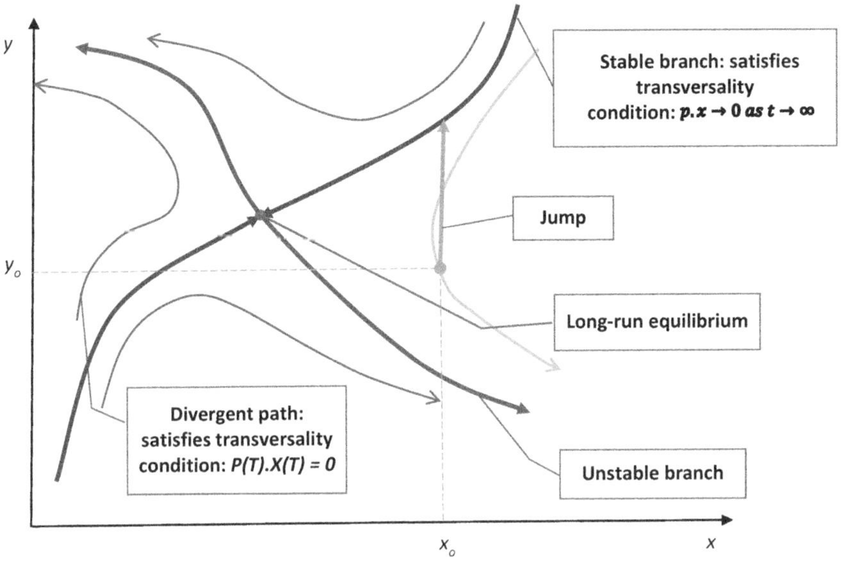


**Fig. 9.3** Dynamic stability of economic models: standard approach (phase diagram)

on as an unconvincing afterthought. In economic models the slow flow is usually interpreted as a moving equilibrium, while the fast flow is interpreted as disequilibrium behaviour.

The economist's standard methodology is illustrated in Fig. 9.2 as a flow chart and in Fig. 9.3 as a phase diagram. Returning to the egg analogy of Sect. 1, imposing a transversality condition is equivalent to forcing robustness by gluing the egg to a plate. It would then stand on its end, but far more forces then mere gravity would be involved.

# 4 Two Economic Examples

## 4.1 Economic Growth Models

Economic growth models often have the form described in Sect. 3. The state variables are typically stocks such as physical capital, human capital or "knowledge", so-called backward-looking variables whose levels are determined by their history and which therefore cannot jump. The key economic assumptions of such a model are embodied in an equation such as (9.2). But that is not enough to close the model and generate a unique solution. So an infinite horizon, controlling agent is introduced into the model, often interpreted as a "representative household", sometimes in an elaborate "overlapping generations" framework. In the Uzawa-Lucas two-sector model of growth with human capital (Uzawa 1965; Lucas 1988) there are two backward-looking variables (physical capital and human capital) and two jump variables (consumption and a variable $v$ which indicates the proportion of human capital allocated to the final output sector), generating a four-dimensional saddle-point model. In dimension higher than two the possibility arises of eigenvalues with non-zero imaginary parts, indicating cyclical solution paths but all the issues, raised above in the two-dimensional context, continue to manifest themselves. In two dimensions, complex eigenvalues can only occur in conjugate pairs, which must have real parts with the same sign. So there can be no "cyclical saddle-points" in two dimensions (which is immediately obvious from geometrical intuition).

The analysis proceeds according to the standard methodology described above. The economic assumptions of the model are embodied in an equation similar to Eq. (9.2). They concern the dynamic interaction between a final goods sector and an "education sector" in a model where physical and human capital are distinct factors of production. The analysis generates a saddle-point phase portrait in four dimensions. Because of the higher dimensionality, the stable and unstable branches become stable and unstable *manifolds* respectively. Happily the Blanchard-Kahn condition is satisfied: the unstable manifold has dimension two, and there are two jump variables ($C$ and $v$). So we know there exists a unique jump which would place the economy on the stable manifold and guarantee to convergence to the long-run equilibrium. But the issues of Sect. 3 are immediately apparent. We are asked to imagine the infinitely long-lived "representative household" suddenly changing its consumption level and its allocation of human capital between final goods and education sector, in order to satisfy a transversality condition. While the plausibility of the underlying economics, embodied in Eq. (9.2), is open to debate, the "add-on" jump variable/transversality condition assumptions are wholly implausible and are doing much of the work of driving the model's conclusions. From the methodological perspective this presents the economist with a well-known issue: the Duhem-Quine problem (see Cross 1982). Empirical testing of the Uzawa-Lucas model (and most mainstream economic growth models) would entail jointly testing the economics of Eq. (9.2) along with the jump variable/transversality assumptions. Suppose we have data which refute an implication of the model; is the underlying economics of Eq. (9.2) now rejected? Not necessarily: it may be the jump variable/transversality assumptions which are at fault.

Further examples of endogenous growth models which rely on saddle-point dynamics include Romer's (1990) model of purposeful invention and the Aghion and Howitt (1992) Schumpeterian endogenous growth model. Both are analysed in Barro and Sala-i-Martin (2004), along with a discussion of the transversality condition.

## 4.2 Rational Expectations Models

The assumption of rational expectations is now an essential feature of many mainstream macrodynamic models. Following Muth (1961) economists typically assume that agents' "subjective expectation will be equated with the true mathematical expectation implied by the model itself". So agents are assumed to be "forward looking": they may make errors, but only random and unsystematic ones. The assumption of rational expectations is a behavioural hypothesis, possibly a reasonable working hypothesis. It is open to question, and there are alternative expectations hypotheses available, but in practice, the Duhem-Quine problem, discussed above, re-asserts itself. The rational expectations hypothesis is typically embedded in a macrodynamic model with a saddle-point structure, so that it can only be empirically tested jointly with the jump variable/transversality paraphernalia discussed in Sect. 3. A particular difficulty with the rational expectations hypothesis is that it does not specify how far into the future individuals are assumed to look. This proves crucial when we consider the solutions to rational expectations models. A further problem arises from the higher moments of the statistical distribution of the relevant variables. Most rational expectations models circumvent these issues by invoking the idea of *certainty equivalence,* so that actual values of future variables can be replaced with current expectations of those future variables. This allows the consideration of a single market relevant expectation, and rational expectations boil down to perfect foresight. But this useful simplification is only possible if the model is linear, with zero mean additive error terms. We return to the issue of linearization in Sect. 5.

A canonical rational expectations model (see Buiter and Miller 1981; Eastwood and Venables 1982; Neary and Purvis 1982) might have the price level ($p$) as a backward-looking variable, dependent on slowly changing wage contracts, and the exchange rate ($e$) as a jump variable, set almost instantaneously by "smart speculators" with the latest IT. The reduced form of such a model has a linear saddle-point structure such that *every* solution path is consistent with rational expectations (in fact with perfect foresight). So the problem of Sect. 3 asserts itself. Given an initial condition for the backward looking variable, the transversality condition is invoked to supply a terminal condition "at infinity", ensuring convergence to the long-run equilibrium. Eastwood and Venables (1982) tell us:

> The stable branch plays an important role in the analysis to follow, since we rule out *by assumption* all paths which do not converge to a steady state. The uniqueness of the path (actually followed by the economy) evidently depends crucially on *the assumption that* rational agents anticipate convergence to a steady state. (emphasis added)

Buiter and Miller (1981) elaborate further:

> The *assumption* of the transversality condition that rational agents will not choose an unstable solution [i.e. a divergent solution path] mean[s] that the jump variable ... will always assume the value required to put the system on the unique convergent solution trajectory. (Emphasis and comment added)

Neary and Purvis (1982) (in the context of a three-dimensional saddle-point model) reinforce the position with:

> This gives rise to a typical saddlepoint structure ... the single positive root contributes a direction of instability, but exchange rate speculators *are assumed* to choose an initial value of e (exchange rate) and hence of $\pi$ ('real' exchange rate) which ensures that the model converges towards a long-run equilibrium. (Emphasis added)

Note that the Blanchard-Kahn condition is satisfied in this model: the unstable manifold has dimension one and there is one jump variable (the exchange rate). Note also that in a typical rational expectations model it is a price (the exchange rate) that jumps, whereas in a typical growth model it is a quantity (such as consumption) that jumps. The former may seem more plausible, but both types of model suffer from the Duhem-Quine problem, and neither offers a credible justification for the jump variable/transversality mechanism.

# 5 Linearization

As discussed in Sect. 3, the economists' standard methodology relies on linearization of a dynamical system by (sometimes unacknowledged) appeal to the Hartman-Grobman theorem. This theorem provides a means to calculate a local, linear, topological (homeomorphic) approximation to the phase portrait of a non-linear dynamical system in the neighbourhood of any point (provided that all the eigenvalues of the linearization have non-zero real parts). The point in question is usually a long-run equilibrium in economic models. This procedure has three apparent advantages:

(a) By calculating the eigenvalues and eigenvectors of the linearization, the long-run equilibrium can be characterized.
(b) In dimension higher than two, complex eigenvalues indicate the presence of cyclical behaviour.
(c) It allows the certainty equivalence principle to be applied.

But the linear approximation is local and topological, thus presenting some major difficulties. To quote Buiter (2009) again:

> ... any potentially policy-relevant model would be highly non-linear, and ... the interaction of these non-linearities and uncertainty makes for deep conceptual and technical problems. Macroeconomists are brave, but not that brave. So they took these non-linear stochastic dynamic general equilibrium models into the basement and beat them with a rubber hose until they behaved. This was achieved by completely stripping the model of its non-linearities.

We turn first to the limitations arising from the local nature of the linear approximation. Consider the non-linear dynamical system (9.9):

$$\left.\begin{aligned} \dot{x} &= y \\ \dot{y} &= -x + y - y^3 \\ x(0) &= x_0, y(0) = y_0 \end{aligned}\right\} \tag{9.9}$$

Its phase portrait is that of a stable limit cycle (Fig. 9.4). The blue closed curve indicates regular cyclical motion. All other solution paths converge towards the limit cycle.

This dynamical system has one long-run equilibrium at the origin. Linearizing in the neighbourhood of this equilibrium yields the dynamical system (9.10):

$$\left.\begin{aligned} \dot{x} &= y \\ \dot{y} &= -x + y \\ x(0) &= x_0, y(0) = y_0 \end{aligned}\right\} \tag{9.10}$$

Calculation of the eigenvalues of (9.9) reveals the solution paths to be unstable spirals (Fig. 9.5).

The linearized model diverges to infinity and would therefore be deemed of little economic interest. *Near the origin* the original system and its linearization do have homeomorphic flows, as the

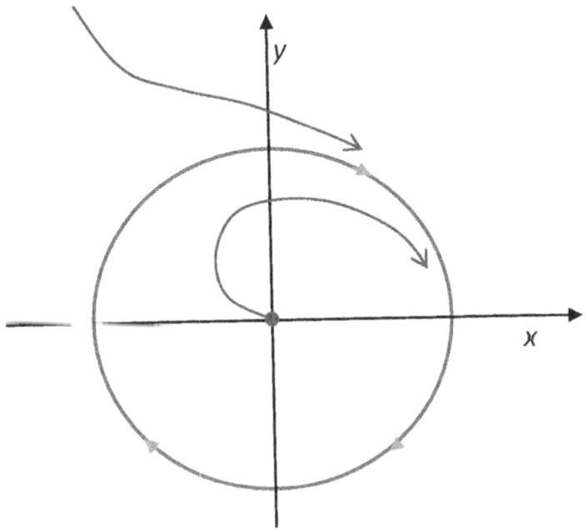


**Fig. 9.4** Stable limit cycle

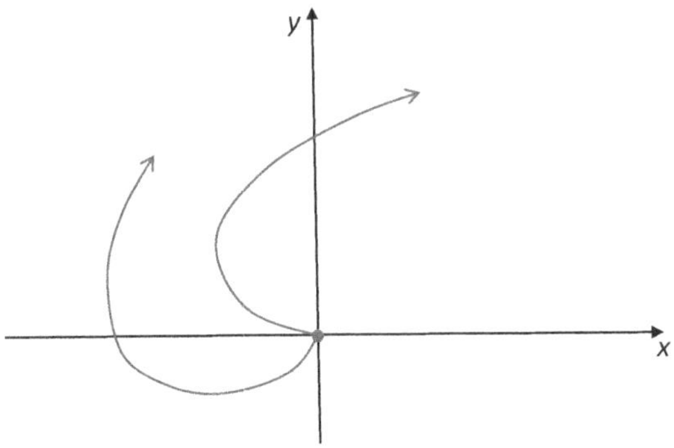


**Fig. 9.5** Unstable spirals

Hartman-Grobman theorem requires. But this equivalence is only local, and does not provide a picture of the system's global behaviour. Analysed globally the system of Eq. (9.9) may well be of economic interest, indicating some form of persistent, regular cyclical behaviour.

The contrast between global and local dynamics is exemplified clearly by George and Oxley (2008). They develop a model of inflation, keeping close to macroeconomic orthodoxy. Asset market equilibrium under perfect foresight, market clearing and strictly controlled money growth are assumed, along with a standard demand for money function. Note that the strict money growth assumption rules out Cagan-type explanations (Cagan 1956) of hyperinflation. But there is one deviation from orthodoxy: a variable returns to scale production function. Similar nonlinearities could arise from a technical progress function of Kaldorian type. This generates a model which, for some parameter values, has multiple equilibria: there are three cases:

1. growing economy with two stable equilibria
2. growing economy with a single stable equilibrium
3. contracting economy with two stable equilibria

Linearizing and imposing the jump variable/transversality mechanism leads to the standard mainstream result: in the long run the inflation rate equals the rate of money growth. Analysing the model globally presents a quite different picture. Now the model converges (robustly) to a stable equilibrium, and along solution paths there are hyperinflationary bubbles. Numerical simulation indicates long-run inflation rates of 2000%–3000%, with a money growth rate of 5%. The methodological issue is clear. Empirical observation of hyperinflationary bubbles would confirm the non-linear model but refute the linearized version. Empirical analysis by George and Oxley (1991) indicates the presence of hyperinflationary bubbles which track the simulation results for several countries including Germany, Greece, Hungary, Argentina, Mexico and Uruguay. This analysis confirms the non-linear model and refutes its linearization.

Further methodological problems arise when we turn attention to the jump variables. As discussed in Sect. 3, the economist's standard methodology includes the method of comparative dynamics. Suppose a parameter shock occurs, such as a change in the rate of money growth. The consequences of such a shock are typically analysed by calculating the new long-run equilibrium and characterizing the adjustment path from old to new equilibrium. But the original model and its linearization may easily imply very different adjustment paths. This is illustrated in Fig. 9.6.

The linearization implies a downward jump in $y$ to establish convergence, while the original system implies an upward jump. Empirical observation of the former jump confirms the linearization but refutes the original model, vice versa for the latter observation.

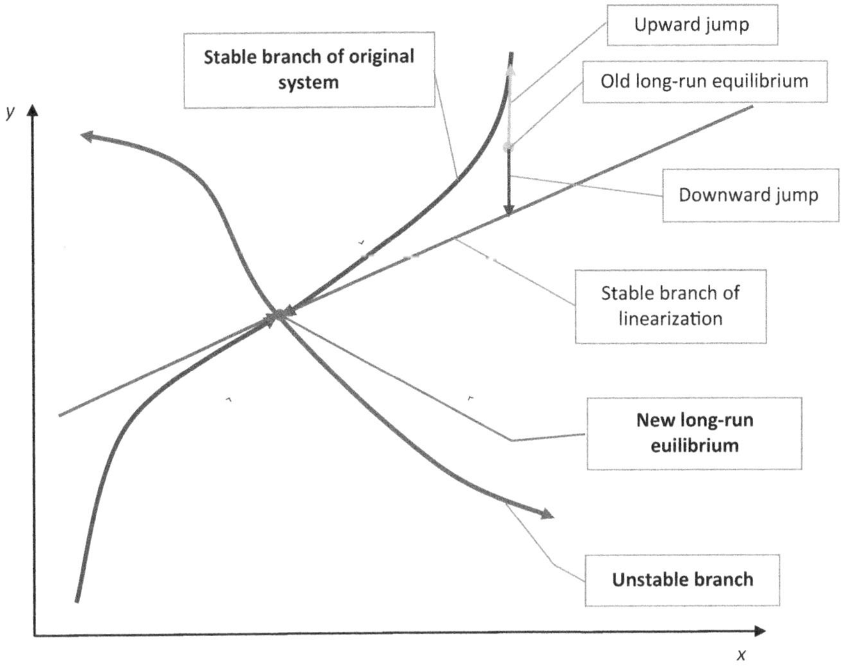


**Fig. 9.6** Non-linear saddle-point versus its linearization

# 6 Conclusions

I propose that robustness be regarded as a necessary (though not sufficient) property for an economic model to be considered scientifically valid. Without this property, meaningful empirical testing would be impossible. Models relying on saddle-point dynamics typically do not possess this property and are therefore not even candidates for empirical testing. Many macroeconomic models (including growth models, exchange rate models and models of inflation) secure robustness by invoking a suite of additional assumptions, involving infinite horizon optimization, jump variables and transversality conditions. This procedure immediately raises the Duhem-Quine problem of empirical testing, and moreover, these additional assumptions are usually highly implausible, lacking any credible real-world interpretation.

For reasons of mathematical convenience, macroeconomic models are often analysed by means of local linear approximation. This process may easily divert attention from economically important features of the model such as cyclical behaviour or hyperinflationary bubbles. It also raises potential methodological problems (in addition to Duhem-Quine) because the linearization can quite easily make predictions diametrically opposed to those of the original model.

The solution to these problems is to embrace non-linear dynamic models in macroeconomics, and to analyse them without recourse to local linearization. This would mean dropping the Certainty Equivalence Principle. Since most non-linear dynamical systems cannot be solved analytically, this approach would require the use of qualitative analysis and simulation methods. The mathematics required is now in the textbooks (see e.g. Azbelev et al. 2007) and the journals (see e.g. Iserles and Terjeki 1995) and simulation packages are now readily available, so a brave new world of credible and empirically testable non-linear macroeconomic models is surely just around the corner. That world has already been explored by the more perspicacious members of the economics profession, notably including Stefano Zambelli (2011).

**Acknowledgements** I am grateful to Les Oxley for insights into macroeconomic modelling, and for allowing me to draw upon research we have conducted jointly. Precursors of this chapter have been presented at the European University Institute, Italy, Uppsala University, Sweden and the University of Melbourne, Australia. I am grateful for the invitations to those seminars and for the constructive comments made. Any remaining errors or omissions are entirely my own.

## References

Aghion, P., & Howitt. (1992). A Model of Growth Through Creative Destruction. *Econometrica, 60*, 323–351.

Arrowsmith, D. K., & Place, C. M. (1992). The Linearization Theorem. In D. K. Arrowsmith & C. M. Place (Eds.), *Dynamical Systems: Differential Equations, Maps, and Chaotic Behaviour*. London: Chapman and Hall.

Azbelev, N. V., Maksimov, V. P., & Rakhmatullina, L. F. (2007). *Introduction to the Theory of Functional Differential Equations: Methods and Applications.* New York: Hindawi Publishing Corporation.

Barro, R. J., & Sala-i-Martin, X. (2004). *Economic Growth* (2nd ed.). London: MIT Press.

Baumol, W. J. (1958). Topology of Second-Order Linear Difference Equations with Constant Coefficients. *Econometrica, 26*, 258–285.

Blanchard, O., & Kahn, C. (1980). The Solution of Linear Difference Models under Rational Expectations. *Econometrica, 48*, 1305–1311.

Buiter, W. (2009). *The Unfortunate Uselessness of Most 'State of the Art' Academic Monetary Economics.* Vox CEPR Policy Portal. Retrieved 2019, from https://voxeu.org/article/macroeconomics-crisis-irrelevance

Buiter, W., & Miller, M. (1981). Monetary Policy and International Competitiveness: The Problem of Adjustment. In W. Eltis & P. Sinclair (Eds.), *The Money Supply and the Exchange Rate*. Oxford: OUP.

Cagan, P. (1956). The Monetary Dynamics of Hyperinflation. In M. Friedman (Ed.), *Studies in the Quantity Theory of Money*. Chicago: University of Chicago Press.

Cross, R. (1982). The Duhem-Quine Thesis, Lakatos and the Appraisal of Theories in Macroeconomics. *Economic Journal, 92*, 320–340.

Eastwood, R., & Venables, A. (1982). The Macroeconomic Implications of a Resource Discovery in an Open Economy. *Economic Journal, 92*, 285–299.

George, D. A. R. (1981). Equilibrium and Catastrophes in Economics. *Scottish Journal of Political Economy, 28*, 43–61.

George, D. A. R., & Oxley, L. (1991). Fixed Money Growth Rules and the Rate of Inflation: Global Versus Local Dynamics. *Scottish Journal of Political Economy, 38*, 209–226.

George, D. A. R., & Oxley, L. (1994). Linear Saddlepoint Dynamics on Their Head. *European Journal of Political Economy, 10*, 389–400.

George, D. A. R., & Oxley, L. (2008). Money and Inflation in a Nonlinear Model. *Mathematics and Computers in Simulation, 78*, 257–265.

Halkin, H. (1971). Necessary Conditions for Optimal Control Problems with Infinite Horizons. *Econometrica, 42*, 267–272.

Hartman, P. (1960). A Lemma in the Theory of Structural Stability of Differential Equations. *Proceedings of the American Mathematical Society, 11*, 610–620.

Iserles, A., & Terjeki, J. (1995). Stability and Asymptotic Stability of Functional-Differential Equations. *Journal of the London Mathematical Society, 51*, 559–572.

Lucas, R. E. (1988). On the Mechanisms of Economic Development. *Journal of Monetary Economics, 22*, 3–42.

Muth, J. F. (1961). Rational Expectations and the Theory of Price Movements. *Econometrica, 29*, 315–335.

Neary, P., & Purvis, D. (1982). Sectoral Shocks in a Dependent Economy: Long-Run Adjustment and Short-Run Accommodation. *Scandinavian Journal of Economics, 84*, 97–121.

Oxley, L., & George, D. A. R. (2007). Economics on the Edge of Chaos. *Environmental Modelling and Software, 22*, 417–425.

Poston, T., & Stewart, I. (1978). *Catastrophe Theory and Its Applications.* London: Pitman.

Romer, P. M. (1990). Endogenous Technological Change. *Journal of Political Economy, 98*, S71–S102.

Rosser, J. B. (1991). *From Catastrophe to Chaos: A General Theory of Economic Discontinuities.* Boston: Kluwer.

Uzawa, H. (1965). Optimal Technical Change in an Aggregative Model of Economic Growth. *International Economic Review, 6*, 18–31.

Zambelli, S. (2011). Flexible Accelerator Economic Systems as Coupled Oscillators. *Journal of Economic Surveys, 25*, 608–633.

# 10

# The Economic Intuitions at the Base of Stefano Zambelli's Technical Contributions

G. C. Harcourt

As I explained to Vela (5 December 2019), I was in despair about being able to write anything suitable as a tribute to Stefano, mainly because of the highly technical nature of his fine contributions. So I suggested to Vela that I base my contribution on that of our friend and mentor, the late Dick Goodwin, to Harcourt and Riach (eds.), *A 'Second Edition' of the General Theory*, vol. 1, Routledge, 1997, Ch 10. Vela (5 October 19) most graciously agreed. In two pages Dick wrote a succinct but profound essay on the difficulties of tackling dynamics within the structure of Maynard Keynes's analysis in The General Theory, Keynes 1936, C.W. vol. 7, 1973. Dick wrote: "[A]t any one time the economy is subject to a large number of different stimuli in various stages of decay. The sum of these coexisting diminishing effects will be, for any particular historical stretch, highly complicated, irregular time series" (Goodwin 1997, p. 162). I think Zambelli has been tackling a similar set of issues.

G. C. Harcourt (✉)
School of Economics, UNSW, Sydney, NSW, Australia
e-mail: gch@unsw.edu.au



K. Velupillai (ed.), *Keynesian, Sraffian, Computable and Dynamic Economics*,
https://doi.org/10.1007/978-3-030-58131-2_10

Let me put it this way: at any moment of time decision-makers have to decide on what employment to offer and, in imperfect competition, what prices to set or maintain, in order to produce the goods and services that match what they think the demands for these will be. They also have to decide what orders for capital goods, and changes in stocks, to implement and/or what constructions they should do themselves. They also have to decide on how to finance these various activities.

All the results of these various decisions are combined with ongoing processes arising from similar past decisions. Some of these are about to be or actually are fulfilled, some are part of the way through, and some have just begun. The basic problems that I believe Zambelli (and others of course) is tackling is how to capture these complicated real-world phenomena in models which are tractable yet do not depart in any significant way from the economic processes being explained. This rules out assumptions which are mathematically tractable but unrelated to the economic intuitions involved. Yet the resulting economic analysis has to be so simplified that what is going on can be understood and so acted upon when designing policy.

I have often argued that the growth cycle models of Goodwin and Kalecki's last *Economic Journal* article in 1968, "Trend and business cycle reconsidered", are the most promising ways forward. Though they differ in details, their essence is captured by Kalecki's statement: "In fact, the long-term trend is only a slowly-changing component of a chain of short-period situations; it has no independent entity [or existence]" (Kalecki 1968, p. 263). This in turn is consistent with Zambelli's own approaches.

What has to be avoided is the modern theory of using representative agent models in systemic analysis so that the fallacy of composition can take its rightful place. I believe all Zambelli's contributions fall neatly beneath these rubrics and aim to achieve comprehensive ways of tackling those devilishly difficult problems. Bob Solow (2010) touched on these issues as well when he wrote in Stefano's Festschrift for Vela (Zambelli 2010) "how to knit the short run and long run together. It is not as if there is a time interval called the short run and another called the long run, with some kind of movement of transition between them, instead there are slow and fast processes going on all the time and they influence one another. The analogy with Marshall's terminology is close" (pp. 55–56).

So Stefano is a worthy member of the club which contains some of the greatest and deeper thinkers of our discipline.

## References

Goodwin, R. M. (1997). Keynes and Dynamics. In Chapter 10 of G. C. Harcourt and P. A. Riach (Eds.), *A 'Second Edition' of The General Theory* (Vol. 1, pp. 162–163). London and New York: Routledge.

Harcourt, G. C., & Riach, P. A. (Eds.). (1997). *A 'Second Edition' of The General Theory, Volume 1*. London and New York: Routledge.

Kalecki, M. (1968). Trend and Business Cycle Reconsidered. *Economic Journal, 78*, 263–276.

Keynes, J. M. (1936). *The General Theory of Employment, Interest and Money*. London: Macmillan, C.W., Vol. VII, 1973.

Solow, R. M. (2010). Not Growth, Not Cycles, But Something in Between. In Chapter 4 of S. Zambelli (Ed.), *Compatible, Constructive and Behavioural Economic Dynamics: Essays in Honour of Kumaraswamy (Vela) Velupillai* (pp. 55–61). London and New York: Routledge, Taylor & Francis Group.

Zambelli, S. (Ed.). (2010). *Compatible, Constructive and Behavioural Economic Dynamics: Essays in Honour of Kumaraswamy (Vela) Velupillai*. London and New York: Routledge, Taylor & Francis Group.

# 11

# The Foreseeable Future

Brian Hayes

Imagine a chocolate crisis. A fungal blight attacks cacao trees throughout the Tropics, and within a year or two production of chocolate ceases, perhaps forever. But you are prepared. On hearing the first rumors of chocapocalypse, you began stockpiling Hershey bars, and now you have 10,000 of them in a freezer in the basement. They amount to a metric ton of chocolate, enough to last a lifetime if you allocate them wisely.

Your next task, therefore, is to formulate a rational plan for rationing your chocolate. The simplest idea is to consume the same amount every day. If you expect to live another 50 years, the daily allocation works out to about 50 grams, or half of a Hershey bar. Another approach calls for eating a fixed percentage of the remaining stock each year. If your annual consumption is 5 percent, you will get 164 grams per day during the first year. By the 50th year the allocation will have dwindled down to less than 8 grams per day, but you'll never run out entirely (assuming that Hershey bars are infinitely divisible).

B. Hayes (✉)
Amherst, MA, USA
e-mail: brian@bit-player.org


K. Velupillai (ed.), *Keynesian, Sraffian, Computable and Dynamic Economics*,
https://doi.org/10.1007/978-3-030-58131-2_11

You are cheerfully weighing these options when a disconcerting thought flits through your mind: What about the children? Don't they deserve a share of your accumulated treasure? As it happens, you have no children, and so their claims on your hoard of chocolate (and on your sentiments) are purely hypothetical. But you do have hopes of starting a family someday, and so it seems reckless to ignore posterity.

How much of your wealth should you consume and how much should you reserve for future generations? Economists, ethicists, and mathematicians have suggested a number of ingenious approaches to answering this question, some of which I shall mention below. For now, however, let us consider only the two extreme possibilities: all or nothing.

Eating the whole stash yourself has the obvious attraction of maximally satisfying your own appetites. And you can concoct various rationales to justify this "mine, all mine!" choice. The kids will be born into a world without chocolate (except in your freezer), and so they won't know what they're missing. Indeed, it might be considered cruel to let them acquire a taste for the stuff. Besides, it's probably not good for their health; let them eat broccoli instead.

In spite of these imaginative arguments, you can't escape the feeling that the maximally selfish policy is going to carry a high cost in guilt, shame, and diminished self-respect. After all, what you are contemplating is taking candy from children, an act that elicits universal opprobrium.

At the other extreme, you could save all 10,000 Hershey bars for your offspring, consuming none of the chocolate yourself. A selfless gesture of this kind might well be seen as noble, or even heroic. We have all heard stories of the good parent in desperate circumstances—marooned in a snowstorm, adrift in a lifeboat, trapped in a besieged city—who gives up his or her own paltry rations so that a child can have one more mouthful. But there's a paradox in this tale of self-sacrifice. If the right thing for you to do is to forgo consumption and save everything for your children, then those children, following the same ethical reasoning, must reach the same conclusion and save it all for *their* children. No one ever gets to eat a morsel of chocolate.

* * *

**Peak Oil** My fable of the chocolate crisis was inspired by reflections on a different commodity: petroleum. In the 1950s, the geologist M. King Hubbert predicted that oil production in the United States would reach a peak in the 1970s, followed by a steady decline (Hubbert 1956). For the world as a whole, production was expected to continue growing after the US peak, but only for about 20 years; then global output would also begin falling off. Thus the age of petroleum would be a brief blip in the course of human history. In 1971 Hubbert wrote: "The time span required to produce the middle 80 percent of the ultimate cumulative production is approximately the 65-year period from 1934 to 1999—less than the span of a human lifetime." (Hubbert 1971)

By the middle of the 1970s the idea that the world might soon be running out of oil seemed all too plausible. Gasoline prices suddenly doubled, and drivers were waiting in mile-long queues to fill the tank. Although the immediate causes of these market disruptions were mostly political and economic, genuine constraints on capacity were also a factor. US oil production had reached a maximum in 1970 (consistent with Hubbert's prediction) and was gradually tapering off. There were still large reserves elsewhere, but the price spikes and the long lines at the gas pumps provided a sharp warning signal that the resource is finite.

Other alarms were sounding at the same time—one of the loudest being *The Limits to Growth*, a book published in 1972 that sold 30 million copies. *The Limits to Growth* was based on a suite of computer models developed by an international group of 17 collaborators directed by Dennis Meadows and drawing heavily on earlier work by Jay W. Forrester (Meadows et al. 1972). The models sought to describe the dynamics of a "world system," including sectors for the human population, industrial activity, agriculture, natural resources, and pollution. The standard version of the model showed that various measures of human well-being—such as life expectancy and per capita food supply—would take a nosedive by the middle of the twenty-first century. This disaster of "overshoot and collapse" would be caused primarily by the exhaustion of nonrenewable resources such as fuels, minerals, and arable land.

On an earlier occasion I have written about my personal response to this dire forecast: "When *The Limits to Growth* appeared in 1972, I was a young man not long out of adolescence. I read the book with fascinated horror, with total credulity, and also with rising anger. The anger was directed against my parents' generation, which it seemed to me had enjoyed a whopper of a party and had left nothing in the house for the next tenants but an empty larder and a mess to clean up" (Hayes 1993).

I now read those words with a measure of chagrin. Even if I had a legitimate grievance against my elders, I would have done better to look forward rather than backward—to focus on what my own generation could do to brighten the outlook for the future. At that moment in the 1970s I was myself the parent of a young child. If the prophecies of Hubbert and the Meadows group proved to be correct, my daughter would be among those paying a heavy price. By the time she reached her adult years, petroleum products would be scarce, and perhaps too precious to burn. The responsible course would be to conserve the existing supply while mounting an international effort to develop alternative sources of energy. There was much discussion of such plans, but it seemed to me that nations were mainly intent on securing the largest possible share of the remaining petroleum for their own use.

* * *

**Ramsey's Formula** What do we owe posterity? This is a question I didn't have the wit to ask when I was in my 20s, but Frank Plumpton Ramsey did. He was only 25 when he published a detailed mathematical analysis of intergenerational obligations[1] (Ramsey 1928).

Ramsey asked how much of our income we are morally entitled to consume and enjoy, and how much we should set aside as capital for the use of future generations. He based his answer on utilitarian principles, looking to maximize the sum of the benefits afforded to all individuals across all generations. In taking this sum, he noted, "We do not discount later enjoyments in comparison with earlier ones, a practice which is ethically indefensible and arises merely from the weakness of the imagination."[2]

[1] At age 21 Ramsey had been elected a Fellow of Kings College, Cambridge. He died in 1930 before reaching his 27th birthday.

[2] Later in the paper Ramsey does consider the effect of discounting. He finds that the result depends crucially on how the discount rate for future utilities compares with the interest rate, or the discount rate for money.

Thus your grandchild's pleasure in eating a chocolate bar counts exactly the same as your own. Ramsey also assumed that all your descendants are as honest and ethical as you are; none of them will cheat the future by consuming more than their fair share.

Within this framework, Ramsey was able to offer quantitative advice on balancing our entitlements in the present against our obligations to the future. In his economic model, the fundamental activity of generating income, or new wealth, requires inputs of labor $a$ and capital $c$, combined according to some unspecified function $f(a,c)$. A fraction $x$ of the income is consumed by each generation; the rest becomes capital for future use. Consumption is assumed to be pleasurable; it has utility $U(x)$. Labor, in contrast, is disagreeable; it has disutility $V(a)$. Thus the net "rate of enjoyment" is $U(x) - V(a)$. This quantity has an upper bound $B$, which Ramsey called *bliss*. (Once you have everything you want, further consumption cannot make you any happier.) A final element in the analysis is the marginal utility of consumption, $u(x)$, the additional benefit conferred by consuming one more unit of income.

Here is Ramsey's result. If you would maximize utility summed across all generations, the optimal rate for accumulating capital is given by the expression:

$$\frac{B-\left[U(x)-V(a)\right]}{u(x)}$$

Here the numerator goes to zero as the society becomes wealthier and approaches the state of bliss, but the marginal utility of consumption in the denominator can also be expected to diminish with greater wealth. Choosing plausible values for the various parameters in the model implies quite a high rate of savings—perhaps greater than 50 percent. In other words, if we are to be fair to our descendants, we should be consuming less than half of what we earn.

Ramsey's call to sacrifice for the sake of the children appeals to our better instincts, helping humanity make steady progress toward bliss. Nevertheless, the actual economic behavior of nations and individuals reflects quite different impulses. No society, as far as I know, has ever sustained a savings rate anywhere near 50 percent. In modern times, a rate of 10 percent is considered praiseworthy.

* * *

**Discounting the Future** Ramsey's analysis has been a point of departure for many later studies of intergenerational equity. Authors admire it, but they also find much to quibble with. One issue is Ramsey's refusal to admit a discount rate greater than zero. He justifies this choice on moral grounds, insisting that future lives matter just as much as present ones. But there are also potent counterarguments. The compounding of investments made today should make future generations far richer than we are, and so it can be argued that we should be allowed to consume a larger fraction of our (meager) income. Would we ask a 2020 laborer to forgo a second crust of bread so that a 2120 epicure can enjoy a second bottle of champagne?

In the 1960s Tjalling C. Koopmans explored other peculiarities of the no-discounting principle (Koopmans 1960, 1963). Ramsey's model holds population constant through all generations; when Koopmans examined a variant model with population growth, he found there is no optimal solution when the discount rate is set to zero. Under these conditions it is always better to defer consumption until the last (and largest) generation—but with an infinite time horizon, that generation never comes. "There seems to be no way," Koopmans writes, "in an indefinitely growing population, to give equal weight to all individuals living at all times in the future."

In spite of these and other objections, the ethical basis of Ramsey's disdain for discounting the future remains a powerful force. In 2010, during a symposium sponsored by the Algorithmic Social Science Research Unit of the University of Trento, I had the pleasure of dining in the company of several distinguished economists and talented students. I took the opportunity to ask those at the table, "What is the appropriate discount rate on grandchildren?" Without a moment's hesitation, Stefano Zambelli declared: "Zero percent." No one disagreed.

Although a commitment to intergenerational fairness motivated Ramsey's position on discounting, that goal can be undermined by his choice of a utilitarian accounting scheme for human happiness. He measured the overall well-being of a population across time by summing the utilities experienced by each successive generation. Under this procedure, the sequences 5 + 5 + 5 and 0 + 0 + 15 are equally meritorious. Is it morally acceptable for early generations to endure unremitting toil and deprivation so that their distant descendants can enjoy transcendent bliss?[3] Such an injustice seems hard to excuse even when it increases the total or average enjoyment of the society as a whole.

In 1971 the philosopher John Rawls proposed a different framework for guiding the choices of social and economic planners (Rawls 1971). Rather than maximizing the sum of individual utilities, he argued, we should act to maximize the well-being of those who have the least. In a society with a fixed amount of wealth, the only way to satisfy this max-min criterion is to make everyone equal, but that's not the only possibility in a more dynamic economy. Under the Rawls criterion, some people can be allowed to have more than others if that inequity serves to elevate the lowest stratum.

Can the Rawlsian theory of justice tell us what provisions we should make for succeeding generations? Rawls himself avoided applying the max-min rule in this context, but in 1974 Robert Solow investigated how it might work (Solow 1974). The results were peculiar and largely unappealing. When balancing the interests of contemporaneous groups, it's always possible (at least in principle) to alter the allocation of labor, capital, and consumption so as to maximize the welfare of the least-favored group. But the asymmetric nature of time complicates this kind of solution when the parties involved live in different eras. A hypothetical planner standing outside of time might determine that the generation of 2080 should send some wealth back in time to the generation of 2020—but

[3] The sharpest version of this question was framed by Fyodor Dostoevsky in *The Brothers Karamazov*: "Imagine that you are creating a fabric of human destiny with the object of making men happy in the end, giving them peace and rest at last, but that it was essential and inevitable to torture to death only one tiny creature—that baby beating its breast with its fist, for instance—and to found that edifice on its unavenged tears, would you consent to be the architect on those conditions? Tell me, and tell the truth."

how is that transfer to be accomplished? Because the past cannot be altered, the only feasible arrangement that satisfies the max-min criterion is for every generation to maintain exactly the same standard of living. Progress is forbidden. Striving to give your children a life better than your own is a form of unfairness.

* * *

**Exhaustible Resources** The only inputs to Ramsey's economic model are labor and capital, which can always be fully exploited to produce income. Excluded from the analysis is the constraining effect of natural resources, which may also be needed for production, and which exist in only limited quantities. Harold Hotelling addressed this issue just a few years after Ramsey's work was published (Hotelling 1931). Given a finite and nonrenewable supply of some commodity, such as a mineral, he sought the optimum schedule of exploitation. (Of course "optimum" may be defined differently by the owner of a mine trying to maximize profits and by a planner concerned with maximizing benefits to society as a whole.)

The fundamental problem here is trying to make a finite resource last forever. Hotelling noted: "Problems of exhaustible assets are peculiarly liable to become entangled with the infinite. Not only is there infinite time to consider, but also the possibility that for a necessity the price might increase without limit as the supply vanishes." Nevertheless, in Hotelling's model even the total exhaustion of a "necessity" never leads to a social collapse. When the price of a scarce commodity rises, the market sees an incentive to develop an alternative. In this way labor and capital can eventually produce a substitute for any resource.

The Meadows group in *The Limits to Growth* took a different view of resource exhaustion: In their model it is permanent and irremediable, impairing all subsequent industrial and agricultural production, and thereby depressing the worldwide standard of living. In 1974 some of the questions raised by *Limits* were taken up from an economics perspective in a Symposium on the Economics of Exhaustible Resources (Heal et al. 1974). Solow's paper on the Rawlsian approach to intergenerational economics appears in the proceedings of this symposium. I want to mention two other interesting contributions.

Koopmans considers the case of a truly essential resource, one for which some minimum nonzero rate of consumption is necessary to sustain human life, and no substitute exists (Koopmans 1974). If this resource is finite, the population relying on it must eventually perish. To maximize the community's lifespan, the resource should be depleted at the minimal rate needed to support life. Koopmans points out that this constant minimal rate is the optimal exploitation strategy only if we adopt a discount rate of zero, thus valuing consumption in later periods the same as consumption now. Setting the discount rate to any level greater than zero favors accelerated consumption in the present and leaves less for the future; as Koopmans says, this policy "advances the doomsday."

Partha Dasgupta and Geoffrey Heal study the role of natural resources in an economy where the laws of nature are a little less harsh (Dasgupta and Heal 1974). They describe a world where the exhaustion of an essential resource is not a death sentence, provided that the society invests heavily enough in economic growth to make substitute resources affordable. With increased inputs of labor and capital, we can let the remaining quantity of the resource approach zero while the efficiency of extraction and use diverge toward infinity. In this way, the society can survive indefinitely with an arbitrarily small reserve of the resource. Dasgupta and Heal solve the optimization problem that gives the best possible schedule of capital accumulation needed to compensate for the depletion of the resource. Dasgupta later refined these ideas in (Dasgupta 2005).

* * *

**What the Future Wants** These mathematical models of economics *sub specie aeternitatis* are ingenious and fascinating intellectual exercises. They provide important insights, revealing sharp boundaries between feasible and infeasible modes of behavior. But do the models offer reliable guidance for setting economic policy all the way out to their infinite time horizon? Of course not!

Some prescriptions of the models are too delicate for successful implementation. For example, prolonging resource use into the indefinite future requires an exquisite balance between two exponential functions, with capital investment growing as $e^t$ and the resource stock diminishing as $e^{-t}$. We know how to maintain such a balance in the idealized realm of mathematics, but not in the messy world of mines and mills and markets. Another example: One of Koopmans's theorems rules out a zero discount rate because "there is not enough room in the set of real numbers to accommodate and label numerically all the different satisfaction levels that may occur in relation to consumption programs for an infinite future." The idea that subtle properties of the real number line might have a bearing on the practical deliberations of economic planners is delightful—and preposterous.

Furthermore, even if models like these can tell us *how much* to invest for the needs of future generations, they say nothing about the difficult question of *where* to invest it. The models describe an economy with a single commodity that serves as both a consumer good and capital equipment capable of producing more output. I like to think of this commodity as a kind of machine tool whose parts are made of edible gingerbread or sugar candy. The only choice here is how much of the machine to eat and how much to put to work in production. The real economy demands that we make an endless stream of choices about what to consume and where to invest. When we try to do a favor for the future, should we develop new technologies, build infrastructure, create works of art, plant forests, cure diseases, explore distant planets, erect cathedrals? To answer wisely we need to know what the people of the future will want, or perhaps what they *should* want—what's good for them. History suggests we have little chance of getting that right if we are looking very far beyond our own lifespan.

I live in a part of North America where European settlers arrived in the seventeenth century. They promptly set about clearing the forests, plowing the land, damming the rivers, exterminating the wolves and bears and eagles, releasing various exotic species into the wild, driving out or annihilating the indigenous human residents, bringing in enslaved people from Africa, and imposing their own religion on everyone they encountered. No doubt the colonists sincerely believed they were creating a better world for their descendants, but now we see things differently. We struggle to undo much of their work: restoring the forests and the native wildlife, eliminating the invasive species, removing the dams to let the rivers run free, and somehow making amends to the displaced and dispossessed people.

More recent generations have not done much better at guessing what the future wants. In the middle years of the twentieth century city planners ripped up trolley tracks and built superhighways into the heart of the city. Their successors are tearing down the highways and installing new light-rail transit systems hardly distinguishable from the former trolley lines.

Consider again at the state of the world in the 1970s, when we faced an energy crisis and various other environmental perils. Looking back from the present day—with 2020 hindsight—it appears that Hubbert's prediction of "peak oil" was utterly wrong. Although US petroleum output did diminish after 1970, it has rebounded strongly in recent decades, so much so that the US is now the largest oil-producing nation in the world. Global production has also continued to climb.[4] (Oil and gas output are currently depressed as a result of the coronavirus pandemic, but the downturn was brought on by softening demand, not by exhaustion of resources.)

What accounts for this dramatic turnaround? Whether or not Hubbert was wrong, *I* was wrong. My youthful ire over the world's complacency was misdirected. Over the past 50 years the world has actually done quite a good job of coping with the oil-depletion crisis. Early measures such as lower speed limits and incentives for building more efficient vehicles reduced the rate of growth in consumption. New technologies such as horizontal drilling and hydraulic fracturing augmented the supply. So did drilling in the Arctic and in the deep oceans. This outcome is an impressive testimony to the effectiveness of both government policymaking and market forces. The only trouble is, we solved the wrong problem.

[4] This criticism of Hubbert's forecast is in some ways unfair. His estimates were based on drilling methods and locations considered standard in the mid-twentieth century. He explicitly excluded oil reserves at high latitudes, from deep ocean basins, and from oil associated with shale and sand deposits. Most of the new production comes from precisely those sources. On the other hand, Hubbert's broad declaration that the "age of petroleum" would soon end suggests he did not believe that any of these sources could be exploited in the near term. In this respect he truly was wrong.

It's now clear that getting more oil out of the ground was not the ideal response to the fuel shortages of the 1970s. The imperative now is not to find more carbon-based energy sources but to avoid burning those we have, in a last-ditch effort to avert a climate catastrophe. So far, progress in that direction is imperceptibly slow. And thus another angry new generation, represented forcefully and eloquently by Greta Thunberg, steps forward to complain that the world's inaction is putting their future in jeopardy.

* * *

**Attention Span** Setting aside theoretical flights of fancy and historical object lessons, the big question remains: How many Hershey bars should we save for our children, and for their children, and for their children, and so on? How far into the future should we project our plans and predictions?

We denizens of the modern world are often criticized for our short attention span—but we don't dwell on it. No doubt many of us focus too much energy on the quarterly earnings report, the 24-hour news cycle, the millisecond stock trade. However, gazing into the distant future can also be dangerous, when you try to steer beyond the reach of your headlights. Formulating plans for a national economy based on how mathematical models behave when $t \to \infty$ is nonsensical.[5] (Infinity is the one value of $t$ that we know with logical certainty we'll never experience.)

How about $t = 10{,}000$ years? That's the temporal horizon favored by a group of thinkers organized as the Long Now Foundation (Brand 1999). Ten thousand years is equivalent to roughly 400 human generations. I suppose it does no harm to daydream about the lives of my (great$^{398}$)-grandchildren, but when I try to shape my actions today with the aim of doing what's best for them, I am paralyzed. Should I water the flowers, producing seeds that through some long and intricate chain of transmission might eventually bloom in their homes? Or should I conserve the water, which for all I know they might desperately need? I would like to help them, or at least avoid hurting them, but I don't know how. The

[5] There's nothing wrong with seeking a "sustainable" plan, one that could in principle be continued forever. But sustainability can be established without invoking the infinite, namely by considering $t_n$ and $t_{n+k}$ for finite $n$ and $k$.

Long Now group are well aware of this conundrum. They respond that they do not advocate planning or predicting the future, but rather "taking responsibility" for it. "The difference is between trying to control the future and trying to give it the tools to help itself." But I'm afraid this advice leaves me still muddled. I have no idea what tools the future needs, or what I can do to provide them.

Ramsey framed our challenge in terms of sacrificing now for then, *nunc pro tunc*. But saving for the extremely remote future, 400 generations onward in the growth of the human family tree, requires no more than a token sacrifice. The most paltry savings, when compounded over 10,000 years, will yield a fortune. I would be happy to invest a dollar in a bond paying 3 percent per annum, redeemable in the year 12020. It would then be worth $10^{128}$ dollars, a fabulous sum indeed. Unfortunately, no such financial instrument is on offer.

There are circumstances where we really must think carefully about the consequences of our actions for the inhabitants of the Earth 10,000 years hence. The disposal of radioactive wastes is the best-known example. Another comes from the belated recognition that the planet's climate system is much less stable than we had supposed, and that our own actions can tip it into another regime that might last for millennia. But these are exceptional cases, highlighting the dreadful consequences of mistakes we might make. On a day-to-day basis, if we want to do something positive to help our descendants, we have a better chance of success if we look to that part of the future we can actually foresee. Although I cannot put a precise bound on the range of accurate foresight, I strongly suspect the number of generations encompassed can be expressed with a single decimal digit.

One possibility is to adopt a rule attributed to the constitution of the Iroquois Federation in eastern North America, which was probably formed before first contact with Europeans. Leaders of the federation were instructed to consider the consequences of their actions through the seventh generation.[6] This principle invites us to extend our vision to the

[6] The story has been popularized by a brand of soaps called Seventh Generation, and its authenticity has been questioned. Published versions of the constitution include no such statement, but these are twentieth-century documents. They may not capture everything present in an oral tradition that goes back to the fifteenth-century CE, or perhaps earlier.

outer limits of the human lifespan: It is just barely possible for someone to know their great-great-great-great-great-grandchild.

The theory of evolution by natural selection suggests an even narrower scope. Evolution is a game where we keep score by counting offspring. The most successful organism, by the rules of this game, is the one that projects the most copies of its genes into the next generation. However, if you are designing a life-form to compete in an evolutionary contest, there is a hazard in adopting this criterion of success. You might invent a very prolific species that produces immense numbers of offspring but then cannot rear them; they all die in infancy. This is a recipe for quick extinction. A better strategy takes a slightly longer view, rewarding the organism that maximizes the number of *grand*children. When this algorithm is applied consistently, from one generation to the next, it sets in motion a process that favors continuing improvement into the indefinite future. Doing what's best for your grandchildren may well be a decent rule of thumb for thinking about how we can help the future.

I will also note that two generations beyond the present was the time frame chosen by John Maynard Keynes in his essay "Economic Possibilities for Our Grandchildren" (Keynes 1930). This short, informal work was a pep talk for the British people, written in the early months of the Great Depression. However bleak the immediate outlook, Keynes proclaimed, riches and leisure are surely coming for everyone, guaranteed by the engine of technological innovation and the fuel of compound interest. Your grandchildren will enjoy them. If he had claimed that good times were just around the corner, no one would have believed him. If he had promised paradise in 10,000 years, no one would have cared.

## References

Brand, S. (1999). *The Clock of the Long Now: Time and Responsibility*. New York: Basic Books.

Dasgupta, P. (2005). Three Conceptions of Intergenerational Justice. In H. Lillehammer et al. (Eds.), *Ramsey's Legacy*. Oxford: Oxford University Press.

Dasgupta, P., & Heal, G. (1974). The Optimal Depletion of Exhaustible Resources. *The Review of Economic Studies, 41*, 3–28.

Hayes, B. (1993). Balanced on a Pencil-Point. *American Scientist, 81*(6), 510–516.
Heal, G., et al. (1974). Symposium on the Economics of Exhaustible Resources. *The Review of Economic Studies*, Vol. 41.
Hotelling, H. (1931). The Economics of Exhaustible Resources. *Journal of Political Economy, 39*(2), 137–175.
Hubbert, M. K. (1956). *Nuclear Energy and the Fossil Fuels, American Petroleum Institute Drilling and Production Practice*. Proceedings of the Spring Meeting, San Antonio, TX, pp. 7–25.
Hubbert, M. K. (1971). The Energy Resources of the Earth. *Scientific American, 225*(3), 61–70.
Keynes, J. M. (1930). Economic Possibilities for Our Grandchildren. Reprinted in Pecchi, L., & Piga, G. (Eds.). (2008). *Revisting Keynes: Economic Possibilities for Our Grandchildren*. Cambridge, MA: The MIT Press.
Koopmans, T. C. (1960). Stationary Ordinal Utility and Impatience. *Econometrica, 28*(2), 287–309.
Koopmans, T. C. (1963). On the Concept of Optimal Economic Growth. In Pontificia Academia Scientiarum. (1965). *Study Week on the Econometric Approach to Development Planning* (pp. 225–300). Amsterdam: North-Holland Publishing Co. Also: Cowles Foundation Discussion Paper No. 163, Cowles Foundation for Research in Economics at Yale University, New Haven.
Koopmans, T. C. (1974). Proof for a Case Where Discounting Advances the Doomsday. *The Review of Economic Studies, 41*, 117–120.
Meadows, D. H., Meadows, D. L., Randers, J., Behrens, W. W., & III. (1972). *The Limits to Growth: A Report for the Club of Rome's Project on the Predicament of Mankind*. New York: Universe Books.
Ramsey, F. P. (1928). A Mathematical Theory of Saving. *Economic Journal, 38*, 543–549.
Rawls, J. (1971 [1999]). *A Theory of Justice*. Cambridge, MA: Belknap Press of Harvard University Press.
Solow, R. M. (1974). Intergenerational Equity and Exhaustible Resources. *The Review of Economic Studies, 41*, 29–45.

# 12

# Uniqueness in Planar Endogenous Business Cycle Theories

Ragupathy Venkatachalam and Ying-Fang Kao

## 1 Introduction

Economic dynamics has been an important theme in theoretical pursuits from the classical economists to today. Attempts to incorporate dynamic phenomena, and in particular sustained fluctuations into economic theory, began getting prominent around the turn of the twentieth century.

This chapter draws from some of the themes discussed in Venkatachalam's PhD thesis (Venkatachalam 2013), written under the guidance of Vela Velupillai and Stefano Zambelli at the University of Trento. We are grateful to both of them for numerous conversations and their influence over the years, without implicating them for any of the errors. We thank Jessica Paul for the editorial help. All errors remain our own.

R. Venkatachalam (✉)
Institute of Management Studies, Goldsmiths, University of London, London, UK
e-mail: r.venkatachalam@gold.ac.uk

Y.-F. Kao
Experimentation Team, Machine Learning and AI Division, Just Eat, London, UK



K. Velupillai (ed.), *Keynesian, Sraffian, Computable and Dynamic Economics*,
https://doi.org/10.1007/978-3-030-58131-2_12

The corpus of the prevailing economic theory was predominantly static and tied to the notion of equilibrium. These attempts arguably culminated in the birth of modern macroeconomics, in particular business cycle theory, monetary theory, theory of economic policy and growth theory. Developments to this end saw a major surge in theoretical innovations, particularly those in mathematical applications, especially in the 1930s and the immediate decades that followed the Second World War. Major contributors include Wicksell, Fisher, Frisch, Kalecki, Tinbergen, Keynes, Hayek, Myrdal, Lindhal, Hawtrey, Aftalion, Schumpeter, *Hicks*, *Kaldor*, Harrod, Samuelson, Hansen, Leontief, Solow and *Goodwin*, among others.

If we focus our attention on business cycle theory, it is perhaps useful to classify the different visions to reconcile dynamic phenomena into static equilibrium theory as two types: exogenous and endogenous theories. The exogenous view relies on factors outside the system that disturb an economy which is in equilibrium or steady state as the major driver of fluctuations. In this view, studying business cycles translates to understanding how positive or negative stochastic shocks to a variable, for example technology, translates to output or employment fluctuations. This view is still quite influential in the empirical and policy fronts in orthodox macroeconomic theory in the form of *impulse response* investigations.

The endogenous tradition in cycle theories, on the other hand, focuses on the structure of relationships between different economic variables *within* the capitalistic economic systems. There are many different strands under this broad view. Overall, the nature of relationships between economic variables are such that they make the system prone to sustained fluctuations, even if they are insulated from the disturbances. *Exogenous shocks* may very well have an impact in the endogenous view; however, they play a subordinate role at best. They are not central to explaining the persistent cyclical tendencies of the economic system. The unifying theme is that the sources of these fluctuations are from within the system, which does not have any self-regulating mechanisms to bring itself back to a stable equilibrium or continue to evolve without cycles.

In the development of endogenous cycle theories in the mathematical mode, the presence of non-linear relationships between different variables proved to be a crucial ingredient. Consequently, formalisms from the theory of non-linear oscillations (in the formative years) and non-linear dynamical systems theory (in the later years) were utilized for building mathematical models. They demonstrated different long- and short-term properties of the system and their capacity to oscillate by resorting to the application of different existence theorems. In particular, the *Poincaré-Bendixson theorem* and *Levinson-Smith theorem* were widely used to demonstrate persistent fluctuations in the form of limit cycles.[1] In addition to the existence, questions concerning the number of such *limit cycles* are also important. If more than one such attractor is present, it is always possible for an economy to head toward one of the undesirable attractors. In such cases, there may be a need to steer it away from these basins with the aid of policy. From an algorithmic perspective, whether these mathematical objects (i.e., limit cycles) that are proved to exist and their properties (e.g., their uniqueness) are computable is also a relevant question.

*Stefano Zambelli* is a deep scholar in the *endogenous business cycle* tradition, especially in studying them via careful numerical approximations and simulations. Together with *Vela Velupillai*, he has also advanced a computable approach to studying economic dynamics. We were fortunate to learn these issues from him and later work with him on several aspects of his broad research programme.

In this chapter, we examine some of the *uniqueness theorems* employed in business cycle theories. We confine our attention to the Non-linear, Endogenous Theories of Business Cycle (NETBC), in particular, to the pioneering models of Goodwin, Kaldor, Hicks and their variations. We focus on the uniqueness proofs concerning the attractors (limit cycles) in these models. Section 2 provides a survey of different uniqueness theorems that were used in Kaldor's trade cycle model. In Sect. 3 Goodwin's non-linear cycle model is considered and we apply a sufficiency theorem for the non-linear accelerator model, with just one non-linearity. We point out the connection this theorem has with Goodwin's own contribution.

[1] See Ragupathy and Velupillai (2012).

Section 4 addresses the issues concerning the algorithmic decidability of properties of attractors and uniqueness in particular. To this end, we use the framework of computable analysis that provides one way to pose decidability questions for continuous time models.

## 2 Uniqueness Proofs in NETBC

In the planar models of NETBC, the qualitative nature of the attractors that underpin these theories is fairly obvious, namely limit cycles.[2] Important pioneering models in this tradition are Goodwin (1951), Kaldor (1940) and Hicks (1950). These models were broadly in the Keynesian tradition. Their unifying thread was the presence of non-linearities in how different economic variables were related. For example: relationship between income, savings and investment; presence of limits to investment and growth due to natural economic constraints such as full employment. This non-linearity played a crucial role in explaining the observed, sustained fluctuations in aggregate variables such as output and employment. Mathematically, what these economic theories sought to explain (viz., sustained fluctuations of aggregate economic variables over time) were translated to demonstrating the presence of periodic solutions at a local or a global level. These theories were formulated in terms of models using differential or difference equations as dynamical systems. The early models that were formulated in continuous time were mostly reduced to one or the other special case of the Liénard equation:[3] *van der Pol equation* (in the case of Kaldor's model) or the *Rayleigh equation* (Goodwin 1951)), which were known to possess stable periodic solutions. Later models were formulated in terms of dynamical systems and attention shifted to demonstrating the existence of sustained

[2] There is also the case of 'centers', which is associated with the growth cycle model of Goodwin (1967).

[3] Liénard equation is written as

$$\ddot{x} + f'(x)\dot{x} + g(x) = 0.$$

oscillations by means of existence proofs. Theorems such as the Poincaré-Bendixson theorem were used to establish the necessary and sufficient conditions for the presence of limit cycles.

Compared to the use of existence proofs in NETBC, studies providing results concerning the number of possible attractors have been relatively few. The proof of existence and uniqueness was established in some of the early models by invoking the Levinson-Smith theorem. While Poincaré-Bendixson guarantees the existence of *at least* one limit cycle for planar dynamical systems, the Levinson-Smith theorem establishes the sufficient conditions under which a *Liénard equation* (a special case of a second-order differential equation) can have a unique isolated periodic solution (limit cycle). There are a couple of observations that may be relevant here. First, uniqueness theorems that are used often provide only sufficient conditions and not the necessary conditions for the presence of a unique limit cycle. Presupposing that a cycle already exists for a given system, these theorems provide the conditions for such a cycle to be unique. Therefore, proof of existence is provided first and these sufficiency conditions are provided for the strip in which the limit cycle exists. Second, it is relatively easier to provide sufficient conditions, than to prove the existence of a limit cycle. The more general mathematical problem concerning the upper bound on the number of limit cycles for a planar polynomial vector field (as a function of the degree of the polynomial) concerns the second part of *Hilbert's* $16^{th}$ *problem*. This problem remains unresolved to date. Consequently, a 'complete' characterization of the nature and number of attractors, even for Liénard equation (which is a special case of the planar polynomial vector fields), is still beyond reach.

## 2.1 Uniqueness of Limit Cycle: Kaldor's Model

In the early mathematical models of NETBC, the proof of uniqueness of the limit cycle in the planar models has involved reducing the dynamic model to a generalized Liénard equation and invoking the Levinson-Smith theorem, which provides sufficient conditions for the existence and uniqueness of limit cycles. Depending on the way in which one approximates the economic assumptions into a mathematical model, the number of limit cycles can vary. Therefore, any categorical statement regarding the presence of a unique limit cycle must be evaluated in the light of the approximation involved.

We provide a survey of the studies that employ uniqueness theorems in NETBC. We restrict our attention to analytical proofs for establishing uniqueness and therefore do not focus on studies which use numerical simulations and other approximate methods In the case of Kaldor's model, the issue of the uniqueness of attractors has been taken up for different versions of the model by Ichimura (1955), Lorenz (1987) and Galeotti and Gori (1989). The earliest application of sufficient conditions to guarantee a unique limit cycle was by Yasui (1953), who applied the Levinson-Smith theorem to his version of Kaldor's model. In this case, the model was reduced to a van der Pol–type equation, which is a special case of the Liénard equation.

**Theorem 12.2.1 (Levinson Smith Theorem, Gandolfo (2005), p. 440)** *Consider a two-dimensional differential equation system*

$$\begin{aligned} \dot{x} &= y - f(x) \\ \dot{y} &= -g(x) \end{aligned}$$

*which is represented as a second-order differential equation,*

$$\ddot{x} + f'(x)\dot{x} + g(x) = 0$$

*The above equation has a unique periodic solution if the following conditions are satisfied.*

1. $f'(x)$ *and* $g(x)$ *are* $C^1$
2. $\exists x_1 > 0$ *and* $x_2 > 0$ *such that for* $-x_1 < x < x_2 : f'(x) < 0$ *and* $\geq 0$ *otherwise.*
3. $xg(x) > 0 \ \forall x \neq 0$
4. $\lim_{x\to\infty} f(x) = \lim_{x\to\infty} G(x) = \infty$ *where* $f(x) = \int_0^x f'(s)ds$ *and* $G(x) = \int_0^x g(s)ds$
5. $G(-x_1) = G(x_2)$

Ichimura (1955) discussed the possibility of applying the above theorem to a particular case of his model in which he attempted to synthesize the theory of Kaldor, Goodwin and Hicks. However, he perceptively noted that the *symmetry condition* ($G(-x_1) = G(x_2)$) may not hold for his system and therefore the uniqueness of the limit cycle was not certain. Lorenz (1987) later took up the Kaldor model and explicitly addressed the question of uniqueness. He observed that Kaldor's model (as formalized by Chang and Smyth (1971)) does not reduce to a generalized Liénard equation and therefore the Levinson-Smith theorem cannot be applied. In particular, he argued that the assumption concerning symmetry of $G(x)$ may be too restrictive from an economic point of view. He contended that it is not possible to apply the Levinson-Smith theorem unless one of the following assumptions are made: investment is assumed to be independent of capital stock or that changes in capital stock is entirely determined by savings, which is independent of the level of capital. This is because in the Kaldor model as long as one assumes that the investment function is dependent on both capital stock and income, the resulting second-order differential equation is not a Liénard equation. The main argument is that it was not possible to retain all the assumptions of the original economic model without making further simplified assumptions to satisfy the mathematical requirements of the theorems invoked.

In response to this, Galeotti and Gori (1989) contended that it is possible to make use of other uniqueness theorems for Kaldor's trade cycle model and demonstrated the presence of a unique limit cycle. By making convenient assumptions and appropriate transformations, they showed that Kaldor's system is reducible to a Liénard system.

$$\begin{aligned} \dot{x} &= y - F(x) \\ \dot{y} &= -g(x) \end{aligned} \tag{12.1}$$

The existence of a limit cycle is proved using the theorem by Fillipov and they provided the sufficiency conditions for the uniqueness of the limit cycle for this model through the following theorem.

**Theorem 12.2.2 (Zhang Zhi-Fen[4])** *Suppose the system* (12.1) *above satisfies the following conditions:*

1. *There exists* $a \geq 0$ *such that,* $F_1(z) \leq 0 \leq F_2(z)$ *for* $0 \leq z \leq a$, $F_1(z) \not\equiv F_2(z)$ *for* $0 < z \ll 1$, $F_1(z) > 0$ *for* $z > a$; $F_2^{'}(z) \leq 0$ *for* $z \in \{z > 0 | F_2(z) < 0\}$
2. $F_1^{'}(z)$ *is non-decreasing for* $z > a$
3. *if* $F_1(z) = F_2(u)$ *with* $a < z < u$, *then* $F_1^{'}(z) \geq F_2^{'}(u)$

*Then the system has at most one limit cycle, which, if exists, must be stable.*

The above theorem is utilized by applying the *Fillipov transformation.*[5]

However, in the process of doing so, they overlook the essential message that there is a tendency among economists to force their economic intuitions to the demands of the existence-uniqueness theorems.

Goodwin (1951) did not 'prove' the existence or uniqueness of the limit cycle by invoking theorems of these kind, instead demonstrating the presence of single stable limit cycle (for an S-shaped characteristic) by using geometric methods (Lienard integration). This was later addressed by Sasakura (1996), pp. 1771–73:

> In Goodwin's (1951) model there has been something mysterious to business cycle theorists, since, in spite of the simple structure, the question: "Does the model have really a unique stable limit cycle?" could not be solved in general circumstances. In this paper I gave a correct answer to the

[4] Galeotti and Gori refer to Zhi-Fen (1986b) and Zhi-Fen (1986a). Since the second reference is difficult to access, we refer the reader to Theorem 1, section 2 of Xianwu et al. (1994) for the proof.

[5] Fillipov transformation is done as follows:

$$z_1 = \int_0^x g(t)dt \quad \text{if } x \geq 0; F_1(z_1) = F(x) as\ x \geq 0$$
$$z_2 = \int_0^x g(t)dt \quad \text{if } x \leq 0; F_2(z_2) = F(x) as\ x \leq 0$$

$z_i$ is the integral curve of $g(x)$ and therefore instead of the trajectory of (12.1) in the right and left half-planes, due to the transformation, one deals with the integral curves $\frac{dz}{dy} = F_i(z) - y, i = 1,2$. Uniqueness in this case is established by way of a comparison argument involving $F_1(z)$ and $F_2(z)$ for $z > 0$.

question: 'Yes, as was expected.' The model has a unique stable limit cycle in an economically meaningful region.

He demonstrated the uniqueness of the limit cycle by using the following theorem which provides the sufficient conditions:

**Theorem 12.2.3 (Luo Ding-Jun Uniqueness Theorem)** *For the system*

$$\dot{x} - y - F(x)$$

$$\dot{y} = -x$$

*if* $F'(x) - F(x)/x \geq 0$ *(or* $\leq 0$*) for all* $x \neq 0$*, and* ***in the strip where the limit cycle exists*** *the left side of the above formula is not identically zero, then the system has at most one limit cycle. (Ye et al. (*1986*), 139–140)*

The above theorems comprehensively cover almost all the uniqueness results that were employed within this tradition.

## 3 Uniqueness of Limit Cycle and Goodwin's (1951) Model

There has been a fair amount of ambiguity on the number of limit cycles that are associated with the Goodwin model. On the one hand, Sasakura points out the 'academic belief' that was held about the presence of a unique limit cycle for this model. Flaschel (2009) also resonates the same belief for his version of Goodwin's model but, at the same time, makes the puzzling remark[6] that there could be multiple limit cycles:

> ...**We state without proof that a [Goodwin] system such as the one we depicted earlier will not only have a closed orbit, but will in fact exhibit just one limit cycle, which will be a globally stable attractor for all other trajectories** of this dynamical system in the above depicted domain.

[6] In chapter 3, footnote 75, *Flaschel*'s remark about uniqueness may be slightly misleading and his reference to Ye et al. (1986) is inaccurate. It is misleading because the uniqueness theorems discussed in Ye et al. (1986) deal with 'sufficiency' conditions and not 'necessary' conditions.

> For economic purposes, **it is, however, not necessary to have a unique and stable limit cycle under all circumstances**. Figure 3.13 shows that all points close to the boundary of the box as well as points close to the stationary state of the dynamics cannot lie on the limit cycle, but will be attracted by one (not necessarily the same) in the interior of the box.
> - Flaschel (2009, pp. 97–98, emphasis added).

In this section, we will take a closer look at Goodwin's model in the light of the above discussion on the uniqueness of limit cycle and hope to clarify some of these ambiguities.

## 3.1 Goodwin's Non-linear Model

We briefly sketch the business cycle model developed by Goodwin (1951). In this model, cyclical fluctuations result from the interaction of the dynamic multiplier with a non-linear accelerator. Let $y, \alpha, \dot{k}, \beta, \in$ be the income, marginal propensity to consume, change in capital stock, autonomous consumption and lag in consumption for the changes in income, respectively. The multiplier relation can be written as:

$$y = \frac{1}{1-\alpha}(\beta + \dot{k} - \in \dot{y})$$

By introducing a lag between the time at which investment outlays are made and their realization (θ—the time to build parameter), we have

$$(1-\alpha)y(t+\theta) + \in \dot{y}(t+\theta) = O_A(t+\theta) + O_I(t+\theta)$$

where,

$$O_A(t+\theta) = \beta(t+\theta) + l(t+\theta)$$

and

$$O_I(t+\theta) \simeq O_D \simeq \psi(\dot{y})$$

Here $O_A$ is the sum of autonomous investment and consumption outlays and $O_I$ is the induced investment $\psi(\dot{y})$ (the nonlinear accelerator or the flexible accelerator). This investment function is assumed to be non-linear.[7] We then have

$$(1-\alpha)y(t+\theta) + \in \dot{y}(t+\theta) = O_A(t+\theta) + \psi(\dot{y}(t)) \tag{12.2}$$

We shall call this the *Canonical Goodwin Equation*. From here, based on the kind of approximation we would prefer, we can have different final equations and, consequently, the nature and the number of attractors can vary.

Taking the *Canonical Goodwin Equation* and approximating the equation through Taylor-series expansion for the $(t+\theta)$ terms and retaining only the first two terms of $y$ and $\dot{y}$ variable,[8] we have:

$$\in \theta\ddot{y} + [\in +(1-\alpha)\theta]\dot{y}] - \varphi(\dot{y}) + (1-\alpha)y = O_A(t+\theta) \tag{12.3}$$

This is a second-order non-linear difference-differential equation. Goodwin shifts the time co-ordinate of the autonomous injections by $\theta$ units and arrives at:

$$\in \theta\ddot{y} + [\in +(1-\alpha)\theta]\dot{y}(t)] - \varphi(\dot{y}) + (1-\alpha)y = O_A(t) \tag{12.4}$$

The delay term here can be viewed as a periodic forcing to the differential system by the injection of autonomous investment. This equation corresponds to a Rayleigh-type equation with external forcing[9] and to the best of our knowledge, there is no general result characterizing the attractors completely or establishing that this system has a unique limit cycle. As in the case of the forced van der Pol equation, results are known only for

[7] Goodwin also introduces a lag in investment and decision outlays—the time lag between decisions on investment and actual investment outlays. However, it is assumed that $O_I(t+\theta) \simeq O_D(t)$.

[8] That is, without taking $O_A(t+\theta)$ term into account.

[9] In this case, constant and periodic.

some special cases of the forced Rayleigh-type equation. However, Goodwin himself went on to further approximate this equation by assuming that $O_A$ to be constant $O^*$ and redefined the variable $y$ in terms of $z$, representing deviations from the equilibrium value $\frac{O^*}{(1-\alpha)}$. The system is assumed to have a *cubic characteristic*, that is, the non-linear accelerator is assumed to be an S-shaped function, with two non-linearities representing the built-in economic constraints.

$$\in \theta \ddot{z} + [\in +(1-\alpha)\theta]\dot{z}(t)] - \varphi(\dot{z}) + (1-\alpha)z = 0 \tag{12.5}$$

To this, he adds the requirement that the equilibrium is locally unstable and that $d\varphi(0) / d\dot{z} > \in +(1-\alpha)\theta$. By defining the following variables, $x = \sqrt{\frac{1-\alpha}{\in \theta}} z / \dot{z}_0$ and $t_1 = \sqrt{\frac{1-\alpha}{\in \theta}} t$, the above equation can be reduced to a dimension-less form,[10] to the following equation.[11]

$$\ddot{x} + \chi(\dot{x}) + x = 0 \tag{12.6}$$

$$where, \chi(\dot{x}) = \frac{[\in +(1-\alpha)\theta]\dot{z}(t)] - \varphi(\dot{z})}{\sqrt{(1-\alpha)\in \theta}}$$

Goodwin states:

> Consequently the system oscillates with increasing violence in the central region, but as it expands into the outer regions, it enters more and more into an area of positive damping with a growing tendency to attenuation. It is intuitively clear that it will settle down to such a motion as will just balance the two tendencies, although proof requires the rigorous methods developed by Poincaré.

[10] Refer Goodwin (1951) pp. 12–13.

[11] $\dot{z}_0$ is any unit to measure velocity.

...Perfectly general conditions for the stability of motion are complicated and difficult to formulate, but what we can say is that any curve of the general shape of $X(\dot{x})$ [or $\varphi(\dot{y})$] will give rise to **a single, stable limit cycle.**

Goodwin (1951, pp. 13–14,emphasis added.)

He uses the graphical integration method of Liénard—a geometric method and not a proof of existence and uniqueness—to establish the presence of a limit cycle. However, whether there will be 'single, stable limit cycle' for more complicated functional forms of non-linear accelerator is not addressed.

We can rewrite the above system as given below:

$$\begin{aligned} \dot{x} &= u - \Theta(x) \\ \dot{u} &= -x \end{aligned} \tag{12.7}$$

where,

$$\Theta(x) = \sigma\tau(x)$$

$$\sigma = \frac{1}{\sqrt{(1-\alpha) \in \theta}}$$

and

$$\tau(x) = [\in +(1-\alpha)\theta]\dot{x}(t)] - \varphi(\dot{x})$$

Does this system have a unique limit cycle? The answer to that question depends on the approximation of the non-linear investment function. For example, Matsumoto (2009) shows that assuming $\varphi(\dot{x}) = vtan^{-1}(x)$ (an odd function), the system can have single or multiple limit cycles depending on the values of $\theta$ and the local instability condition $\epsilon + (1 - \alpha)\theta - v < 0$ on $\Theta(x)$.

Approximating the non-linear accelerator $\varphi(\dot{x}) = vtan^{-1}(x)$ by $x - \frac{1}{3}x^3$ would have a different result on the number of limit cycles as opposed to taking the higher-order terms by say the fifth-order expression, where $\tau(x) = x - \frac{5}{3}x^3 + \frac{2}{5}x^5$, which has two limit cycles.[12] For the above Liénard form representation of the Goodwin model, the number of limit cycles for the system will depend on the degree of $\Theta$ function. Therefore, the approximations play a crucial role, and it is necessary to have them correspond to the actual shape of the investment function and be compatible with the economic assumptions.[13] Goodwin was aware of this and notes:

> Finally, it should be noted that, while I have assumed a particular shape for $\varphi(\dot{y})$, the power of the Liénard construction is shown by the fact that an equation containing any given curve may be easily integrated. Therefore, whatever sort of investment function is found actually to hold, that type may be completely analysed in its cyclical functioning. If we look closely into this problem, we find that what is really necessary is to take individual account of many different industries because, while one industry may still have excess capacity, another may be short of fixed capital. Therefore, the combined operation may depend as much on the points at which different industries fire into investment activity as on the actual shape of the X function for each industry or any conceivable aggregation of all of them.
>
> -(Goodwin 1951, p. 17)

Instead of approximations of the investment functions, if one resorts to higher-order approximations around the time lag parameter $\theta$, it would result in multiple limit cycles as well. Overall, the uniqueness of the limit cycle in Goodwin's model and its independence from initial conditions is not so straightforward.

## 3.2 Sasakura's Proof

Sasakura (1996) starts his analysis by taking the following equation mentioned in the last section:

[12] For $\sigma = 0.08$. Refer Matsumoto (2009) for the details of the approximation.

[13] For example, Matsumoto notes that the fifth-order approximation specified above does not have asymptotic bounds that correspond to the ceiling and the floor and the same goes for the values of $\theta$ being small or large.

$$\in \theta\ddot{Y} + [\in +(1-\alpha)\theta]\dot{Y}(t)] - \varphi(\dot{Y}) + (1-\alpha)Y = \beta + l \quad (12.8)$$

He then replaces it with the following, mathematically equivalent system of the previous equation:

$$\begin{aligned} \dot{Y} &= (1/\in)\big(I-(1-\alpha)y+\beta\big) \\ \dot{I} &= (1/\theta)\big(\varphi[\dot{y}(t)]+l-I\big) \end{aligned} \quad (12.9)$$

Here $I = \dot{K}$ and income is not in terms of deviations from its equilibrium value, but its absolute value. By restricting the domain of income and investment values to an economically meaningful region, he proved the existence of a limit cycle for this region using the Poincaré-Bendixson theorem. He considers the dimensionless form (Eq. 12.6)

$$\ddot{z} + \zeta'(z)\dot{z} + z = 0 \quad (12.10)$$

Let $u = \dot{z}$ and $v = -z$

$$\dot{u} = v - \zeta(u)$$

$$\dot{v} = -u$$

and uses a theorem that provides sufficient conditions for uniqueness of the limit cycle for this system. Since this theorem does not require any assumptions regarding symmetry, the functional form of the induced investment (or the characteristic) need not be restricted to being symmetric around the origin. From the economic point of view, the meaning of this asymmetry is quite clear.

**Theorem 12.3.1 (Luo Ding-Jun Theorem)** *For the system*

$$\dot{x} = y - F(x)$$

$$\dot{y} = -x$$

> *if $F'(x) - F(x) / x \geq 0$ (or $\leq 0$) for all $x \neq 0$, and* ***in the strip where the limit cycle exists*** *the left side of the above formula is not identically zero, then the system has at most one limit cycle. (Ye et al. 1986, pp. 139–140)*

The intuitive meaning of the condition is the following: if the marginal propensity to invest due to an increase in income is less than the average propensity in the strip where the limit cycle exists, such a cycle will be unique, within that strip.

### 3.2.1 One-Sided Oscillator

Since the approximations and the assumptions that go into defining the shape of the investment function are crucial in Goodwin's model, we shall examine alternative considerations regarding the shape of non-linear accelerator. The *non-linear accelerator* in Goodwin (1951) is motivated by the fact that aggregate capital accumulation in an economy cannot go on unhindered forever, since the built-in constraints of the economic system come in to play at some point. In the multiplier-accelerator mode, this means that the operation of the accelerator mechanism (changes in investment as induced by changes in income) is restricted during the upswing by having reached the desired level of capital (which is a function of income) or by hitting full employment of economic resources. In the downswing, the fact that net investment in fixed capital cannot be lower than the amount required corresponding to rate(s) of depreciation poses a natural lower bound. These constraints have traditionally been dubbed as the *ceiling* and the *floor* of the economic system. This means that there are two economically plausible non-linearities, or two plausible bends on either end of the accelerator, in the model of the economy. In Hicks' model, exogenous, autonomous growth factors are superimposed onto a disequilibrium model of fluctuations which incorporates both the ceiling and the floor. Goodwin(1951) model also had two built-in constraints on either side of the accelerator, therefore utilizing two non-linearities in order to explain sustained oscillations. In terms of the mathematical structure, this means that the dimensionless form (Eq. 12.6) of the reduced master equation has a cubic characteristic.

However, the presence of two bounds is not a necessary condition for showing persistence of cycles in this class of planar models. It was persuasively argued by Goodwin in his review of Hicks' book that economic intuition would suggest that *either* the ceiling (full employment) *or* the floor (lower limit on disinvestment, which is zero) would be sufficient to guarantee the presence of sustained oscillations.[14] In terms of the mathematical structure, this meant that a single non-linearity would be enough to have sustained oscillations, which until then was not thought to be possible. This was shown to be a mathematically plausible by Goodwin himself and thus was born the '*one-sided oscillator*'.[15]

Now, if we approximate the investment function with a piecewise linear function with only one non-linearity—either a ceiling or a floor—it is still possible to show the presence of a limit cycle.[16] Let us consider the case where the accelerator becomes inflexible after having reached a ceiling:[17]

$$\phi(\dot{y}) = \begin{cases} \kappa \dot{y} & \text{if } \kappa \dot{y} \le \dot{k}^U \\ \dot{k} & \text{if } \dot{y} > \kappa \dot{k}^U \end{cases}$$

Here $\kappa$ is the accelerator co-efficient and $\dot{k}^U$ is the investment level once the system reaches the ceiling. This can be appropriately modified in case one

---

[14] He notes:

> Either the 'ceiling' or the 'floor' will suffice to check and hence perpetuate it. Thus, the boom may die before hitting full employment, but then it will be checked on the downswing by the limit on disinvestment. Or again it may, indeed it ordinarily does, start up again before eliminating the excess capital as a result of autonomous outlays by business or government. Goodwin (1950, p. 319).

[15] A detailed discussion of this discovery can be found in Velupillai (1998).

[16] See: Sordi (2006), which focuses on the simulation aspects of the cycle more than the proof of uniqueness.

[17] Note that this ceiling, given by desired capital level given the income level, need not necessarily coincide with the full employment ceiling. This ceiling can come into effect even before the full employment ceiling is reached.

wants to shift the focus to the floor and on the downswing. Let us measure income in terms of the deviations from its equilibrium value and express

$$\tau(\dot{|}) = \begin{cases} -[\kappa - (\in +(1-\alpha)\theta)]\dot{z} & \text{if } \dot{z} \leq \dot{k}^U / \kappa \\ -[\dot{k}^U - (\in +(1-\alpha)\theta)]\dot{z} & \text{if } \dot{z} > \dot{k}^U / \kappa \end{cases}$$

When we substitute this and following the time translations $x = \sqrt{\frac{1-\alpha}{\in\theta}} z / \dot{z}_0$ and $t_1 = \sqrt{\frac{1-\alpha}{\in\theta}} t$, we arrive at the Eq. 12.5 and reduce it to the dimensionless[18] form, the characteristic of which is as follows:

$$\ddot{x} + \zeta(\dot{x}) + x = 0$$

where,

$$\zeta(\dot{z}) = \frac{\tau(\dot{x}\dot{z}_0)}{\dot{z}_0\sqrt{(1-\alpha)\in\theta}}$$

The above dimensionless equation can be rewritten as:

$$\begin{aligned} \dot{x} &= -u - \zeta(x) \\ \dot{u} &= x \end{aligned} \tag{12.12}$$

The proof of existence is given by a theorem by *de Figueiredo*, making use of the Poincaré-Bendixson theorem. (de Figueiredo 1960, Theorem 1, p. 274).

---

[18] The piecewise linear characteristic above can be approximated by a function to smoothen the discontinuity (Refer Le Corbeiller (1960)) and we have the following second-order differential equation.

$$\ddot{z} - \rho(2 - e^{-\dot{z}})\dot{z} + z = 0 \tag{12.11}$$

Under the instability condition assumed by Goodwin, that is, $\kappa > \epsilon + (1-\alpha)$ and for appropriate parameter values, we can establish the presence of sustained oscillations.

**Theorem 12.3.2 (de Figueiredo's Existence Theorem)** *Consider the system* (12.12) *above and let*

1. $\zeta(0)=0$
2. $\zeta'(0)$ *exists and is negative and provided there exists a* $y_0 > 0$ *such that*
3. $\zeta(\dot{x}) > 0$, $min(\dot{x} \geq y_0)$
4. $2 > -min\zeta'(\dot{x}) < \zeta'(-\dot{x}), (\dot{x} \leq -y_0)$ *except for values of* $\dot{x}$ *at which* $\zeta'(\dot{x})$ *undergoes simple discontinuities.*

*Under the above conditions, the system has* ***at least*** *one periodic solution.*

Given the above conditions for existence, the sufficient conditions for uniqueness of the periodic orbit are provided by the following theorem:

**Theorem 12.3.3 (de Figueiredo's Uniqueness Theorem)** *Suppose the aforementioned system satisfies the above conditions for existence and therefore has a periodic solution. Let there exist a* $y_1 > 0$ *such that following conditions hold:*

1. $\zeta(y_1) = \zeta(0) = 0$
2. $\dot{x}\zeta(\dot{x}) < 0, (0 < |\dot{x}| < y_1)$
3. $\zeta(\dot{x}) > 0, (\dot{x} > y_1)$
4. $\zeta'(\dot{x}) \geq \frac{1}{\dot{x}} \zeta(\dot{x}), \dot{x}\langle 0, \dot{x} \rangle y_1$ *except at values of* $\dot{x}$ *where* $\zeta'(\dot{x})$ *undergoes simple discontinuities. Then the system has a unique periodic solution, except for translations in t.*

A more general theorem for uniqueness is given in de Figueiredo (1970) for a generalized Liénard system.

**Theorem 12.3.4**

$$\dot{x} = y - F(x)$$

$$\dot{y} = -g(x)$$

*Suppose the above system has a periodic solution. Let* $xg(x) > 0$ *for* $x \neq 0$ *and the following conditions hold for g, G and F:*

1. *f and g are real valued functions which are* $C^1$ *(Lipschitz condition, which in turn, guarantees the local uniqueness of the solution of the system)*
2. $\lim_{x \to 0}[g(x)/x]$ *exists and is* $\neq 0$
3. $G(x) \to \infty$ *as* $x \to \pm\infty$
4. $2G(x) + y^2 - F(x)y \neq 0 \ \forall (x, y) \neq (0, 0)$

*If the inequality* $2G(x)f(x) - F(x)g(x) \geq 0$ *holds on the interval* $x < 0$, $x > x_0$, *where* $x_0$ *is a positive constant such that* $xF(x) < 0$ *on* $0 < |x| < x_0$, $F(x) > 0$ *on* $x > x_0$ *and* $G(x_0) = G(-x_0)$, *then the above system has a unique periodic orbit (except for time translations along t axis).*

***Remark 12.3.5*** For $g(x) = x$, the above inequality reduces to $f(x) - F(x)/x \geq 0$. Note that this is the same condition that ensures the uniqueness of periodic orbit in *Sasakura*'s use of Luo Ding-Jun's theorem.[19]

Some remarks here may be pertinent. It is legitimate to wonder if we are merely providing yet another sufficiency theorem that is applicable to one of the non-linear models of business cycle, then may be some justification is warranted. This is not meant to be an exercise in showing that a

[19] On Sasakura's theorem, Sordi (2006) remarks:

> ' a good starting point is the recent contribution by Sasakura (1996), where the existence of a unique stable limit cycle in Goodwin's model (for the general case of asymmetric non-linearity of the investment function) is rigorously proved.'

Although de Figueiredo's work and Goodwin's role in the discovery of the one-sided oscillator are mentioned, this study overlooks the fact that the sufficient conditions in Sasakura's theorem are in fact the same conditions (see above) that de Figuerido obtained in his thesis, where the one-sided oscillator played a crucial role. Sasakura mentions about the one-sided oscillator, but does not discuss similarities of the sufficient conditions. Moreover, in footnote 3, Sasakura (1996) notes that 'one of the referees suggested another easier method for proving at least the uniqueness and stability parts as follows: This is to compute the derivative of the *Poincaré map* and show that (2) is hyperbolic and orbitally asymptotically stable. Then uniqueness drops out easily too'. This is the way de Figuerido proves uniqueness in his 1970 paper.

certain sufficiency theorem can be applied, by searching in the compendium of results on sufficiency conditions for unique limit cycles. The motivation is the contrary—to show that economic intuition ought to come first, as in the case of Goodwin's review of Hicks' book. The economic intuition that the accelerator was dead during the downswing motivated to Goodwin to come up with the one-sided oscillator as a mode of clarifying his economic intuition. This was acknowledged by de Figueiredo and Le Corbeiller. de Figueiredo provided sufficient conditions for the unique limit cycles as early as 1958. The economic interpretation of these sufficient conditions are exactly the same as the ones we seem to have 'rediscovered' after almost 40 years! In addition, the aim was also to show that a more general, economically grounded, yet parsimonious explanation for the persistence of the cycle can be provided within the framework of Goodwin's non-linear cycle model. If one wishes to prove uniqueness and existence and so on, it is possible, but that however was not the concern for Goodwin. In our view, he seemed to be much more interested in unearthing the *nature* of the cycle.

Proving existence and uniqueness which has preoccupied the theorists of NETBC seems to have limited the potential that non-linear theories of the cycle hold. This meant not having to dig deep to uncover the nature of the cycles, their properties, amplitude, frequency and so on, instead merely proving that there are cycles, without providing any explicit method to either find or analyse them. Goodwin's disinterest in proving existence may have been partly because he was concerned with solving or simulating them (geometrically). In contrast, the approximations and simplifications in NETBC often got trapped in the practice of reducing models to equations with known results on uniqueness.

> we discuss three different accounts of the original model derived from alternative assumptions...
>
> In each case the corresponding dynamics is written in Lienard form, **so as to apply a classical result of A. Fillipov** and a more recent theorem of the Chinese mathematician Zhang Zhi Fen.
>
> ...Indeed in business-cycle Kaldor's systems, which can be driven to Lienard form, several periodic orbits are ruled out: even with an imperfect

> knowledge of the initial state, the limit cycle to which the economy will eventually tend is univocally determined.
>
> Galeotti and Gori (1989, pp. 137–38, emphasis added.)

Rather than exploring ways to generalize the models, for example to higher dimensions, removing first approximations and so on, the above quote clearly captures the way in which NETBC modeling activities were directed.

> Lorenz repeatedly underlines the ad hoc' character of these further assumptions and their lack of economic meaning ...it is very important, in our opinion, to underline the fact that the empirical relevance of systems presenting a certain number of limit cycles cannot be deduced from the 'realism' of the formal conditions, which are known to guarantee such a dynamical morphology.
>
> In particular, in the case discussed, if the mathematical hypotheses employed in proving existence and uniqueness of a limit cycle do not appear economically justifiable, this cannot imply that models reducible to Lienard [sic] form, which exhibit a unique periodic orbit, are necessarily 'unrealistic'.
>
> Galeotti and Gori (1989, p. 137)

Expecting realism of formal conditions is one thing, demanding that the economic assumptions be modified to suit these requirements is quite another. This practice always came at the cost of resorting to ad hoc assumptions which compromised the rich economic intuitions in these models. Galeotti and Gori assume that either savings or investment is a function of income level alone and independent of the level of capital stock. But this does not escape the criticism posed by Lorenz that these assumptions are economically restrictive. These simplifications are done so that the model is reducible to the general Liénard form, so that already-available theorems can be readily applied. Even when moving on to higher dimensions and other generalizations, the same temptation to trail behind mathematical results is likely to prevail, for example, in the use of bifurcation theory.

# 4 Algorithmic Decidability and Uniqueness

We will now examine some issues related to computation in the context of dynamical systems and differential equations, which are widely used for modeling economic dynamics. This has implications for computational approaches to studying endogenous economic dynamics as well. We will largely focus on the methodology of computational dynamics in the context of continuous time models or flows.

By computational or algorithmic models, we refer to algorithms in the sense in which they are formally understood in computability theory. This should not be confused with the use of numerical procedures to solve economic models. The focus of the algorithmic approach is therefore on computation, and the kind of numbers and processes that are involved in it. If we choose to retain continuous time models and solve them using numerical methods, we need to understand the scope and limitations of this approach. In order to pose questions concerning computation, we first need to provide computational meaning (in the sense in which '*computability*' was defined by *Alan Turing*) to continuous time dynamic models in macroeconomics. By imposing a computability structure, we can ask whether questions about their long-run dynamic properties can be answered algorithmically. Questions concerning the extent of predictability of future events and states of the economy arise naturally in this context. A subset of questions that are of interest include the following:

1. Is it possible to characterize the attractors of dynamic economic models algorithmically? Are their *domains of attraction* computable?
2. Given knowledge of the attractors, can we 'decide' whether and when the economy would reach a given attractor?
3. Can we 'decide' the number of attractors algorithmically?

This brings us to the interface between economic theory, computability theory and dynamical systems. First, almost all the theoretical models in economic dynamics are defined on real number domains and the functions are real valued functions, whereas the mathematics of digital computers deals with numbers and functions that are defined on natural or rational numbers. It is also worth noting that not all real numbers are computable—when we simulate these models on digital computers, we are in fact dealing with functions that are defined over natural, rational or algebraic numbers. Second, the natural data type of the economic system are themselves rational numbers, at best. Many results that are valid for dynamics defined over real domains do not easily carry over to dynamics defined over rational numbers. The functions over these numbers also need to be equipped with computational content. There are several ways to attempt to bridge the gap between the world of discrete and that of the continuous.

In order to provide a computational structure to dynamical systems, we appeal to definitions and results from *computable analysis* so as to keep the discussion relevant to continuous time models that are widely used in economic dynamics. That means, while talking about computation, we do not impose restrictions such as that the numbers have to be natural or rational (or computable reals) alone, as in classical computability theory. Instead, we resort to computation over real numbers and topological spaces using *Type-2 machines*. There are several important properties in dynamics (and also other parts of economic theory) that are algorithmically undecidable (see Velupillai (2009)). Since we are interested in endogenous models of economic dynamics and the role of non-linearity, the emphasis will be on non-linear dynamical systems and the algorithmic undecidabilities associated with them. We also discuss the decidable fragments of these models and the assumptions that may be necessary (or sufficient) for them to be decidable. We do not address questions related to computational complexity here. We provide a brief introduction to the notion of computability in continuous time models in the following subsection. We then discuss *decidability* of attractors, in particular about the decidability of the number of attractors, which is related to uniqueness.

## 4.1 Continuous-Time Models and Computability

Many models in endogenous business cycle theories are formulated in continuous time and we need to endow them with computational content. Only then can the questions that we raised in the previous section be framed as decision problems concerning economic dynamics. In a *decision problem*, we are interested in a 'yes' or 'no' decision using an *effective procedure*. Typically, this involves a problem that has many individual sub-problems and one looks for a general method or procedure to answer each of those problems. For example, to decide whether an arbitrary Diophantine equation is solvable is a more general problem with countably infinite sub-problems. Instead of addressing the solvability of each specific problem, one looks at whether there is a general method to decide. If there is no such method available, then each problem or a subclass of problems might need a specific decision procedure. Some of these sub-problems might not be decidable as well.

Before proceeding, we need to formally define what we mean by a 'procedure', which leads us to the definition of an algorithm, provided by the work of Turing, Church and others. The conventional definition of an algorithm in computability theory is over discrete mathematical objects. This can be viewed as a theory for (discrete) computation on words in some alphabet $\Sigma$.[20] According to the *Church-Turing thesis*, the set of intuitively computable functions are precisely those that are computable via Turing machines. Turing machines themselves are discrete dynamical systems in their own right, and the operation of a Turing machine can be viewed as the evolution of a corresponding discrete dynamical system. Since most models of the economy are formulated in terms of continuous-time dynamical systems that are often defined over (compact) metric spaces, we need a way to tackle this problem for continuous time systems.

For continuous time systems, there is a need for a bridge between the structure on which traditional computability theory is defined ($\mathbb{N}$, which

[20] In a digital computer, one can think of an alphabet as being composed of $\{0,1\}$. But it need not necessarily be restricted to binary alphabets and can be generalized to more expressive ones. See Collins (2010).

are countable) and continuous systems (defined on sets in $\mathbb{R}^n, n = 1, 2..$ for example, which are uncountable). Notions such as enumerable, recursively enumerable, co-recursively enumerable, semi-decidable, recursive are central to understanding the notion of computability of the functions defined over sets.

**Definition 12.4.1 (Recursively Enumerable Set)** A set $S \subset \mathbb{N}$ is said to be recursively enumerable if and only if it can be accepted by a Turing machine.

**Definition 12.4.2 (Recursive Set)** A set $S \subset \mathbb{N}$ is recursive if and only if both the set $S$ and its complement $S^c$ are recursively enumerable.

The idea of enumerability deals with listing the elements of a set, while recursive sets have the property that the problem of membership is solvable for them. There are at least two possible ways to extend the notion of computation to continuous time dynamic models. The first is to extend the theory of computability to continuous-time systems. In classical computability theory, the set $S \subset \mathbb{N}$ and we need to extend it to subsets of $\mathbb{R}$ and functions defined on these sets. The second is to simulate the continuous time model using continuous-time analog machines. The former is the subject of computable analysis or recursive analysis, which extends computability to continuous objects. On the other hand, the analog computation of continuous time models has a fairly long and established history, even within economics. See Velupillai (2011) for a detailed account of this tradition.[21]

In computable analysis, 'representations' or naming systems provide a way to link continuous objects (such as real numbers, continuous functions) to other objects that have an explicit computational content or meaning. It is instructive to think of this as a code word that links

[21] One of the more well-known theoretical models of a universal continuous-time analogue machine is perhaps Claude Shannon's General Purpose Analog Computer (GPAC). The computational power of computable analysis and GPAC is shown to be equivalent, at least in the case of real computable functions over compact domains (Bournez et al. 2007). However, there seems to be no explicit agreement on the class of computable functions via different models of analog machines, as opposed to the case of digital computation, where we have the Church-Turing thesis.

elements in one domain to those in another. Using these representations, we can induce computability on sets, and the results of the computation can be interpreted in light of these representations. This allows us to carry out accurate computations with arbitrary finite precision.

When dealing with real numbers, we require an infinite amount of information to describe an object exactly. We also need to be able to reliably approximate these infinite objects in $\mathbb{R}$ using finite information, and use them for computation or find other ways to overcome this problem. It is possible to extend the traditional notion of computability on words of an alphabet ($\Sigma \rightarrow \Sigma$) to sequences of words on an alphabet( $\Sigma^{\omega} \rightarrow \Sigma^{\omega}$). Since real numbers can be represented via infinite sequences, computability can now be defined for mappings between infinite sequences. This is referred to as Type-2 computability or Type-2 effectivity (see Weihrauch (2000), Ch:2 for more details), where infinite sequences act as representations for a real number. Note that Type-2 computability is still explicitly based on Turing computability and it is only as powerful. The infinite amount of computation associated while dealing with infinite inputs and outputs (sequence of decimals, for example) can be finitely approximated to any desired level of precision in this framework and can be simulated using digital computers.

These representations can be extended to topological spaces as well (Weihrauch 2000; Brattka and Weihrauch 1999), and concepts such as effective or computable topological spaces, admissible representations and names, computability over real numbers, computability over closed, open and compact sets, can be appropriately defined (Chapters 2–5, Weihrauch (2000)). This approach relies heavily on the nexus between continuity and computability of functions. Please refer to the appendix for some basic definitions concerning computable analysis that are utilized in this chapter.

**Definition 12.4.3** 1. A sequence $\{r_n\}$ of rational numbers is called a $\rho$-name of a real number $x$ if there are three functions $a$, $b$ and $c$ from $\mathbb{N} \rightarrow \mathbb{N}$ such that for all $n \in \mathbb{N}$,

$$r_n = (1)^{a(n)} \frac{b(n)}{c(n)+1} \text{ and } | r_n - x | \frac{1}{2^n}$$

2. A double sequence $\{r_{n,k}\}_{n,k\in\mathbb{N}}$ of rational numbers is called a $\rho$-name for a sequence $\{x_n\}_{n\in\mathbb{N}}$ of real numbers if there are three computable functions $a$, $b$, $c$ from $\mathbb{N}^2 \to \mathbb{N}$ such that, for all $k$, $n \in N$, $r_{n,k} = (1)^{a(k,n)} \dfrac{b(k,n)}{c(k,n)+1}$ and $\left| r_{n,k} - x_n \right| \dfrac{1}{2^k}$
3. A real number $x$ (a sequence $\{x_n\}_{n\in\mathbb{N}}$ of real numbers) is called computable if it has a computable $\rho$-name, that is, there is a Type-2 machine that computes the $\rho$-name without any input.

**Definition 12.4.4 (Computable Functions)** Let $A$, $B$ be sets, where $\rho$-names can be defined for elements of A and B. A function $f: A \to$ B is computable if there is a Type-2 machine such that on any $\rho$-name of $x \in A$, the machine computes as output a $\rho$-name of $f(x) \in B$.

**Definition 12.4.5** 1. An open set $E \subseteq \mathbb{R}^m$ is called **recursively enumerable** (r.e. for short) open if there are computable sequences $\{a_n\}$ and $\{r_n\}, a_n \in \mathbb{Q}^m$ and $r_n \in \mathbb{Q}$, such that

$$E = \bigcup_{n=0}^{\infty} B(a_n, r_n).$$

2. A closed subset $K \subseteq \mathbb{R}^m$ is called **r.e. closed** if there exist computable sequences $\{b_n\}$ and $\{s_n\}, b_n \in \mathbb{Q}^m$ and $s_n \in \mathbb{Q}$, such that $\{B(b_n, s_n)\}_{n\in\mathbb{N}}$ lists all rational open balls intersecting K.
3. An open set $E \subseteq \mathbb{R}^m$ is called **computable** (or recursive) if $E$ is r.e. open and its complement $E^c$ is r.e. closed. Similarly, a closed set $K \subseteq \mathbb{R}^m$ is called computable (or recursive) if K is r.e. closed and its complement $K^c$ is r.e. open.
4. A compact set $M \subseteq \mathbb{R}^m$ is called **computable** if it is computable as a closed set and, in addition, there is a rational number $b$ such that $\|x\| \leq b \forall x \in M$.

## 4.2 Attractors of Dynamic Economic Models and Computability

Having extended the notion of computability to real numbers and topological spaces via representations, we can now turn to dynamic economic models formulated in these spaces. It should be remembered that these extensions do not enable us to compute more than what is computable by a Turing machine. This should not be interpreted as advocating for or dismissing the use of continuous time economic models. Rather, we are interested in exploring what properties can be declared computable in this class of economic models. In macroeconomic dynamics, given certain assumptions regarding the relationships between different economic variables, we are interested in exploring and characterizing certain long-term properties of an economic system such as steady state paths, equilibrium points, limit cycles, periodic or chaotic attractors and their stability properties. If more than one attractor is possible, then we need understand the conditions under which the system tends to one or the other, that is, their respective domains of attraction. This can be viewed as the characterization of the $\omega$ limit set associated with a given dynamic economic model. In the case of endogenous economic dynamics, the focus will be on the algorithmic characterization of equilibrium points and periodic attractors, as has been the major focus of this tradition.

In the context of aggregate economic dynamics, we may ask: given a representation of an economy as a (non-linear) dynamical system, can we algorithmically characterize features concerning the periodic attractors? It turns out that many long-run properties associated with these models are, in general, *undecidable*. Therefore, exhaustive algorithmic classification of attractors is generally not possible. Since this is not a big surprise for the case of continuous time models, we focus on a class for which these properties are known to be decidable. Fortunately, the major class of economic models of endogenous dynamics—which happen to be planar systems—do seem to have important properties that are algorithmically decidable under certain stability conditions. In non-linear models, Poincaré-Bendixson theorem helps to classify the attractors on the plane. In higher dimensions, the attractors can be highly complicated, and we do not have general results for classifying them as we do on the plane. Some formal definitions concerning dynamical systems and related notions are provided below.

**Definition 12.4.6 (Dynamical System)** A dynamical system describes the evolution of points on a state space over time. Let X be an open subset of $\mathbb{R}^n$. A dynamical system on X is a $C^1$ function

$$\phi : \mathbb{R} \times X \rightarrow X,$$

where $\phi_t(x) = \phi(t, x)$ and $\phi_t$ satisfies the following conditions:

1. $\phi_0(x) = x$ for all $x \in X$
2. $\phi_t \circ \phi_s(x) = \phi_{t+s}(x)$ for all $s, t \in \mathbb{R}$ (in case of discrete time systems $s, t \in \mathbb{N}$) and $x \in X$.

The evolution rule $\phi$ is a map (for discrete-time system) or can be written as a differential equation (for a continuous-time, $C^1$ system).

**Definition 12.4.7 ω limit Set** Let $\phi(t, x)$ be the flow of the above dynamical system and z be a point on this trajectory. z is called a $\omega$ limit point of the trajectory of the dynamical system if there exists a sequence $t_n \rightarrow \infty$ such that $lim_{n \rightarrow \infty} \phi(t_n, x) = z$. The $\omega$ limit set of x,$\omega(x)$, is the set of all $\omega$-limit points $z \in X$.

**Definition 12.4.8 (Invariant Set)** A set $L \subset \mathbb{R}^n$ is called an invariant set if $\phi(t, x) \in L$, for all $x \in L$ and $t \rightarrow \infty$.

**Definition 12.4.9 (Attracting Set)** The closed invariant set $L$ is called an **attracting set** of the flow $\phi(t, x)$ if $\exists$ some neighbourhood V of L, such that, $\forall x \in V$ and $\forall t \geq 0$, $\phi(t, x) \in V$ and $\phi(t, x) \rightarrow L$ as $t \rightarrow \infty$.

**Definition 12.4.10 (Domain of Attraction)** Domain of attraction of the attracting set L of $\phi(t, x)$ is defined as follows:

$$\Theta_L = \bigcup_{t \le 0} \phi_t(V)$$

the union of all neighbourhoods V of the attracting set, for which $\forall x \in V$ and $\forall t \ge 0$, $\phi(t, x) \in V$ and $\phi(t, x) \to L$ as $t \to \infty$

For now, let us assume that we know the qualitative properties of the possible attractors for the economic model. This is what is usually done when one invokes the Poincaré-Bendixson theorem to prove the existence of limit cycles. Computability and decidability questions about the $\omega$-limit set can be analysed in different ways. One is to compute the attracting set—such as fixed points and limit cycles, explicitly. The second is to algorithmically decide whether a trajectory belongs to the domain of attraction of a given attractor. There is also the issue of explicitly computing the domain(s) of attraction for members of the $\omega$-limit set.

When we ask such questions about attractors, we are essentially asking whether the set is recursive. By providing a computable structure, we endow the set with the property of recursive enumerability. That is, there is a rule or an algorithm or a partial recursive function to list the successive members of this set. In order for this set to be decidable, we require an algorithm that will decide whether a given element belongs to the set or not in finite time. It is intuitive that all recursive sets are recursively enumerable, but the converse is not true. By establishing a correspondence between the economy formulated as a dynamical system and a Turing machine, we can study the dynamic trajectories of an economy via the evolution of a Turing machine.

## 4.3 Decidability of Attractors in Planar Models

Planar, non-linear models form an important class of models in the tradition of endogenous business cycle theory. What is the status of these models when it comes to algorithmic decidability and computability of attractors? Although several of their properties are undecidable, there are some decidable fragments. Graça and Zhong (2011) conclude that attractors and their basins of attractions are *semi-computable* if we assume that the system is stable. They work within the framework of computable analysis and Type-2 machines.

**Definition 12.4.11 (Semi-Computable Functions)** A function $\psi : A \rightarrow O(\mathbb{R}^m)$, (where $O(\mathbb{R}^m) = \{O \mid O \subseteq \mathbb{R}^m$ is open in the standard topology} is called **semi-computable** if there is a Type-2 machine such that on any $\rho$-name of $x \in A$, the machine computes as output two sequences $\{a_n\}$ and $\{r_n\}$, $a_n \in \mathbb{Q}^m$ and $r_n \in \mathbb{Q}$, such that $\psi(x) = \bigcup_{n=0}^{\infty} B(a_n, r_n)$.

**Definition 12.4.12 (Type-2 Machine, Weihrauch (2000), p. 15)** Let $\Sigma^*$ be the set of finite words over some arbitrary finite alphabet $\Sigma$. Similarly, let $\Sigma^\omega$ be the set of infinite sequence of symbols from some arbitrary finite alphabet $\Sigma$, which has at least two elements. A Type-2 Machine M is a Turing machine with k input tapes together with a type specification ($Y_1$, $Y_2 \ldots . Y_k$, $Y_0$) with $Y_i \in (\Sigma^*, \Sigma^\omega)$, giving the type for each input tape and the output tape.

Since the attractors cannot be computed in general, we need to explore the conditions under which they become computable. Stability becomes a crucial condition for ensuring the computability of attractors. They employ the notion of computability on closed, open and compact sets as outlined earlier, following the work of Brattka and Weihrauch (1999) and Weihrauch (2000).

**Theorem 12.4.13** *Let $x' = f(x)$ be a planar dynamical system. Assume that $f \in C^1(\mathbb{R}^2)$ and that the system is structurally stable. Let $K \subseteq \mathbb{R}^2$ be a computable compact set and let $K_{cycles}$ be the union of all hyperbolic periodic orbits of the system, which is contained in K. Then, given as input ρ-names of f and K, one can compute a sequence of closed sets $\{K^n_{cycles}\}_{n \in \mathbb{N}}$ with the following properties:*

1. $K^n_{cycles} \subseteq K$ *for every* $n \in \mathbb{N}$
2. $K^{n+1}_{cycles} \subseteq K^n_{cycles}$ *for every* $n \in \mathbb{N}$
3. $\lim_{n \to \infty} K^n_{cycles} = K_{cycles}$

This means that, under the assumption of structural stability (together with the Lipschitz property), if one can supply the $\rho$ names of $f$ and the compact set $K$ as input, there is an algorithm which can tell, in finite time, whether $f$ has a periodic orbit of the above dynamical system in the compact set $K$. Since the periodic orbits are only *semi-decidable* in this case, one may need an infinite amount of time, countably calibrated, to conclude that $K$ does not contain a periodic orbit. The same is true for the equilibrium points of the above dynamical system. This is a necessary consequence of dealing with a recursively enumerable, but not recursive, set.

## 4.4 Decidability of the Number of Attractors

We are now ready to address the issue of the algorithmic decidability of the number of attractors associated with a given planar dynamical system. Deciding whether the attractor (limit cycle in our case) is unique is a special case of this problem. Since the models invoking these theorems often assume compactness, we grant these assumptions and ask whether the number of attractors for a given economy (formulated as a planar dynamical system) is algorithmically decidable. We can consider a situation that is general enough by allowing the function to be analytic.

**Proposition 12.4.14** *Consider a non-linear model of an economy, formulated as a planar dynamical system* $\dot{x} = \psi(x)$ *on a compact subset* $K \subseteq \mathbb{R}^2$*. Consider the case where* $\psi$ *is described by an analytic function and assume that the system is structurally stable.*

1. *The possible limit sets (hyperbolic equilibria and hyperbolic limit cycles) are necessarily finite.*
2. *Given the* $\rho$ *names of the compact set* $K \subseteq \mathbb{R}^2$ *and the analytic function* $\psi$*, the problem of deciding the number of equilibria and limit cycles is in general undecidable.*

***Proof 12.4.15*** *The first part follows from* Dulac's theorem *(Perko (*2001*), pp. 205–6). The second part follows from Graça and Zhong (*2011*), theorems 20 & 21.*

Thus, we note that within the framework of computable analysis it not possible to algorithmically decide the number of attractors, in general. The precise number and position of limit cycles of planar polynomial vector fields is the subject of Hilbert's $16^{th}$ problem, which is yet to be resolved.

# 5 Conclusion

We examined various uniqueness theorems utilized in the developments that followed some of the pioneering contributions in the non-linear endogenous business cycle models. We have argued that there has been a tendency to straightjacket economic models to fit the mathematical requirements in several cases. We also highlighted some issues concerning the algorithmic decidability of properties of attractors, such as their uniqueness. This brings us to the question of whether a methodology strongly reliant on existence-uniqueness-stability aspects which may have their legitimate place in dynamical systems theory are relevant at all for endogenous economic theories. We believe that an excessive reliance on existence-uniqueness-stability mode of theorizing stunted the possibilities for exploring the rich avenues that these endogenous theories possessed. Stefano Zambelli's work on carefully studying the dynamic possibilities of economies within the framework of coupled oscillators through numerical simulations shows us a way to overcome some of these limitations (Zambelli 2015). It may be entirely possible to devise methods that are suited for the specificities and nuances of the economic system and their evolution as a continued transformation of its own structure. Dynamical systems of the sort analysed earlier have a *given* structure and one searches for associated attractors and their properties. The key aspect of economic dynamics is the continual change in structure, composition/dimension with birth of new products, sectors, technologies and evolving demand patterns.

Zambelli's painstaking development of a theory of production, extending the research of Piero Sraffa in innovative ways, where distribution issues are at the core, has already broken ground (Zambelli 2018a,b). His sustained advocacy of computable economic dynamics, together with Velupillai, which pays close attention to the actual nature of the domain of economic quantities, that is, rational numbers, and algorithms provides promising avenues for further research. In this Zambelli seems to be in elite, enviable company of Alan Turing for his philosophy toward studying economic problems. Turing noted (in the context of morphogenesis) that rigid (classical) mathematical requirements that one adopts at the initial stages of developing a theory ought to give way to more powerful computational methods, even if it is at the cost of an all-embracing theory:

> Most of an organism, most of the time, is developing from one pattern into another, rather than from homogeneity into a pattern. One would like to be able to follow this more general process mathematically also. **The difficulties are, however, such that one cannot hope to have any very embracing theory of such processes, beyond the statement of the equations. It might be possible, however, to treat a few particular cases in detail with the aid of a digital computer.** This method has the advantage that it is not so necessary to make simplifying assumptions as it is which doing a more theoretical type of analysis. ...The essential disadvantage of the method is that one only gets results for particular cases. **But this disadvantage is probably of comparatively little importance**. - Turing (1952, pp. 71–72, emphasis added.)

## References

Bournez, O., Campagnolo, M. L., Graça, D. S., & Hainry, E. (2007). Polynomial differential equations compute all real computable functions on computable compact intervals. *Journal of Complexity, 23*(3), 317–335.

Brattka, V., & Weihrauch, K. (1999). Computability on subsets of Euclidean Space I: Closed and Compact subsets. *Theoretical Computer Science, 219*(1–2), 65–93.

Chang, W. W., & Smyth, D. (1971). The existence and persistence of cycles in a non-linear model: Kaldor's 1940 model re-examined. *The Review of Economic Studies, 38*(1), 37–44.
Collins, P. (2010). *Computable analysis with applications to dynamic systems.* Centrum wiskunde & informatica, working paper (MAC-1002).
de Figueiredo, R. (1960). Existence and uniqueness of the periodic solution of an equation for autonomous oscillations. In L. L. Cesari & S. Lefschetz (Eds.), *13, Contributions to the Theory of Nonlinear Oscillations* (Vol. 5, pp. 269–284). Annals of Mathematical Studies, no. 45. Princeton, NJ: Princeton University Press.
de Figueiredo, R. (1970). Existence and uniqueness results for liénard's equation. *IEEE Transactions on Circuit Theory, CT-17*(3), 313–321.
Flaschel, P. (2009). *The macrodynamics of capitalism* (2nd Edition). Berlin: Springer.
Galeotti, M., & Gori, F. (1989). Uniqueness of periodic orbits in lienard-type business-cycle models. *Metroeconomica, 40*(2), 135–146.
Gandolfo, G. (2005). *Economic dynamics.* Heidelberg: Springer.
Goodwin, R. (1950). A non-linear theory of the cycle. *The Review of Economics and Statistics, 32*(4), 316–320.
Goodwin, R. (1951). The nonlinear accelerator and the persistence of business cycles. *Econometrica,19*(1), 1–17.
Goodwin, R. (1967). A growth cycle. In C. Feinstein (Ed.), *Socialism, capitalism and economic growth: essays presented to Maurice Dobb* (pp. 54–58). Cambridge: Cambridge University Press.
Graça, D., & Zhong, N. (2011). Computability in planar dynamical systems. *Natural Computing, 10*(4), 1295–1312.
Hicks, J. (1950). *A contribution to the theory of the trade cycle.* Oxford: Clarendon Press.
Ichimura, S. (1955). Toward a general nonlinear macrodynamic theory of economic fluctuations. In *Post-keynesian economics by K. K. Kurihara* (pp. 92–226). London: George Allen & Unwin.
Kaldor, N. (1940). A model of the trade cycle. *The Economic Journal, 50*(197), 78–92.
Le Corbeiller, P. (1960). Two-stroke oscillators. *IRE Transactions on Circuit Theory, CT-7*(4), 387–398.
Lorenz, H.-W. (1987). Strange attractors in a multisector business cycle model. *Journal of Economic Behavior & Organization, 8*(3), 397–411.

Lundberg, E. (1937). *Studies in the theory of economic expansion.* London: P.S. King & Son.

Matsumoto, A. (2009). Note on Goodwin's 1951 nonlinear accelator model with an investment delay. *Journal of Economic Dynamics and Control, 33*(4), 832–842.

Perko, L. (2001). *Differential equations and dynamical systems.* New York: Springer.

Ragupathy, V., & Velupillai, K. (2012). *Existence proofs in nonlinear endogenous theories of the business cycle on the plane – the origins.* ASSRU discussion paper DP-10-2012/1.

Sasakura, K. (1996). The business cycle model with a unique stable limit cycle. *Journal of Economic Dynamics and Control,20*(9–10), 1763–1773.

Sordi, S. (2006). 'Floors' and/or 'Ceilings' and the persistence of business cycles. In T. Puu & I. Sushko (Eds.), *Business cycle dynamics - models and tools.* Berlin: Springer–Verlag.

Turing, M. A. (1952). The chemical basis of morphogenesis. *Philosophical Transactions of the Royal Society of London. Series B, Biological Sciences, 237*(641), 37–72.

Velupillai, K. (1998). The vintage economist. *Journal of Economic Behavior and Organization, 37*(1), 1–31.

Velupillai, K. (2011). The phillips machine and the epistemology of analogue computation. *Economia Politica [Journal of Analytical and Institutional Economics], XXVII*(Special issue), 39–62.

Velupillai, K. V. (2009). Uncomputability and undecidability in economic theory. *Applied Mathematics and Computation, 215*(4), 1404–1416.

Venkatachalam, R. (2013). *Studies in endogenous macroeconomic dynamics.* Ph. D. thesis, University of Trento, Italy.

Weihrauch, K. (2000). *Computable Analysis – An Introduction.* Berlin: Springer-Verlag.

Xianwu, Z., Zhi-Fen, Z., & Suzhi, G. (1994). On the uniqueness of the limit cycle of the generalized Liénard equation. *Bulletin of the London Mathematical Society, 26*(3), 213–247.

Yasui, T. (1953). *Self-excited oscillations and the business cycle.* Cowles commission discussion paper no. 2065.

Ye, Y.-Q., Sui-lin, C., Lan-sun, C., Ke-cheng, H., Ding-jun, L., Zhi-en, M., et al. (1986). *Theory of limit cycles* (Vol. 66). Providence, RI: Translations of Mathematical Monographs, American Mathematical Society.

Zambelli, S. (2015). Dynamical coupling, nonlinear accelerator and the persistence of business cycles. *Cambridge Journal of Economics, 39*(6), 1607–1628.

Zambelli, S. (2018a). The aggregate production function is NOT neoclassical. *Cambridge Journal of Economics, 42*(2), 383–426.
Zambelli, S. (2018b). Production of Commodities by Means of Commodities and non-uniform rates of profits. *Metroeconomica, 69*(4), 791–818.
Zhi-Fen, Z. (1986a). On the number of limit cycles of lienard equation. *Quaderni dell'Istituto Mathematico U. Dini, Università di Firenze, Firenze, A.A*, 85–86.
Zhi-Fen, Z. (1986b). Proof of the uniqueness theorem of limit cycles of generalized Lienard equations. *Applicable Analysis, 23*(1–2), 63–76.

# 13

# Nonlinear Endogenous Business Cycles: Zambelli-Goodwin Excursions in Cellular Automata Worlds

Cassey Lee

## 1 Introduction

The study of the economy as a complex system has been undertaken in a number of ways. One of the earliest approach—the mathematical theories of nonlinear endogenous business cycles—can be traced to the early works of Hamburger (1930, 1931, 1934) and Goodwin (1951).[1] The mathematical formulation of these theories was shaped by both the mathematics used originally in physics and the prevailing economic theories and models. The main mathematical tools used were differential and difference equations.

When a leading theorist has his attention diverted to business cycle analysis, the result is usually a happy one, as witness the examples provided by Schumpeter, Pigou, J.M. Clark, Harrod and Haberler. Goodwin (1950, p. 316)

[1] See Venkatachalam and Vellupilai (2012) and Rosser (2016).

C. Lee (✉)
ISEAS—Yusof Ishak Institute, Heng Mui Keng Terrace, Singapore



K. Velupillai (ed.), *Keynesian, Sraffian, Computable and Dynamic Economics*,
https://doi.org/10.1007/978-3-030-58131-2_13

An alternative approach to modelling the economy as a complex system entails the use of computational methods that feature local interactions leading to aggregate fluctuations. Some of the early pioneers include Schelling (1978) and Bak et al. (1993). A useful approach to modelling local interactions is cellular automata (CA). Initially discovered in the 1940s by Stanislaw Ulam and John von Neumann, the cellular automata is a powerful tool that can be used to study endogenous economic fluctuations.

There are several reasons that make cellular automata a useful approach to study nonlinear endogenous business cycles. Cellular automata can generate four classes of dynamical behaviour: fixed point, periodic, complex and chaotic (Wolfram 1984). Langton's (1992) conjecture on the computability correspondence of these four classes suggests that not only can cellular automata be used to study nonlinear dynamics, but it can also anchor such a study on a computability foundation. Another appealing feature of this approach is its microfoundations—not of the representation agent type but through the use of decentralized local interactions.

The goal of this chapter is to explore how nonlinear endogenous business cycles—an area of interest to Stefano Zambelli (2011a, 2011b, 2015) and in the footsteps of Goodwin (1952)—can be studied using cellular automata. The outline of the rest of the chapter is as follows. Section 2 will discuss the relationship between cellular automata and nonlinear dynamics. Section 3 explores the use of CA to study the flexible accelerator model. Section 4 concludes.

## 2 Cellular Automata and Nonlinear Dynamics

Cellular automata (CA) is a useful computational model to study spatial dynamics involving multiple agents. A CA model comprises a set of regular arrays of cells in one, two or higher dimensions. Each cell can assume a finite number of states, the simplest being binary states (1,0). The evolution of a CA is determined by its *transition function*, which specifies how the state of each cell changes over iterations. More specifically, the state of each cell at a given iteration $t + 1$ is dependent on the states of the same cell and the states of neighbouring cells at iteration $t$:

$$c_i(t+1) = \lambda\left[c_{i-1}(t), c_i(t), c_{i+1}(t)\right] \tag{13.1}$$

In the case of *one-dimensional CA* (also known as *elementary CA*), the transition function for cell $i$ or $c_i$ at iteration $t + 1$ can be expressed as follows:

$$c_i(t+1) = \left[c_{i-1}(t) + c_i(t) + c_{i+1}(t)\right] \bmod 2 \tag{13.2}$$

where $c_{i-1}$ is the state of cell $i$'s left neighbour, $c_{i+1}$ the state of its right neighbour and mod 2 the remainder after division of the sum by 2.[2] This can be graphically represented as follows:

| $c_{i-1}$ | $c_i$ | $c_{i+1}$ |
|---|---|---|

Wolfram (1984) has classified the long-term (asymptotic) CA behaviour into four types:[3]

- Class I: fixed point—where CA cells evolve to a uniformly constant state.
- Class II: periodic—where CA cells evolve towards continually repeating a periodic structure.
- Class III: chaotic—where CA cells evolve in a chaotic and aperiodic manner.
- Class IV: complex—where CA cells evolve in such a way that persistent and localized structures are produced that move about and interact with each other.

Graphical depictions of the four classes for a one-dimensional CA are presented in Fig. 13.1.[4] The rows in these diagrams are in one of the two available states (white, black). These diagrams summarize how CA systems evolve spatially over time.

---

[2] See Schiff (2008, p. 43).

[3] This is also known as CA rule classification.

[4] Random initial conditions are used in the simulations.

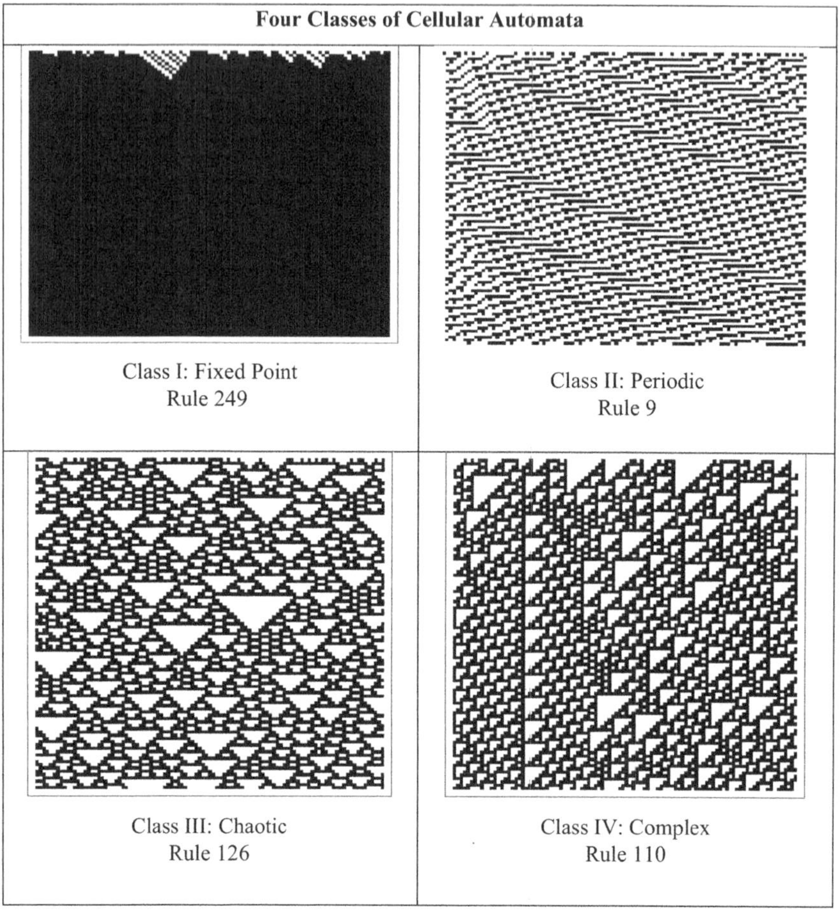


**Fig. 13.1** Four classes of cellular automata. (Source: Author)

CAs are essentially discrete dynamical systems. Economists are generally less familiar with such space-time depictions of dynamical systems. If the states are assigned two numbers, 0 (white) and 1 (black), a time series plot can be generated based on an aggregate function which sums up the total number of cells with state equal 1. This is depicted in Fig. 13.2.

The "microfoundation" for these four classes of dynamical behaviour resides in their transition functions. A sample of transition functions/rules for each of the four classes are summarized in Table 13.1. A more

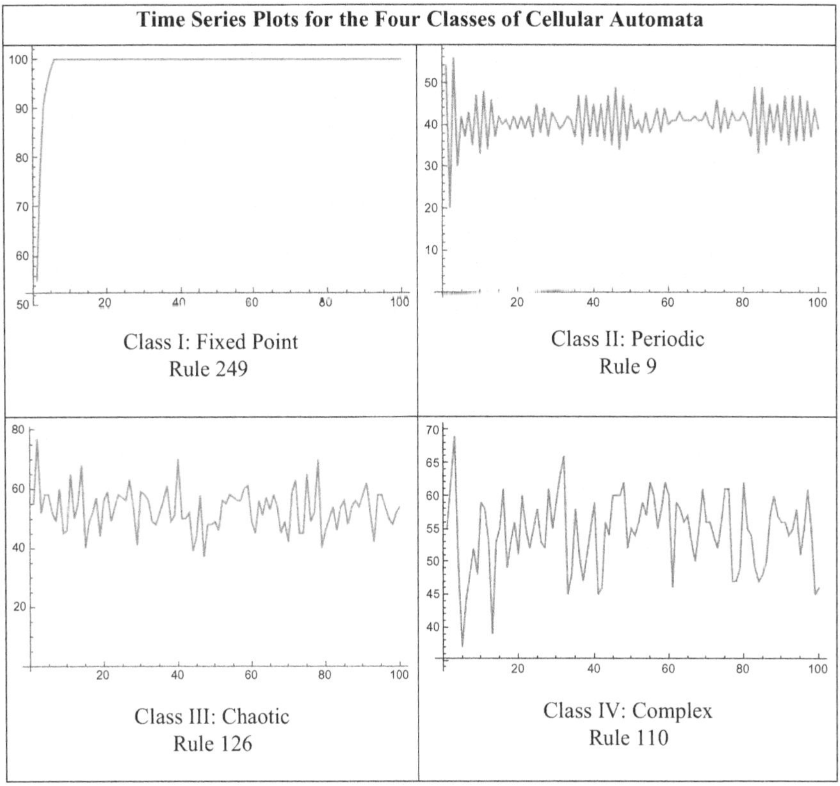


**Fig. 13.2** Time series plots for the four classes of cellular automata. (Source: Author)

**Table 13.1** Transition functions for dynamic classes

| Class | Rule | Algebraic form | Rule icon |
|---|---|---|---|
| I: Fixed point | 249 | Mod[1 + $q$ + $pq$ + r + $pr$, 2] |  |
| II: Periodic | 9 | Mod[(1 + $p$) (1 + $q$ + $r$), 2] | 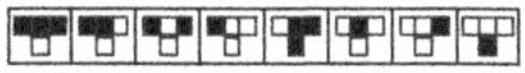 |
| III: Chaotic | 126 | Mod[$p$ + $q$ + $pq$ + $r$ + $pr$ + $qr$, 2] | 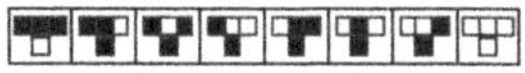 |
| IV: Complex | 110 | Mod[$q$ + $r$ + $qr$ + $pqr$, 2] |  |

Source: http://atlas.wolfram.com/01/01/rulelist.html

detail example of how a transition rule is applied under Rule 249 for different states is presented in Table 13.2. For an elementary CA with two states (0,1) and three neighbours (*p*, *q*, *r*), there a total of 256 transition rules. The classification of CA into different classes of dynamical behaviour has preoccupied scholars since the publication of Wolfram (1984). There have been a number of attempts to refine the classification of CA behaviour. One much-cited early example is Li and Packard (1990). Table 13.3 summarizes and compares the original classification provided by Wolfram (1984) with that of Li and Packard (1990).

The classification of the dynamical behaviour of CA continues to be an important area of research.[5] As the original classification by Wolfram (1984) is based on patterns of long-term evolution observed from simulations, it can be difficult to classify CA that requires length iterations before observable differences emerge. This is particularly true for Class III and Class IV—it can be difficult to distinguish between the two. More fundamentally, the problem of CA classification based on the long-term evolution of CA pattern is undecidable (Sutner 2009). This should not be considered to be a limitation of the CA approach to exploring business cycles.

**Table 13.2** Computation using algebraic form for Rule 249

| No. | $p$ | $q$ | $r$ | $1 + q + pq + r + pr$ | Mod2 |
|---|---|---|---|---|---|
| 1 | 1 | 1 | 1 | 1+1+(1*1)+1+(1*1) = 5 | 1 |
| 2 | 1 | 1 | 0 | 1+1+(1*1)+0+(1*0) = 3 | 1 |
| 3 | 1 | 0 | 1 | 1+0+(1*0)+1+(1*1) = 3 | 1 |
| 4 | 1 | 0 | 0 | 1+0+(1*0)+0+(1*0) = 1 | 1 |
| 5 | 0 | 1 | 1 | 1+1+(0*1)+1+(0*1) = 3 | 1 |
| 6 | 0 | 1 | 0 | 1+1+(0*1)+0+(1*0) = 2 | 0 |
| 7 | 0 | 0 | 1 | 1+0+(0*0)+1+(0*1) = 2 | 0 |
| 8 | 0 | 0 | 0 | 1+0+(0*0)+0+(0*0) = 1 | 1 |

Source: http://atlas.wolfram.com/01/01/rulelist.html

[5] See Sutner (2009) for a review of this. There have been more formalistic attempts of classifying CA, for example, based on topological and measure theoretic means (Kurka 1997; Sutner 2009). Other approaches include Langton's $\lambda$ parameter and Gutowitz's mean field parameters and Wuensche's Z parameter.

**Table 13.3** Classes of elementary cellular automata dynamics

| Class | Transition rules |
|---|---|
| I. Fixed point | Wolfram (1984):<br>0, 4, 16, 32, 36, 48, 54, 60, 62<br>Li and Packard (1990)—null (homogeneous fixed points):<br>0, 8, 32, 40, 128, 136, 160, 168<br>Li and Packard (1990)—fixed point (non-homogeneous fixed points):<br>2, 4, 10, 12, 13, 24, 34, 36, 42, 44, 46, 56, 57, 58, 72, 77, 78, 104, 130, 132, 138, 140, 152, 162, 164, 170, 172, 184, 200, 204, 232 |
| II. Periodic | Wolfram (1984):<br>8, 24, 40, 56, 58<br>Li and Packard (1990): periodic<br>1, 3, 5, 6, 7, 9, 11, 14, 15, 19, 23, 25, 27, 28, 29, 33, 35, 37, 38, 41, 43, 50, 51, 74, 108, 131, 133, 134, 142, 156, 178 |
| III. Chaotic | Wolfram (1984):<br>2, 6, 10, 12, 14, 18, 22, 26, 28, 30, 34, 38, 42, 44, 46, 50<br>Li and Packard (1990)—locally chaotic:<br>26, 73, 154<br>Li and Packard (1990)—chaotic and unbounded:<br>18, 11, 30, 45, 54, 60, 90, 105, 106, 129, 137, 146, 150, 161 |
| IV. Complex | Wolfram (1984):<br>20, 52 |

Source: Wolfram (1984), Li and Packard (1990)

## 3 Zambelli-Goodwin Excursions in Cellular Automata Worlds

> In my view economies impossibly complex as to defy any completely satisfactory analysis: rather the best that can be hoped for is a number of different approaches, each of which yields valuable but incomplete insights into the various aspects of the system. Goodwin (1983, p. vi)

The CA is essentially a discrete dynamical system that can generate a wide range of dynamical behaviour. Thus, it can be another approach to study nonlinear endogenous business cycles. Depending on the transition rule used, CA simulations can exhibit nonlinear behaviour without any exogenous shocks. Given the importance of transition rules in CA, an exploration of business cycle modelling using CA could focus on interpreting their microfoundations—more specifically, what the various transition rules represent and mean.

In our business cycle excursion into a CA world, we follow the paths taken by Zambelli (2011a, 2015) and Goodwin (1951), which use the flexible accelerator model within a Keynesian framework. An aggregated version of such a model comprises the following equations (discrete version) representing national income (Y), consumption (C) and investment (I):

$$Y_t = C_t + I_t \tag{13.3}$$

$$C_t = \alpha Y_{t-1} \tag{13.4}$$

$$I_t = \varphi\left(vY_{t-1} - K_{t-1}\right) \tag{13.5}$$

where $K$ is capital stock, $\alpha$ marginal propensity of consumption and $v$ the capital-output ratio.

The CA is an agent-based model in which consumption and investment activities are all undertaken at the micro level, involving consumers and producers. Thus, economic activity is thus a coupling of consumption and investment activities. This follows the tradition of economic dynamic coupling embraced by Zambelli (2011a, 2011b, 2015) and Goodwin (1947), albeit with a different twist. Instead of dynamic coupling between national economies, the coupling takes place between different forms of economic activities within an economy (assumed to be a closed one). Figure 13.3 provides a depiction for a model comprising three layers of interacting one-dimensional CAs, each arranged in a circle.

The basic structure of our model is one in which there are a fixed number of N economic agents that are assumed to be located along a circle (see Fig. 13.3).

## 3.1 Consumption

For simplicity, consumption is modelled as a binary state, namely, 0 or 1. In a typical one-dimensional or elementary CA, the state of consumption

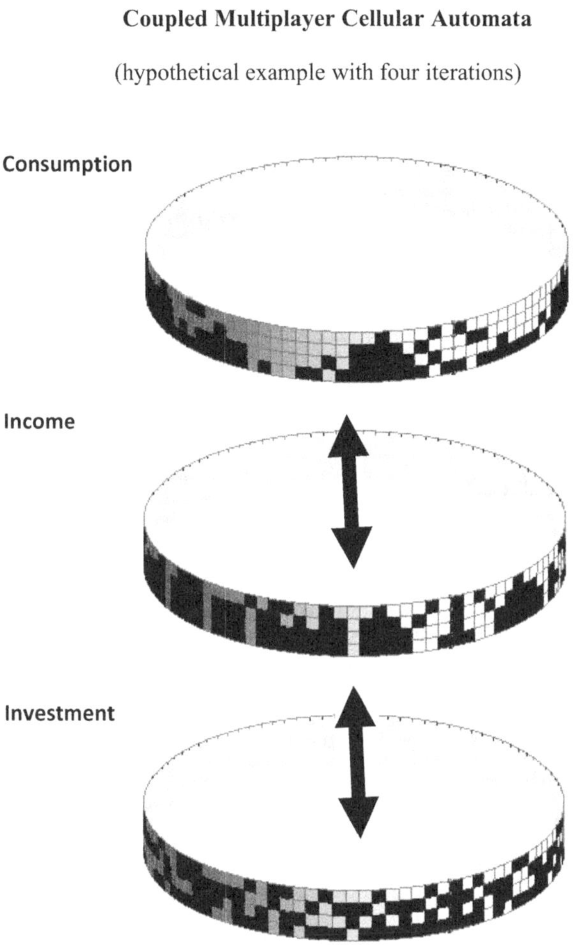


**Fig. 13.3** Coupled multilayer cellular automata (hypothetical example with four iterations). (Source: Author)

($x$) of a given agent $i$ at time $t + 1$ is dependent on income level $y$ at time $t$, namely:

$$x_i(t+1) = \gamma\left[\alpha_{i-1} y_{i-1}(t), \alpha_i y_i(t), \alpha_{i+1} y_{i+1}(t)\right] \tag{13.6}$$

where $\alpha$ is the marginal propensity of consumption, with $0 < \alpha < 1$ and $i = 1, 2, \ldots, N$.

The consumption of each individual $i$ at time $t + 1$ is dependent on his/her income at time $t$ as well as the income levels of two neighbouring agents at time $t$. The latter could be a general barometer of the overall conditions of the economy as observed by the agent locally.

## 3.2 Investment

In the aggregated model of the flexible accelerator, investment at time $t + 1$ is a function of the previous level of economic activity ($Y$) and previous capital stock ($K$). In a real economy, the number of firms are smaller than the number of consumers/workers. The mapping of consumers/workers to firms is an important assumption. A simplistic assumption would be to set the number of firms equal to the number of consumers (the upper limit); that is, each consumer is also a producer that undertakes investment. The individual investment function can be represented as follows:

$$z_i(t+1) = \varphi\left[v_{i-1} y_{i-1}(t), v_i y_i(t), v_{i+1} y_{i+1}(t), -k_{i-1}(t), -k_i(t), -k_{i+1}(t),\right] \tag{13.7}$$

## 3.3 Transition Rules and Macrodynamics

The long-term evolution of consumption and investment in the CA model is obviously determined by the transition rules. The functional form for consumption is straightforward, as it is determined by past income (though it differs slightly from the aggregated version). The investment function is a bit more complicated, as it draws from the interactions of two lagged variables, namely, income and capital stock. The dynamics of coupling takes place in the investment function.

There are eight possible configurations for the lagged income and two possible outcomes for consumption (0, 1). Thus, there are 256 ways in which the combination of the lagged income levels ($y_{i-1}$, $y_i$, $y_{i+1}$) can be mapped into consumption ($x_i$), that is, $2^8 = 256$.

For the investment function, the number of possible combinations for the three lagged income variables and three lagged capital variables is greater at 64, that is, $2^6$. The number of possible transition rules for the investment function is very large at more than 18 quintillion, or more precisely: $2^{64}$ = 18,446,744,073,709,551,616. One possible way to reduce the complexity of the model is to assume investment is only determined by three lagged income variables and one lagged capital stock variable or alternatively, one lagged income variable and three lagged capital variables. Either of the two assumptions will reduce the number of transition rules to 65,536, which is still a big number.

Aside from the large number of transition rules, the interpretation of transition rules is also a challenging problem. For example, algebraically, Rule 249, which belongs to Class I, has the following rule: $1 + q + pq + r + pr$ (see Table 13.1). If this rule is used for a consumption function, the consumption function would assume the following form (here presented without the coefficients ($\gamma$, $\alpha$) and modulo (2)):

$$x_i(t+1) = 1 + y_{i-1}(t) + \left[y_{i-1}(t)y_i(t)\right] + y_{i+1}(t) + \left[y_{i-1}(t)y_{i+1}(t)\right] \quad (13.8)$$

The above consumption equation is a quadratic equation with no obvious interpretation. Agent *i*'s consumption at time $t + 1$ depends only on the incomes of his/her neighbours at time t. The first multiplicative term in the equation implies that agent i's own income at time t also plays a role, but this role depends on the income of one of his/her neighbour (agent $i$ - 1).

Obviously, it would be problematic to interpret all 456 transition rules in this manner. An alternative approach would be to let theory drive the choice of transition rule(s) rather than experiment with all transition rules.

**Table 13.4** Transition rule classification for Mod(1 + $c_{i+1}(t)$, 2)

| $c_{i-1}(t)$ | $c_i(t)$ | $c_{i+1}(t)$ | $c_i(t+1)$ |
|---|---|---|---|
| 1 | 1 | 1 | 0 |
| 1 | 1 | 0 | 0 |
| 1 | 0 | 1 | 1 |
| 1 | 0 | 0 | 1 |
| 0 | 1 | 1 | 0 |
| 0 | 1 | 0 | 0 |
| 0 | 0 | 1 | 1 |
| 0 | 0 | 0 | 1 |
| Base 2 → Base 10 | | | |
| 00110011 → 51 | | | |

Source: Author

Drawing from Eq. (13.4), the transition rule would assume the following form:

$$x_i(t+1) = \text{mod}\left[1 + \alpha_i y_i(t), 2\right] \tag{13.9}$$

If the value of $\alpha$ is 1, the above transition rule is Rule 51 in the table for the 256 transition rules for elementary CA (see derivation in Table 13.4). Rule 51 is a Class II CA which exhibits periodic behaviour. This can be seen in the pattern generated by simulations in Fig. 13.4.

In macroeconomic theory, the value of $\alpha$, which is the agent's marginal propensity of consumption, is often less than 1. If we vary the value of $\alpha$, the dynamics of the CA will vary as well. As the value of $\alpha$ decreases, the dynamics of the CA changes from a periodic one (Class II) to a fixed point (Class I).

It should be useful to experiment with different economic assumptions that have corresponding different transition rules. For example, it could be meaningful to assume that an agent's consumption depends on his/her income as well as those of others. In addition, simulations could also be carried out on a population of heterogeneous agents with different transition rules (different degrees of bounded rationality). Agents could also change the transition rules used over time.

One glaring weakness of the above excursions into consumption dynamics is that the evolution of income has not been really addressed.

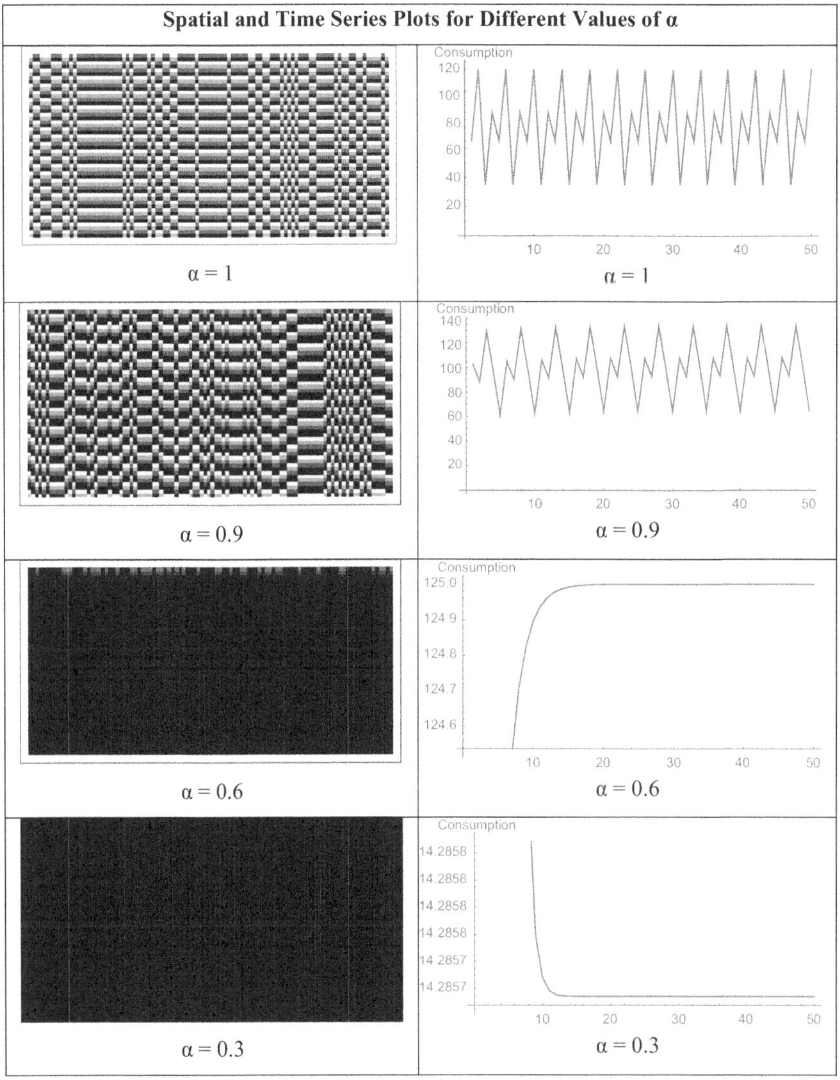


**Fig. 13.4** Spatial and time series plots for different values of $\alpha$. (Source: Author)

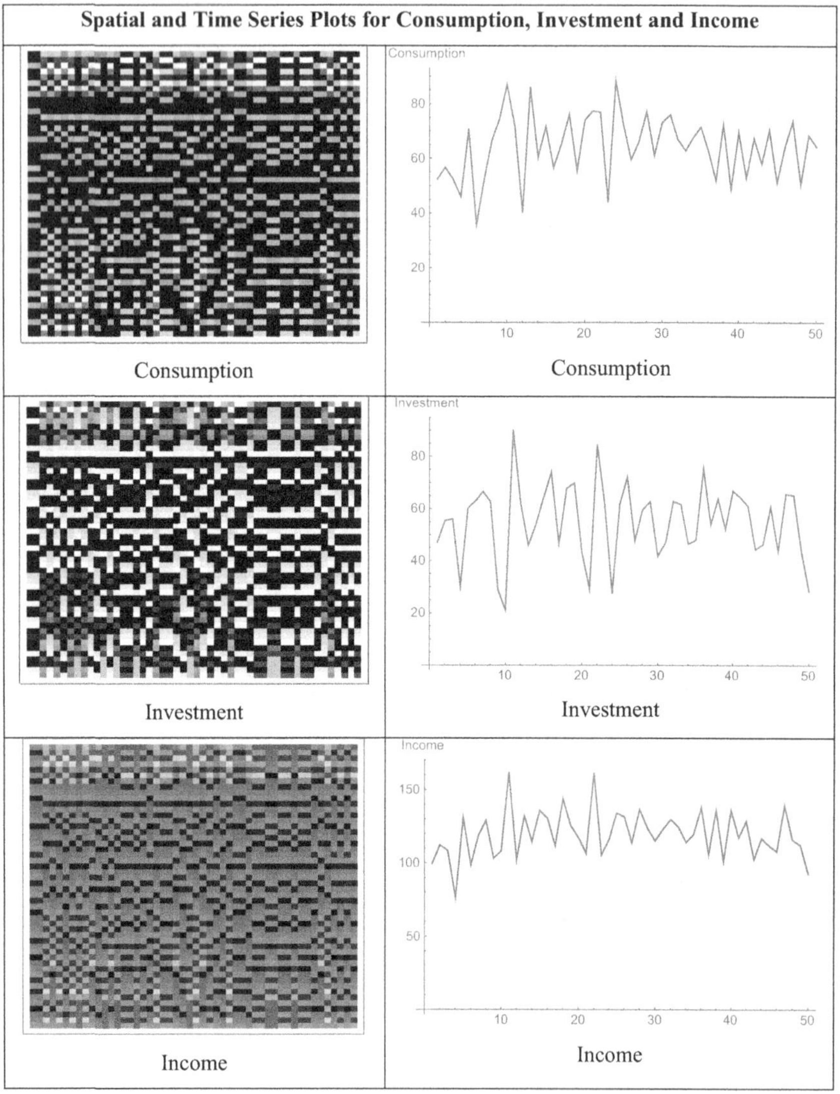


**Fig. 13.5** Spatial and time series plots for consumption, investment and income. (Source: Author)

The investment function was not fully integrated in a meaningful way into the earlier simulations. Income in the above model is akin to an impulse represented by an initial income configuration that is randomly generated. To have a full model of the economy, both the investment and consumption functions have to be included (as in Eqs. 13.3–13.5). In such a model, investment interacts with lagged income, which in turn is driven by lagged consumption and investment.

A simplistic model would be to assume that an individual's investment decision is only dependent on his/her own income and capital level in the previous period:

$$z_i(t+1) = \varphi\left[v_i y_i(t) - k_i(t)\right] \tag{13.10}$$

The individual consumption function is assumed to as in Eq. 13.9. The simulation results are summarized in Fig. 13.5. The resulting dynamics is a complex one. Even more complex models can be generated with richer consumption and investment functions that incorporate spatial interactions between agents. Beyond the elementary CA model, business cycles could also be modelled in two-dimensional CA models, for example, mapped in a sphere or torus. These can be avenues for future research.

Finally, one area which we have not explored here is the computability aspects of CA models. CA models lend themselves to computable-theoretic analysis. The undecidability of Class III and Class IV behaviours for some of the transition rules can provide a greater understanding of the limits of formal models of business cycles.

## 4 Conclusions

An excursion into the study of business cycles using cellular automata is an exciting and challenging endeavour that can potentially yield rich insights. The spatio-temporal patterns that can be generated using CA are complex and rich. Using a CA approach, the microfoundations of business cycles can be studied via the CA transition rules. Since the number of possible transition rules is vast, economic theory could provide some guide to narrow this down. The CA approach to studying business cycles is also amenable to computability analysis. In this regard, some classes of business cycle behaviour are likely to be undecidable. Finally, another important area that has not been explored here within the framework of CA is the number-theoretic aspects of macrodynamics associated with the links between transition rules and the generation of number sequences.

## References

Bak, P., Chen, K., Scheinkman, J., & Woodford, M. (1993). Aggregate Fluctuations from Independent Sectoral Shocks: Self-Organized Criticality in a Model of Production and Inventory Dynamics. *Ricerche Economiche, 47*, 3–30.

Goodwin, R. M. (1947). Dynamical Coupling with Especial Reference to Markets Having Production Lags. *Econometrica, 15*(3), 181–204.

Goodwin, R. M. (1951). The Non-Linear Accelerator and the Persistence of Business Cycles. *Econometrica, 19*(1), 1–17.

Goodwin, R.M. (1952). A Non-Linear Theory of the Cycle. *The Review of Economics and Statistics, 32*(4), 316–320.

Goodwin, R.M. (1983). Essays in Linear Economic Structures. London: Macmillan.

Hamburger, L. (1930). Een Nieuwe Weg Voor Conjunctuur-Onderzoek, Een Nieuwe Richtlijn Voor Conjunctuur-Politiek. *De Economist, LXXIX*, 1–38.

Hamburger, L. (1931). Analogie des Fluctuations économiques et des Oscillations de relaxation. Institut de Statistique de l'Universite de Paris, Supplément aux Indices du Mouvement des Affaires, Janvier, 1–35.

Hamburger, L. (1934). Note on Economic Cycles and Relaxation Oscillations. *Econometrica, 2*(1), 112.

Kurka, P. (1997). Languages, equicontinuity and attractors in cellular automata. *Ergodic Theory and Dynamical Systems, 17*(2), 417–433.

Langton, C. (1992). Life at the Edge of Chaos. In C. Langton, C. Taylor, J. Farmer, & S. Rasmussen (Eds.), *Articial Life II*. Redwood City, CA: Addison Wesley.

Li, W. and Packard, N. (1990). The Structure of the Elementary Cellular Automata Rule Space. *Complex Systems, 4*(3), 281–297.

Rosser, J. (2016). Economic Dynamics. In G. Faccarello & H. D. Kurz (Eds.), *Handbook on the History of Economic Analysis Volume III*. Cheltenham: Edward Elgar.

Schelling, T. (1978). *Micromotives and Macrobehavior*. New York: W.W. Norton.

Schiff, J.L. (2008). Cellular Automata: A Discrete View of the World. Hoboken, NJ: Wiley.

Sutner, K. (2009). Classification of Cellular Automata. In A. Adamatzky (Ed.), *Cellular Automata: A Volume in the Encyclopedia of Complexity and System Science* (2nd ed.). New York: Springer.

Venkatachalam, R., & Vellupilai, K. (2012). Origins and Early Development of the Nonlinear Endogenous Mathematical Theory of the Business Cycle. *Economia Politica, 24*(1), 45–80.

Wolfram, S. (1984). Universality and Complexity in Cellular Automata. *Physica D, 10*, 1–35.

Zambelli, S. (2011a). Flexible Accelerator Economic Systems as Coupled Oscillators. *Journal of Economic Surveys, 25*(3), 608–633.

Zambelli, S. (2011b). Coupled Dynamics in a Phillips Machine Model of the Macroeconomy. *Economia Politica, 28*(4), 171–186.

Zambelli, S. (2015). Dynamical Coupling, the Non-Linear Accelerator and the Persistence of Business Cycles. *Cambridge Journal of Economics, 39*(6), 1607–1628.

# 14

# *Chipping off* to Compute Sraffa's Standard Ratio

Francesco Luna

## 1 Introduction

It was in the fall of 1991 that I curiously entered the classroom where Professor Velupillai was delivering his course on the History of Economic Thought for the graduate program in Economics at UCLA. Rumor had it that he was a fascinating speaker and storyteller. After the ritual introductions, Vela pointed at a big black-bearded fellow to his right, joyously announcing that there was another Italian in the room. That is how I met Professor Zambelli, nearly 30 years ago. The detail is not irrelevant: he belonged to a previous "period" of Vela's scientific (and esthetic) endeavors: the "non-linear dynamics" period. This is at least what I believed after getting to know the dynamic duo, Vela and Stefano. However, unlike Picasso's pictures of the "blue period", Professor Zambelli kept on changing, thematically expanding, and branching out from the initial colorful imprinting sketch. For example, his almost mythical programming skills put him in the perfect position to code various Turing machine

F. Luna (✉)
IMF, Institute for Capacity Development, Washington, DC, USA



K. Velupillai (ed.), *Keynesian, Sraffian, Computable and Dynamic Economics*,
https://doi.org/10.1007/978-3-030-58131-2_14

configurations and dance along a group of busy beavers, busier than any one of them. Yes, computability theory and the 90s ... that was the current "period" for Vela's journey and the one I belong to (if I am allowed such arrogance).

In a clearly appropriate nonlinear dynamics evolution of research, Zambelli's most recent interests have reverted almost to the starting point focusing once more on the work of Sraffa.[1] When I started thinking of this note, I was not aware of this revolution and my effort was designed only to entice Professor Zambelli into looking once more at that part of his research career.

However, given my current occupation and employer, I realized that reading Sraffa while working on various aspects of "inclusive growth" is absolutely appropriate. It is so because of the potentially revolutionary perspective that distinguishing value production from distribution can have in a world of wide and increasing inequality, especially in times of deep global macroeconomic crises: a perspective that has been lost by most of the profession.

In 1993, as "stagier" at the Observatoire français des conjonctures économiques (OFCE) in Paris, I had the chance to work for Jean-Paul Fitoussi on several notes elaborating the argument that a fair income distribution is—among other things—a precondition for sustained growth.[2] The examples employed in Fitoussi's writings were the "Asian tigers" of the early 90s and it seems that the argument shared those countries' crisis without ever recovering, at least on this side of the Atlantic. In fact, the more recent literature wave on "growth[3]" going under the name of "inclusive growth" is all based on "redistribution" and, in some more radical versions, on "pre-distribution". Distribution is, in the eyes of most economists (but not Zambelli's, I should add), the exclusive task and privilege of the market: the ultimate institution. And, although the profession recognizes its limitations—imperfection, incompleteness, externalities,

[1] I thank our common friend and adventurer, Charlotte Bruun, for mentioning this part of Stefano's latest production.

[2] See for example Fitoussi (1996).

[3] Even at the International Monetary Fund (IMF), see for example Ostry et al. (2008).

public goods, and so on—the possibility of encompassing distribution in the policy perimeter is not (yet, or any more) part of the discussion or analysis.

The rest of the chapter is organized in three sections. The first one presents an algorithm to compute the Standard ratio following the "instructions" suggested on page 22 of PCMC:

> It can be said that in any actual economic system there is embedded a miniature Standard system which can be brought to light **by chipping off unwanted parts**.

The exercise is performed in a "constructive" spirit[4] and wants to add a specific example of how the "vague" instructions contained in the text are actually sufficient to reach a solution to the system of equations. As Velupillai (2008) points out, such an approach is more in line with Sraffa's intention and mathematical methodology. The routine is applied, as an instance, to the interindustry matrix presented on page 21 of PCMC and the result compared with Sraffa's solution on page 22.[5] The following part proposes another version of the algorithm and compares the two on a large set of simulations over an increasing number of industries. The concluding section points at some interesting findings, suggests other possible questions to ask about the effect of process innovation on the Standard ratio, and draws some conclusions.

## 2 The "Chipping Off" Algorithm

The algorithm should be based on the instruction to "chip off unwanted parts". The goal is to reach a configuration where the ratio of each commodity's output to the total amount of that commodity used as input in

[4] I do not dare to call it "constructivist" as I am not versed on that sort of mathematics.

[5] The algorithm is explained and implemented first in "Excel" (that file can be obtained from the author), while the simulations are performed in python and the code is provided in the appendix. Again, the Jupyter notebook files can be obtained from the author.

the whole system is the same for each industry. Such a common ratio is the "Standard ratio" in Sraffa's terminology and the industry configuration that achieves it is called the Standard system. Finally, the Standard commodity is an "index" commodity composed of the proportion of each good in that aggregate. Sraffa's example is the following:

| | Iron in ton | Coal in ton | Wheat in qr | Labor share | Total production of |
|---|---|---|---|---|---|
| Iron | 90 | 120 | 60 | 3/16 | 180 |
| Coal | 50 | 125 | 150 | 5/16 | 450 |
| Wheat | 40 | 40 | 200 | 8/16 | 480 |
| Output/Input | 1.00 | 1.58 | 1.17 | | |

In the starting situation, it takes 90 tons of iron, 120 tons of coal, and 60 quarters of wheat plus 3/16th of the labor force to produce 180 tons of iron. Similarly, each row describes the physical inputs necessary for the production of one specific commodity (after iron, coal, and wheat). Labor is normalized so that the sum is equal to one. To continue with the example of iron, the ratio of production output to the total amount of iron used up as input in the system is 1; for example, 180 tons produced and 180 tons (90 + 50 + 40) used as input by all industries.

It is clear that, if it exists (and given the assumptions in PCMC it does exist), the Standard ratio ($R$) will have to lie somewhere between the maximum and the minimum ratios of the starting set: that is, $1 \leq (1 + R) \leq 1.58$: the search for "$R$" requires chipping off the activity of those industries that show "high" ratios. What's left is to code Sraffa's "macro" instructions to compute the Standard ratio and supporting the Standard system:

| | Iron in ton | Coal in ton | Wheat in qr | Labor share | Total production of |
|---|---|---|---|---|---|
| Iron | 90 | 120 | 60 | 3/16 | 180 |
| Coal | 30 | 75 | 90 | 3/16 | 270 |
| Wheat | 30 | 30 | 150 | 6/16 | 360 |
| Total inputs | 150 | 225 | 300 | 12/16 | |
| Output/Input | 1.20 | 1.20 | 1.20 | | |

The Standard ratio is hence 20 percent. As for the Standard commodity, it is a composite employing this proportion of each commodity: of 1 of iron, 1.5 of coal, and 2 of wheat according to the relation: 150/225/300 (which, of course, is the same as 180/270/360).[6] The Standard ratio is the measure of the surplus produced in the economy and the amount that will be distributed between profits and labor. For the modern economists who study and discuss models of "inclusive growth", the too often forgotten lesson of this approach is that distribution is separate from value production: there is no notion of marginal productivity as the foundation of wages and profits. Hence, distribution cannot be an after-thought, but rather, the result of socio-political negotiations and one of the fundamental objects of study of the economic discipline that, in several countries, is still called "Political Economy".

Here is the first proposed algorithm to compute *R*.[7] Consider every industry and calculate the current ratio (*CR*: output to total input) for each one of them. The activity level of all those industries for which the ratio is above the minimum one will be reduced according to this formula:

$$q_J = 1 - 0.5 * \left( !R_J - \min\left( !R \right) \right) / \, !R_J$$

and clearly, the activity of the industry that expresses the minimum current ratio will not be modified. For example, "iron" $CR = 1$ is the smallest and its activity will not be reduced. As for "coal", its level of production will be multiplied by $q_c$ = 1 - 0.5*(1.58 - 1)/1.58 = 0.816667 and the wheat industry by $q_w = 0.927083$. This implies that after the first step, the input-output matrix looks like this:

| | Iron in ton | Coal in ton | Wheat in qr | Labor share[8] | Total production of |
|---|---|---|---|---|---|
| Iron | 90 | 120 | 60 | 3/16 | 180 |
| Coal | 40.83 | 102.08 | 122.50 | 0.26 | 367.50 |
| Wheat | 37.08 | 37.08 | 185.42 | 0.46 | 445.00 |
| Output/Input | 1.07 | 1.42 | 1.21 | | |

[6] As a "rule", on page 23, Sraffa suggests "to take as unit of the Standard commodity the quantity of it that would form the net product of a Standard system employing the whole annual labour of the actual system". So, for this specific example, the Standard commodity would be composed of 40 tons of iron, 60 tons of coal, and 80 quarters of wheat.

[7] It should be noted that Velupillai (2008) suggests a set of broad steps to reach the result. My routines exemplify step 2 and the stopping rule. By constructions, my simulations make sure that each industry produces more than the simple replacement amount, hence step one is not called for.

[8] As the activity level is reduced in the chipping off process, the notional labor employed falls below 1. Once the Standard ratio is obtained, according to Sraffa's framework, to calculate the total net product, all industries will be boosted in the same proportion so as to bring back labor to 100 percent without changing the ratios between produced commodities.

As the *CR*s converge to the Standard ratio the smallest $q_J$ will be closer and closer to 1. In the simulations performed, the stopping rule is min($q$) ≥ 0.99999.

In this specific case, the algorithm stops after 20 steps to this configuration:

| | Iron in ton | Coal in ton | Wheat in qr | Labor share | Total production of |
|---|---|---|---|---|---|
| Iron | 89.98 | 119.98 | 59.99 | 0.19 | 179.97 |
| Coal | 29.99 | 74.99 | 89.98 | 0.19 | 269.95 |
| Wheat | 30.00 | 30.00 | 149.98 | 0.37 | 359.96 |
| Output/Input | 1.20 | 1.20 | 1.20 | | |

which is, apart from some rounding discrepancy,[9] the solution found on page 23 of PCMC as given above.

## 3 The Challenger and the Match

As noticed, the Standard ratio must lie between the initial maximum and minimum current ratios (*CR*). Then, an alternative version of the algorithm could take as "moving target" for the search, the average of the ratios rather than the minimum. In this case, each industry's activity level is updated according to:

$$q_J = 1 - 0.5 * \left(\mathrm{CR}_J - \text{average } \left(\mathrm{CR}\right)\right) / \mathrm{CR}_J$$

which implies that the adjustment is some sort of generalized "chipping off:" the level of activity of those industries whose *CR* is below average will be increased (a "negative chipping off"). As there is only one Standard ratio for each interindustry matrix, the solution will be the same and attention can be focused on the efficiency of the two versions of the algorithm (Fig. 14.1).

Before proceeding, the next graphs exemplify the behavior of the two algorithms in the context of an artificial economy composed of ten industries (Fig. 14.2).

[9] Clearly the level of precision can be improved at will by increasing the initial stopping rule value.

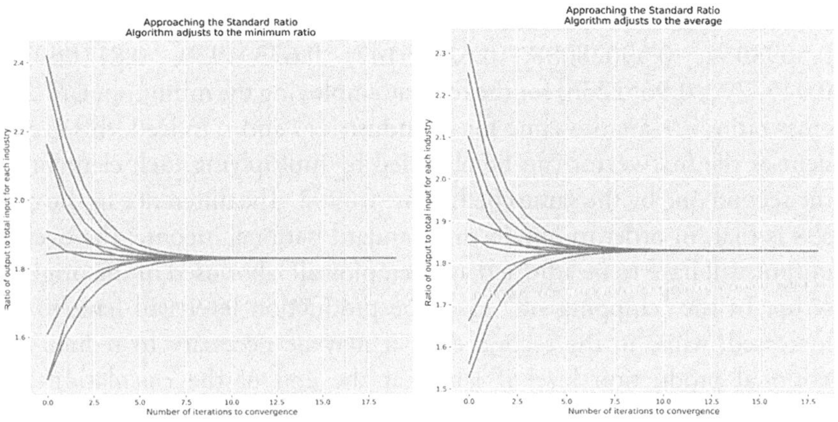


**Fig. 14.1** Approaching the Standard Ratio

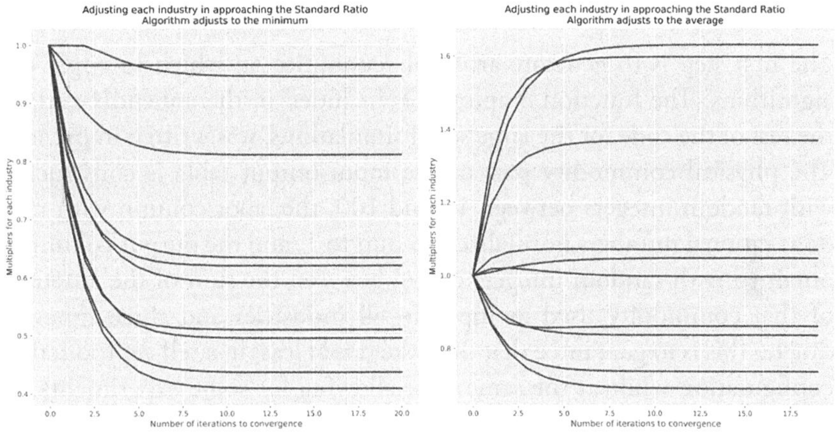


**Fig. 14.2** The adjustment dynamics of the two algorithms

As mentioned, while the *CR*s will tend to the same Standard ratio, the industries' multipliers adjust along different paths. However, it is clear that the final values will determine the same proportions among commodities hence the same Standard commodity. In the example depicted above, the final series of multipliers are respectively: [0.69105146, 0.73794837, 0.83726986, 0.86170621, 0.99773858, 1.04804979, 1.07154601, 1.37090584, 1.59862146, 1.63147955] for the routine using the average *CR* and [0.40883811, 0.4365872, 0.49534836, 0.5098054, 0.59028088, 0.62005147, 0.63394928, 0.81105933, 0.9457792, 0.9652236] for the routine employing the minimum *CR*. The cross ratios $r_i/r_j$ are the same for all industries $i$ and $j$. Indeed, this is evident as the first vector can be obtained by multiplying each element of the second one by the same coefficient: 1.6902. The difference in the two sets is that, in order to obtain the Standard national income, the overall output will have to be adjusted as to employ all labor used in the original setup. In the "chipping off" case, the production level will have to be increased, while in the second case, it may be necessary to reduce the notional production level if labor, at the end of the calculations, is greater than 1.

## 3.1 The Setup

The first step is to generate artificial economies on which to apply the algorithms. The function employed is included in the appendix and, as the rest of the code for the large set of simulations, was written in python. The physical commodity part of the input-output table is constructed with random integers between 10 and 100, the labor column with random rational numbers normalized to sum to 1, and the output column is obtained with random integers drawn between the sum of the amounts of that commodity used as input in all industries and three times as much. This is to guarantee that the system is at least in a self-reproduction configuration while at the same time allowing for some experiments on the effect of "productivity" on the Standard ratio.[10]

For each economy size ranging from 3 to 20 industries, I ran both algorithms on the same set of 10,000 input-output matrices. For each simulation, I recorded the Standard ratio obtained and the number of iterations to satisfy the stopping criterion. For the full 10,000 set of simulations performed on each matrix size, I also recorded the time taken to completion. The Standard ratio by each algorithm is the same, the average and median for each economy size is depicted in the next figure (Fig. 14.3):

[10] We experimented with factors ranging from 2 to 5: the results will be briefly mentioned below.

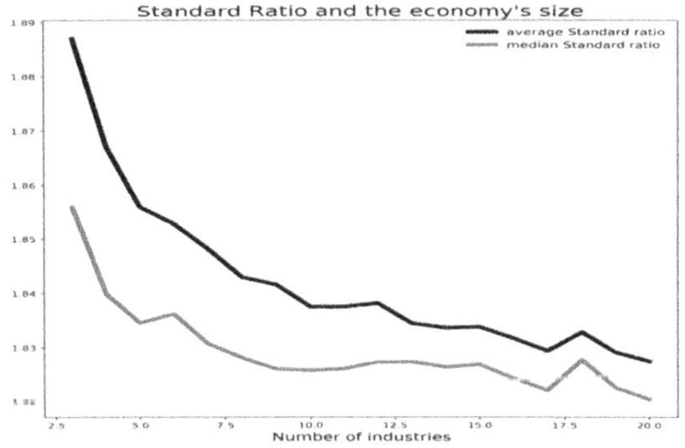


**Fig. 14.3** Standard ratio and the economy's size

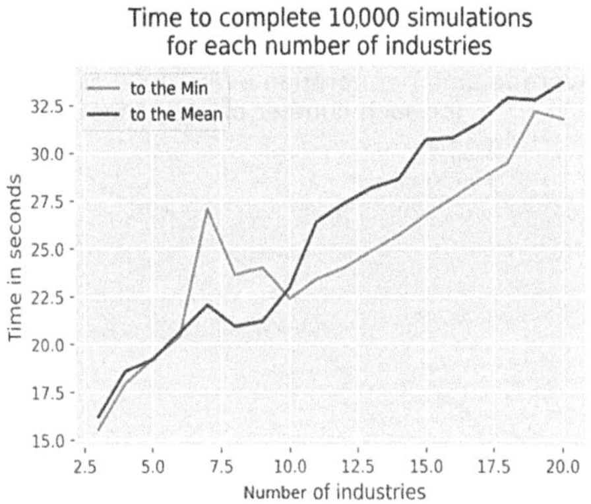


**Fig. 14.4** Time to complete 10,000 simulations for each number of industries

Although the trend is very "gentle", it appears that the Standard ratio tends to diminish with the size of the economy (the number of industries). I will take up this observation in the next section.

Going back to the comparison of the two routines, the first dimension I will consider is the time to complete the simulations (Fig. 14.4).

It appears that, as the dimension of the input-output matrix increases, the original algorithm pointing at the min shows some consistent advantage. Is it perhaps because the number of iterations to convergence is on average smaller? (Fig. 14.5)

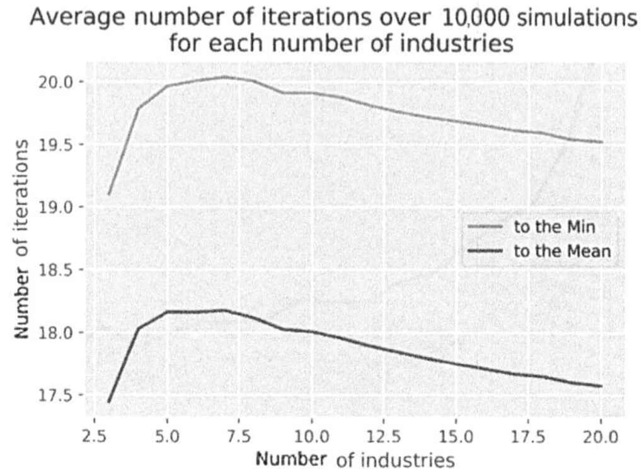


**Fig. 14.5** Average number of iterations over 10,000 simulations for each number of industries

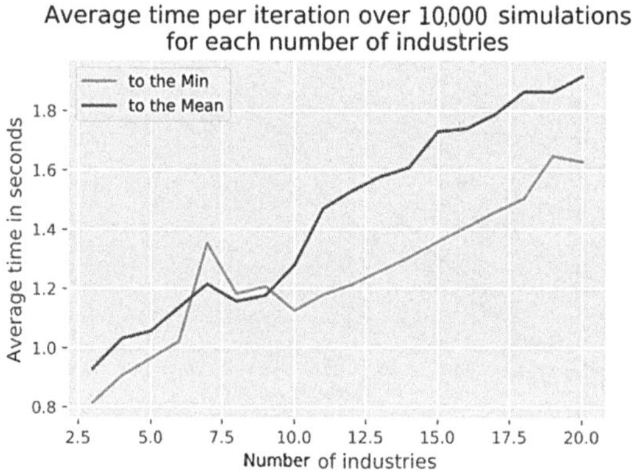


**Fig. 14.6** Average time per iteration over 10,000 simulations for each number of industries

Surprisingly, on average, the algorithm targeting the mean converges with two fewer iterations than the alternative. This seems to indicate that the time per iteration must be quite smaller in the case of the "chip off" routine. Indeed, this is the case as shown in the following graph. The result should not be very surprising as the calculation of the average is more CPU intensive than the identification of the minimum element in a rather short list (Fig. 14.6).

# 4 Surprising Findings

There are two interesting results that I would like to point at: the most intriguing one, from an economic perspective, is the fact that, for a given (average) productivity, the Standard ratio is inversely correlated to the number of industries in the economy. Although marginal, Fig. 14.3 shows that on average the Standard ratio for an economy with 20 industries is about 5 percentage points lower than for an economy with 3 industries. Pursuing further this finding, it turns out that also the standard deviation diminishes with size and the whole distribution becomes less spread: the sample variance diminishes as the fan diagram (Fig. 14.7) clearly shows. I am tempted to infer that the Standard ratio may converge "in the limit" to a particular middle value that is a function only of the average productivity.

The other interesting finding (from Fig. 14.5) is that the largest number of iterations is found for an economy composed of five or six industries: the Standard ratio is identified in fewer steps for larger sets of industries. This could be simply the result (from the point of view of the algorithm) of having more levers to act upon, with a given overall space to search. Clearly, as noted, each iteration takes longer, so the overall time employed increases steadily as shown in Fig. 14.4.

## 4.1 An Economic Policy Question

The question that arises from the first surprising result is policy related. Which innovation will impact more effectively the Standard ratio? A boost in productivity in the less productive sectors of the economy or, vice versa, in the already technologically more advanced industries? Even forgetting for a moment the distribution issues attached to it, an increase in the Standard ratio is—if you allow me the expression—welfare enhancing for the economy as a whole. Hence, it becomes a very important political decision where to invest public resources in R&D. Especially considering the entrepreneurial role played by the state as documented by Mazzucato (2013).

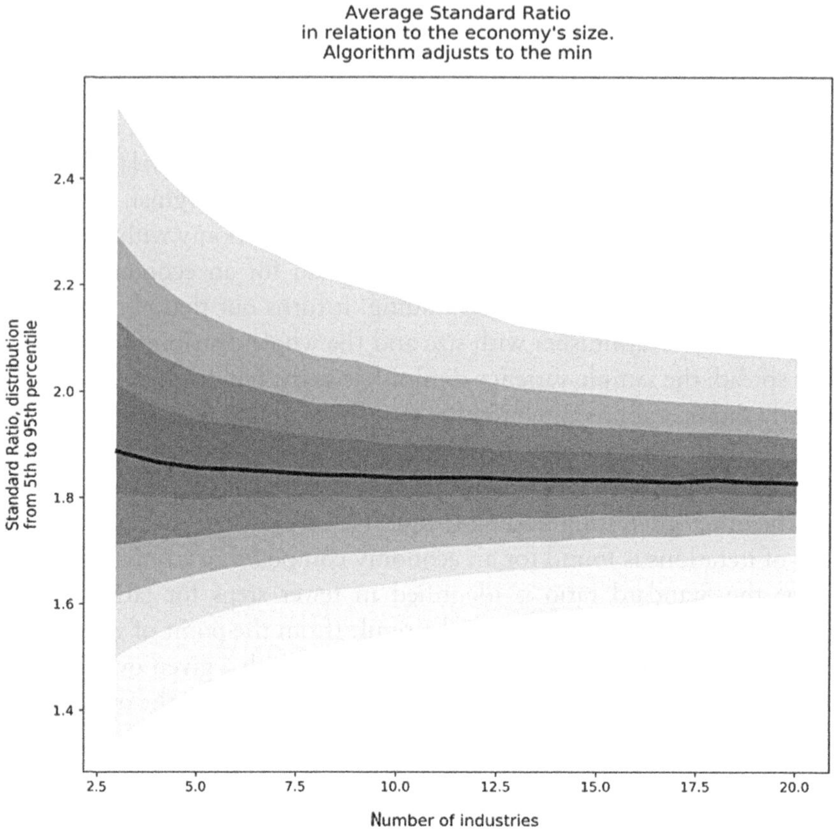


**Fig. 14.7** Average Standard ratio in relation to the economy's size. Algorithm adjusts to the min

My prior was quite strong. As the Standard ratio is somewhere "in the middle" of the productivity range spanned by the industries, an innovation that expands that range should lead to an increase in the Standard ratio as well. Following this reasoning, a positive productivity shock on the more productive sector, by pushing outward the upper bound of the range, should indeed be more effective; after all, on the lower bound, there could be another industry only marginally more productive than the lowest, hence the overall range may not be significantly affected, on average.

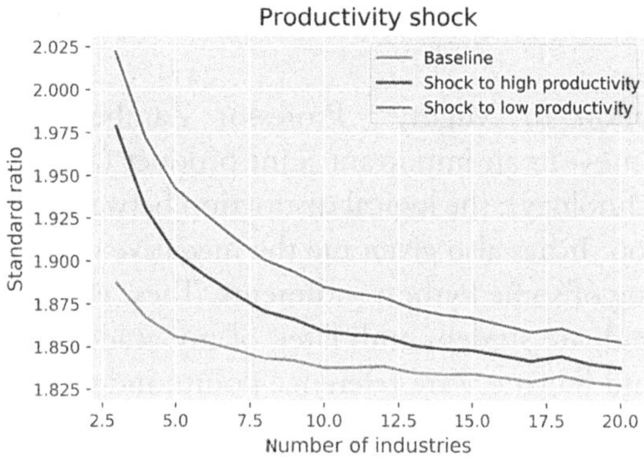


**Fig. 14.8** Productivity shock

The result of the simulations clearly contradicts the prior, as shown in Fig. 14.8. Consistently, an increase of 20 percent in the productivity of the least productive industry results in a significantly higher increase in the average Standard ratio for each economy's dimension considered (from 3 to 20 industries). The sample elasticity of the Standard ratio to a change in productivity is, on average, about 0.14 for a productivity shock to the least productive and half as much (0.072) for an equivalent shock affecting the most productive industry.

It may seem somewhat difficult to think that innovation could boost the productivity of very "mature" industries, like the textiles, let's say, but as Romer (1993) with the famous example of the shirt factory shows, there could be in fact much unexplored territory at least in process innovation. Some experts may also rightly note that especially an innovation in these traditional industries will most likely translate only in increased rents for the entrepreneur because of institutional hysteresis. Indeed, this could happen even in the "world" described by Sraffa since, as shown by Zambelli (2018) and contrary to Sraffa's initial persuasion, the economy's Standard ratio is compatible with different net-product sharing arrangements in each industry.

# 5 Conclusions

This contribution to Mighty[11] Professor Zambelli's Festschrift has resulted—for me—in an important joint product (and the return of an intellectual technology): the logical distinction between value production and distribution. It has also given me the incentive to go back to coding and the learning of some Python rudiments. These elements were part of my life as a graduate student and, later, of my academic career. In both periods Vela and Stefano were reference points and compass for creative research endeavors and I am grateful for the chance to relive that experience for a while.

For over two decades now, my work has focused on macroeconomic policy: design and, more recently, capacity development (the new buzzword for training and more). Naturally, what is defined as "macro-relevant" has changed over time. It now includes "gender", "climate", and soon "pandemics" at the intersection of globalization and the environment. My computability "imprinting" has been a source of pride and frustration all along. Frustration because, over and again, I have seen policy designs justified on the basis of some theoretically uncomputable model. But also pride for the diverse perspective I can offer when I teach young country officials and talk about policy measures as algorithms, as routines to "construct" solutions, or when I describe institutions as inherent procedures to obtain some "satisfactory" result.

According to Pasinetti (2013), PCMC is the third and final part of what Sraffa had planned to be a magnum opus: after the analysis of the Classics to give the appropriate history of thought context and the consequent criticism of the marginalist approach, he had planned his "constructive[12]" contribution. At some point, probably while editing Ricardo's

[11] This is how Vela would refer to Professor Zambelli during his Trento years.

[12] Pasinetti clearly does not use the term constructive (twice on page, 165) in its mathematical connotation—in the same place he mentions the Perron-Frobenius theorems—but the coincidence is striking.

work, Sraffa realized the initial "grand programme" was too large and focused on the third part. He produced PCMC. Sraffa's project is still relevant and the implications of his work still to be fully understood and disseminated. Hence, I am glad Stefano Zambelli is investing on this intellectual adventure and hope this minimal[13] contribution of mine will trigger more research on his part.

I will conclude with a quote extracted from Sraffa's notes which synthesizes (only as Sraffa knew how to do) the current state of affairs in our discipline: "Political Economy was a science of things. Economics is a science of illusions"[14]

**Post Scriptum**

There is at least one thing that Professor Zambelli and I have in common: the love for rock. True, in his case it is mainly for "rocking horses[15]" and for me it is about musical performance.

# Appendix

This function generates the input-output matrix including labor and output produced. Its only argument is the number of industries in the economy.

```
   def mat(ind): #ind is the number of industries
       E = np.random.randint(10,100, size=(ind,ind)) #generates
the initial matrix
       input = np.sum(E, axis = 0) #calculates the total of
each input used by the system
```

[13] I was tempted to say "marginal".

[14] As reported in Sinha (2016), p. 70. It refers to Sraffa's collections of unpublished notes housed in the Wren Library, Trinity College at the University of Cambridge. That specific notes is archived as D3/12/10: 61 (1–3) according to the original methodology employed by the archivist, Jonathan Smith.

[15] Zambelli (2007).

```
l = np.random.random(ind) #generates the labor vector
employed by industry
s = np.sum(l)
l = l/s #to normalize the random labor inputs so the sum
is equal to one, ie. all labor is employed
v = l.reshape(ind,1)
out = np.arange(ind) #variable to hold the total output
for each industry
for i in range(ind):
out[i] = np.random.randint(input[i], 3*input[i]) #
generates output to make sure that it is larger than the
sum of input used up in the system
production = out.reshape(ind,1) #simply reshapes the
vector as a column
InOut = np.hstack((E, v, production)) # assembling the
three pieces
return InOut
```

This function implements the "chipping off" idea. The moving target is the minimum current ratio: all industries above the minimum ratio will chop off part of the difference.

```
def passo(I_O):
    ind = I_O[:,0].size #"array_name".size returns the
    integer number of elements in array_name
    tot_in = np.sum(I_O, axis = 0) # sum all elements by
    column: these are the total input of each commodity
    cic = tot_in[:ind] # select only the material input
    (no labor)
    ratio = I_O[:, ind+1]/cic # calculates the Current
    ratio:  total output divided by total input of that
    commodity used in the system
    erre = np.ones(ind)
    erre -= .5*((ratio - np.min(ratio))/ratio) # calculates
    the new level of activity of each industry
    for b in range(ind):
    I_O[b]*=erre[b]
    return(erre, I_O)
```

This function implements the algorithm targeting the mean of the *CR* in order to adjust each industry's activity level, looking for the Standard ratio. The activity level of those industries whose *CR* is above the mean will be reduced and vice versa if it is below.

```
def passom(I_O):
    "'By construction, the number of rows of this matrix
    identifies the number of industries in the economy"'
    ind = I_O[:,0].size #"array_name".size returns the
    integer number of elements in array_name
    tot_in = np.sum(I_O, axis = 0) #sum all elements by
    column: these are the total input of each commodity
    cic = tot_in[:ind] # select only the material input
    (no labor)
    ratio = I_O[:, ind+1]/cic # calculates the current
    ratio: output of industry i divided by total input of i
    used by the system
    erre = np.ones(ind)
    erre -= .5*((ratio - np.average(ratio))/ratio) #
    determines how much should be "chopped off" or augmented
    for b in range(ind):
    I_O[b]*=erre[b]
    return(erre, I_O)
```

This is the main body of the program that runs 10,000 simulations for each economy size (from 3 industries up to 20).

```
np.random.seed(1963)# random seed to allow replicability of
the simulations
Number_of_simulations = 10000
Number_of_Industries = 3 #starting number
Max_Num_of_Industries = 20 # max dimension we simulate
heading = np.arange(Number_of_Industries-1, Max_Num_of_
Industries+1)
tempi = np.array([0]) #will record the time taken to find the
solutions to the simulations for each economy size
archive = np.arange(Number_of_simulations).
reshape(Number_of_simulations,1)
Media_StdRatio = np.arange(Number_of_simulations).
```

```
reshape(Number_of_simulations,1)
   while Number_of_Industries <= Max_Num_of_Industries:
       start = time.time()
       record = np.empty((Number_of_simulations,1))
       StdRatio = np.empty((Number_of_simulations,1))
       for sup_ind in range(Number_of_simulations):
           counter = 0
           #adjustor = .5 #indicates the speed of adjustment of
the gradient to the Standard Ratio
           ro = np.zeros(Number_of_Industries)
           InOut = mat(Number_of_Industries) #creation of the
initial input-output matrix
           while counter <= 99 and np.min(ro) <= .99999: #this
is where the "gradient" search takes place
               ro, InOut = passom(InOut)# this is for the
version targeting the mean. Simply substituting "passo" will
implement the simple "chopping off" variant
               counter += 1
           record[[sup_ind]] = counter #record the number of
iteration necessary to reach the solution in each case
           StdRatio[[sup_ind]] = InOut[0,Number_of_
Industries+1]/np.sum(InOut[:,0])
       crono = time.time() - start
       Number_of_Industries +=1
       archive = np.hstack((archive, record)) #stack the
records for each size of the economy: Number_of_Industries
       Media_StdRatio = np.hstack((Media_StdRatio, StdRatio))
       tempi = np.hstack((tempi, crono))
   heading[[0,0]] = Number_of_simulations
   tempi[[0,0]] = Number_of_simulations
   data1 = np.array(np.hstack((np.vstack((tempi, archive)),
np.vstack((heading, Media_StdRatio)))))
   np.savetxt('risultati-prod-m3-d3_20.dat', data1)
```

## References


Fitoussi, J.-P. (1996). Anatomie de la croissance molle. *Revue de l'OFCE, 59*(1), 213–244.

Mazzucato, M. (2013). *The Entrepreneurial State: Debunking Public vs. Private Sector Myths*. London: Anthem Press.

Ostry, D. J., Berg, A., & Zettelmeyer, J. (2008). *What Makes Growth Sustained?* IMF Working Paper Series, WP/08/59.

Pasinetti, L. (2013). Piero Sraffa and the Future of Economics: A Personal Evaluation. In E. S. Levrero, A. Palumbo, & A. Stirati (Eds.), *Sraffa and the Reconstruction of Economic Theory* (Vol. 3). Palgrave Macmillan.

Romer, P. M. (1993). *Two Strategies for Economic Development: Using Ideas and Producing Ideas*. Proceedings of the World Bank Annual Conference on Development Economics 1992, Supplement to the World Bank Economic Review, March, 63–91.

Sinha, A. (2016). *A revolution in Economic Theory. The Economics of Piero Sraffa*. Palgrave Macmillan.

Velupillai, K. (2008). Sraffa's Mathematical Economics: A *Constructive* Interpretation. *Journal of Economic Methodology, 15*(4), 325–342.

Zambelli, S. (2007). A Rocking Horse That Never Rocked: Frisch's 'Propagation Problems and Impulse Problems. *History of Political Economy, 39*(1), 145–166.

Zambelli, S. (2018). Production of Commodities by Means of Commodities and Non-uniform Rates of Profits. *Metroeconomica, 69*(4), 791–819.

# 15

# Observations on Computability, Uncertainty, and Technology

J. Barkley Rosser Jr

## 1 Introduction

Stefano Zambelli is one of very few economists to have studied in depth issues relating computability of economic models (Zambelli 2010, 2012) to technical change (Zambelli 2004, 2005) and more indirectly to the nature of Sraffian economic models (Zambelli 2018). A centerpiece of this panorama was concern with that most Keynesian of concepts, uncertainty. Uncertainty is most certainly uncomputable. Nevertheless economic agents act, and must do so on the basis of guesses and approximations, which may be computed, even as certainty always remains out of reach. This becomes even more salient when decisions are made to change technology. Outcomes cannot be known in advance. And the implications of changing technology in one sector for other sectors also can rarely be seen clearly in advance. Economies effectively stumble forward as their agents change how they operate without fully understanding what they are doing or where it will lead.

J. Barkley Rosser Jr (✉)
James Madison University, Harrisonburg, VA, USA
e-mail: rosserjb@jmu.edu



K. Velupillai (ed.), *Keynesian, Sraffian, Computable and Dynamic Economics*,
https://doi.org/10.1007/978-3-030-58131-2_15

## 2 Computational Complexity and Uncertainty

Underpinning concerns about computability of economic models as studied by Zambelli (2010) is the question of incompleteness as identified by Gödel (1931) and then applied by Church (1936) and Turing (1936). Self-referencing in Gödel's Incompleteness Theorem plays a central role in generating unresolvable contradictions within systems stabling incompleteness. The classic form of this is the Cretan Liars Paradox, but there are others. Such paradoxes when appearing in a computer program introduce infinite do-loops that run back and forth without halting. This halting problem becomes the basis for uncomputability, with this holding for real numbers (Blum et al. 1998) as well as for the rational numbers that are actually used in computer models of the sort that concern Zambelli, although Zambelli (2011) would consider real computation as it occurs in analogue computers such as the Phillips Machine.

It is generally accepted that the case where halting problems occur and programs cannot end represents the most extreme case of computational complexity. But computationally complex systems include many more cases, with a variety of competing ways to measure the degrees of such complexity, with many of these having been explicated by Velupillai (2000, 2005, 2009). Also it is well understood and widely accepted that computational complexity can underlie uncertainty.

A deep thread in this matter involves relations between probability and information content. An important foundational concept has been that of *Shannon information*, which in turn derives from Shannon entropy (1948). If $p(x)$ is the probability density function of a set of $K$ states denoted by values of $x$, then the Shannon information content is given by

$$SI(x) = \ln(1/p(x)). \tag{15.1}$$

This is regularly understood to be a useful representation of the number of bits in an algorithm to compute the relevant associated code. It became the foundation for the highly influential formulation by Kolmogorov (1965) of *Kolmogorov complexity* (sometimes known as Kolmogorov entropy) measuring the minimum number of bits in an algorithm that does not prefix any other algorithm $a(x)$ that a universal Turing machine would require to compute a binary string of information, $x$, given by

$$K(x) - \min la(x)l, \tag{15.2}$$

with $l$ denoting the length of the algorithm in bits.

This formulation has deep links to ones also by Solomonoff (1964) as well as by Chaitin (1966, 1987). Solomonoff was also trying to link information with probability and drew especially on Keynes's (1921) view of these matters. Chaitin would emphasize the importance of the minimum length description, tying it to his number Ω, the probability that a program will halt, which is the foundation of his broader work on *algorithmic complexity* (Chaitin 1987; Rosser 2020). This links back to the question of incompleteness, and Velupillai (2009, p. 72) has argued that Chaitin's emphasis on incompleteness inappropriately narrows the conceptualization of computational complexity. In any case, these are all themselves uncomputable.

A computable measure is that of stochastic complexity formulated by Rissanen (2005). This draws on these earlier measures and defines a likelihood function for a given structure of parametric density functions on k parameters and indexed data strings, $x$. From this a logarithmic measure can be constructed known as *stochastic complexity*, which can be interpreted as representing the shortest code length for the indexed data, $x$, that can be obtained with the given structure of parametric density functions or model class. While this measure has the virtue of being computable, it has probably been used less frequently than some of these other measures.

Whichever of these measures of degrees of computational complexity one favors, it is widely viewed that four distinct levels of such complexity exist, even as there remain important unsolved problems regarding the nature of these levels (Wolfram 1984; Mirowski 2007). At the lowest level are linear systems, often described as not being computationally complex. They are generally solvable with algorithms of relatively short length. Qualitatively more complex are polynomial systems, or *P*. While usually involving substantially longer algorithms than linear ones, these are generally able to be solved by most current computers in a reasonable time. Generally accepted as the next qualitative level up are the non-polynomial systems, or *NP*. It remains unproven whether or not these are really different levels, with this problem initially identified independently in the 1950s by Gödel and Nash, although their work on this was highly classified for many decades. In any case, *NP* systems are solvable in finite time, but take far longer than *P* ones, with the Busy Beaver problem studied by Rado (1962) an example of much interest to Zambelli (2004, 2012). At the highest level of computational complexity are those that cannot be solved, that suffer from the halting problem, with some holding that only these are truly computationally complex.

The most difficult unresolved problem in this is indeed the matter of whether or not $P = NP$, something the vast majority of those who consider the matter accept, but the proof of which has yet to be found. Curiously in Nash's long-classified initial discussion of this matter he foresaw the promise and the problem. He considered the distinction to have relevance for problems of encryption and decryption and declared that he believed that indeed the two categories are distinct. But he noted that he was unable to prove that they were, and that this seemed to be a hard problem. Indeed it is hard enough that it remains unsolved, and its Chaitin probability, Ω, continues to change.

Teasing us in regard to this problem are studies of the apparent boundaries between these probably distinct conditions. A curious example is the theorem of Maymin (2011) that shows that under certain conditions about information, markets are efficient if and only if $P = NP$, which, as already noted, very few believe. Following on this, da Costa and Doria (2016) have used the O'Donnell algorithm (O'Donnell 1979) to study the functioning of markets in this likely boundary zone. This algorithm is exponential and thus not *P*, but one that is slowly growing and thus "almost *P*." This holds for if $P < NP$ is provable for any strictly stronger than Primitive Recursive Arithmetic (PRA) while PRA itself cannot prove it. This is known as the *counterexample function to the P = NP problem.* The sorts of economics problems that appear to involve *NP* solvability include the traveling salesman problem, well-known to be highly computationally complex. In any case, da Costa and Doria show that when the

O'Donnell algorithm behaves as an "almost *P*" system, this implies an outcome of "almost efficient markets." Arguably we are dealing here with an outcome that walks on the edge of the unknown, if not the unknowable.

This links to the problem of uncertainty in various ways. One figure who deeply studied computational complexity in various of its forms and considered how this implies limits on the knowledge of humans and how they deal with this lack of certainty induced directly by such complexity was Herbert Simon (1955, 1957). While Simon emphasized more conventional issues such as people simply lacking information relevant to decisions they must make, he was also fully aware of the deeper sorts of problems we have been discussing here arising from the work of Church, Turing, and others. Simon saw these deep problems of uncomputability by humans themselves, not just computers, as the most fundamental reason why at best people must operate with bounded rationality. Ironically it was his study of these problems with humans that led him to study artificial intelligence in computers themselves (Simon 1969). In any case, in a world of bounded rationality, one is dealing with an unavoidable degree of uncertainty. A more extended discussion of these issues is in Velupillai (2019).

Of course one of the deepest students of the nature of uncertainty in the economy was Keynes (1921, 1936). A fundamental source of uncertainty for Keynes came from the nature of the interactions between people regarding their expectations and more particularly how their expectations depend on their expectations about what the expectations of others are. His classic statement of the problem came with his discussion of the beauty contest problem in Chapter 12 of *The General Theory* (Keynes 1936). It has long been posed as fundamental to understanding financial markets, which was clearly Keynes's main thrust when he wrote about it, but its application and implications go well beyond that context. To the extent one's behavior depends on one's expectation of what the expectations of others are, and their expectations depend on what one's own expectations are, a situation of potentially self-referencing infinite regress is opened up that has the potential for being uncomputable and the basis for Keynes's fundamental uncertainty (Rosser 2004).

About the same time, Oskar Morgenstern (1935) considered a similar problem in the form of the Holmes–Moriarty problem, which also has a potentially uncomputable infinite regress problem of reflexivity. In "The Final Problem" Moriarty is trying to catch Holmes as he travels from Victoria Station through Canterbury to Dover, hoping to catch him at one of those stations. Each contemplates the expectation of the other regarding where each will try to get off, and there is no end to levels of this set of expectations of expectations. Like Keynes's beauty contest, it is an $n$-level game, but there is no end to how high $n$ can go, which is completely arbitrary. It was Morgenstern's concern about this problem that pushed him to collaborate with von Neumann in working on game theory (von Neumann and Morgenstern 1944), with in effect a potential solution being found by means of mixed strategies: each agent simply tosses a coin.

However, even as tossing a coin may be a Nash equilibrium solution, there still arises the problem from a computability perspective of how the agents come to this solution. It turns out that if one poses the problem as contemplating best reply functions, a hyper-rational Turing machine will find the problem to be uncomputable with the infinite regress problem reappearing to pose a classic self-referencing halting problem (Koppl and Rosser 2002). Koppl and Rosser posed that the way out of this was to fall back on what Keynes proposed as the way out of the beauty contest problem as well, to rely on "animal spirits" to make the decision.

Binmore (1987) considered the self-referencing problem and proposed that it be resolved using a form of Bayesian updating. This can be viewed as operating within a greater degree of ignorance, which has a similarity to the bounded rationality of Simon. But this form of updating will only operate properly under certain conditions as shown by Diaconis and Freedman (1986), notably that the basis is continuous and the problem is posed in a finite dimensional space. Otherwise there may be convergence to a cycle rather than a point, bouncing back and forth between two incorrect probabilities, again posing the problem of probability and information. An example might be a coin tossing that jumps back and forth between 1/3 and 2/3 without ever converging on 1/2, with Nyarko (1991) having studied such problems. Again, one may have to fall back on either an arbitrary heuristic a la Simon or more purely intuition a la the animal spirits of Keynes in order to act in the face of an uncomputably based uncertainty.

# 3 Technology and Computability

Zambelli (2004, 2018) has shown concern about relations between technology and computability by analyzing characterizations of technology, based on Sraffa (1960). He has pushed the model beyond its usual limits by considering such variations as allowing multiple profit rates, although this arguably violates steady state equilibrium conditions usually assumed for such systems. The Sraffian framework allows for a perspective on technology and the choice of techniques that more clearly highlights deeper issues than the more standard neoclassical framework allows. Much of this arises from the avoidance of using aggregate capital concepts with a more precise characterization of technology. It must be recognized here that at least some neoclassical economists have accepted this at least in principle (Samuelson 1966), but that recognition has generally been made by theorists, while empirical neoclassical modelers have tended to fall back on using Solow-style aggregate production functions with aggregate capital and simply ignoring these complications.

Of course, much of the attention the Sraffian framework has received has been due to its usefulness for examining various capital theoretic paradoxes such as reswitching within it. These have been and are important questions, but the Sraffian framework also allows one to see into other aspects of capital theory that reveal issues of technical choice. Indeed, there are potentially problems related to computability that can be depicted within the framework not so easily depicted in more conventional models and frameworks.

One matter the Sraffian framework allows to be revealed is that of the nature of continuity and discontinuity when looking at technique choice and the relations between different techniques along the wage-profit frontier of optimal techniques. In particular, that techniques may appear near each other on the wage-profit frontier does not mean they are near each other in any real sense, with ratios of factor inputs possibly being quite different. In short, while the wage-profit frontier may be continuous, indeed smooth, this does not mean that there is continuity across the techniques as one moves along the frontier. Realization of this has been known for a long time (Pasinetti 1969; Garegnani 1970; Harris 1973). Thus, in particular from Pasinetti (1969) we have the following:

> For vicinity of any two technique on the scale of variation of the rate of profit does not imply closeness of the total values of their capital goods. It is therefore not true that, as the number of techniques becomes larger and larger, the differences in the values of capital goods per man and outputs per man of any two neighboring techniques necessarily becomes smaller and smaller. These differences might well remain quite large, no matter how infinitesimally near to each other two techniques are on the range of variation of the rate of profit. In other words, continuity in the variation of techniques as the rate of profit changes, does not imply continuity in the variation of the values of capital goods per man and of net outputs per man. This in fact seems to be one of the most important results emerging from the reswitching of techniques discussion. It seems to reveal capital theory as a field unsuitable to the application of calculus and infinitesimal analysis, and thus of marginal analysis.

Let us consider this from a generalized Sraffa–von Neumann approach that allows to describe more precisely techniques and their relations to the optimizing wage-profit frontier. We shall assume these all exhibit constant returns to scale. Let $A$ be a non-negative $n$ by $m$ matrix of inputs and $B$ a non-negative $n$ by $m$ matrix of outputs with $n$ commodities and $m$ activities, $C$ be an $n$ by 1 vector of final consumption, $x$ is a positive $n$ by 1 vector of activity levels, y and z are $n$ by 1 vectors, $p$ is a 1 by $n$ positive price vector, $\delta$ is a 1 by $n$ vector of depreciation rates, $r$ is the rate of profit, $w$ is the wage rate, $A_0$ is a 1 by $n$ vector of labor inputs, and $L(t) = L(0)e^{gt}$ is the labor force at time $t$ with g its growth rate, The set of possible techniques $T = (\alpha, \beta, \ldots)$ will include only viable techniques fulfilling $y(\alpha) = A(\alpha)x(\alpha) = B(\alpha)x(\alpha) - c(\alpha)$ for at least one $x(\alpha)$.

In equilibrium for technique $\alpha$, the quantity system is given by

$$(1+g)A(\alpha)x(\alpha) \leq B(\alpha)x(\alpha) - C(\alpha), \tag{15.3}$$

and the dual price system is given by

$$wA_0 + (1+g)pA(\alpha) > pB(\alpha). \tag{15.4}$$

The wage-profit curve is given by

$$W = [A_0(\alpha)]^{-1} p(\mathrm{r})[B(\alpha) - (1+r)A(\alpha)]. \tag{15.5}$$

Endpoints are given by respectively setting $r$ and $w = 0$, with that for $w = w^*$ given by

$$w^* = [A_0]^{-1} p_\alpha(0)[B(\alpha) - A(\alpha)] \tag{15.6}$$

with this equaling maximum steady state per capita consumption when g = 0, and that for $r = r^*$ given by

$$r^* = 1/\lambda^*(\alpha), \tag{15.7}$$

where $\lambda^*(\alpha)$ is the maximum eigenvalue of $A(\alpha)[I - \delta A(\alpha)]^{-1}$, with $r^*$ also being the maximum rate of balanced growth, the von Neumann ray.

The wage-profit frontier (WPF) is the outer envelope of the set of wage-profit curves for all viable techniques in $T$, namely WPF = $W(r)$ = $(w, r^\wedge)$ such that for all $r^\wedge$ there exists a viable $\alpha$ in $T$ for which

$$\begin{aligned} &P(\alpha)[B(\alpha) - (1+r^\wedge)A(\alpha)][A_0]^{-1} \\ &\geq p(\beta)[B(\beta) - (1+r^\wedge)A(\beta)][A_0]^{-1}, \end{aligned} \tag{15.8}$$

for all viable $\beta$ in $T$ that are not $\alpha$.

Paradoxes of capital arise when there exist non-monotonic relations between $r$ and steady state per capita consumption as $r$ is varied for comparisons of steady state equilibria along the WPF, with reswitching being one such example, but not the only one. Rosser (1983) shows that the presence of such paradoxes, especially reswitching, where a given technique appears at distinct and separate points on the WPF, can lead to discontinuities in dynamic paths under certain circumstances. We also note that these non-monotonicties also occur between $r$ and the ratio of the value of capital to labor along the WPF in a comparative manner, where that ratio is given by

$$K / L = \left[\left(pC / L\right) - w\right] / \left(r - g\right). \tag{15.9}$$

While Pasinetti and others have seen that an apparently smooth WPF might well be enveloping an underlying set of possibly highly discontinuous relations, others have decided that if this is not the case then the non-monotonicities associated with various capital theoretic paradoxes can be avoided. In particular, such a claim was made by Yeager (1976). However, Rosser (1978) showed a counterexample based on an "eccentric reswitching" model in which variations in capital-labor ratios are smooth across the entire WPF, yet one finds a fundamental non-monotonicity, with the relationship between $K/L$ and $r$ reversing at the midpoint of the WPF and every technique except that appearing at the midpoint appears exactly twice on the WPF, once on each side of the midpoint, thus exhibiting reswitching. Garegnani (1970) also presented a similar case where there is smooth variation between techniques on the WPF surface even as the system exhibits non-monotonocities and reswitching.

Let us now consider more thoroughly how varied the sets of techniques can be that can be represented within this Sraffian framework and how there might be a link to computability issues, opening up how this can complicate the problem of technique choice and the dynamic paths economies can take. For this we shall draw on and extend arguments first presented in Rosser (1991, Chap. 8). This can be viewed as drawing forth more fully the conceptualization presented by Pasinetti regarding the possibility of deep discontinuities even with a smooth WPF.

So within the Sraffian tradition it has long been a practice to argue that techniques can be considered as appearing in a "book of blueprints." Needless to say, this book may have an infinite number of pages, as there may be an infinite number of techniques. However, the cardinality of this infinite set of techniques may be up in the air. The image of a book with a set of successive discrete pages suggests that they may be counted, that the set may be of cardinality $\aleph_0$. Assuming the continuum hypothesis holds then the next infinity up will have cardinality $\aleph_1$ and will be the continuum. Indeed, that is what we expect the cardinality of the set of points on the WPF to be, a continuum, with each one associated with a technique, one out of the book of blueprints that now has a continuum of pages.

But this represents a narrowing of the possibilities involved here. As shown earlier, each possible technique is associated with a wage-profit curve, a function. As it turns out the set of functions, or the broader set of curved lines on a plane. The cardinality of such a set can in general be yet higher; it can be $\aleph_2$. It may be that for each point on the WPF there may be an infinite set of wage-profit curves associated with an infinite set of techniques passing through that point. Not only that, the cardinality of this set may not be merely countable or a continuum, but an even higher cardinality, that associated with the set of curved lines in a plane, although this may require broader technical possibilities.

Here we return to the problem of possible non-computability. An economy may face a particular wage-profit pair. But this may not allow a computation to unequivocally select a technique. Not only may there be more than one possible technique, there may be a higher order infinite set of techniques. It may be that there are even sub-sets within these infinite techniques, all associated with a single point on the WPF. The techniques may be separated into *technique clusters*. These may include infinite sets of techniques that only slightly differ from one another in a physical sense, possibly representable as sets of neoclassical production functions or relations resembling those. The idea of technique clusters has been used in microeconomics, such as to compare TVs and VCRs. But here we are talking about technologies describing entire economies. In any case, through a given point on a WPF, there may be multiple technique clusters passing, each exhibiting reasonably continuous variations within themselves, but possibly highly discontinuous changes across each other, with their possibly being an infinite set of these clusters with a cardinality higher than the continuum.

This is not precisely analogous to computational complexity, but it resembles it in the sense that some problems of computational complexity as noted in the previous section can involve disjunctures between different levels of such complexity, such as trying to solve an *NP* system using a *P* level algorithm. We do not think that it can be done, even if that has not been definitively proven yet.

We present below in Fig. 15.1 a WPF with only four different wage-profit curves, each associated with a very different technique. They exhibit the basic idea posed by Pasinetti, where we see techniques appearing near each other on the WPF, but exhibiting very different shapes and characteristics implying deep discontinuities between each other.

This brings us back to the problem of how to decide what to do in the face of such profound uncertainty. These are decisions that are not properly computable and thus must be made on the basis of other means, whether some form of Simonian bounded rationality or more intuitively along the lines of Keynesian animal spirits. We close this discussion by noting a historically inspired comment by Joan Robinson (1975, pp. 38–39):

> When investment us being planned, whether for a single plant or for a socialist economy the choice of technique is made by groping amongst incomplete information. There are no read-blue-printed techniques to choose from. When the technique to be installed is designed to give a higher output per man than that formerly in use, it must be a recent innovation or an adaptation from one already known in the broad, not in detail.

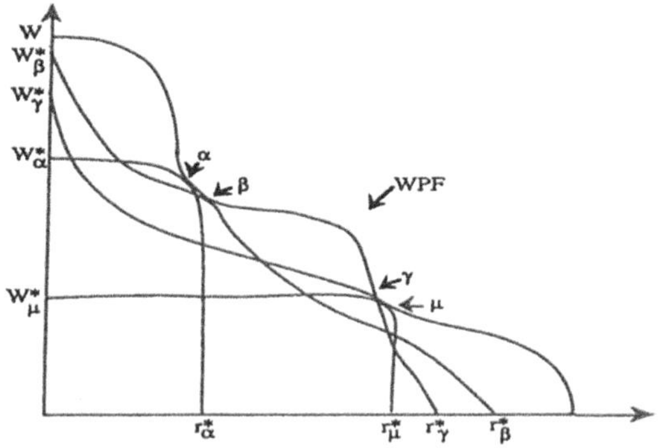


**Fig. 15.1** Continuous technologies with discontinuous profit-capital intensities

The blueprints are drawn when the technique is chosen, and it will rarely turn out, after the event, that exactly the best possible choice was made.

There is no such phenomenon in real life as accumulation taking place in a given state of technical knowledge. The idea was introduced into economic theory only to give a meaning to the concept of the marginal productivity of capital, just as the pseudo-production function was constructed in order to show that it has no meaning.

# 4 Conclusions

Computational complexity profoundly implies uncertainty as its level rises. This is intimately tied to the deep considerations of links between information and probability as studied by such figures as Shannon, Solomonoff, Kolmogorov, Chaitin, and Rissanen. Chaitin's probability of a program halting encapsulates this, even as it possibly oversimplifies it. And the fullest uncertainty arises when the highest level of computational complexity is in place when reflexive self-referencing implies infinite do-loops and the presence of a halting problem. This problem, deeply associated with Gödelian incompleteness as realized by Church and Turing and others, forecloses any strictly computational solution of problems when it appears. But even short of that, when systems are *NP* as with the busy beaver problem, solutions may be extremely difficult to achieve. This is why Nash viewed the use of such systems as useful for encryption problems, although we know that some *NP* problems may not be so difficult, with such systems implying possibly even better behaved economies. In any case, when uncertainty due to computational complexity becomes too great, agents must rely on either some sort of procedural rationality along lines suggested by Simon or in more difficult cases fall back on more intuitive animal spirits as suggested by Keynes.

Somewhat similar issues can arise in the problem of choosing techniques. The Sraffian framework offers a perspective in which examining available techniques as they array along a wage-profit frontier can highlight comparisons. But this also reveals that simplistic assumptions held in much of neoclassical analysis may not hold. Non-monotonic relations between capital-labor ratios and profit rates may occur that can imply possible erratic dynamic behavior. Apparently smooth systems with techniques lying infinitesimally close to each other on the frontier may represent highly different techniques revealing the frontier to be a surface hiding profound discontinuities. Indeed, the set of possible techniques may well be of a cardinality of infinity higher than the continuum, making computability of selecting a technique highly complex. The matter of technical choice may come to possess the sorts of problems discussed in the earlier portion of this chapter. Thus the problem of technical choice may also ultimately depend not only possibly on some heuristic approach, but ultimately on reliance in the end on intuitive animal spirits of a Keynesian sort.

## References

Binmore, K. (1987). Modeling Rational Players I. *Economics and Philosophy, 3*, 9–55.

Blum, L., Cucker, F., Shub, M., & Smale, S. (1998). *Complexity and Real Computation*. New York: Springer-Verlag.

Chaitin, G. J. (1966). On the Length of Programs for Computing Finite Binary Sequences. *Journal of the ACM, 13*, 547–569.

Chaitin, G. J. (1987). *Algorithmic Information Theory*. Cambridge: Cambridge University Press.

Church, A. (1936). A Note on the Entscheidungs Problem. *Journal of Symbolic Logic, 1*, 40–41, correction 101–102.

da Costa, N. C. A., & Doria, F. A. (2016). On the O'Donnell Algorithm for NP-Complete Problems. *Review of Behavioral Economics, 3*, 221–242.

Diaconis, P., & Freedman, D. (1986). On the Consistency of Bayes Estimates. *Annals of Statistics, 14*, 1–26.

Garegnani, P. (1970). Heterogeneous Capital, the Production Function and the Theory of Capital. *Review of Economic Studies, 37*, 407–436.

Gödel, K. (1931). Über Formal Unentssheidbare Satz der Principia Mathematica und Verwandte Systeme I. *Monatshefte für Mathematik und Physik, 38*, 173–198.

Harris, D. J. (1973). Capital, Distribution, and the Aggregate Production Function. *American Economic Review, 63*, 100–113.

Keynes, J. M. (1921). *Treatise on Probability*. London: Macmillan.
Keynes, J. M. (1936). *The General Theory of Employment, Interest and Money*. London: Macmillan.
Kolmogorov, A. N. (1965). Three Approaches to the Quantitative Definition of Information. *Problems of Information Transmission, 1*, 4–7.
Koppl, R., & Rosser, J. B., Jr. (2002). All That I Have to Say Has Already Crossed Your Mind. *Metroeconomica, 35*, 339–360.
Maymin, P. Z. (2011). Markets are Efficient if and only if P = NP. *Algorithmic Finance, 1*, 1–11.
Mirowski, P. (2007). Markets Come to Bits: Evolution, Computation, and Markomata in Economic Science. *Journal of Economic Behavior and Organization, 63*, 200–242.
Morgenstern, O. (1935). Voltommene Vorastlicht und Wirtschaftslichees Gleichgewicht. *Zeitschrift für Nationalökonomie, 6*, 337–357.
von Neumann, J., & Morgenstern, O. (1944). *Theory of Games and Economic Behavior*. Princeton: Princeton University Press.
Nyarko, Y. (1991). Learning in Mis-Specified Models and the Possibility of Cycles. *Journal of Economic Theory, 55*, 416–427.
O'Donnell, M. (1979). *A Programming Language Theorem That Is Independent of Peano Arithmetic*. Proceedings of the 11th Annual ACM Symposium on the Theory of Communication, 179–188.
Pasinetti, L. L. (1969). Switches of Technique and the Rate of Return in Capital Theory. *Economic Journal, 74*, 508–531.
Rado, T. (1962). On Non-Computable Functions. *Bell System Technical Journal, 41*, 877–884.
Rissanen, J. (2005). Complexity and Information in Modeling. In K. V. Velupillai (Ed.), *Computability, Complexity and Constructivity in Economic Analysis* (pp. 85–104). Victoria: Blackwell.
Robinson, J. (1975). The Unimportance of Reswitching. *Quarterly Journal of Economics, 89*, 32–39.
Rosser, J. B., Jr. (1978). Continuity and Capital-Reversal: Comment. *Economic Inquiry, 16*, 143–146.
Rosser, J. B., Jr. (1983). Reswitching as a Cusp Catastrophe. *Journal of Economic Theory, 31*, 182–193.
Rosser, J. B., Jr. (1991). *From Catastrophe to Chaos: A General Theory of Economic Discontinuities*. Boston: Kluwer.
Rosser, J. B., Jr. (2004). Epistemological Implications of Economic Complexity. *Annals of the Japan Association for Philosophy of Science, 31*, 3–18.

Rosser, J. B., Jr. (2020). Incompleteness and Complexity in Economic Theory. In S. Wuppuluri & F. A. Doria (Eds.), *Unraveling Complexity: The Life and Work of Gregory Chaitin* (pp. 345–367). Singapore: World Scientific.
Samuelson, P. A. (1966). A Summing Up. *Quarterly Journal of Economics, 80*, 568–583.
Shannon, C. E. (1948). A Mathematical Theory of Communication. *Bell Systems Technical Journal, 27*, 379–423, 623–656.
Simon, H. A. (1955). A Behavioral Model of Rational Choice. *Quarterly Journal of Economics, 60*, 99–118.
Simon, H. A. (1957). *Models of Man: Social and Rational*. New York: John Wiley.
Simon, H. A. (1969). *The Sciences of the Artificial*. Cambridge: MIT Press.
Solomonoff, R. J. (1964). A Formal Theory of Inductive Inference Parts I and II. *Information and Control, 7*(1–22), 224–254.
Sraffa, P. (1960). *Production of Commodities by Commodities: A Prelude to a Critique of Economic Theory*. Cambridge: Cambridge University Press.
Turing, A. M. (1936). On Computable Numbers with an Application to the Entscheidungsproblem. *Proceedings of the London Mathematical Society, 2*, 230–265.
Velupillai, K. (2000). *Computable Economics*. Oxford: Oxford University Press.
Velupillai, K. V. (2005). A Primer on the Tools and Concepts of Computable Economics. In K. V. Velupillai (Ed.), *Computability, Complexity and Constructivity in Economic Analysis* (pp. 148–197). Victoria: Blackwell.
Velupillai, K. V. (2009). A Computable Economist's Perspective on Computational Complexity. In J. B. Rosser Jr. (Ed.), *Handbook of Complexity Research* (pp. 36–83). Cheltenham: Edward Elgar.
Velupillai, K. V. (2019). Classical Behavioural Finance Theory. *Review of Behavioral Economics, 6*, 1–18.
Wolfram, S. (1984). Universality and Complexity in Cellular Automata. *Physica D, 10*, 1–35.
Yeager, L. B. (1976). Toward Understanding Some Paradoxes in Capital Theory. *Economic Inquiry, 14*, 313–346.
Zambelli, S. (2004). Production of Ideas by Means of Ideas: A Turing Machine Metaphor. *Metroeconomica, 55*, 155–179.
Zambelli, S. (2005). Computable Knowledge and Uncertainty: A Turing Machine Metaphor Applied to Endogenous Growth Models. In K.V. Velupillai (Ed.), *Computability, Compleixty and Constructivity in Economic Analysis* (pp. 233–263). Victoria: Blackwell.
Zambelli, S. (2010). Computable and Constructive Economics, Undecidable Dynamics and Algorithimic Rationality. In S. Zambelli (Ed.), *Computable, Constructive and Behavioural Dynamics* (pp. 15–45). London: Routledge.

Zambelli, S. (2011). Coupled Dynamics in a Phillips Machine Model of the Macroeconomy. *Economia Politica, Special Issue, 28*, 171–186.
Zambelli, S. (2012). Computable Economics: Reconstructing the Nonconstructive. *New Mathematics and Natural Computation, 8*, 113–122.
Zambelli, S. (2018). Production of Commodities by Means of Commodities and Non-Uniform Rates of Profit. *Metroeconomica, 69*, 383–426.

# 16

# Marx and the Other Sraffa: The Insignificant Empirical Effect of Price-Value Deviations on Economic Aggregates

Anwar Shaikh

## 1 The Visible Sraffa[1]

Sraffa's elegant and elliptical book transformed the treatment of prices of production. His stated agenda was to ground a critique of some central propositions of neoclassical theory, particularly its reliance on the notion of an aggregate production function whose marginal products of labor and "capital" determines wage and profit rates, respectively (Sraffa 1960, pp. v–vii). From the neoclassical perspective, "[w]hat a social class gets is, under natural law, what it contributes to the general output of society" (Clark 1891).

[1] I wish to express my gratitude to Riccardo Bellofiore and Scott Carter for their illuminating work on Sraffa's archives. My use of the phrase "the Other Sraffa" is a reference to the conference 'The Other Sraffa: Surprises in Archive?' at the University of Bergamo in December 2010 and to the subsequent volume (Bellofiore and Carter 2014).

A. Shaikh (✉)
Department of Economics, New School for Social Research,
New York, NY, USA


K. Velupillai (ed.), *Keynesian, Sraffian, Computable and Dynamic Economics*,
https://doi.org/10.1007/978-3-030-58131-2_16

Robinson (1953) pointed out that the quantity of "capital" was itself the aggregate price of a heterogeneous bundle of capital goods. Since individual prices of production depend on the profit rate, the aggregate price of capital goods could not also determine the profit rate. Sraffa provided the formal foundation for this argument, which in turn became a central focus of the famous Cambridge Capital Controversies (Harcourt 1969; Cohen and Harcourt 2003).

Sraffa's impress led to many neo-Ricardian representations of Marx. Marx's great emphasis on the length of the working day as the proximate source of a surplus product in pre-capitalist societies, and of surplus value in capitalist societies, disappears from view under the assumption that the number of workers was a proxy for their total labor time (Bellofiore 2014, pp. 207, 214). This Ricardian element is present in Sraffa's own formulation, in which a surplus product is represented as coming into existence due to an advance in technology (Sraffa 1960, pp. 6–7). It is a particularly curious formulation given the well-known history of working class struggles about conditions of work, and the fact that even today the length and intensity of the working day vary enormously between countries. In most advanced capitalist countries, through a long struggle, workers have achieved a 40-hr working week at a moderate pace. In China and some other developing countries, a common practice is "996": 9am to 9pm, six days a week (72-hrs) at a break-neck pace. This is a non-trivial point, since comparisons among "techniques" would then have to account for variations in the conditions of labor extraction (Shaikh 2016, pp. 206–220).[2]

A common neo-Ricardian claim is that Marx's "erroneous transformation algorithm" arose because he "did not have the method of simultaneous equations at his disposal" (Gehrke and Kurz 2006, p. 214). Yet in Marx's presentation of his algorithm, he is careful to state that it is a *first* step because any deviations of prices from values implies that costs previously expressed in labor value terms must be further adjusted to reflect the new prices.

[2] A longer and or more intense working day would count as a lower labor coefficient and hence as a lower unit labor value. Since Sraffa prices equal labor values at $r = 0$, this would lower their absolute levels.

> We had originally assumed that the cost-price of a commodity equaled the value of the commodities consumed in its production. But for the buyer the price of production of a specific commodity is its cost-price, and may thus pass as cost-price into the prices of other commodities. Since the price of production may differ from the labor value of a commodity, it follows that the cost-price of a commodity containing this price of production of another commodity may also stand above or below that portion of its total value derived from the value of the means of production consumed. It is necessary to remember this modified significance of the cost-price, and to bear in mind that there is always the possibility of an error if the cost-price of a commodity in any particular sphere is identified with the value of the means of production consumed by it. Our present analysis does not necessitate a closer examination of this point. (Marx 1967b, Chapter IX, pp. 164–165)

In other words, his derivation is the beginning of an *iterative* process. Iteration has been around since Gauss (1823), and even today is commonly utilized in computer calculations. The steps involved could easily have been implemented by Marx, and have been shown to lead to the standard simultaneous equation solution (Shaikh 1977; Morishima and Catephores 1978).

Another often-mentioned point in that literature is that, for any common total output price (i.e. for any common price-level), the deviations of prices from values can yield aggregate profits different from aggregate surplus value.[3] In the algebraic domain, this is touted as the definitive criticism of Marx. Yet the very *same* problem arises when we consider prices (market, monopoly, etc.) different from Sraffian prices: aggregate profits will then differ from aggregate competitive profits. It follows that all models of pricing have a "transformation problem". Once again, it is most curious that neo-Ricardian followers of Sraffa have overlooked this obvious point. I have argued that in all cases this difference is the net result of balance-of-payments transfers between the capital and

[3] Sraffa shows that this problem arises solely from the difference between actual output proportions and standard ones. In the latter case, all aggregates have the same internal proportions (i.e. they are the same vector except for scale), so that any sets of prices will yield the same ratios. Hence keeping the value of money constant (keeping the price production of aggregate output equal to its value) will make all other price aggregates equal to their value counterparts.

non-capital circuits on which Marx himself places great emphasis (Shaikh 2016, Ch. 6).

My present concern relates to the preceding point along a different dimension: at an empirical level, how relevant is the putative complexity of prices of production, and how important are the effects of price-value deviations on economy-wide aggregates? It turns of that the Other Sraffa, brought out from his archive lair, has a lot to say on this.

## 2 The Other Sraffa

The material in Sraffa's archives, now publicly available thanks to the efforts of a dedicated band of scholars such as John Eatwell, Jonathan Smith, Giancarlo de Vivo, Murray Milgate, and Scott Carter and Riccardo Bellofiore, came as a shock to some of Sraffa's followers, particularly those whose comments about Marx and the labor theory of value (LTV) had been critical and dismissive. Yet according to "anecdotal evidence put forward by his friends and colleagues, … [Sraffa] was always an adherent of the LTV" (Bellofiore 2014, p. 205), the "role of Marx in the construction of Sraffa's 1960 book turns out to be more profound than could previously have been guessed before the opening of the Sraffa Archive, and Sraffa's reference to Marx's value theory persists even after the publication of the book" (Bellofiore and Carter 2014, p. 19).

In the late 1920s, Sraffa was critical of the labor theory of value as he understood it. By 1927 he had "discovered the Quesnay–Smith–Ricardo 'surplus approach' whose ultimate result was to be a restatement of Marx" and by the 1940s had read Marx's *Theories of Surplus Value* and *Capital* Volume II and obviously Volume III containing Marx's transformation from labor values to prices of production. In the early 1940s, as he was getting back to work on his book, "Sraffa was convinced that his study would have shown that Marx was unequivocally correct." (Bellofiore 2014, pp. 210–212). Commenting on Bortkiewicz's simultaneous equation solution for prices of production, Sraffa say: "[T]he real objection (though somewhat vaguer) is this: that B[ortkiewicz]'s point of view, for the sake of obtaining absolute exactness *in a comparatively trifling matter*, sacrifice (by concealing it) the essential nature of the question—that is, that commodities are produced *by labour* out of commodities. (D1/91/16; emphasis added)". We also know that Sraffa underlined a passage in T.A. Jackson's *Dialectics: The Logic of Marxism*, which says "Capitalist production is therefore a system of producing commodities *from* commodities (raw materials, machinery etc.) *by means* of commodities (*the labour power* of wage labourers)" (Bellofiore and Carter 2014, p. 214, emphasis added). This is a direct reference to Marx's central points that labor-power becomes a commodity under capitalism. It provides a different perspective on the title of Sraffa's *The Production of Commodities by Means of Commodities.*

Marx did not live to write Volumes II and III of *Capital.* Engels compiled the material in those books, after of a long and arduous effort, from a mass of notes that Marx left behind. Vol III of *Capital* appeared more than a decade after Marx's death (Marx 1967b, Prefaces, 1967a). To this day, we do not know much about the excluded material. With this in mind, there is a striking correspondence in Marx's (incomplete) published material between his notion of a "standard" industry whose price of production need not deviate from its value and Sraffa's own standard industry with exactly the same property. Marx first establishes that the formation of a common rate of profit implies that the prices of production of individual industries will deviate from their labor values. As previously noted, he goes on to say that these deviations must be fed back onto costs previously measured in terms of labor values. But, one particular industry will be exempt from price-value deviations because it has a special "structure" with a particular composition: "The capital invested in some spheres of production has a *mean, or average, composition*, that is, it has the same, or almost the same composition as the average social capital ... In these spheres the price of production is exactly or almost the same as the value of the produced commodity expressed in money. *If there were no other way of reaching a mathematical limit, this would be the one*". This average composition is an "ideal average, i.e., an average that does not really exist, i.e., a[n] *ideal as a standard* ...In the case of [such capital] ... the price of production is ... the same or almost the same as the value, and the profit the same as the surplus value produced by them ... with the same, or approximately the same *structure* " (Marx 1967b, Ch X, pp. 173–174, emphasis added).

So the industry of a mean, or average composition, "the ideal as standard", has a composition that is different from the "social average". Yet Marx goes on to say that sum of "the profit on the social average capital is equal to the sum of surplus value", which does not follow (op. cit.). We do not know whether in his unpublished notes he meant this as an exact statement or as an empirically valid statement as Sraffa insists. However, we can say that just as the profit rate and aggregate profit corresponding to prices of production theoretically differ from the value rate of profit and surplus value, respectively, so too will Sraffian total profit and the profit rate differ from those measured at market, monopoly, prices. Those who insist that price-value deviations invalidate Marx's theory of surplus value should at least have the grace to admit, under their own logic, that there is a *universal* transformation problem (Shaikh 2016, pp. 217–226).

Sraffa also begins from a situation in which individual prices equal labor values. In Marx's case this is because he chooses labor values as his starting point to establish that the creation of profit (Vol I) is independent of transfers of any sort (Shaikh 2016, pp. 208–212). In Sraffa's case it is because he starts at a point at which the wage share happens absorb all net national product per worker (hr.), in which case the profit share and profit rate are zero and his prices equal labor values. He next considers a lower wage share, so that a positive rate of profit arises. Then prices cannot remain equal to values because in "deficit" industries with high capital-labor ratios the saving in wage costs would not be sufficient to generate a normal rate of profit, while in "surplus" industries with low capital-labor ratios the same effect would be more than sufficient. But, "[t]here would be a "critical proportion of labour to means of production ... which marked the watershed between 'deficit" and 'surplus' industries", and this critical proportion would fall somewhere between the lowest and highest capital-labor ratios. In the elegant argument that follows, Sraffa establishes that one can construct a composite sector whose price would remain equal to its labor value (its initial price) regardless of the level of the rate of profit, and whose output-capital ratio evaluated at prices of production remain equal to its labor value equivalent. This *standard* industry is ideal in two senses: because it does not exist as such; and because it serves as the fulcrum for the analysis of changes in the wage (profit) relation.

By construction, the standard output-capital ratio is invariant to changes in distribution. When wages are zero and all net output goes to profit, the common rate of profit is at its maximum. Then all industries, including the standard one, will have the same output-capital ratio. Since the output-capital ratio of the standard industry is invariant, it is also the maximum rate of profit. As a result, the wage share in the standard sector would be linearly related to the actual profit rate. In the actual system the output-capital ratio would not be invariant and the relation between wage share and the profit rate would not be a straight line (Sraffa 1960, pp. 12–23).

In the 1940s, Sraffa had hypothesized that the aggregate output-capital ratio was indeed constant, and hence equal to the maximum rate of profit. He "thought that his inquiry would vindicate the 'Old Moor'". Even after his 1960 book in which he had shown that his "Hypo" was not exactly true in theory, he "maintained a positive judgment on Marx's transformation procedure and ...[viewed the] results of his book in terms of capitalist exploitation within an amended Marxian discourse" (Bellofiore 2014, p. 199).

Sraffa's "Hypo" drove his research for several years because it would have provided a simple relation between the wage share and a uniform rate of profit at *any* given output proportions, that is, in the actual economy. Let $Y(r)$, $K(r)$ represent actual net output (net national product) and capital stock in prices $p(r)$ calculated at some rate of profit ($r$), $L$ represent total hours of labor, and $\omega$, $r$ represent equalized money wages and profit rates. Then $\omega L$ is the aggregate wage bill, $rK(r)$ is aggregate profit, and from the national accounting identity $Y(r) \equiv \omega L + rK(r)$. Denoting the wage share as $w(r) \equiv \frac{wL}{Y(r)}$ and the output-capital ratio as $R'(r) = \frac{Y(r)}{K(r)}$ gives a relation between the two at any given rate of profit for arbitrary output proportions:

$$w(r) = 1 - \frac{r}{R'(r)} \tag{16.1}$$

If $R'(r)$ was constant at all rates of profit, in keeping with Sraffa's Hypo, then it would have to be equal to the maximum rate of profit $R$ corresponding to a zero wage share. In this case, the actual wage share would be a linear function of the rate of profit. Conversely, if $R'(r)$ did not vary much, which we will see is the empirical case, this would explain the virtually universal finding that actual wage-profit curves were near-linear.

Sraffa's Hypo was originally "based on the "statistical compensation of large numbers" (D3/12/35: 28)" (Perri 2014, p. 109). Indeed, in his unpublished notes Sraffa himself says that

> the propositions of M[arx] are based on the assumption that the composition of any large aggregate of commodities (wages, profits, constant capital) consists of a random selection, so that the ratio between their aggregates (rate of surplus value, rate of profit) is approximately the same whether measured at 'values' or at the prices of production corresponding to any rate of surplus value… . This is obviously true.

In response to Eaton's (1960) review, Sraffa defends Marx again: "It is clear that M[arx]'s pro[position]s … are based on the assumption (*justified in general*) that the aggregates are of some average composition. This is in general *justified in fact*, and since it is not intended to be applied to detailed minute differences it is all right … This should be good enough till *the tiresome objector arises*. If then one must define which is the average to which the comp[osition] should conform for the result to be *exact* and not only approximate, it is the S[tandard] Comm[odity]" (Bellofiore 2014, pp. 220–221, emphasis added).

# 3 Empirical Investigations

> Although it is often said that economics is too much like physics, to a physicist economics is not at all like physics. The difference is in the scientific method of the two fields: theoretical economics uses a top-down approach in which hypothesis and mathematical rigor come first and empirical confirmation comes second. Physics, in contrast, embraces the bottom up 'experimental philosophy' of Newton, in which 'hypotheses are

> inferred from phenomena, and afterward rendered general by induction' … if economics were to truly make empirical-verification the ultimate arbiter of theories … [this] would force it to open up to alternative approaches. (abstract)[4]

Early Sraffian literature concentrated on elaborations of Sraffa's mathematics (Steedman 1977; Schefold 1989). Over time a portion of the literature shifted to the empirical investigation of actual relative prices of production and of actual wage-profit frontiers (Krelle 1977; Ochoa 1989; Shaikh 2012, 2016, Ch. 9; Bienenfeld 1988; Chilcote 1997; Mariolis and Soklis 2010; Mariolis and Tsoulfidis 2011; Iliadi et al. 2014; Shaikh 1984). This growing body of evidence showed that wage-profit curves and even individual price curves are near-linear. Han and Schefold (2006) found that in actual European tables reswitching and reverse capital deepening were rare. On the other side, it has been shown that such results do not reinstate the neoclassical aggregate production function that was Sraffa's own focus (Shaikh 2016, pp. 431–433, 440). In this regard, Zambelli's two papers (2004, 2018) are particularly innovative. In the first paper he generates artificial economies consisting of different numbers of commodities with many different viable methods of production (blueprints) for each and finds that only about 40 percent are even look like aggregate production functions. In the second paper, he uses actual production methods from 30 countries over 15 years to create a vast set of potential economies. Here his conclusion is more draconian: as-if aggregate production functions are never neoclassical over the whole domain, isoquants are never neoclassical, and the capital-labor ratio is seldom appropriately (negatively) sloped.

I wish to take up a different question: In the context of actual systems, is Sraffa correct to say that statistical considerations validate Marx's notion that price aggregates are essentially equivalent to corresponding labor value aggregates?

Actual US input-output tables for 1947, 1958, 1963, 1967, 1972 (71-order) and 1998 (65-order)[5] were used to calculate vectors of

[4] J. Doyne Farmer is Professor of Mathematics at Oxford University where he is Director of the Complexity Economics at the Institute for New Economic Thinking at the Oxford Martin School.

[5] Sources and methods for the 1947–1972 data are in Shaikh (1998) Appendix 15.2, and for 1998 are in Shaikh (2012) Data Appendix. In order to isolate the effects of changes in *relative* prices on

intermediate input, workers consumption, surplus product, net output and capital stock.[6] Each of these was measured at prices of production corresponding to the *observed* rate of profit (displayed in the first line in each table) in that year and in direct prices (prices proportional to labor values). The *ratios* of the aggregate production price of each bundle to its direct price are called ConstCap, VarCap, SurplusProd, NetOutput, SV (Surplus Product/Variable Capita), rop (rate of profit = Surplus Product/ Capital), and R1 (Output/Capital), respectively. Each ratio was calculated for the circulating capital case in which the capital stock is equal to ConstCap and the fixed capital case in which the capital stock is fixed capital. Since Sraffa prices equal labor values at a zero rate of profit ($r = 0$), *the preceding ratios also represent the effect on each variable of moving from r = 0 to r = robserved.* In the circulating capital case, average price-value ratios of various aggregates range between 0.95 and 1.03 (Table 16.1), while in the fixed capital case they range between .097 and 1.05 (Table 16.2). As Sraffa had predicted, *in actual conditions there is no*

**Table 16.1** Ratios of price and value aggregates at observed rates of profit and profit share: Circulating capital

| Matrix size | 71 | 71 | 71 | 71 | 71 | 65 | |
|---|---|---|---|---|---|---|---|
| | 1947 | 1958 | 1963 | 1967 | 1972 | 1998 | *Average* |
| *Observed rate of profit (robserved)* | *0.32* | *0.32* | *0.36* | *0.40* | *0.36* | *0.23* | *0.33* |
| *Observed profit share (robserved/R)* | *0.32* | *0.30* | *0.35* | *0.39* | *0.35* | *0.22* | *0.32* |
| ConstCap | 1.02 | 1.02 | 1.03 | 1.04 | 1.03 | 1.02 | *1.03* |
| VarCap | 0.99 | 0.98 | 0.97 | 0.97 | 0.96 | 0.99 | *0.98* |
| SurplusProd | 0.98 | 0.98 | 0.97 | 0.97 | 0.98 | 0.98 | *0.98* |
| NetOutput | 1.00 | 0.98 | 0.97 | 0.97 | 0.97 | 0.98 | *0.98* |
| SV | 1.03 | 1.00 | 1.00 | 1.00 | 1.02 | 0.99 | *1.01* |
| rop | 0.97 | 0.96 | 0.94 | 0.94 | 0.95 | 0.96 | *0.95* |
| R1 | 0.97 | 0.96 | 0.94 | 0.94 | 0.94 | 0.96 | *0.95* |

various aggregate bundles, we must keep the price *level* constant. Total market price is defined as the market value of gross output, and total direct price and total price of production at any given profit rate are scaled to match total market price. This keeps the value of money the same across all three types of prices.

[6] US data has several advantages. The data is good, the time span is long, US economy is relatively closed (from 1977–2007 almost 90 percent of goods are produced domestically), and there are good domestic approximations to the input-output structure of imported commodities.

**Table 16.2** Ratios of price and value aggregates at observed rates of profit and profit share: Fixed capital

| Matrix sze | 71 | 71 | 71 | 71 | 71 | 65 | |
|---|---|---|---|---|---|---|---|
| | 1947 | 1958 | 1963 | 1967 | 1972 | 1998 | *Average* |
| *robserved* | *0.24* | *0.18* | *0.21* | *0.23* | *0.19* | *0.11* | *0.19* |
| *Observed profit share (robserved/R)* | *0.29* | *0.26* | *0.28* | *0.31* | 0.28 | *0.27* | *0.28* |
| ConstCap | 1.02 | 1.03 | 1.04 | 1.04 | 1.03 | 1.03 | *1.03* |
| VarCap | 0.98 | 0.99 | 0.98 | 0.99 | 0.98 | 1.01 | *0.99* |
| SurplusProd | 0.98 | 0.96 | 0.95 | 0.94 | 0.96 | 0.98 | *0.96* |
| NetOutput | 0.98 | 0.97 | 0.97 | 0.97 | 0.97 | 0.96 | *0.97* |
| SV | 0.99 | 0.97 | 0.97 | 0.96 | 0.97 | 1.00 | *0.98* |
| rop | 1.04 | 1.04 | 1.05 | 1.05 | 1.04 | 0.98 | *1.04* |
| R1 | 1.04 | 1.06 | 1.07 | 1.08 | 1.06 | 1.00 | *1.05* |

**Table 16.3** Ratios of price and value aggregates in observable range r/R = 0.2 to 0.4, circulating capital

| | 1947 | 1958 | 1963 | 1967 | 1972 | 1998 | *Average* |
|---|---|---|---|---|---|---|---|
| ConstCap | 0.99 | 1.04 | 0.95 | 1.02 | 1.02 | 1.02 | *1.00* |
| VarCap | 1.01 | 1.03 | 1.01 | 0.98 | 0.98 | 0.99 | *1.00* |
| SurplusProd | 1.01 | 1.01 | 1.02 | 0.98 | 0.99 | 0.98 | *1.00* |
| NetOutput | 1.01 | 1.01 | 1.02 | 0.98 | 0.98 | 0.98 | *1.00* |
| SV | 1.01 | 1.00 | 1.01 | 1.00 | 1.01 | 0.99 | *1.00* |
| rop | 1.02 | 1.05 | 1.04 | 0.97 | 0.97 | 0.96 | *1.00* |
| R1 | 1.02 | 1.03 | 0.97 | 0.97 | 0.97 | 0.97 | *0.99* |

*effective difference between aggregates*. The last line in Tables 16.1 and 16.2 represent the price-value ratio of net output-capital that was Sraffa's singular focus: over 1948–1998, in the circulating capital case the ratios range from 1.00 to 1.08; in the fixed capital case they range from 0.97 to 1.03, with an average of 0.99.

Across 29 advanced countries (27 European countries plus the USA and Canada), the observed profit share r/R varies between 0.25 and 0.32 (Shaikh 2016, T. 9.5, p. 388). Taking the range of r/R = 0.20–0.40 as feasible outer bounds of potential profit shares, I examine how much each ratio changes between the lower and upper bounds. Tables 16.3 and 16.4 show there is effectively no difference over the socially feasible range of the profit share: in the circulating capital case, the final and beginning

**Table 16.4** Ratios of price and value aggregates in observable range r/R = 0.2 to 0.4, fixed capital

| Ratios between r/R = 0.20 and r/R = 0.40 | 1947 | 1958 | 1963 | 1967 | 1972 | 1998 | *Average* |
|---|---|---|---|---|---|---|---|
| ConstCap | 1.01 | 1.02 | 1.02 | 1.02 | 1.02 | 1.02 | *1.02* |
| VarCap | 0.99 | 0.99 | 0.99 | 0.99 | 0.99 | 1.00 | *0.99* |
| SurplusProd | 0.98 | 0.97 | 0.97 | 0.97 | 0.97 | 0.96 | *0.97* |
| NetOutput | 0.99 | 0.98 | 0.98 | 0.98 | 0.98 | 0.98 | *0.98* |
| SV | 0.99 | 0.98 | 0.98 | 1.01 | 0.98 | 1.02 | *0.99* |
| rop | 1.03 | 1.03 | 1.04 | 1.03 | 1.03 | 0.98 | *1.02* |
| R1 | 1.03 | 1.04 | 1.03 | 1.05 | 1.04 | 0.99 | *1.03* |

ratios are essentially the same, while in the fixed capital case they range between 0.97 and 1.03.

Next, we consider all the preceding variables over the full range of r/R from 0 to 1. Each variable is normalized to its corresponding labor value, and since Sraffa prices equal labor values at r/R = 0, each ratio begins at 1 and spreads out as r/R increases. In theory, the paths could be complicated. However, as shown in Fig. 16.1, in all years almost all the empirical paths of the variables are near-linear, with only a few have some smooth curvature. Most ratios vary less than ten percent over their whole level, with only a few around fifteen percent.

As previously noted, in the 1940s Sraffa had hypothesized that the capital ratio would be constant over the range. He subsequently showed that it was not. At r/R = 0, Sraffa prices are equal to labor values, so all initial output-capital ratios represent the ratio of the labor value of net output (living labor hours) to the labor value of the capital stock. These will be different according to the industry involved. Then as the profit share varies, all output-capital ratios approach the same ratio R, which is the output-capital ratio of the standard industry (Sraffa 1960, pp. 16–17). Figure 16.1 had already established the smoothness and modest non-linearity of these paths. Table 16.5 shows that the average variation of the output-capital ratio in the circulating capital case is 0.86, while that of the fixed capital case it is 1.17. This is for the full, socially impossible range of the profit share, with workers living on air at one end and capital euthanized at the other. Tables 16.3 and 16.4 had already demonstrated that within a socially feasible range the output-capital ratio hardly varies:

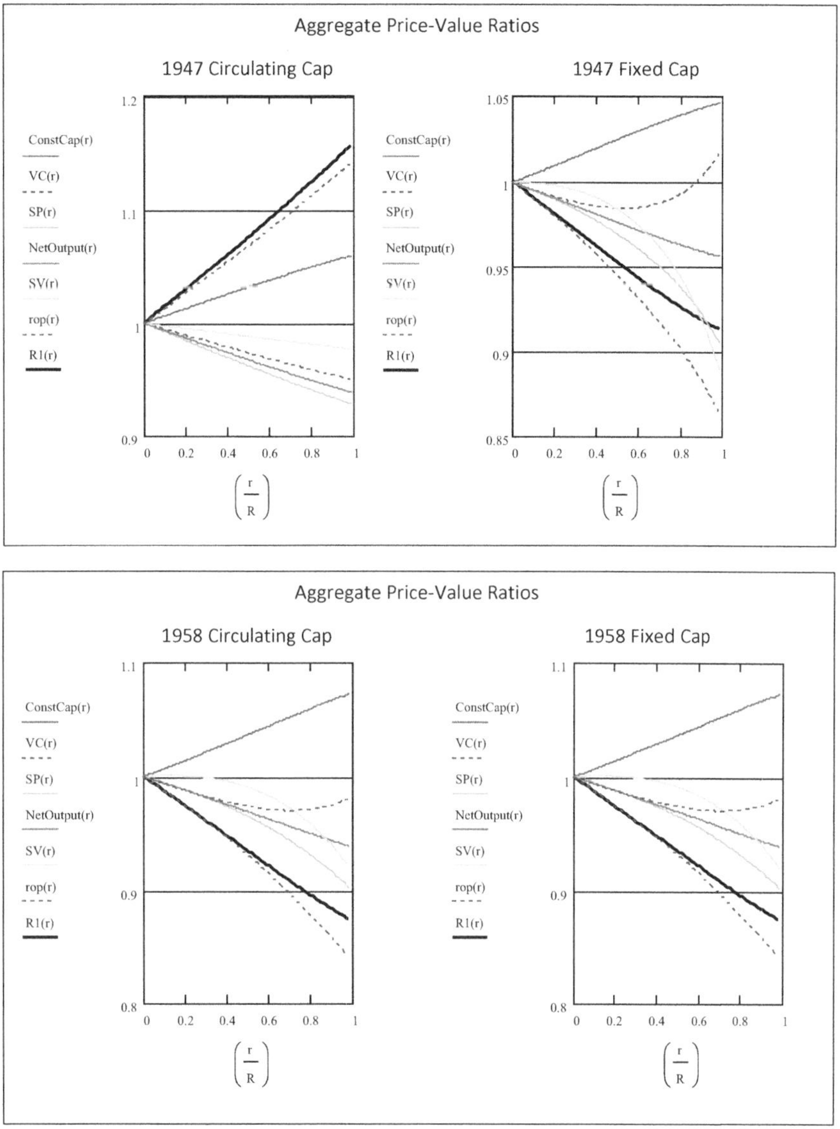


Fig. 16.1 Aggregate price-value ratios

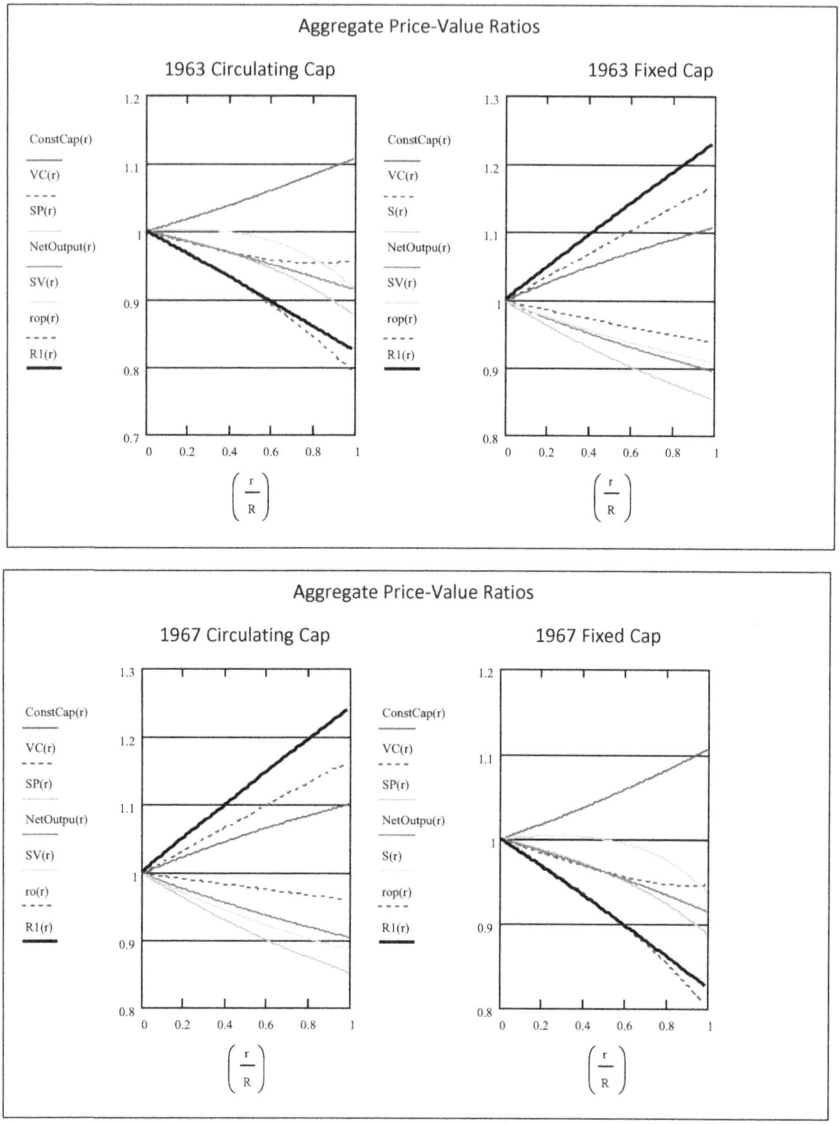


**Fig. 16.1** (continued)

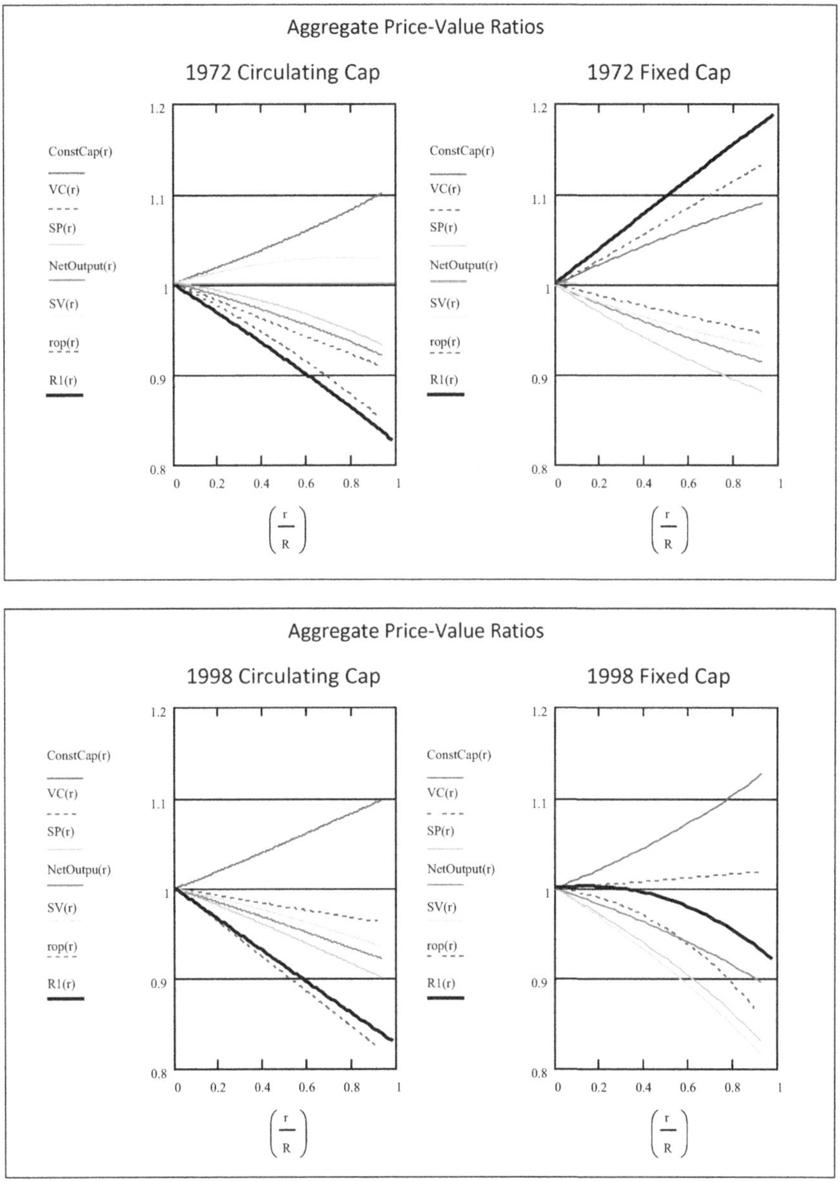


**Fig. 16.1** (continued)

**Table 16.5** Sraffa's hypo: Output-capital ratio over full range (r/R = 0 to 1)

| | 1947 | 1958 | 1963 | 1967 | 1972 | 1998 | *Average* |
|---|---|---|---|---|---|---|---|
| Circulating capital | 0.91 | 0.92 | 0.86 | 0.83 | 0.83 | 0.83 | *0.86* |
| Fixed capital | 1.15 | 1.21 | 1.29 | 1.24 | 1.19 | 0.92 | *1.17* |

*in advanced capitalist countries, Sraffa's Hypo is completely correct.* This in no way detracts from the beauty of his subsequent formulation. It just says that theory must always be tempered by the actual properties of its object of investigation—precisely as Sraffa does.

Finally, I would like to affirm my debt to my student Eduardo Ochoa for his pathbreaking PhD dissertation and subsequent publication (Ochoa 1984, 1989). The input-output tables and related variables for 1947–1972 that I have utilized were his constructions. He begins with a classical fixed capital model of prices of production with a given wage basket of commodities and corresponding sectoral and average rate of profit in each year. He calculates the Marxian rate of surplus value, the labor value profit rate, and direct and vertically integrated ratios of fixed capital to living labor. He finds a high degree of correspondence between direct prices (prices proportional to labor values), market prices and prices of production (the latter calculated at the observed rate of profit). The rates of profit measured in these different prices are very close. In retrospect, this further evidence confirming the Other Sraffa's sense about the empirical validity of Marx's approach. Finally, Ochoa turns to a fixed capital model of Sraffa prices over their full range finds wage-profit curves to be generally smooth and near-linear—suggesting that reswitching would be a rare empirical phenomenon in US data. This is despite the fact that the composition of the actual output vector is very different from that of Sraffa's standard commodity (Ochoa 1984, Chs. V–VII).

## 4 Summary and Conclusions

The 1960s Sraffa is right to say that the theoretical output-capital ratio will vary with the profit share r/R. And the Other Sraffa is right to say that this variation is insignificant at an empirical level, which validate Marx's intuition.

The Sraffian literature originally concentrated on elaborations of Sraffa's mathematics emphasizing "wiggly" prices and wage-profit curves. As work shifted to empirical investigation, a growing body of evidence found wage-profit curves and even individual price curves are near-linear, so that reswitching and reverse capital deepening were rare at the observed empirical level. At the same time, it was emphasized that these results do not reinstate the neoclassical aggregate production since the price of production of capital and net output itself depended on the rate of profit.

At a more detailed level, at the observed rate of profit, the price-value ratios of intermediate inputs, the wage basket, the surplus product, net product, profit-wage ratio, rate of profit, and output-capital were close to 1 in both circulating and fixed capital models. The price-value ratio of net output-capital that was the Sraffa's singular focus: over 1948–1998, in the circulating capital case the ratios range from 1.00 to 1.08; in the fixed capital case they range from 0.97 to 1.03, with an average of 0.99. Further, since the observed profit share ranges in 29 advanced countries between 0.25 and 0.32, r/R = 0.20–0.40 was taken as feasible outer bounds. Once again, there is effectively no difference the output-capital ratio over the socially potential range.

The last step was to consider all the preceding variables over the full range of r/R from 0 to 1. In theory, the paths could be complicated. However, in all years almost all the empirical paths of all variables were near-linear, with only a few have some smooth curvature. Most ratios vary less than ten percent over their whole level, with only a few around fifteen percent. Between the two full limits, in the circulating capital case the average variation of the output-capital ratio is 0.86, while in the fixed capital case it is 1.17. These are algebraic limits of course. Within any feasible range the output-capital ratio hardly varies. This reminds us theory must always be concerned by the actual properties of its object of investigation. This is the greatest beauty of Sraffa's contribution.

## References

Bellofiore, R. (2014). The Loneliness of the Long Distance Thinker. In R. Bellofiore & S. Carter (Eds.), *Symposium: New Directions in Sraffa Scholarship*. Houndmills, Basingstoke, Hampshire RG21 6XS: Palgrave Macmillan.
Bellofiore, R., & Carter, S. (Eds.). (2014). *Towards a New Understanding of Sraffa: Insights from Archival Research*. Houndmills, Basingstoke, Hampshire RG21 6XS: Palgrave Macmillan.
Bienenfeld, M. (1988). Regularities in Price Changes as an Effect of Changes in Distribution. *Cambridge Journal of Economics, 12*, 247–255.
Chilcote, E. (1997). Interindustry Structure, Relative Prices, and Productivity: An Input-Output Study of the U.S. and O.E.C.D. Countries. Ph.D., New School for Social Research.
Clark, J. B. (1891). Distribution as Determined by a Law of Rent. *Quarterly Journal of Economics, 5*, 229–318.
Cohen, A. J., & Harcourt, G. C. (2003). Retrospectives: Whatever Happened to the Cambridge Capital Theory Controversies? *The Journal of Economic Perspectives, 17*, 199–214.
Eaton, J. (1960). Il modello di Sraffa e la teoria del valore-lavoro. *Società, XVI*.
Gehrke, C., & Kurz, H. D. (2006). Sraffa on von Bortkiewicz: Reconstructing the Classical Theory of Value and Distribution. *History of Political Economy, 38*, 91–149.
Han, Z., & Schefold, B. (2006). An Empirical Investigation of Paradoxes: Reswitching and Reverse Capital Deepening in Capital Theory. *Cambridge Journal of Economics, 30*(5), 737–765.
Harcourt, G. C. (1969). Some Cambridge Controversies in the Theory of Capital. *Journal of Economic Literature, 7*, 369–405.
Iliadi, F., Mariolis, T., Soklis, G., & Tsoulfidis, L. (2014). Bienenfeld's Approximation of Production Prices and Eigenvalue Distribution: Further Evidence from Five European Economies. *Contributions to Political Economy, 33*, 35–54.
Krelle, W. (1977). Basic Facts in Capital Theory. Some Lessons from the Controversy in Capital Theory. *Revue d'Economie Politique, 87*, 282–329.
Mariolis, T., & Soklis, G. (2010). On Constructing Numeraire-Free Measures of Price–Value Deviation: A Note on the Steedman–Tomkins Distance. *Cambridge Journal of Economics, 35*, 613–618.
Mariolis, T., & Tsoulfidis, L. (2011). Eigenvalue Distribution and the Production Price-Profit Rate Relationship: Theory and Empirical Evidence. *Evolutionary and Institutional Economics Review, 8*, 87–122.

Marx, K. (1967a). *Capital, Vol II*. New York: International Publishers.
Marx, K. (1967b). *Capital, Vol III*. New York: International Publishers.
Morishima, M., & Catephores, G. (1978). *Value, Exploitation and Growth Marx in the Light of Modern Economic Theory*. London: McGraw-Hill.
Ochoa, E. M. (1984). Labor Values and Prices of Production: An Inter-Industry Study of the U.S. Economy, 1947–1972. PhD Dissertation, New School for Social Research.
Ochoa, E. M. (1989). Values, Prices, and Wage-Profit Curves in the U.S. Economy. *Cambridge Journal of Economics, 13*, 413–429.
Perri, S. (2014). The Standard System and the Tendency of the (Maximum) Rate of Profit to Fall – Marx and Sraffa: There and Back. In R. Bellofiore & S. Carter (Eds.), *Towards a New Understanding of Sraffa: Insights from Archival Research*. Houndmills, Basingstoke, Hampshire RG21 6XS: Palgrave Macmillan.
Robinson, J. (1953). The Production Function and the Theory of Capital. *The Review of Economic Studies, 21*, 81–106.
Schefold, B. (1989). *Mr Sraffa on Joint Production and Other Essays*. Routledge.
Shaikh, A. (1977). Marx's Theory of Value and the Transformation Problem. In J. Schwartz (Ed.), *The Subtle Anatomy of Capitalism*. Santa Monica: Goodyear Publishing Company.
Shaikh, A. (1984). The Transformation from Marx to Sraffa: Prelude to a Critique of the Neo-Ricardians. In E. Mandel (Ed.), *Marx, Ricardo, Sraffa*. Verso.
Shaikh, A. (1998). The Empirical Strength of the Labor Theory of Value. In R. Bellofiore (Ed.), *Marxian Economics: A Centenary Appraisal*. London: Macmillan.
Shaikh, A. (2012). The Empirical Linearity of Sraffa's Critical Output-Capital Ratios. In C. Gehrke, N. Salvadori, I. Steedman, & R. Sturn (Eds.), *Classical Political Economy and Modern Theory: Essays in Honour of Heinz Kurz*. Abingdon: Routledge.
Shaikh, A. (2016). *Capitalism: Competition, Conflict, Crises*. New York: Oxford University Press.
Sraffa, P. (1960). *Production of Commodities by Means of Commodities*. Cambridge: Cambridge University Press.
Steedman, I. (1977). *Marx After Sraffa*. London: New Left Books.
Zambelli, S. (2004). The 40% Neoclassical Aggregate Theory of Production. *Cambridge Journal of Economics, 28*, 99–120.
Zambelli, S. (2018). The Aggregate Production Function Is NOT Neoclassical. *Cambridge Journal of Economics, 42*, 383–426.

# 17

# Corn-Model, Subsistence Economy and the Empirical Economy

Ajit Sinha

## 1

In this chapter I argue that the nature of Sraffa's problem of the determination of prices and the rate of profits for an empirical economy that produces surplus can be understood by breaking it into Sraffa's two insights for much simpler systems: 'corn-model' and 'subsistence economy'.

In the corn-model, corn is the only basic good. In this system if, for example, 20 kg corn seed-capital results in 40 kg corn harvest and 10 kg corn is paid as wages after the harvest, then the rate of profit is equal to 50%. In this case, the rate of profit is determined by production equation and the given wages. The first point to note is that this rate of profit is independent of prices. The second point to note is that this rate of profit is independent of demand considerations—it does not matter whether the capitalists desire to consume the 10 kg corn left with them or invest them in the next production cycle or let it be eaten by rats. In other

A. Sinha (✉)
Thapar School of Liberal Arts and Sciences, Patiala, India



K. Velupillai (ed.), *Keynesian, Sraffian, Computable and Dynamic Economics*,
https://doi.org/10.1007/978-3-030-58131-2_17

words, the question of 'realization' of profits is not relevant to the determination of the rate of profits.

In a 'subsistence economy' there is no surplus output, and so no question of the determination of the rate of profits arises. But the system is made of *n* basic goods produced by *n* industries. So the problem for this system is to determine the price ratios or the exchange ratios between the goods and the industries so that the system can reproduce itself—solving the problem of price determination is essential for this system. In this system as well, the equations of production has sufficient information to determine those unique prices that would allow the system to reproduce itself. Yet again, demand plays no role.

Now, an empirical system[1] of *n* basic goods that produces surplus is, in a sense, a combination of 'corn-model' and 'subsistence economy'. I shall argue that with the help of the Standard system and the Standard commodity, Sraffa proves that the insights of the two simple systems mentioned above also hold for the more complex cases of the surplus producing *n*-commodity basic goods system; therefore, the notions of effectual demand and the centre of gravitation are irrelevant.

## 2

Let us take Sraffa's (1960) example of an empirical system of production that has produced surplus:

$$90\text{t.iron} + 120\text{t.coal} + 60\text{qr.wheat} + 3/16\,\text{labour} \rightarrow 180\text{t.iron}.$$

$$50\text{t.iron} + 125\text{t.coal} + 150\text{qr.wheat} + 5/16\,\text{labour} \rightarrow 450\text{t.coal}\;(\mathbf{I})$$

[1] By 'empirical system', I mean a system based on observed data of inputs and outputs of an empirical economy. To the extent that the observations can never be either complete or exact, the results based on such incomplete and inexact data would be off the true empirical values. But Sraffa's equations are not designed as a tool for planning or empirical predictions. It is designed to serve a theoretical purpose, which is to show that any interconnected system of basic goods has a structural property that can be derived from objective information available in the data and prices of commodities are tied to those structural relations and thus are independent of human subjectivities.

$$40t.\text{iron} + 40t.\text{coal} + 200qr.\text{wheat} + 8/16\,\text{labour} \rightarrow 480qr.\text{wheat}.$$

---

$$180t.\text{iron} + 285t.\text{coal} + 410qr.\text{wheat} + 1\,\text{labour} \rightarrow 180t.\text{iron} \\ +450t.\text{coal} + 480t.\text{wheat}.$$

In terms of its price equations the system is represented by:

$$\left(90p_i + 120p_c + 60p_w\right)\left(1 + r_i\right) + 3/16\,\mathbf{w} = 180p_i.$$

$$\left(50p_i + 125p_c + 150p_w\right)\left(1 + r_c\right) + 5/16\,\mathbf{w} = 450p_c \;(\mathbf{I})$$

$$\left(40p_i + 40p_c + 200p_w\right)\left(1 + r_w\right) + 8/16\,\mathbf{w} = 480p_w.$$

---

$$\left(180p_i + 285p_c + 410p_w\right)\left(1 + R\right) + \mathbf{w} = 180p_i + 450p_c + 480p_w.$$

Where p's are prices of respective goods and r's are the industrial rates of profit for those goods, **w** is the wage rate. R is the weighted average rate of profits for the system as a whole. In order to keep the conceptual clarity between a 'subsistence' or 'non-surplus' system and a 'surplus' system, we assume **w** = 0. This gives us the equation system as:

$$\left(90p_i + 120p_c + 60p_w\right)\left(1 + r_i\right) = 180p_i.$$

$$\left(50p_i + 125p_c + 150p_w\right)\left(1 + r_c\right) = 450p_c \;(\mathbf{I'})$$

$$\left(40p_i + 40p_c + 200p_w\right)\left(1 + r_w\right) = 480p_w.$$

---

$$\left(180p_i + 285p_c + 410p_w\right)\left(1 + R\right) \\ = 180p_i + 450p_c + 480p_w.$$

Let us multiply the first equation of (I′) by 4/3 and the second equation by 4/5. This does not change the mathematical properties of our equation system, that is, the values of either r's or p's are not affected by rescaling. We obtain:

$$
\begin{aligned}
(120p_i + 160p_c + 80p_w)(1 + r_i) &= 240p_i. \\
(40p_i + 100p_c + 120p_w)(1 + r_c) &= 360p_c \ (\mathbf{II}) \\
(40p_i + 40p_c + 200p_w)(1 + r_w) &= 480p_w.
\end{aligned}
$$

---

$$
\begin{aligned}
&(200p_i + 300p_c + 400p_w)(1 + R*) \\
&= 240p_i + 360p_c + 480p_w.
\end{aligned}
$$

This is Sraffa's Standard system associated with (I′). Sraffa (1960) has demonstrated that there always exists a vector of multipliers, such as in this case (4/3 4/5 1), that converts any given empirical system of equations to a Standard system and that the Standard system is *unique* to the given empirical system. In other words, all systems have an associated one and only one Standard system. The importance of system (II) or the Standard system is its aggregate equation. Because, it has only one (a composite) commodity on both its left hand side as well as its right hand side. This composite commodity is made up of iron, coal and wheat in fixed proportion given by (2:3:4)—Sraffa called it the Standard commodity. Thus from the aggregate equation of system (II), we can derive the value of the weighted average rate of profits of this system, R*, without the knowledge of either p's or r's. In our example, it turns out to be: R* = 1/5 or 20%. Thus the aggregate of the Standard system is the surrogate of our 'corn'.

Now we will show that prices determined by the subsistence system (III) given below are the prices that must prevail in the given empirical system (I′) and the average rate of profits determined by the Standard system (II) must also prevail in the empirical system (I′).

First we show that the average rate of profits determined in system (II) must also prevail in system (I′). Since the unknown R of (I′) is the weighted average rate of profits of this system of equations, all industrial rates of profits must be either equal to R or some more than R and some less than R. First, suppose they are equal to R.[2] If $r_i$, $r_c$ and $r_w$ are not all equal to R, then this would generate a new set of prices, which we refer to as p'. This turns our equation system (I′) to:

$$\left(90p'_i + 120p'_c + 60p'_w\right)(1+R) = 180p'_i.$$

$$\left(50p'_i + 125p'_c + 150p'_w\right)(1+R) = 450p'_c \quad (\mathbf{I''})$$

$$\left(40p'_i + 40p'_c + 200p'_w\right)(1+R) = 480p'_w.$$

---

$$\left(180p'_i + 285p'_c + 410p'_w\right)(1+R) = 180p'_i + 450p'_c + 480p'_w.$$

Now by rescaling this system back to the Standard system by multiplying the first equation by 4/3 and the second by 4/5, we derive:

$$\left(120p'_i + 160p'_c + 80p'_w\right)(1+R) = 240p'_i.$$

$$\left(40p'_i + 100p'_c + 120p'_w\right)(1+R) = 360p'_c \quad (\mathbf{II'})$$

$$\left(40p'_i + 40p'_c + 200p'_w\right)(1+R) = 480p'_w.$$

---

$$\left(200p'_i + 300p'_c + 400p'_w\right)(1+R) = 240p'_i + 360p'_c + 480p'_w.$$

[2] During the Winter 1927–1928 while writing his 2nd equation, that is the equation of a system producing surplus, Sraffa put it this way: 'But since we have (in the no-surplus system) a spare equation, we can use it to determine, simultaneously with value, *the ratio that total surplus bears to total initial stocks of the community*.' (Sraffa Archive n.d.: D3/12/6: 17, emphasis added, quoted in Sinha 2016, p. 57). Then he goes on to put equal rate of profits for all industries to solve for it.

Since in this case all the industries receive their rate of profits equal to R, it implies that its weighted average must also be equal to R. But we know from the physical relation of the aggregate of (II') that it is equal to R* and its value is fixed independently of prices at 20%. Therefore, R must be equal to R*. Since the Standard system (II) is unique to the empirical system (I′), any rescaling of the empirical system (I′) must also be associated with the same Standard system (II). Let us assume that other rescalings of the empirical system (I′) generate separate weighted average rates of profits of their own as R', R", etc. Now, by a similar reasoning as above, it can be shown that R', R", etc. must also be equal to R*. But the condition that the average must remain fixed with respect to arbitrary rescaling of equations is possible if and only if $r_i = r_c = r_w$ to begin with; QED. Thus the condition of the 'uniform rate of profits' in Sraffa's equation system has nothing to do with the notion of equilibrium or the centre of gravitation of Classical economics.

It should be noted that Sraffa's proposition that 'the rate of profits must be uniform' follows directly from his demonstration that there always exists a rescaling vector that converts a given system of equations to a Standard system and that the Standard system is unique to the given system of equations of basic goods. The demonstration crucially depends on the fact that the value of R* is known without the knowledge of p's and r's. Without this we will have no means of showing that the average rate of profits of Sraffa's system of basic goods must remain constant with respect to rescaling of individual equations.

Zambelli (2018) has worked out all possible sets of prices that are compatible with the condition of reproduction of a Sraffian system, where the condition of reproduction is taken to be the set of prices that ensures non-negative rate of profits for all industries. In this case, the set of prices associated with the uniform rate of profits is just one such set and is not an essential condition for the reproduction of Sraffa's system. In the classical tradition all such prices that are associated with unequal rates of profits are called the 'market' prices. The idea that 'market' prices can generate unequal rates of profits is based on the notion that prices are given from outside the system of equations. In this case the integrity of Sraffa's basic goods system breaks down since industrial rates of profits can be determined by applying those prices to each industry individually.

This is possible if the industries could be completely vertically integrated—i.e., industries can be treated as independent silos exchanging only their 'final goods' with each other. In this case there is no basic good, labour is the only primary factor of production. Sraffa, however, showed that in the case of a basic goods system, it is impossible to completely vertically integrate an industry—there always will remain a *commodity residue* along with labour. Thus, when wages go to zero, the rate of profits must reach a finite maximum, given the 'commodity residue'. However, in the case of completely vertically integrated industries, when wages go to zero then the rate of profits must go to infinity. This is the fundamental difference between the two separate conceptualisations of the systems of production. The existence of the maximum rate of profits reveals that the system of production is a structure of relations between commodities and can never be reduced to labour alone—*production of commodities is always by means of commodities* and its structural properties are revealed by the Standard system.

Now I will show that the subsistence system associated with the Standard system (II) determines the prices that must prevail in the empirical system (I′). Remove the surpluses from the Standard system (II). This gives us a subsistence system (III):

$$\begin{aligned} (120p_i + 160p_c + 80p_w) &= 200p_i. \\ (40p_i + 100p_c + 120p_w) &= 300p_c \quad (\mathbf{III}) \\ (40p_i + 40p_c + 200p_w) &= 400p_w. \end{aligned}$$

---

$$(200p_i + 300p_c + 400p_w) = (200p_i + 300p_c + 400p_w)$$

The relative prices or the p's are completely and uniquely determined in this subsistence system by the equations.

Now multiply all the equations of system (III) with 1.2. We know that this does not change the properties of the equation system and therefore the values of p's determined by it. This gives us equation system (IV):

$$(120p_i + 160p_c + 80p_w)(1 + 1/5) = 240p_i.$$
$$(40p_i + 100p_c + 120p_w)(1 + 1/5) = 360p_c \quad \textbf{(IV)}$$
$$(40p_i + 40p_c + 200p_w)(1 + 1/5) = 480p_w.$$

---

$$(200p_i + 300p_c + 400p_w)(1 + 1/5) = (240p_i + 360p_c + 480p_w)$$

Given that we have already established that in the Standard system (II), $r_i = r_c = r_w = R^* = 1/5$, equation system (IV) is identical to the Standard system (II). Thus the prices determined by the subsistence system (III) must prevail in the Standard system (II) as well. And we have already established that the prices prevailing in the empirical system (I′) are identical to the prices prevailing in the Standard system (II). Hence prices prevailing in the subsistence system (III) must also prevail for the empirical system (I′).

## 3

It can also be shown that any system with positive wages can also be analysed into its two components in terms of its 'corn economy' that determines its rate of profits and a 'subsistence economy' that determines its prices. Here we will work out only one example. Let us take the Standard net product of our equation (II), $(40p_i + 60p_c + 80p_w) = 1$, as the numeraire in which we measure our wages and prices. Let us suppose that **w** in our equation (I) is given by $(20p_i + 30p_c + 40p_w)$. This converts the equation system (I) to:

$$(90p_i + 120p_c + 60p_w)(1 + r_i) + 3/16 * (20p_i + 30p_c + 40p_w) = 180p_i.$$
$$(50p_i + 125p_c + 150p_w)(1 + r_c) + 5/16 * (20p_i + 30p_c + 40p_w)$$
$$= 450p_c \quad \textbf{(V)}$$

$$(40p_i + 40p_c + 200p_w)(1 + r_w) + 8/16 * (20p_i + 30p_c + 40p_w) = 480p_w.$$

$$\overline{\hspace{10cm}}.$$

$$(180p_i + 285p_c + 410p_w)(1 + R) + 20p_i + 30p_c + 40p_w$$
$$= 180p_i + 450p_c + 480p_w.$$

Which is equivalent to:

$$(90p_i + 120p_c + 60p_w)(1 + r_i) = 180p_i - 3/16 * (20p_i + 30p_c + 40p_w)$$

$$(50p_i + 125p_c + 150p_w)(1 + r_c)$$
$$= 450p_c - 5/16 * (20p_i + 30p_c + 40p_w)(\mathbf{V'})$$

$$(40p_i + 40p_c + 200p_w)(1 + r_w) = 480p_w - 8/16 * (20p_i + 30p_c + 40p_w)$$

$$\overline{\hspace{10cm}}.$$

$$(180p_i + 285p_c + 410p_w)(1 + R) = 160p_i + 420p_c + 440p_w.$$

Let us once again multiply the first equation by 4/3 and the second equation by 4/5 of the equation system (V′), i.e., apply the vector of multipliers (4/3 4/5 1).[3] This converts our equation system (V′) into its Standard counterpart given by:

$$(120p_i + 160p_c + 80p_w)(1 + r_i) = 240p_i - 1/4 * (20p_i + 30p_c + 40p_w)$$

$$(40p_i + 100p_c + 120p_w)(1 + r_c) = 360p_c - 1/4 * (20p_i + 30p_c + 40p_w)(\mathbf{VI})$$

[3] I am indebted to Yoann Verger for working out the multipliers for the Standard system with positive wages given in terms of the Standard commodity.

$$\left(40p_i + 40p_c + 200p_w\right)\left(1 + r_w\right) = 480p_w - 1/2 * \left(20p_i + 30p_c + 40p_w\right)$$

---

$$\left(200p_i + 300p_c + 300p_w\right)\left(1 + R *\right) = 220p_i + 330p_c + 440p_w.$$

Clearly the ratio of net output to total capital $(20p_i + 30p_c + 40p_w)/(200p_i + 300p_c + 400p_w) = R^* = 1/10$ or 10%. Now following the reasoning already given for the case with **w** = 0, we can conclude that the rate of profits of equation system (V) must be equal to 10%.

Now, to solve for prices, we remove the surplus of 10%, which gives us the subsistence system:

$$\left(120p_i + 160p_c + 80p_w\right) = 1/1.1 * \left[240p_i - 1/4 * \left(20p_i + 30p_c + 40p_w\right)\right].$$

$$\left(40p_i + 100p_c + 120p_w\right) = 1/1.1 * \left[360p_c - 1/4 * \left(20p_i + 30p_c + 40p_w\right)\right] \quad (\mathbf{VII})$$

$$\left(40p_i + 40p_c + 200p_w\right) = 1/1.1 * \left[480p_w - 1/2 * \left(20p_i + 30p_c + 40p_w\right)\right].$$

---

$$\left(200p_i + 300p_c + 300p_w\right) = 200p_i + 300p_c + 400p_w.$$

Following the above reasoning in the case of w = 0, the price solution for the equation system (VII) must also be the solution for the equation system (V).

## References

Sinha, A. (2016). *A Revolution in Economic Theory: The Economics of Piero Sraffa*. Cham: Palgrave Macmillan.

Sraffa, P. (1960). *Production of Commodities by Means of Commodities*. Cambridge: Cambridge University Press.

Sraffa, P. (n.d.). *Sraffa-Archives*. Cambridge: Trinity College, University of Cambridge.

Zambelli, S. (2018). Production of Commodities by Means of Commodities and Non-uniform Rates of Profits. *Metroeconomica, 69*(4), 791–819.

# 18

# The *Zambelli* Attractors of Coupled, Nonlinear *Macrodynamics* and *Knot* Theory

Kumaraswamy Velupillai

## 1 Introductory Notes

Zambelli pointed out (2012, p. 231; italics added):

> "It has been shown that when the economic systems are viewed as *coupled oscillators*, a rich variety of behaviours can be expected to occur.

In three significant, relatively mature, contributions, Zambelli (2011, 2012, 2015), tackled the problem of studying, by means of *simulations*, *approximations* and *computations*, the *attractors of the coupled dynamics of macroeconomies*. He harnessed, most interestingly and enlighteningly, the four attractors of nonlinear dynamical systems (Ott 2002, especially Chaps. 5 and 6), the four-classes of Wolfram's cellular automaton dynamical systems (Wolfram 1983), the Fermi–Pasta–Ulam (*FPU*) experiments

I am inspired, in the subject matter of this chapter, by Zambelli and Goodwin, particularly Goodwin (1947, 1951, 1990)—as, indeed, Zambelli was (and still is—I think).

K. Velupillai (✉)
Solna, Sweden


K. Velupillai (ed.), *Keynesian, Sraffian, Computable and Dynamic Economics*,
https://doi.org/10.1007/978-3-030-58131-2_18

and *quasi-periodic* behaviour (Fermi et al. 1955), the Goodwin coupled market dynamics (Goodwin 1947), the Phillips Machine representation (Phillips 1950) and the flexible accelerator model (Goodwin 1951), in studying the attractors of coupled national economies.

The harnessing was done with finesse and panache by Zambelli's mastery of the triptych of *effective*[1] tools: *approximation, simulation* and *computation*.[2]

In this chapter, I want to concentrate on the background and motivation for what I think is Zambelli's derivation of a sequence of *limit cycles*—or *closed, non-intersecting, curves*[3] on the plane ($R^2$)—as attractors in dynamically coupled macroeconomies, in the above three articles.

In particular, Figs. 2 and 8 in the two earlier chapters by Zambelli intrigued me; I wondered whether they were not the *unknot*—sometimes referred to as the *trivial knot*—and, if so, it should be possible to write a program—an algorithm—for the *Reidemeister moves* that will result in the *unknot*, starting from the original 'loops'!

The applications of *knot theory* to *dynamical systems* is not new; in particular, the knot structure of the 'chaotic' attractors generated by the Lorenz and Rössler equation systems have been known at least since 1983. Zambelli's work with all kinds of attractors was *always* based on concrete macroeconomic systems and examples of abstracting properties of macroeconomies—whether it be Frischian, Keynesian, Goodwinian or Phillipsian. On the other hand, as perceptively noted in Smale (1998, p. 12; italics added):

> Geometric, structurally stable, chaotic attractors in dynamics are in my paper (Smale 1967), But these *did not arise from any physical system.*

[1] In the sense that an *intuitive* concept is equated to a *mathematical* definition, later called the *Church-Turing Thesis*, which was a guiding principle of modelling in all of Zambelli's work (at least that I can claim any knowledge of).

[2] *Computation* as in formal *computability theory.*

[3] Closed, non-intersecting, curves—or limit cycles—on the plane can easily be of the most 'bizarre' shape and size (Ross and Ross 2009).

Ralph Abraham—a pioneer, with Steve Smale (and a *few* others), in dynamical systems theory (and a friend of Zambelli's), observed:

> The chaotic attractor of *mathematical theory* began with Birkhoff in 1916. The chaotic attractor of *simulation experiment* arrived with Lorenz in 1962. ... The *identification* of these two objects has not yet succeeded, despite many attempts during the past twenty years. Of course, everyone (including myself) expects this to happen soon ....

(Abraham 1985, p. 117; italics added)

This kind of observation resulted in Smale's formulation, as the 14th of 18 problems for the twenty-first century,[4] of the above *identification* (ibid.):

> Is the dynamics of the ordinary differential equations of Lorenz[5] that of the geometric Lorenz attractor ... .?

In the early years of this century, the *identification* was *proved*, using *interval arithmetic* and in the mode that Appel and Haken (1976) demonstrated the validity of the *four colour theorem* (Tucker 2002). Proving the identification 'legitimizes' the application of knot theory to dynamical systems like the ordinary differential equations (ODEs) of Lorenz and Rössler—but the particular methods used by Tucker are, broadly speaking, constructive; moreover, the ODE Solvers used in the proof are based on rigorous computation. It is not an existence proof in the sense of classical mathematics.

---

[4] Smale's essay was in response to V. I. Arnold's query, 'inspired in part by Hilbert's list of 1900', on behalf of the International Mathematical Union.

[5] They are:

$$\dot{x} = -10x + 10y$$

$$\dot{y} = 28x - y - xz$$

$$\dot{z} = -\frac{8}{3}z + xy$$

Tucker's answer to Smale's 14th, and to Abraham's identification, and the methods used therein, should appeal to Zambelli in his work on the attractors of coupled national economies, invoking precise approximations, simulating them with and without forcing terms and employing the ODE Solvers of Matlab, with various algorithms and studying the dependence of the long-term solutions—attractors—on a family of initial conditions on the basis of rigorous computations.

However, it must be acknowledged that Zambelli—consciously—works with digital computers, whereas the simulations—for example by coupling two Phillips machines—is by analogue computers; similarly, the ODE Solvers of Matlab, which Zambelli uses felicitously, discretize differential equations. Therefore, the simulation results are not entirely faithful to the analogue computing tradition of ODE Solvers, nor a precise equivalent of the Tucker framework, mathematical method of proof and ordinary differential equations.

Of course, other kinds of attractors—point and strange, in particular—have been emphasized in the Zambelli *oeuvre*, but these will, if at all, be mentioned only in passing. They have their importance—especially point attractors, Wolfram's fourth class (or universally computable Turing Machine simulable attractors) and quasi-periodic orbits, in his earlier work (Frisch's *non-rocking* rocking horse and in considering the FPU and Cellular Automaton attractors). Strangely (sic!) he has not been too enthusiastic[6] about investigating the properties and dynamics of strange attractors, from a numerically computable angle, or as a simulation exercise.

Thus, two important *caveats* by Zambelli have to be remembered:

I. "A non-linear [coupled] dynamical [economic] system such as the above may converge to *point attractors*, *limit cycles* or *chaotic attractors*. A combination of a low capital–output ratio, low marginal propensities to consume and import, low levels consumption and investment lags would make the equilibrium vector a point attractor. For other sets of

[6] I could, of course, be wrong on this; after all, I do not have all Zambelli's expertise on this (and other issues).

parameters, *limit cycles* and *chaotic attractors* could exist." (Zambelli 2015, p. 1614; italics added)

II. "In the context of the analysis conducted here, it is *not important* to verify whether the variables will show chaotic behaviours, but whether the two economies could or would evolve synchronously. For certain sets of the parameters, the two economies will be highly synchronized, while for others highly asynchronized[7]." (Zambelli 2012, p. 217; italics added)

In the above article of 1985, Abraham went on to state (ibid., pp. 117–118; underlining in the original):

> "Nevertheless, there is an important reason to consider the loathsome alternative [to the *identification*]: the quasi-periodic paradox".

In 1991, Goodwin *erroneously* thought that the dynamics of coupled markets he had considered in 1947 depicted chaotic behavior in the sense of the Lorenz Attractor (Goodwin 1947, pp. 201–202, 1991); the *identification problem* remained open in 1991). Goodwin in serendipitously 'hitting upon' the quasi-periodic paradox, anticipated the *Seifert conjecture* (Seifert 1950) and its falsification (Kuperberg 1999). Zambelli, however, was *never* enthusiastic about chaotic behavior of coupled macroeconomies—as is evident from the above references and quotes. Zambelli was more interested in the set of initial conditions that resulted in synchronous dynamic behavior of coupled national economies.

When the three Lorenz ODEs (see footnote 5) were used to generate the experimental *Lorenz attractor*, Birman and Williams (1983, p. 48) found that it contained several well-known knots.[8] Since at least 1983, a rich source of research has tended to investigate the type and number of knots inherent in dynamical systems modeled as ODEs; moreover, in discussing the decomposition of knots, the significance of the *Jordan*

[7] In the original 'asynchronized' appears as 'a synchronized'!

[8] The main reason for including a reference to this pioneering paper is its mention of the *trefoil* knot (of which more, below) in the trajectory of the *Lorenz attractor*.

*Curve Theorem*, even if only tangentially, was mentioned in Murasugi (2008, pp. 18–19, note 6).[9]

The *knot problem*, the *four colour theorem* and the *Poincaré conjecture* were related (Wilson 2014, pp. 128–130); Haken was instrumental in the comprehensive algorithmic solution of the first two (Haken 1961; Appel and Haken 1976; and, perhaps, a significant part of the third—before it was completely solved by Perelman). However, the $\mathbf{P} \stackrel{?}{=} \mathbf{NP}$ problem, the *Jordan Curve Theorem*, its constructive and algorithmic solutions, and the solution to *Fermat's Last Theorem* are also related, to *some* of them—and, hence, to *all* of them!

I know of only James Alexander (1922, 1928), among leading mathematicians, to have worked on any two of the above problems, theorems or conjectures explicitly; but I am sure many others, from Poincaré and Brouwer to Smale and Conway, must have done so.

In my very insignificant way, I shall try to relate the *classical knot theory* to the constructive and algorithmic *Jordan Curve theorem*. In this I was inspired by Zambelli's experimental results in investigating the dynamics of coupled macroeconomies and Conway (op.cit., p. 50; italics in the original) enunciating a philosophy:

> "[Y]ou take something you've learnt in one place, and apply it to something else, somewhere where it's not obvious that there is any mathematics, and there *is*."

This is about life and Brouwer's intuitionistic constructivism was about discussing *How Mathematics Is Rooted in Life* (van Dalen 2013, 2008)—and in this sense I think it is a way of paying respect to Zambelli's *lifelong* pursuit of the algorithmic mathematics of economics. Zambelli, more than anyone I personally know, extolled the virtues of De Finetti's pursuit of the meaning of the *theory of probability* that he developed (De Finetti

[9] As a novice to the mathematical theory of knots, I have found the three books of Adams (2004), Murasugi (ibid.) and Burde and Zieschang (2003) most illuminative and pedagogically enlightening. It is *only* in Murasugi (ibid.) I found any mention of the connection between aspects of knot theory and the *Jordan Curve theorem*, which lies at the heart of the *Poincaré-Bendixson* theorem (on the plane—but more on this later).

1974) in *life*—as Lindley[10] in his enthusiastic *Foreword* to the book wrote (p. ix; italics added):

> "[T]his is a book about *life*."

## 2 *Elementary* and *Reidemeister Moves and Codes* in *Classical*[11] Knot Theory

When Conway (2005, p. 42; italics added) stated that:

> "*All* knot deformations can be reduced to *a sequence* of these three [Reidemeister] *moves*."

he made a prescient observation: knot theory is *simple* and *intrinsically dynamic*. Any theory is simple, if looked at from the vantage point of 'first principles'—as Convey himself did.

Knot theory in general, but *classical* knot theory in particular, can be approached from geometric, topological, algebraic, arithmetical or combinatorial viewpoints—and it has been so studied ever since Gauss, as mathematics itself evolved. It has also graph theoretic, dynamical system or invariant polynomial representations. Although knot theory is permeated with algorithms—witness, for example, Haken's important contributions—it has never, at least to my (admittedly limited) knowledge, been either modeled as a Universal Turing Machine programmable theory (accepting some version of the Church-Turing thesis[12]), or the proofs of its theorems demonstrated constructively (in any of its many senses—my preference is for Brouwer–Bishop version).

For the purposes of this chapter—actually, for the purpose of *any* formal paper—it is sufficient to consider *a knot as a closed curve in three dimensions, not crossing itself*—where the closed curve meets any other

[10] I had the great pleasure to be present at Lindley's *lecture*!

[11] By classical knot theory I mean only that no considerations of virtual knots are involved; virtual knots are like complex or imaginary numbers, which I don't consider for algorithmic reasons.

[12] Although I prefer Emil Post's term of *law*, for *thesis*, so that the analogy with *the second law of thermodynamics*, in particular, can be imagined.

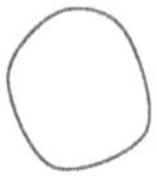

Fig. 18.1 *Unknot* or the *Trivial Knot*

part of itself, it 'passes' under or over it; when, and where, it meets itself, and passes under or over it, is called a *crossing*.

The *unknotted* closed curve—also known as the *trivial* knot—in 3-dim space, *projected* on the 2-dim plane, has *no* crossings (Fig. 18.1):

Note that *all manipulations* of classical knots are done on their *projections* in the plane.

On the other hand, the (left-handed) *trefoil knot* has one knot, and three crossings, at 1, 2 and 3; it passes over itself at 1, under itself at 2 and, again, over itself at 3 (Fig. 18.2). Thus, the Gaussian code for the *left-handed* trefoil knot—like the Gödel #—would be ***O1U2O3U1O2U3***.[13]

The mirror-image of the left-handed trefoil knot is the *right-handed* trefoil knot (Fig. 18.3), which has the Gaussian code, for the same type of numbering: ***U1O2U3O1U2O3***.

Interpreting ***O*** & ***U*** as ***L***(eft shift) & ***R***(ight shift) operations of a Turing Machine program, and representing the (integer) numbers in terms of binary codes of 0s and 1s, and the stop rule to be called into action when the ordering exhibits cyclicity, enables one to implement the Gaussian code algorithmically—remembering, of course, that only *finite* (classical) knots are considered.

There is no loss of generality in assuming that all knots are formed in polygonal spaces; hence, their projections are piecewise linear (PL) simplexes.

## 2.1 Elementary Knot Moves (Fig. 18.4)

a) Suppose C is a point that does not lie on the given knot, **K**; if the Δ **ABC** does not intersect the projection of the knot, **K**, with the

[13] ***O***: over-cross; ***U***: under-cross;

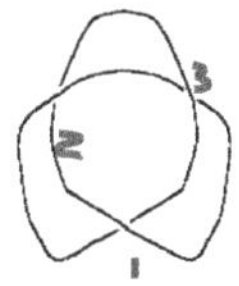


**Fig. 18.2** (left-handed) *Trefoil Knot* with three crossings

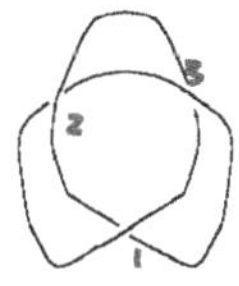


**Fig. 18.3** (right-handed) *Trefoil Knot*

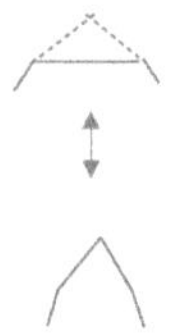

**Fig. 18.4** *Elementary* moves

exception of the line **AB**, then it can be removed and the two edges **AC** & **CB** can be added;

b) Conversely, if ∃, in the polygonal space that contains **K**, a Δ **ABC** that does not intersect it, *s.t.*, its two adjacent sides, say **AC** & **CB** are (possibly) on **K**, then these two sides can be 'deleted' and **AB** can be added;

## 2.2 Reidemeister Moves (Fig. 18.5)

**Definition:** *Two planar knot diagram projections of knots in 3-dim space are equivalent* (see footnote 15) ***iff*** *they are connected by a* ***finite sequence*** *of Reidemeister moves,* $\Omega_i$ *or* $\Omega_i^{-1}$, $i = 1, 2, 3$

With these preliminaries in place, the following definitions and results pertaining to classical knots can be stated:

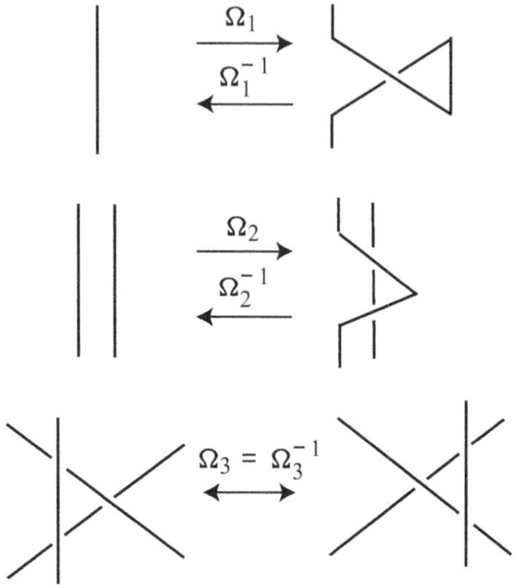


**Fig. 18.5** *Reidemeister* moves (This figure is from the text of Burde and Zieschang (op.cit., p. 10, Figure 1.9), although *any* of the texts mentioned earlier, including the article by Conway (2005), should have it. The reason for taking it from Burde and Zieschang, ibid., is that the proof is particularly perspicacious and makes its constructive algorithmic sense evident, which is why I have bold italicized the terms ***finite sequence*** in the definition)

1. No non-trivial knots with *less than* 3 crossings are possible;
2. *Any* projection of a knot, by changing *some*—not all—crossings from ***O*** to ***U***, or *vice versa*, can be shown to *equivalent*[14] to the projection of the trivial knot; this can easily be seen from one of the trefoil knots, and entails its unknotting.
3. *All* knots are *ambient isotopic*.
4. *Composite, factor and prime knots* are considered *as if* the knots were **integers**.
5. *Orientation* of knots are akin to those endowments of vectors.
6. Only a conjunction of *Elementary* and **Reidemeister** moves are allowed, in showing the feasibility of unknotting *any* given knot.

[14] See Murasugi (op.cit., definitions 1.2.1 or 1.3.1, pp. 8 & 11).

7. Both of these moves are *constructively algorithmic*; i.e., Turing Machine programmable (without any assumption of the validity of the Church-Turing thesis).[15]
8. *Knots* are the sets that make up *links*; in this paper, all definitions and results (and theorems and proofs) that are relevant for knots are also valid for links.[16]

These eight properties, in addition to the definitions of knots (and links) in the rest of this section, are more than sufficient to interpret, in an unambiguous constructively algorithmic way, the Zambelli results on the structure of experimental attractors of coupled dynamical macro-economies. These are stated as propositions in this section—but one observation must be made before that. It is that the *average*—i.e., representative—*reasonable*[17] individual, whether he or she be on the *Clapham Omnibus*, does not model national economies in terms of *differential, difference or mixed differential-difference, integral, linear or non-linear, dynamic equations*; but *she or he could play with knots*, without any expertise on simulation, approximation or computation of ODE solvers, whether using *Matlab* or any other software package of algebraic digital, or even analog, programs.

**Proposition 1** (referring to figures 2 & 3 of Zambelli 2011)

These two projected closed curves can be made into, and are equivalent to, the trivial knot.

**Proof** By the definition of the *Reidemeister* moves, in addition to 1, 3 & 6; and 7 makes it constructively algorithmic.

**Proposition 2** (referring to figures 8 & 9 of Zambelli 2012)

All of the projected closed curves can be made into, and are equivalent to, the trivial knot; in addition, the unknots are linked without intersections.

[15] See Bishop (1967, p. 6).

[16] Coupled economies or sectors are, in fact, collections of *non-intersecting* knots, i.e., *links*.

[17] Not necessarily *rational* – *Captain Ahab* in *Melville*'s **Moby Dick**, immediately comes to mind!

**Proof** The first part is demonstrated exactly as in proposition 1; the second part is based, additionally, on the validity of 7 and by simple visual inspection.

**Remark 1** The Zambelli-Goodwin *like* statement of Étienne Ghys, on proofs in modular knot theory, is worthwhile remembering, in the context of the 'formal' demonstration of the above two propositions (Mackenzie 2009, p. 13; italics added):

> "A *proof* for me is *not always fully formalized*. I had [the proposition] all clear in my head. I was sure it was true, I knew why it was true, and I was beginning to write it down. But for me, *putting it in a picture* was a confirmation that it was *more true* than I thought."

**Remark 2** I read 'picture' as the results of computational experiments with approximations and simulations in the case of Zambelli and the geometry of dynamics in Goodwin's case.

## 3 *Jordan Curve* Theorem, *Existence of Limit Cycles and the Unknot*

Classical knot theory and the Jordan Curve theorem, on the plane, have at least one thing in common: they are both about simple closed curves. As Berg et al. (1975, p. 225, bold italics in the original) perceptively observed:

> "The main concern of the *Jordan curve theorem* is the *construction* of a path joining two points and missing a curve. ….. ***Given any three points off a Jordan curve, two of them can be connected by a path missing the curve.*** The *constructive* approach requires finding an explicit, *finite* procedure for *computing* the path."

However, with the possible exception of Alexander's fundamental frameworks and results of the 1920s and the recent fine textbook of Murasugi, these two important fields do not seem to have fertilized each other.

One of the main results of the previous section was that all of the theorems (or propositions) of classical knot theory are proved in constructively algorithmic modes. In this I am only reflecting the visions of Hales (2014) and Dowek (2015). However, I did not emphasize (enough) that classical knot theory is about finite processes and entities; the fact remains that the Jordan Curve theorem, even when it is proved constructively, with and without the assumption of the Church-Turing thesis, is (partly at least) about non-finite sets and processes.

However, there is no justification for the kind of way Sternberg (2010, Chap. 10, particularly §10.6), in an otherwise excellent book, presents the proof of the important Poincaré-Bendixon theorem as depending on the non-constructive Jordan Curve theorem.[18] After all, in an admittedly 'formidable paper' (Berg et al., op.cit., p. 225), there was an intuitionistic constructive proof, by Brouwer (1925), of the Jordan Curve theorem (even in the case of infinite sets—but it is 'potential infinity', in the case of constructive and Turing-type algorithmic mathematics).

Lefschetz (op.cit., p. 30) makes two unqualified assertions (underlining in the original):

1. "[The Jordan-Schoenflies theorem] is a classical theorem of topology ..."
2. "A Jordan curve is *merely* a 1-sphere, that is the homeomorph of *a circle*."

Of course, a classical knot is also 'merely a 1-sphere', nothing other than the 'homeomorph of a circle'; but more importantly it is, like classical knots, a theorem of *combinatorial topology*, at least in the expert hands

[18] There is even less justification for the admirable Lefschetz (1975, p. 30, italics added) to write:

> "As the *proof* is definitely *arduous* no attempt will be made to give it here."

But what measure of *arduous* does Lefschetz use? Zambelli told me he can compute the devil's staircase in a fraction of a second, using Matlab software, whereas he required several orders of magnitude greater, about thirty years ago (using the same software of the early 1990s). That which Lefschetz considered 'arduous' in 1975, is less so, in 2019, given the improvements in software and hardware.

of Hales (2007). Hence, the Jordan curve that Hales constructs in piecewise linear, as is the case with classical knots.

Hales, in the excellent algorithmic approach to the Jordan Curve theorem above, has computed (Hales, ibid., p. 883):

> "The formal proof of the Jordan curve theorem in HOL [Higher Order Logic]-light consists of 138 definitions, 1381 lemmas, and over 44,000 proof steps spread over 59,000 lines of computer code. There are approximately 20 million primitive logical inferences in this proof of the Jordan curve theorem."

This puts in proper perspective the notion of 'arduous' used by Lefschetz in 1975 (and, in particular, the non-computable Bourbaki's need for over one trillion symbols to express the number '1', of course when computers as we know them today, hardly existed (but after Turing's work in the 1930s).

Goodwin (1951) refers to the 'rigorous[19] methods developed by Poincaré' (p. 14) for the required proof of the Poincaré-Bendixon theorem and to the existence of 'the Poincaré limit cycle' (p. 17), in a purely macroeconomic theoretical setup of one country. The 'rigorous methods' and the limit cycles of Poincaré, were neither constructive, nor algorithmic—despite the fact that he—Poincaré—was himself an intuitionist!

Zambelli, on the other hand, demonstrates the existence of [Poincaré] limit cycles as attractors of dynamically coupled macroeconomies, experimentally, in the sense of approximate trajectories of such systems, exhibited in the state space of the ODE solvers of Matlab, implemented in a digital computer.

Neither the 'rigorous methods developed by Poincaré,' nor the existence of the (Poincaré) limit cycles, are demonstrated constructively, algorithmically (with or without assuming the validity of the Church-Turing thesis) or with the methods of an analog computer (so that continuous variables, at least in theory, need not be approximated).

---

[19] I was inspired by Emil Post, again, to think of *rigorous methods* as the infusion of *unconscious assumptions* (Stillwell 2004, p. 6) in an otherwise self-contained system; it was in the context of discussing the *inexact* formalizations of **Principia Mathematica** by Whitehead and Russell, the supposed system of clarity.

However, instead of the concentration on the Poincaré-Bendixon theorem and its proofs, and on the non-constructive, non-algorithmic, existence of Poincaré limit cycles, I shall make use of the fact that the trivial knot is closed curve in 3-dim space and is subject to, in particular, the constructively algorithmic proof of the existence of Zambelli's experimentally generated limit cycles.

**Proposition 3** (referring to Zambelli 2011, Fig. 2 & Fig. 3)

The trivial knots are limit cycles.

**Proof** By inspection and/or construction.

**Proposition 4** (referring to Zambelli 2012, Fig. 7, Fig. 8 & Fig. 9)

The collection of non-intersecting trivial knots, forming links, are a collection of non-intersecting limit cycles.

**Proof** Again, by inspection and/or construction.

**Proposition 5** (referring to Zambelli 2015, Fig. 3, especially in the Y-I, Y-K & Y-Z planes)

The existence of 'average' limit cycles is the same as the algorithmic construction of respective trivial knots.

**Proof** By construction, in the projected planes, of appropriate trivial cycles.

**Proposition 6** (referring to Zambelli 2015, Fig. 3, in the Y-CA plane)

The trivial knot is first unfolded; then, the trivial knot is the limit cycle.

**Proof** The unfoding to reveal the trivial knot is achieved as, for example, in Proposition 2, of §2; the second stage is, again, by inspection and/or construction.

**Remark 3** The Jordan Curve theorem and the Poincaré-Bendixon theorem can both be circumvented to show the *algorithmically constructive* equivalent classical knot to the traditional limit cycle of dynamical systems, whether coupled or uncoupled.

**Remark 4** The traditional '*constructive* approach [which] requires finding an explicit, *finite* procedure for *computing* the path' can be replaced by algorithmically constructive procedures to demonstrate the (constructive) existence of the (classical) unknot (or trivial knot).

## 4 Concluding Notes and a *Conjecture*

I am an adherent and an *aficionado* of the *power of mathematics*, but I am not a mathematician; not even an incompetent one. Zambelli is a competent *applied mathematician*, in the Flato (1992, p. 39) sense—but equating 'physical mathematics' with *applied mathematics*, in that the formalism and methods of *any* independent (of mathematics and physics) defined discipline delineates it—i.e., applied mathematics. Origami, morphogenesis, knots, music (particularly of the atonal, 12-tone, variety), dada performance and surrealist constructions are examples of this kind of physical mathematics. Thom (1975), especially Chap. 7, Adams (2004) and Ball (1996), are instances of this. I would like to 'lump' all of them under the rubric of *craft techniques* in the way knots are viewed by Davidson (2018, p. 6; italics added):

> "*Knots* are diverse and unique. There are literally thousands of different knots, for all sorts of different purposes, and once you're acquainted with them they are easy to use. There are few *craft techniques that have a long heritage* and yet so accessible,,,. *There's something quite magical* about taking a length of rope and transforming it into something that you can use or display around the home."

The triptych of Zambelli's applied mathematics is based on *approximations*, *simulations* and *computations*[20]—or any combination of at least two of them—define these non-physics disciplines.

I was myself inspired to look at knot theory to *untangle* Poincaré's *tangles* in the interaction between stable and unstable manifolds Ekeland 1988, particularly Appendix 1) and the subtle interplay between *homoclinic* and *heteroclinic tangles* in (modern) dynamical systems. I was first drawn to Conway (1970, § 1 & § 3) for this, display of knots in dynamical systems.

Economics deserves to return to a tradition of *magic*, that can be provided by *craft techniques*. Artists, origami modellers, atonal and 12-tone musicians, pottery designers, knitters, weavers, cooks, farmers, gardeners, painters, poets, prose writers, Dada performances,—even architects and medical practitioners (and, of course, many others), although they use computers imaginatively, seem never to forget their *craft heritage* and *magical thinking*. I still think—indeed am convinced—that *all* finite or countably infinite tangles can be untangled by a mastery of the magical craft technique of knot theory, in conjunction with algorithms (whether implemented by means of analog or digital computers).

The applied mathematician in Zambelli, is—I think—motivated by the magic of craft techniques. No layperson I know, formulates the dynamics of coupled or uncoupled economies in terms of differential, or other types of functional equations. At best, 'back-of-the-envelope' calculations are disciplined by formal accounting rules.

Many would like economics to become the craft technique that it should be. It has, after all, more in common with roof thatching—a vanishing art—and weaving, a flourishing craft; it is only a question of time before economics learns the virtue of the magic and craft of knots. These are mathematically constructive processes of an algorithmic nature!

For now, I end with a conjecture:

[20] I would like to emphasise, again, that computation is underpinned by computability theory, especially for Zambelli.

## 4.1 A Conjecture

*I believe that the framework of dynamical systems theory will be superseded, especially in the study of attractors for coupled and uncoupled economies, by the craft technique of knots.*

Zambelli epitomizes the magic of the craft technique of applied mathematics for economics. When, in the last dialogue between *Estragon* and *Vladimir*, in **Waiting for Godot**, Beckett makes them express the dissonance between words and action (italics added), like statics and dynamics in economics, he could have been thinking of a future Stefano Zambelli, and his kind of applied mathematics, which tries to understand the *dynamics* of coupled macroeconomies, equipped with a new *correspondence principle*:

> ESTRAGON: Well, shall we go?
> VLADIMIR: Yes, let's go.
> They do *not* move.

# References


Abraham, R. H. (1985). *Is There Chaos Without Noise?*, chapter 7. In P. Fischer & W. R. Smith (Eds.), *Chaos, Fractals and Dynamics* (pp. 117–121). New York: Marcel Dekker, Inc.

Adams, C. C. (2004). The Knot Book – *An Elementary Introduction to the Mathematical Theory of Knots* (Reprinted with corrections). Providence, RI: American Mathematical Society.

Alexander, J. W. (1922). *A Proof and Extension of the Jordan-Brouwer Separation Theorem. Transactions of the American Mathematical Society, 23*(4), 333–349.

Alexander, J. W. (1928). Topological Invariants of Knots and Links. *Transactions of the American Mathematical Society, 30*(2), 275–306.

Appel, K., & Haken, W. (1976). Every Planar Map Is Four Colorable. *Bulletin of the American Mathematical Society, 82*(5), 711–712.

van Atten, M. (2008). The Foundations of Mathematics as a Study of Life. *Progress of Theoretical Physics, 173*(Supplement), 38–47.

Ball, H. (1996). Flight Out of Time, edited with an introduction and notes by John Elderfield & translated (from *Die Flucht aus der Zeit*) by Ann Reimes, London: University of California Press, Ltd.

Berg, C., Julian, W., Mines, R., & Richman, F. (1975). The Constructive Jordan Curve Theorem. *Rocky Mountain Journal of Mathematics, 5*(2), 225–236.

Birman, J. S., & Williams, R. F. (1983). *Knotted Periodic Orbits in Dynamical Systems – I: Lorenz's Equations. Topology, 22*(1), 47–82.

Bishop, E. (1967). *Foundations of Constructive Analysis*. New York: McGraw-Hill Book Company.

Brouwer, L. E. J. (1925). Intuitionistischer Beweis des Jordanschen Kurvensatzes, Koninklijke Nederlandse Akademie van Wetenschappen (KNAW). *Proceedings*, Vol. 28, pp. 503–508.

Burde, G., & Zieschang, H. (2003). *Knots* (2nd Revised and Extended ed.). New York: Walter de Gruyter.

Conway, J. H. (1970). An Enumeration of Knots and Links, and Some of Their Algebraic Properties. In J. Leech (Ed.), *Computational Problems in Abstract Algebra* (pp. 329–358). Oxford: Pergamon Press.

Conway, J. H. (2005). The Power of Mathematics, chapter 3, pp. 36–50. In A. Blackwell & D. MacKay (Eds.), *Power*. Cambridge, UK: The Darwin College Lectures, Cambridge University Press.

Davidson, L. (2018). *40 Knots and How to Tie Them*. Illustrated by Maria Nilsson. London: Pavilion.

De Finetti, B. (1974). *Theory of Probability – A Critical Introductory Treatment, Volume 1*. London: John Wiley & Sons.

Dowek, G. (2015). Computation, Proof, Machine – *Mathematics Enters a New Age*, translated from the French by Pierre Guillot & Marion Roman. Cambridge: Cambridge University Press.

Ekeland, I. (1988). *Mathematics and the Unexpected*. Chicago: The University of Chicago Press.

Fermi, E., Pasta, J., & Ulam, S., with the assistance of M. Tsingou. (1955). Studies of Non Linear Problems I. Los Alamos Preprint, LA-1940, 7 November.

Flato, M. (1992). The Power of Mathematics, translated (from *Le Pouvoir des mathématiques*) by Maurice Robine. New York: McGraw-Hill, Inc.

Goodwin, R. M. (1947). *Dynamical Coupling with Especial Reference to Markets Having Production Lags. Econometrica, 15*(3), 181–204.

Goodwin, R. M. (1951). The Nonlinear Accelerator and the Persistence of Business Cycles. *Econometrica, 19*(1), 1–17.

Goodwin, R. M. (1990). *Chaotic Economic Dynamics*. Oxford: Clarendon Press.
Goodwin, R. (1991). *Foreseeing Chaos*, Royal Economic Society. *Newsletter*, September, p. 13.
Haken, W. (1961). *THEORIE DER NORMALFLÄCHEN – Ein Isotopiekriterium für den Kreisknoten. Acta Mathematica, 105*, 245–375.
Hales, T. C. (2007). The Jordan Curve Theorem, Formally and Informally. *American Mathematical Monthly, 114*(10), 882–894.
Hales, T. C. (2014). Mathematics in the Age of the Turing Machine. In R. Downey (Ed.), *Turing's Legacy: Developments from Turing's Ideas in Logic* (pp. 252–298). Cambridge: Cambridge University Press.
Kuperberg, K. (1999). Aperiodic Dynamical Systems. *Notices of the AMS, 46*(8), 1035–1040.
Lefschetz, S. (1975). *Applications of Algebraic Topology*. New York: Springer-Verlag.
Mackenzie, D. (2009). A New Twist in Knot Theory. In *What's Happening in the Mathematical Sciences* (pp. 3–17). Providence, RI: American Mathematical Society.
Murasugi, K. (2008). *Knot Theory & Its Applications* (Reprint of the 1996 edition), translated by Bohdan Kurpita. Basel: Birkhäuser.
Ott, E. (2002). *Chaos in Dynamical Systems* (2nd ed.). Cambridge: Cambridge University Press.
Phillips, A. W. (1950). Mathematical Models in Economic Dynamics. *Economica, New Series, 17*(67), 283–305.
Ross, F., & Ross, W. T. (2009). The Jordan Curve Theorem Is Non-trivial. *Journal of Mathematics and the Arts, 5*(4), 213–219.
Seifert, H. (1950). Closed Integral Curves in 3-Space and Isotopic Two-Dimensional Deformations. *Proceedings of the American Mathematical Society, 1*(3), 287–302.
Smale, S. (1967). Differentiable Dynamical Systems. *Bulletin of the American Mathematical Society, 73*(6), 747–817.
Smale, S. (1998). Mathematical Problems for the Next Century. *The Mathematical Intelligencer, 20*(2), 7–15.
Sternberg, S. (2010). *Dynamical Systems*. Mineola; New York: Dover Publications, Inc.
Stillwell, J. (2004). Emil Post and His Anticipation of Gödel and Turing. *Mathematics Magazine, 77*(1), 3–14.
Thom, R. (1975). *Structural Stability and Morphogenesis*, translated from the French edition, as updated by the author, by D. H. Fowler. Reading, MA: W. A. Benjamin, Inc.

Tucker, W. (2002). A Rigorous ODE Solver and Smale's 14th Problem. *Foundations of Computational Mathematics, 2*(1), 53–117.

Van Dalen, D. (2013). *L. E. J. Brouwer – Topologist, Intuitionist, Philosopher: How Mathematics Is Rooted in Life*. London: Springer-Verlag.

Wilson, R. (2014). *Four Colors Suffice – How the Map Problem Was Solved*. (Revised Color ed.). Princeton, NJ: Princeton University Press.

Wolfram, S. (1983). *Statistical Mechanics of Cellular Automata. Reviews of Modern Physics, 55*(3), 601–644.

Zambelli, S. (2011). Coupled Dynamics in a Phillips Machine Model of the Macroeconomy. *Economia Politica, XXVIII*(Special Issue), 171–186.

Zambelli, S. (2012). Flexible Accelerator Economic Systems as Coupled Oscillators, chapter 11. In S. Zambelli, A. Donald, & R. George (Eds.), *Nonlinearity, Complexity and Randomness in Economics: Towards Algorithmic Foundations for Economics* (pp. 211–236). West Sussex; Oxford: Wiley-Blackwell.

Zambelli, S. (2015). Dynamical Coupling, the Non-linear Accelerator and the Persistence of Business Cycles. *Cambridge Journal of Economics, 39*(6), 1607–1628.

# Author Index[1]



[1] Note: Page numbers followed by 'n' refer to notes.


K. Velupillai (ed.), *Keynesian, Sraffian, Computable and Dynamic Economics*,
https://doi.org/10.1007/978-3-030-58131-2

D



E



F

S

# Subject Index[1]

I have tried to confine the Subject Index to approximately the same number of pages as the Name Index (for aesthetic and logistical reasons). I faced several problems, mainly because some of the authors used American spelling of English words and many used English spelling, Also, in order to keep the size from outgrowing the aesthetic criterion, I used the 'subterfuge' of not using all the underlined words and phrases of the authors; in addition, the inevitable 'subjectiveness' was involved in my choices. I hope the distinguished contributors, and the readers of this book, forgive me these infelicities.

Editor



[1] Note: Page numbers followed by 'n' refer to notes.



K. Velupillai (ed.), *Keynesian, Sraffian, Computable and Dynamic Economics*, https://doi.org/10.1007/978-3-030-58131-2

The manufacturer's authorised representative in the EU is Springer
Nature Customer Service Centre GmbH, Europaplatz 3, 69115 Heidelberg,
Germany. If you have any concerns regarding our products, please
contact ProductSafety@springernature.com

Printed and bound by CPI Group (UK) Ltd, Croydon, CR0 4YY
30/09/2026
02225453-0007